GOOD NEWS
FROM
NEW ENGLAND
and Other Writings
on the Killings
at Weymouth Colony

EDITED
by

JACK DEMPSEY
editor of *New English Canaan*
by Thomas Morton of "Merrymount"

Good News from New England
and Other Writings on the Killings at Weymouth Colony.
Edited by Jack Dempsey.
CONTACT:
Dr. Jack Dempsey
45 Broadway
Stoneham MA 02180 USA
781-438-3042; jd37@ici.net
and/or
DIGITAL SCANNING, INC.
344 Gannett Road, Scituate MA 02066
888-349-4433/781-545-2100
www.digitalscanning.com

COVER ILLUSTRATION:
A Bundle of New Arrows Lap'd in a Rattlesnake Skin
and Plimoth's Answer in Powder and Shot
by Michael F. McWade, artist and naturalist
Hardcover ISBN: 1-58218-707-X
Tradepaper ISBN 1-58218-7061
Copyright permissions courtesy of
The John Carter Brown Library,
Brown University, Providence RI (Winslow, Pratt):
Fees paid to The University of Oklahoma Press (Vaughan)
and *The New England Quarterly* (Kupperman).

ALSO BY JACK DEMPSEY:
Ariadne's Brother: A Novel on the Fall of Bronze Age Crete
(1996: ISBN 9602190620; in Greek translation
by Vicky Chatzopoulou; distr. Amazon.com)
& *Ariadne's Website* (http://home.ici.net/~jd37)

New English Canaan, by Thomas Morton of "Merrymount"
(Scituate, MA: Digital Scanning Inc.; Amazon.com)
Thomas Morton of "Merrymount":
The Life and Renaissance of an Early American Poet
NANI: A Native New England Story
(1998: 1-hr. videodocumentary, distributed by
V-Tape/Toronto and Shenandoah Films/Arcata CA)

Merrymount: a different early america (screenplay)

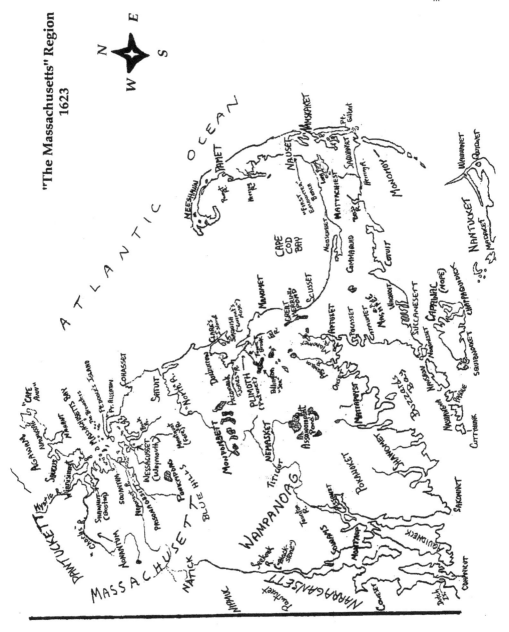

"The Massachusetts" Region
1623

GOOD NEWS
from NEW ENGLAND
and Other Writings
on the Killings at Weymouth Colony

CONTENTS

Detail from "The Waters-Winthrop" Map of Massachusetts Bay
(editor's arrow points to King's Cove location of Weymouth Colony)

"[T]here can be little if any doubt as to where the original settlement was made and the 'pale and houses' stood, [yet] it is also a matter for regret that the ground in the immediate neighborhood should not be preserved and set aside for public uses, with a proper memorial placed upon it....[T]he Legislature of the Commonwealth not impossibly, and the town of Weymouth very probably, might, if the facts were now brought to their notice, be induced to take some action....

"[A]t King's Cove...we saw just 'the lay of the land' which would naturally attract settlers searching for a home in a new country, rising with a gentle slope from a curving beach, in a broad level outstretch of deep soil, well open to the sun upon the east, but sheltered in other directions by higher ground, and having an ample supply of springs of water. Moreover, it was clear...that this spot possessed all the advantages for a trading post...."

Charles Francis Adams, Jr., and Henry W. Haynes,
1891 pamphlet, *The Site of The Wessagusset Settlement of 1622*

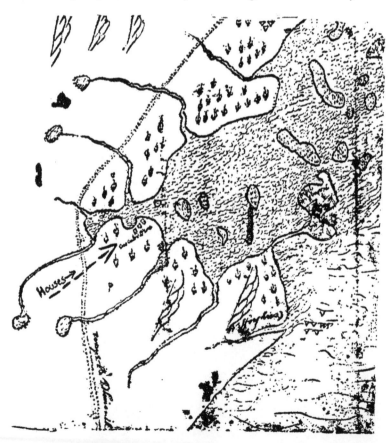

...Reading [Longfellow's poem] The Courtship of Miles Standish, *and looking at the paintings upon the walls of the Memorial Hall at Plymouth and of the Capitol at Washington, it is impossible for anyone at all imbued with the real spirit of the early colonial period not to entertain a hope that the time may come when a school of historical poets and painters shall arise who will deal truthfully and vigorously with these scenes, studying the localities and the authorities carefully and in a realistic spirit, instead of evolving at once facts, dress, features, and scenery from an inner and[,] where not a weak[,] at least a grotesque consciousness. In our early New England scenes the real facts are good enough....*

---Charles Francis Adams, Jr.,
***Three Episodes of Massachusetts History* (1892: I, 95)**

...But, said [Wampanoag Sachem Corbitant], if your love be such, and it bring forth such fruits, how cometh it to pass that when we come to [Plimoth Plantation], you stand upon your guard, with the mouths of your Pieces presented towards us? Whereunto I answered, it was the most honorable and respective entertainment we could give them, it being an order amongst us to receive our best respected friends....But shaking the head he answered that he liked not such salutations.

---Edward Winslow,
***Good News from New England* (1624)**

The world cannot afford to bungle its diplomacy.

---Thomas B. Adams,
President of Massachusetts Historical Society,
1970 (qtd. in Frost, *Immortal Voyage* 78)

And so, by God's goodness, [Captain Standish] brought
away the head of the chiefest of them. And [it] is set on the
top of our fort, and instead of an ancient [flag], we have a
piece of linen cloth dyed in the same Indian's blood, which
was hung out upon the fort when Massasoit was here. And now
the Indians are most of them fled from us....

> ---Captain Emmanuel Altham
> of *The Little James* to Sir Edward Altham, 1623
> in James, ed., *Three Visitors to Early Plymouth* (29)

As a race they have withered from the land. Their
arrows are broken, their springs are dried up, their cabins
are in the dust....Ages hence, the inquisitive white man, as
he stands by some growing city, will ponder on the structure
of their disturbed remains, and wonder to what manner of
persons they belonged. They will live only in the songs and
chronicles of their exterminators. Let these be faithful to
their rude virtues as men, and pay due tribute to their
unhappy fate as a people.

> ---early American school-textbook,
> *McGuffey's Newly Revised Rhetorical Guide* (1853)

dedicated to
Native American friends
who live abundantly
in the presence of the past

CONTEXTS & CHRONOLOGY

Native American "New England" peoples---estimated to be 100,000-135,000 persons through the "early contact" period---continue their various "Eastern Woodland" cultures, including hunting, gathering and agriculture, that build upon "Paleo" (13-6,000 years ago) and "Archaic" Periods (6000-2500 ago), totaling at least 13,000 years on *Nitaukke*: "my land." They have known the region since Europe's "Late Paleolithic" times

1497-1498   John & Sebastian Cabot initiate Early Modern Europe's voyages to "New-found-land" following Columbus' 1490s "discoveries"

1500-1502   Corte-Real of Portugal explores New England coast. Basques and other fishermen soon begin annual voyages, pursuing whales at Belle Isle, trade along mouth of St. Lawrence River

1520?   Joao Fagundes of Portugal sails "Maine" waters, Cape Breton

1524   Verrazanno meets Narragansett, Abenaki Native peoples

1525   Estevan Gomez of Spain coasts Nova Scotia, Cape Cod

1527   John Rut of England sails from Newfoundland to West Indies: he counts 10 fishing ships and lands on Cape Cod (Dexter 46)

1534-1541   Jacques Cartier explores the future "New France"

1562   French attempts to plant in Florida (Brazil 1575)

1569   Mercator's map of the world

1570s   English and Spanish conflict in the Caribbean

1576   Martin Frobisher's first North Atlantic voyage

1583   Future Plimother Myles Standish born: by 1610 an English soldier in The Netherlands, he later meets Wm. Bradford & co.

1584   Ralegh, Barlow in "Virginia": first Roanoke colony; Sir Humphrey Gilbert lost at sea during second Northeast voyage

1585-1587   Davis' voyages continue search for a Northwest Passage

1585-1586   Drake's raids in the "Spanish" Caribbean

1588	England and storms at sea defeat the Spanish Armada
1590	William Bradford (Plimoth leader) born among the early English Puritan congregations of Austerfield, Scrooby
1596	Plimother Edward Winslow born, son of a salt-victualler: he attends King's School, tours Europe, meets Bradford & co. Sir Walter Ralegh's *Guiana* published
1598	Sable Island (Newfoundland) camp fails
1602	Gosnold names "Cape Cod"; camps at Cuttyhunk Island
1603	Pring and others follow Gosnold for sassafrass etc.; Dutch found "New Amsterdam"; Queen Elizabeth dies, James I crowned
1604	French land at St. Croix (Maine), Port Royal (Nova Scotia)
1605	Capt. Waymouth scouts New England for Sir Ferd. Gorges, and kidnaps Native people for information to aid colony efforts. July: Champlain and French at Nauset and other sites in Massachusetts: a fight results in deaths on both sides
1606	voyages of Challons, Pring (2nd): Poutrincourt's French plant at Port Royal, New France. On a voyage south to Cape Cod, the latter's men open fire on Natives at Nauset. Lescarbot's masque *The Theatre of Neptune* is perfomed at Port Royal
1606-1608	with church elder William Brewster, William Bradford and Puritan groups emigrate to The Netherlands to escape Anglican Church repression under James I: they settle at Leyden and John Robinson becomes their most beloved minister
1607	George Popham and Ralegh Gilbert build fortified trading-station at Sagadahoc (Kennebec), "Maine." It fails in 1 year after "mistreatment" of Native trade-partners brings attacks
1608	Champlain and Lescarbot at Quebec and "New France"
1609	voyage of Henry Hudson for The Netherlands. Virginia Company founded. Jesuits at "Mt. Desert" in Maine
1610	John Guy of Bristol and others in Newfoundland; English plantations in Ulster, Ireland, Bermudas by 1611; Samuel Argall at Penobscot Bay and Cape Cod
1611	Captain Harlow kidnaps Native New Englander Epenow and others. Father Pierre Biard in Maine
1613-15	Dutch pursue the fur trade at Manhattan Island and Albany. Captain Argall destroys St. Croix and French missions
1614	Captain John Smith explores and names "New England": fights

and kills Natives at Cohasset and Patuxet (future Plimoth). Captain Hunt abducts 19 Natives from Patuxet (including Squanto/Tisquantum), 7 from Nauset (Dexter 57) for sale as slaves in Malaga. Only Tisquantum makes his way to England.

Captive Epenow (1611) at last escapes back to his people by jumping off an English ship off "Martha's Vineyard."

A French vessel founders off Cape Cod: survivors become Native "servants" and/or marry Native women. Accord- to Pratt, one "had a book" from which he predicts, to Natives incl. Massachusett pneise Pecksuot, that Native peoples will be "driven away" from their lands.

Adriaen Block (Dutch) explores Narraganset Bay, the Connecticutt River, maps the coast from Virginia to Maine

1615-1616   John Mason governs Newfoundland's "swarming fishermen." First report of "plague" or epidemic in Saco, Maine region

c. 1617   Sir Walter Ralegh's "second El Dorado" voyage fails

1616-1618   Nanepashement of Mystic is "Massasoit" or "Supreme Sachem" of southern New England. Pecksuot and Mass. Natives, "upon some distaste given" by French traders at Peddock's Island, attack and burn the ship. "Plague" and/or other European diseases decimate New England Native Americans with up to 90% mortality.

While Patuxet Wampanoag Squanto/Tisquantum is in England, disease wipes out his entire village at future Plimoth. Nanepashemet is killed in a raid by Micmacs, further destabilizing Native New England.

With fewer losses to "plague," the Narragansetts are able to push the plague-decimated Pokanoket Wampanoags under Ousamequin (now "Massasoit" or High Sachem) back east across the Seekonk River, in their ongoing territorial rivalries. Dermer meets Tisquantum working with Newfoundland English and they reach New England in 1619, trade at Nemasket with Wampanoags. At Capawac, Dermer meets the dauntless Epenow, who "laughs" at his former captivity.

"The Pilgrims" (Bradford, Winslow, Standish and families) negotiate with London Merchant Adventurers for "Virginia Company" passage to begin planting in some part of America: they meet merchant Andrew Weston, who tries to arrange contracts. They debate terms and destinations.

1620   Captain Dermer renews trade explorations. At Capawac, Epenow tries to "take" him and a fight breaks out that kills all but one of Dermer's crew: he dies of wounds that summer.

Disputes and delays bring consequences: the "Saints" must plant with a majority of nonPuritan "Strangers," and *Mayflower* does not depart till September, very late in the season. Nor will their leader Robinson be allowed to go with them.

November 9-11: *Mayflower* arrives at Cape Cod: after digging up Native corn-stores and a skirmish with Nauset people at "First Encounter Beach," Bradford and co. make way to Patuxet/New Plimoth, south of Mass. Bay. But more than half the company die of cold, hunger and fevers before Spring

1621   Dutch West Indies Company founded

Spring: Ousamequin/Massasoit sends English-speaking Samoset and Tisquantum to Plimoth to begin relations with Bradford's Plimoth planters. Summer: Plimothers explore from Massachusetts Bay to Cape Cod: in June they meet a Nauset mother demanding return of kidnapped children.
Merchant Thos. Weston's *Sparrow* arrives.
September: Most Mass. Bay Sachems mark a treaty of good will with Plimoth. Nemasket Wampanoag Sachem Corbitant, "too conversant" with Narragansetts, threatens Tisquantum and Ousamequin/Massasoit: Standish intervenes and wounds "several." "The First Thanksgiving."
Before long, diplomatic errors and Tisquantum's affairs result in a "bundle of arrows" taken as a threat to Plimoth. Though Native friend Hobbamock's wife finds "no such" intent in villages, Plimothers begin to build a stockade (Nov.-Feb.).
November: the ship *Fortune* brings 35 of Weston's men, no supply, and a letter demanding company profits

1622   Spring: Tisquantum and Hobbamock maneuver against each other, manipulate local politics. Massasoit demands the former's life but is refused by Plimoth. Native peoples withold trade, "frown" as Plimoth completes stockade. By May leaders resolve to build a fort with cannon, to the neglect of food crops hough rations are short. First "Training Day." *Fortune* is hijacked by the French.
June-July: ships *Charity* and *Swan* arrive with 50-60 men, who select Wessaguscus/Weymouth for their colony-site. It is "not long" before Native peoples report thefts and "abuse."
August: Plimoth learns that Powhatan peoples' attack on Virginia plantations have killed over 300 colonists

Autumn: meagre harvest at Plimoth. On short rations, Weymouthers grow disorderly and increase Native tensions.

Near the end of sailing season, one "Captain Jones" robs and tries to kidnap "some" Nauset Natives (Dec. 17 below) but they escape the run-aground vessel and make "great excla-mation" via Council for New England agent Leo Peddock.

Fall and Winter: starvation at Plimoth/Weymouth compel voyages in search of food from Native peoples:

At Monomoy, Bradford with the *Swan* finds people afraid yet helpful. Tisquantum dies. Bradford continues on to Massachusetts, Nauset, and Mattachiest.

At Nauset, Capt. Standish forces return of some beads. Bradford seeks food at Nemasket and Manomet. Standish threatens Mattachiest (more missing beads).

Dec. 17   Council of New England orders punishment of "Capt. Jones" for robbery and attempted kidnap of Nauset people on Cape Cod.

1623   March: Standish at Manomet sees angry pneise Wituwamat and reports a "conspiracy" afoot. Weymouth planters (incl. Phinehas Pratt) begin to build stockade and houses; but lack of supply causes continued thefts of Native corn.

Winslow seeks to "settle their affections" but is called to the "dying" Massasoit, who recovers from illness. Hobbamock tells Winslow of a widespread "conspiracy."

Amid much Native anger, Weymouth plans to take corn by force: Plimoth dissuades them. Pratt assaults a Native medicine-woman and "discovers" a plot. Unable to secure justice, Native people move dwellings closer to the safety of nearby swamps, and Pratt makes his wilderness journey to warn Plimoth of "conspiracy."

March 23: Plimoth meeting resolves on action "returning their malicious and cruel purposes upon their own heads." Within days, Standish and 10-11 men kill Wituwamat, Pecksuot, "another," and a youth of 18 as other English kill "two." (Bradford says "we killed seven"). Soon, Standish's party skirmish with Obtakiest's braves.

The Massachusetts kill 3 Weymouth men in their village, poss. two more "in their houses" (Pratt). Then the Sachem sues for peace. Standish puts Wituwamat's severed head on a pike over the Plimoth fort. Native contact and trading, and therefore Plimoth's debt-ridden economy, suffer for years until the Mass. Bay Colony at Boston, under John Winthrop's "900 souls," finds itself in need of Plimoth experience and food.

Sir Ferdinando Gorges sends son Robert with new settlers including minister/would-be poet Wm. Morrell and future "old comers" Samuel Maverick, Wm. Blackstone, Wm. Jeffreys and others. Robert Gorges has Thomas Weston arrested at Plimoth, impounds the bark *Swan*. In time, Weston recovers his boat and takes up a profitable trade in Virginia. But Gorges' new people also abandon Weymouth within months, having "scarcely saluted the country," leaving a few English "lone planters" at sites around the Bay.

Before long, Plimoth's Rev. John Robinson chastises
Plimoth for its actions. Phinehas Pratt and other English
attack Native villages at Agawam (Cape Ann) and
"Dorchester," taking food-stores and "prisoners."

1624   June: "the third plantation in the Bay" begins: Captain
Wollaston, gentleman Thomas Morton and 30 servants
consciously avoid Weymouth's site and practices, and in time,
renew relations with Obdakiest/Chikatawbak's Neponsets.

Still later, Chikatawbak treats regularly with the
Puritan colony at Boston (1630), till his death in a second wave
of epidemic in 1633. Though at least one son (Josias) survives
him, by this time the Massachusetts have become "not fifty."
Acc. to Pritchard (56), in 1650 their survivors are sold as slaves
in Jamaica, where they still exist as a people today.

INTRODUCTION

*The value of these contemporaneous documents cannot
be overstated. They are the earliest chronicles of New
England. We have here the first book[s] of our history,
written by the actors themselves.*
---Alexander Young, Preface (xi)
to *Chronicles of the Pilgrim Fathers* (1841)

In March 1623, the struggling English colony of "Pilgrims" at Plimoth, Massachusetts, attacked a supposed "conspiracy" of the region's Native Americans. When it was over, as many as twelve Native people and up to five English from the new nearby settlement at Weymouth had been killed or died of related causes, and Weymouth was no more. Soon, members of both plantations produced written accounts to detail and defend what they had done. This book presents a new edition of those writings and the histories born from them: Plimoth colonist Edward Winslow's 1624 *Good News from New England*; Weymouth colonist Phinehas Pratt's "Declaration of the Affairs" on crucial episodes of this "Wessagusset Conspiracy," "Weymouth Affair" or "Massacre"; and as well, the influential, strongly-varying "further accounts" produced by historians, from Pilgrim William Bradford and Renaissance man Thomas Morton to Charles Francis Adams, Jr. and Karen Ordahl Kupperman. New understandings are still to be gained from those days in 1623, and from the chronicles of indeed "the actors themselves."[1]

---

[1] **GENERAL EDITING NOTE** The original page numbers/printers' folios of all copy-texts appear within bold brackets: for ex., **[37/A]**. Most primary texts are inconsistent in spelling, punctuation, etc., and I have not "improved" where this makes multiple meanings possible. I have broken long paragraphs to increase accessibility, carefully re-presented people's recorded dialogues *verbatim*; and "modernized" only where plain confusion might occur, to preserve at least a savor of Early Modern English and its printing conditions. *Textual* adjustments are fully annotated. I also retain original italics and ellipses (...); and the various spellings of Eastern Algonquian (Wopanaak) words and names, so that readers can better experience early English attempts to comprehend American languages.

The purpose of this book is to gather all relevant texts and evidences into good order, to provide and promote fresh examination of "The Wessagusset Conspiracy" and of the American histories and heritage generated by it. Here are the four main 17th-century accounts (Winslow, Bradford, Pratt and Morton, plus letters from other contemporaries); the two most influential interpretations from the 19th century (Longfellow, Adams); and four investigations (Willison, Vaughan, Kupperman, and Wanakia), each inflected by the return of multiculturalism. Readers can witness the production of that most subtle, perilous and important basis of a "civilization," history; and discern for themselves from these human beings, each with their contexts, agendas, sincerities, contradictions, confusions and/or silences, what were once called the facts and the truth.

It is *not* this book's purpose to attack or disparage yesterday's Pilgrim colonists or today's "interpreters" of Plimoth Plantation; but to present, in the lights of 21st-century scientific knowledge and concepts of culture, fresh line-by-line correlation and analysis of *what evidences there are* concerning this "Affair." Its purpose (to paraphrase James Joyce) is to contribute a chapter in the moral history of the community, and this editor believes that it can, all things considered, promote healing among the descendants of *all* parties.

The sections below introduce "the times" and the peoples involved, within the larger body of knowledge called early Northeast American History.

ACKNOWLEDGMENTS

I will always be grateful to three of New England's most multitalented caretakers of the past: Mr. Bill Bowman of Weymouth; Michael F. McWade, naturalist of the Chikatatawbut Research Station in Massachusetts' Blue Hills; and Connecticutt artist and archaeologist David Wagner. They *are* the "school" looked forward to by Adams above. Bill's, Mike's and David's hours of conversation about old Weechagaskas, seasoned expertise and unspoiled joy in studying all the evidences kept me going---as they keep alive the pasts of this ancient land. I thank Karle Schlieff of Stoneham, Mass., for rare-book-borrowing privileges from his library; and (again) most of all, my mother Irene Geremonte Dempsey and my father John T., who so actively defend the right to write. Any mistakes here are mine.

1) Multiculture, Monologic and Back Again

When England's "Pilgrims" including Edward Winslow, William Bradford, Captain Myles Standish and 100 others on the *Mayflower* arrived in Massachusetts late in the autumn of 1620, they became part of two preexisting American worlds. The most fundamental one all around them (besides, of course, the immeasurable American continent) was a 13,000 year-old, very traditional, and thoroughly interconnected world of Native American peoples. The Plimothers themselves were the cutting edge of a second world already attaching itself to that America, a century-old *transatlantic* one; for throughout a previous period of almost 100 years, and through the first decade of these permanent plantation-style Puritan colonies, seasonal trade and social contacts continued to evolve between Northeastern Native Americans and the fishermen, sailors, fur-traders and explorers of Renaissance Europe.

Over several transatlantic generations of contact and trade, a working body of assumptions, understandings, practices, partnerships and social bonds had been developing between Americans and Europeans, into what another

kind of planter, Thomas Morton, called the country's "humors."[2] Records show
that where these mutual understandings and practices were observed by both
sides, a wary but generally-enduring peace and steady trade became what Colin
Calloway called a "cautious coexistence"; or in J.F. Fausz' phrase, "patterns of
Anglo-Indian aggression and accomodation."

As we discover more of the depth, magnitude, and "validity" of the
Native New England world, and as we get to know that first 100 years of
transatlantic coexistence, we also begin to see America's Puritan "founders" more
completely in their own conceptions and contexts, more *as they saw themselves.* In
their own words about their reasons for living and striving, they were
evangelists: "Saints," as they called themselves, "chosen" to "reform" a sinful
world, which in their case turned out to be America. We discover new
implications in the fact that the planters of Plimoth Colony, like the other first
Puritan colonies after them (Salem 1629, Mass. Bay Boston 1630, etc.), saw and
carried themselves as intentional departures from those long-practiced "humors"
of the transatlantic Northeast. Their aim was radical programmatic reform of
New England's early ways. This Introduction as to how this became the case is
borne out in the histories that follow.

By the 1580s, English plans for America (based on experience in Ireland)
had three main components: conquest, conversion, and (profitable) commerce.
The first such self-declared "reformer" was, in a secular sense, the chief
proponent of colonial enterprise, Richard Hakluyt; whose guiding
"Inducements" argued in 1585---based on English experience so far---that if
Native Americans continued to remain as they were, "content to live naked and
to content themselves with few things, then traffic is not. So then in vain seemeth
our voyage, unless this nature may be altered as by conquest and other good

---

[2] I have detailed this first century of transatlantic contact in *New English Canaan* and *Thomas
Morton: The Life and Renaissance of an Early American Poet.* Hopefully the Chronology and pages
here begin to suggest the dozens of annual transatlantic voyages: by 1615 the English alone
averaged 250 fishing and trade-ships in the Northeast per year (Biggar *Early* 23).

"Pilgrims" refers to the avowedly-Christian members and families of Plimoth who styled
themselves "Saints," though more secular-minded "Strangers" also took part in these events.
Bradford's *History* (edited by Ford *et als*, hereafter FBH) wrote of their departure from Leyden in
1620 (1:124): "So they left the goodly and pleasant city...their resting-place near twelve years. But
they knew they were Pilgrims, and looked not much on those things, but lifted up their eyes to
heaven, their dearest country, and quieted their spirits."

means....our soldiers trained up in the Netherlands, to square and prepare them for our preachers' hands" (in Pennington 181).

These English objectives, each an implicit "reform" of Native Americans, the politically-exiled "Pilgrims" had to wrestle with themselves, because their exile had cut them off from most regular (government-affiliated) means of support. They tried to meet those objectives with Captain Standish's military actions, with some attempts to convert Native people; and by "conversion" too of Native peoples from "dangerous" transatlantic trade-goods---contraband firearms, for example---to wampum, brought to Plimoth by the Dutch in 1627. A trace of this among many in the records appears in Pratt (118) when Massachusett man Pecksuot casually offers "much corn" for "powder and guns"; a bargain in fact almost never refused even into the 1620s, except by Puritan colonies. (Detailed in *Morton* Chs. 5 and 6.)

Plimoth's evangelists hoped to confirm and support their purposes by conversion; but this was founded on incorrect assumptions about Native New Englanders. In Bradford's words, "a great hope and inward zeal they had...for the propagating and advancing of the gospel of the kingdom of Christ in those remote parts....being devoid of all civil inhabitants...only savage and brutish men...little otherwise than wild beasts" (*History* 1:33). Winslow's Epistle to *Good News* thanked Merchant Adventurers for support in "convincing the Heathen of their evil ways, and converting them," and his first page of *Mourt's Relation* (1622: 6) championed "The desire of carrying the Gospel of Christ into those foreign parts, among those people that as yet have no knowledge nor no taste of God." Cushman's "Reasons" likened Plimothers to "the ancient patriarchs" of the Old World's Canaan, "removed from straiter places into more roomy" (245).

However, more like the "patriarchs" than they knew, Plimothers found well-established cultures in the American "Canaan," not subhuman beasts. And, once they realized that Native New Englanders neither needed nor much wanted them, Plimoth's "mission" allowed increasingly less "cautious coexistence" and became more of a collision course. Despite libraries of myth, there is no evidence that "The Pilgrims" believed in or wished to allow "freedom" either for Englishmen unlike themselves, or for Native peoples. Their purpose was to build a place for their own dominant Bible-based "public covenant" (more below). Their desire to return their Christian ways of life to an ancient purity and "libertie" (FBH1:3, 8) meant "liberty" to interpret and live The Bible---*not* the liberty to live *without* The Bible. At the same 1620s time, amid daily records of their pursuit of trade, the Plimothers record almost no effort at conversion; mainly, one such talk (in *Good News*) with Sachem Massasoit's rival Corbitant, who anticlimactically points out that both sides already believe "almost all the same things." Nor do Puritans in general "preach to the Indians" for years to come.

Apparently, the Pilgrims had realized something. They had not been in America five years when Winslow warned off would-be missionaries, to "discourage such as with too great lightness undertake such courses; who peradventure strain themselves and their friends for their passage thither, and are no sooner there, than seeing their foolish imagination made void, are at their wit's end, and...spare not to lay that imputation upon the Country, and others, which [they] themselves deserve" (*News* 85).

Since Plimoth was unable to make religion and profit jump together ("which is rare" as Winslow said), it remains to be seen how a different mixture of English policies took over, while "religion" still played its role; all of this, by programmatic laws and ethnocentric negligence, "changing the culture" of the transatlantic world. And because the Puritans so thoroughly succeeded in wresting control of that landscape and its ensuing written histories, generations of Americans lived a "new" world constructed upon Puritan (*vs.* transatlantic) foundations. Via the cultural work carried on by churches, schools, high and popular literature, business and social instruction underwritten at the root by colonial values, Anglo-Americans made it fundamental to their "national character" to derive and pass on crucial core-assumptions from those "self-reliant" Puritans---not least about Indians, and the righteous uses of "wilderness," violence, and history. There was, more than once, a "right-wing conspiracy" of historians. More often, the lazy or glib acceptance of unexamined "facts" worked to silence the larger story because of the short-term rewards of injustice: "respect," tenure, consciences soothed by the monological drone of "progress" (a word with close ties to "profit": etymology below). As surely as older transatlantic "humors" had created one America, the Puritans' programmatic interventions created another; and theirs became the model for greater hegemonies across the continent.[3]

Despite, however, the newcomers' "historical reformation" that lasted from the 17th century to the shores of the 21st, the Native American and transatlantic worlds remain the insufficiently-recognized mothers of American history and literature. Books and schools that built (seldom consciously) on the medieval European concept of *Monogenesis* made those two early-American worlds seem silent and invisible, at best a "pagan prelude" to the foundations of Christian America. As a result, the majority of America's teaching about early history has gone monologically on without almost two-thirds of the facts for any remotely-objective telling of the story.[4] This is comparable to teaching science without Einstein, to teaching a solar system of five planets because the persons somehow privileged by history to speak are "uncomfortable with" the colors of

---

[3] "We have great Ordnance....But that which is our greatest comfort [is] we have plentie of Preaching, and diligent Catechizing, with strickt and carefull exercise, and good and commendable orders to bring our people into a Christian conversation with whom we have to doe withall....If God be with us, who can be against us?" Higginson, *New-England's Plantation* (1630: rpt. in Force 3: 14). Salisbury *Manitou* (123) treats "coercion" as a "basis for trading."

"As an historian, I would say that the notion of disappearing Indians, or the notion that Indians are doomed to disappear, is embedded in all of the writings of 17th-century English immigrants. And given that the model for writing history comes from the writers of the 1620s and 1630s, it seems to me that we have to...at least consider the possibility, that there is a discourse of 'disappearing Indians' that is foundational to the history of The United States." Nipmuc historian Thomas Doughton, in Dempsey, *NANI: A Native New England Story*.

[4] *Monogenesis*, studied in detail by O'Gorman and Huddleston, was a theory developed partly in response to the clues reaching Europe, via traders and travelers, that the Apostles of Jesus Christ had not, as The Bible claimed, reached "all the ends of the Earth." All "new" peoples being discovered by Christian Europeans were to be understood as "lost" or "degenerate" fragments of themselves, via The Bible's "one original humanity" whose Creation is told in *Genesis* and its "scattering" in the story of the Tower of Babel (*Genesis* 11:9).

This was, in effect, Europe's second attempt to "master Difference" by rewriting worlds past and present; for in the ancient Classical world, "multiculturalism" (that is, a world inevitably diverse) had also been both natural fact and common assumption (see for ex. Herodotus' histories and travels throughout the Mediterranean: he condescends to "other" cultures but reveals no wish to make them Greeks). Even in the slave-powered Roman world, a slave was a *conquered* Other, but still a being *with* its own culture, not a "degenerate" form of oneself needing erasure and reform. Rome was polyglot with distinguished Greek and other "ethnic" slaves who were actually cultural teachers. Medieval Europe's Christians resisted The Renaissance and actively tried to "rewrite" it exactly because of its revival of ancient "relativistic" values and perspectives, just as today's fossils of monologic try to cast multi-culturalism as a passing fashion of "PC" decadence.

four other worlds---which remain nonetheless "out there." The world now knows that this a fundamentally relative universe. "Other" people and cultures are indispensable reference-points for each one, our main and most intelligent chance to know our own behavior. With due poststructural skepticisms into our thinking, we need---given our linguistic, cultural and cosmic limitations each---what Stanley Diamond called "a proper anthropology, the purpose of which is self-knowledge and the means the authentic understanding of others" (in Chiapelli, ed., *First Images*). This is a relative universe and we need to learn to feel at home *where we are*. No longer with "moral bearings" handed down from a transcendental agency, we can (and had better) take readings on what we are by telling *all* the story, all sides in.[5]

As Charles Francis Adams, Jr. expressed it about The Pilgrims, "There is something appalling in the consciousness of utter isolation" (*Three Episodes* 75). What he almost said was, "It is appalling that colonists could consider themselves alone in New England, and it had appalling consequences." Adams knew too well that Plimoth Colony had scarcely made the average fisherman's or fur-trader's effort to know Native New Englanders on their *own* terms---as people, with cultures, families, feelings, memories, motives---and that this was

---

[5] It is important to keep in mind fundamentals of linguistic and hence cultural dynamics. As in Saussure's famous example, both French and German peoples, each with their own languages based in different ecological, social and historical circumstances, perceive something they each call *cow* in a field between them. Each one's word or symbol for that thing is equally arbitrary (it has nothing to do with the *cow itself*), is as unique as any of their other tools for getting things done. Each group's "symbolic approach" to the world is as "valid" as the other's, hence the basis of multiculturalism. At this point, many post-Saussure academics insist with new kinds of deterministic jargon(s) that *neither* party, to some much-debated degree, perceives the cow because of the utterly-circumscribing, self-referential "nature of language" that "always already" affects the human subject. Since theorists remain unable to explain *their own* perception of this "fact," it seems more likely---given that early hominids did evolve five senses, a voice-box, and language itself---that somehow "the cow" (that is, the natural world with its "other peoples" all around each *human symbolic* system) is "really there," the very stimulus of language and its ongoing evolutions.

Thus we may better understand how "cautious coexistence" became a "collision" of cultures (symbolic systems). "Collision" happens when one side tries to force *its own* symbolic system and agenda upon another people. There was no such "ideological effort" during the transatlantic period: most historians mark the "collision" close to and as-of the Puritan. "Outsiders" who stand by their own "realities," like "the cow," are in no way "answerable" to another system's agenda or "destined" (except by many forms of force) to be docile, silent, or invisible. See Wanakia, "Suffering Fools."

not done in the face of the same peoples whose help, alone, enabled Plimoth's "self-reliant" families to survive their first two years in America.

The Plimothers sought treaties to give themselves a sense of security: they sought local trade whose profits would pay for what they built, and they could hardly help recording some of the "human charm" of the peoples they met in both efforts. Beyond this, their connections to "others" were more like a medieval than a Renaissance Europe's. Adams knew, from Plimoth to Quincy in his own day, that it was the colonizers' fondest fantasy to see themselves as "but a pitiful handful...a speck, as it were, of civilized life between the sea on the one side and that impenetrable forest, within which lurked the savage, on the other."[6]

Perceiving the Plimothers' extraordinary and needless isolation from their human neighbors, historians knew but *did not allow the history to know* that, as Adams continued, "it was impossible [that the Plimothers] should not exaggerate rather than diminish the danger." And the ethnocentric melodrama lives on in "mainstream" America. Another example of this cultural damage is the flat-wrong celebration of Puritan Anne Bradstreet as America's first poet in English. Chronologically alone, Bradstreet comes *ninth* among the actual contenders.[7]

------

[6] Contrast the multiple points of view woven into the fabric of secular-minded Morton's *Canaan* with Winslow's *Good News*. Later New England works by Wood and Josselyn put into relief this aspect of Puritan histories, what this Introduction identifies as "selective emphasis." Although Winslow (for ex.) seems to fairly observe much "neutral fact" about Native peoples, the knowledge has no *weight* in or *ethical impact* upon his telling of "the story" itself. In *Canaan*, the details and points of view in specific intercultural incidents accrue into a Native *presence* that must be "answered and accounted for" in the story being told of "human beings in New England." The details reflect *time* spent ("continuance and conversation amongst them"; "the more I looked, the more I liked it," as Morton said, 14 and 53), and the writer's coming to terms with "others." To this editor it seems that the ethnographic portion of *Good News* was mostly the product of "in-house" interviews with Tisquantum and Hobbamock. Winslow had less than a year to write it (from April 1623 when "conspiracy" events concluded to publication in 1624 London), with a 6-weeks voyage between; and he gives no example of his "many apparent deaths" (*News* 1) in Native New England. He does record that when shown Native customs he "tried to make them understand against their practices" (69).

[7] Old traditions continue in New England. In late 2000 an array of historical societies and cultural groups produced a week of events devoted to just this mistaken premise about the Christian "poet of Andover." Politely queried about the homework for the educational enterprise, informed of rich connections between Native peoples and early-American poetry, producers and journalists replied, "another time," "politically correct," and "too intellectual."

See also *The Boston Globe*'s annual preemptive strikes each Thanksgiving and Columbus Days. "Massasoit needed the help...His people were being pressed hard [whatever that means]

Native voices, life-stories, and points of view still wait to be heard between the European lines, wait *to enrich* them, to unlock new dimensions of humanizing values in transatlantic histories. The killings at Weymouth Colony will not go away, because they "would speak" about too many, too-similar events, crucial places and times when assumptions too long-unexamined revealed themselves and, because "realized too late," issued in tragedy. "The Weymouth Massacre" speaks of physical violence, and of violence explained, approved, and encouraged by historians earning their bread at the table of power by twisting the records and the likelihoods between. The story of a mistakenly-hardened, mutual misunderstanding is one thing: to plaster over legitimate questions in fear of moral ambiguity, to fashion a halfbaked us-or-them triumph of one race over generic inferiors is another. A lie cannot underwrite morality. "The Weymouth Paradigm" is a matter of record across the land west of Massachusetts Bay.

Another legacy of these events is America's old yet vibrant "blood pudding" school of "popular entertainment" that came textually out of that old New England standard, the "Indian captivity narrative." Haunted by its uncomprehended histories, dependent upon irrational monsters that obscure its own irrationality, the genre delivers its multiple climaxes as tragic, "unwanted" yet righteous gore: culture as what Jack Frost dubbed "macabre memorabilia."

---

by inland tribes," chime the editors (Nov. 23, 2000). "For several years," from Thanksgiving till "King Philip began his doomed war" as they say, "the Pilgrims and Wam-panoags cooexisted peacefully." Noting that Native Americans have managed to create a Plymouth town plaque "as a reminder of the genocide... and the relentless assault on their culture," *Globe* editors remark: "The best lesson from Winslow's account [of Thanksgiving] is that we humans have a great need to join together to celebrate our material blessings, whether it is a plentiful harvest or a steady job"; and that "the feast is more memorable if we include friends and acquaintances. That is an enduring lesson that will survive the changing interpretations of a complex event."

Since no effort was made to examine those complexities---after all, neither the feast, nor the friendship possible only through justice, outlasted 1621---what *is* the substance of this "enduring lesson"? It hides in plain sight. Control of "media" (dailies and histories) can be used to reinforce paternalistic myths, such as gratitude for "a steady job." This may be what *Globe* advertising for its "family newspaper" calls "a complete picture of your world." The main problem is that "this" is not the 1950s, when Hollywood's unfortunately still-best attempt won an Oscar with *The Plymouth Adventure* starring Spencer Tracy. Not surprisingly, the Oscar was for *Special Effects* used to create a harrowing image of Pilgrim families tossed to and fro in the hold of the seagoing *Mayflower*. "Indians" appear only in the last five seconds, a background-shot in which they "gratefully" saw wood for Plimoth suburbs.

(Jane Tompkins' 1992 *West of Everything* laid bare America's favorite self-image as an innocent hero "forced" to righteous bloodshed.) American blood pudding is a saccharine substitute for real engagement with the past, an infantilization that forfeits "for" people the chance for perception, for Renaissance, new life. That is Hollywood's role as the grease-gun of imperialist realpolitik, bestowing on new generations a spirit-numbing fetish for *everything except the causes* of violence. In contrast to Native societies' general approach to "criminals," which (as A.F.C. Wallace's *Seneca* details) emphasizes the *weakness* of those who harm the group, today's "infotainment" glorifies criminals' power to "disturb"---disturb everything but the turning of community-tragedy into "sensational" commodity. In the language of that marketplace, "The Weymouth Massacre" is "America's Oldest Murder Mystery," and it is not already "a film" because of the identities of the prime-and-only suspects. That's entertainment: everything explodes except the demand that people stand up straight on a crooked foundation.[8]

---

[8] See the Illustrations derived from Frost's rare study *Immortal Voyage*, of the "haunted house" in Weymouth today in which, supposedly, heads of Native victims of the Weymouth Massacre were found and where "the ghost of Wituwamat" supposedly walks. A Thomas Morton would smile at some historical grotesquery, such as finding his diminutive nemesis "Captain Shrimp" Myles Standish's statue atop what is billed today as "the world's tallest historical monument" (at Standish State Forest). But the wax figures and "artist's conceptions" once the main attractions of Plymouth's Pilgrim Hall and Museum---featuring Standish bringing his sword down on a prostrate Indian---stood until very recently as educational homage to "preemptive" violence. The Disney/Demi Moore film *The Scarlet Letter* carries on.

Every Native New Englander of 30 interviewed by this editor for the documentary-film *Nani: A Native New England Story* (1998)---not to mention historically-informed non- Natives of the region---had "always thought" (as one said) that those "cultural attractions" exemplified deliberately-biased history. Though the multicultural balance and quality of most museum-exhibits have improved over time, the topography of today's "living history" museum Plimoth Plantation continues to give the high central ground to the "Pilgrim Village" and a palpable degree of sideshow status to "Hobbamock's Homesite." (I know and respect the excellence achieved throughout Plimoth's programs, but this topography is indeed a "living vestige" of historical hegemonies; as is the fact that though "it's 1627" in Plimoth's main "live" exhibits, neither Wituwamat's head nor Plimoth's blood-soaked "flag" hang over Plimoth gate, and there is still no acknowledgment of either Weymouth or Ma-re Mount colonies.) In the 1620s, as the first map of this book suggests, the Colony's situation was exactly opposite; and in a way "The Affair" occurred *because* Plimoth and Weymouth knew it well.

Later entertainments, from captivity narratives to blood-pudding "frontier romances" studied in Reynolds' *Beneath the American Renaissance,* from wax-figure dioramas to films like *Last of the Mohicans,* continue to register at least that something is missing. Every student will learn from the watershed achievements of Plimoth's exhibit *Irreconcileable Differences,* whose title signifies so much honest cooperative effort to create new dimensions of history. Even so, one

The Weymouth Affair also raises serious questions that a nation of America's stature should be able to answer about its long-declared first-founders. What values did the Pilgrims really practice in the face of their American experiences? How credible today is the scarce-whispered "charge of conscience" that drives all of these writings, that the Weymouth killings were, to say the least, unnecessary? What "cultural work" did the Pilgrim-praising American Republic accomplish by adopting them at its foundations? What can "the mind of Plimoth 1623" tell about the mind of America 2001? Can we come to terms with this history and no longer demonize *any*one?

More than 20 years ago, the distinguished historian Karen Ordahl Kupperman asked us to imagine that "the Brethren could dissemble." Why had "our" historians so seldom made history answer to fresh examination of the evidences, especially where profound human issues were "decided" at last by violence? "Coincidentally," Kupperman was writing about that unique, first-exiled historian Thomas Morton of "Merrymount." Morton had charged that in Puritan New England, one "without" the "new creed" of Christian beliefs would receive neither food nor shelter. So did Kupperman suggest, in challenging the ridicule of Morton and *Canaan*'s "exile," her own explanation for the long life of "nightmare-history": the systematic rewards (for example, *bread, home, tenure*) that keep the "history industry" on good behavior, and are still used to muffle the thunder, minimize the impact, and prevent the healing within the multicultural facts. The stakes are not small when a mouldering spiritual stockade still confines new generations bound for America's leadership in paradigms of righteous (self-interested) violence. "Immoral" Morton was the first American historian denied life, liberty and happiness for recording as best he could a multisided world, and his story follows directly from this one.[9]

---

may wonder if the "differences" really were "irreconcileable," and whether one side more than another held Difference itself as non-negotiable.

[9] Expect this to be dismissed as "progressive presentism," a judging of the past according to present standards [*sic*]. Then read the statements by C.F. Adams, Jr. in the last note to this Introduction, his lecture-comments with *Three Episodes* here, and Vaughan's analysis. There was certainly no lack of "progressive" and *contemporary* voices across the spectrum of European colonizers, from Spain (Las Casas) and France (Lescarbot) to Englishman Morton.

2) The Peoples Involved

As noted, the 17th century's transatlantic world was a network of contacts and traders between two large, very diverse populations---the Native peoples of North America and those of Europe. This section provides a limited portrait of all cultural parties to the events of 1622-23, while much more detail appears through their unfolding actions.

Native Americans of central-coastal Massachusetts and New England[10] were communal in their economics: that is, each group shared "all things" (or most of them) produced by the members, and the many groups traded with each other in a barter (rather than profit-based) relationship.[11] This was sustained

---

[10] Given varying New England landscapes (mountain, upland, riverine, coastal etc.), there were many cultural differences among its peoples. This study intends to refer first to southern *Massachusett* people ("of the big rock region," or "place of the great hill"; also "Great Blue Hill," "because of all the blueberries"). Such were the Neponsets (meaning "Early Summer") living northward of "Weechagaskas" (Dexter 23). It is also spelled Wessaguscus/Wessagusset (Morton, Wood), Wichaguscusset (Winslow *News* 22), Wesaguscosit (Pratt 111)---in Eastern Algonquian/ Wopanaak, "the narrow place" (Horner; Bruchac-Caduto 148); or "at the small salt water cove" (Pritchard 56).

[11] The word *profit* (according to *The Oxford English Dictionary*) originated in Latin and Old French *profit-us*, meaning "advance, progress." Etymological examples of its Early Modern usage include (1466) "A syngler profette hyrtyth and harmyth a comyn wele"; (1500-20) "They think no sin, quhair [where] proffeit cumis betwene"). The word is further defined as "The advantage or benefit (of a person, community or thing)"; as a verb, "to make progress; to advance, go forward; to improve, prosper, grow, increase (in some respect) "; and as "That which is derived from or produced by some source of revenue, *e.g.* ownership of land, feudal or ecclesiastical rights or perquisites, taxes, etc.: revenue, proceeds, returns." *Profit* signifies "The pecuniary gain in any transaction: the amount at which value acquired exceeds value expended: the excess of returns over the outlay of capital...the surplus product of industry after deducting wages, cost of raw materials, rent and charges." As *revenue* it signifies a kind of "second coming" of "value" somehow "beyond" the total expenses of production.

In a *barter* relationship, whatever the costs of each trading-partner's production of their item, the trade itself produces no "surplus" wealth or "advantage" to one side: they establish "fair exchange" of goods/services that both sides equally need. *Profit*, by contrast, is generically "something for nothing": *by definition* it is "value" or wealth that is *not* part of any original outlay. Where, then, does it "come from"? Since physics confirms that nothing can be created from nothing, *profit* must actually emerge from one side's "somehow" receiving more than their share of the goods' finite "value." With reference to the rest of this story, the party somehow being *dis*advantaged by this cannot be expected not to notice. See Kupperman *Major Problems* 27-38.

among groups with (like all families) many serious differences and "running quarrels" by means of an elaborate social fabric of relationships and practices, evolved (like those of Europe) over generations.

Relationships themselves were/are conceived as concentric circles (person/family/clan/tribe/alliance/etc., to infinity), that began with and touched back upon individual identities. These included particular blood-lines traced "to the eighth degree" mostly through the mother; identities conceived in terms of location (for example, the Aquinnah Wampanoag, the Massachusetts inhabiting the Neponset River watershed); different kinds of "transcendent kinship" based in alliances of clans, intertribal adoptions (some of those via kidnap to "replace" lost blood-kin, in so-called "tribute wars"); and "medicine societies" shared by groups of men and women of different origins. Intermarriages, seasonal ceremonies of mutual recognition, "revels" including competitive sports (at which the prizes were given away), and socializing maintained these relationships efficiently. There were also nepotistic "family politics" alliances and "simple" bonds among and across generations, groups or pairs of friends (such as Pecksuot and Wituwamat seemed to be, with the latter's younger brother "in their footsteps").[12] Pritchard (56) describes "seven great confederacies in the New England area south of the Wabanaki": the Pennacook, Massachusett, Wampanoag, Narragansett, Pocumtuck, Nipmuc, and Pequot. While the sheer spectrum of trade-goods/raw materials in archaeological digs proves the region's long-distance connections, too, experienced early observers such as John Pory (c.1622: 13) noted necessary links of language: "many [Native New England] words agree with those of the South Colony [Virginia] and of the eastern shore of [Chesapeake] Bay."

Over decades of recorded contacts with Europe, it was observed that some Sachems began to exert more control over trade conducted in their territories, possibly as part of the attempt to manage their own peoples' changing fortunes in relation to the newcomers. (More detail below.) But the

---

[12] I derive these categories from a 1991 lecture by Wampanoag historican Nanepashemet/ Anthony Pollard, who spoke to the Haffenreffer Museum of Anthropology on Native concepts of "Indian Identity." The recording can be heard via the Nanepashemet Archive at the R.S. Peabody Museum at Phillips Academy, Andover MA. The phrase "transcendent kinship" comes from Barsh's "Nature and Spirit of North American Political Systems."

acknowledged center of Native New England's social structure was and is woman. First, she controlled her own body, sexuality and reproduction. Fresh from his 1627 visit to the Plimoth area, de Rasieres (72) wrote a report that tells much. A Native woman who "addict[ed] herself to fornication," he wrote, was to be "driven" "out of the house" and, "if there be children, they remain with her, for they are fond of them beyond measure." (Few Native women-and-children were observed "without a house.") He noted that "when a man is unfaithful," it "most frequently happens when the wife has a preference for another man." "[They] are very libidinous---in this respect very unfaithful to each other; whence it results *that they breed but few children*" (73: emphasis added). ["It] is a wonder when a woman has three or four children, particularly by any one man."

Second, de Rasieres (cited because his outsider's report corroborates English ones) recorded that the "Sackima" or Sachem required great "expenditure" of hospitality and wealth in conducting trade and diplomacy. "Therefore, the Sackimas generally have three or four wives, each of whom has to furnish her own seed-corn" (73)---that is, women's labors in gathering and gardens were very much the economic base of "his" powers. Women appointed and deposed Sachems, and families knew each other as members of matrilineal clans. One more efficient "summary" by de Rasieres describes the general decision-making process:

> Their political government is democratic. They have a chief Sackima whom they choose by election, who generally is he who is richest in [wampum and other goods], though of less consideration in other respects. When any stranger comes, they bring him to the Sackima. On first meeting they do not speak: they smoke a pipe of tobacco. That being done...[the] stranger then states...what he has to say, before all who are present or choose to come. That being done, the Sackima announces his opinion to the people, and if they agree thereto, they give all together a sigh, "*He!*" and if they do not approve, they keep silence, and all come close to the Sackima, and each sets forth his opinion till they agree.

Native New England religion centered, like the peoples' daily and seasonal practices, around the natural world and human ways of maintaining harmonious relationship with it.[13] Most recognized Kiehtan or Cautantowitt as "The Creator," associated with the southwest, the source of the ancestors and culture, of benign natural forces and the haven of spirits in the afterlife. They also recognized a corresponding spirit "of" the northeast, Chepi or Hobbomock, who embodied the powers of cold, wintry darkness, the malign aspects of "wandering spirits," and who sent human beings visions and shamanic powers (as Winslow's details attest). There is also a "sub-mythology" alive in oral traditions of quasi-demigods such as The Woman Who Fell From the Sky, her part in the world's creation, and her progeny, the giant-magicians Maushop or Gluskap (a proud, semi-comic family-man and helper of human beings), and his gleefully-troublesome twin Lox.[14]

In these "Creation and After" stories traditionally recounted in the snug lodges of midwinter camp (they still take pride telling the generations back to when people walked to Nantucket), a world-class array of characters "human and other" play out a world where people are free to acquire the skills to manipulate the forces and "stuff" of the universe, *manit*---and more or less create their fate. In this symbolic world, death is neither an end (Lox "got over it" many times: Leland 174), nor a bringer of "justice" to a story. Living and dead, right and wrong, good and evil interpenetrate---and teach sophisticated appreciation of each unique being, circumstance, and choice.

Annual agricultural and other surpluses were either consumed in Native villages' autumn social festivals, or stored for winter use (see Russell's indispensable "field-guide," *Indian New England Before the Mayflower* 180). Then "the season's round" took people inland to camps in weather-sheltered forests. There they lived on corn-stores and preserved foods while men more intensively

---

[13] "In Wopanaak, the stars are animate. They are considered alive. The language touches on understanding the religion....In English, you can say about someone, He's a father or he's a friend, but you can't say that in Wopanaak because no person in the circle stands by themselves....Every kinship term depends on someone else in the circle....Land, for example, was considered by the Wampanoags as part of the people, so the word for land has an inalienable ending [that is, an ending signifying spiritual connection]." A Wampanoag quoted in Burrell.

[14] Wallace's *Seneca* provides thorough telling of the widely-known story of The Woman Who Fell From the Sky; and as Leland records New England creation-stories of the birth (from her) of twins Gluskap and Lox, connections appear between the Midwestern "Woman" and New England's gigantic brothers.

tracked and trapped game through January, ice-fishing into the spring, then returning to rivers' weir-works in spawning-season. In addition to Leland's and Simmons' collections of oral traditions evoking ages of relations with land, plants and animals, scholars such as Crosby, Mavor and Dix, Russell Gardner/Great Moose of the Wampanoag, and Kathleen Bragdon have detailed the sacredness of the land itself: "The likelihood that animals in the dark woods or deep waters were transformations of even more powerful beings, and the certainty that the 'natural' world was imbued with power, structured and made sacred hunting and collecting" (Bragdon *Peoples* 195).

> Gift-giving [was important in most Native American societies] in maintaining political and economic alliance networks....Most exchanges, whether internal or external to a village, were articulated in the language of gift-giving. This needs to be reconciled with the knowledge that prior to the introduction of the European fur trade, the Native people of New England killed animals only in proportion as they had need of them. They never made an accumulation of skins of Moose, Beaver, Otter and others....   (Merchant 92-98)

Plimoth's colonists in 1623 consisted of two main groups of "Early Modern" English people, all of them former farmers or tradesmen, a few merchants and gentlemen (such as Winslow), plus their wives and children. About half of Plimoth's people were comparative "secularists" or "Strangers," meaning at least nominally-Christian individuals seeking to colonize America with European economics rather than religion as their driving motive. Plimoth itself had come about through the colony's other main group, its "Saints," as they called themselves. Most basically (individual biographies with selections), these Christians sought to live according to the teachings of Jesus Christ as described in The Bible's New Testament; who, in their belief, had lived and died in the Middle East about 2000 years ago and had been The Only Son of the One True God, come to Earth to atone for the "Original Sin" of the first of all humans, Adam and Eve. That sin---eating fruit from a "forbidden" Tree in The Garden of Eden by which they might "become as gods"---had been caused by a spiritual being antithetical to God and Jesus, called Satan or Lucifer, who ruled over the "underworld" of Hell and "roamed the world seeking the ruin of souls."

The Protestant and especially the Puritans' God had already mysteriously "saved" only a few "Chosen People" for eternal life in His Heaven, while the rest stood preordained for eternal punishment. Nonetheless, the Plimothers believed it their Christian duty to "reform" every born child (see Fischer), plus both "Old English" culture and greater Christianity (in their home-country, the Anglican Church rather than the Catholic). These religious convictions, held in defiance of England's establishment, had resulted in their years of exile in The Netherlands and, after a harsh period of poverty, their *Mayflower* voyage to New England in 1620. In their own minds, they would either succeed in America or see their experimental community come to an end.

On that basis, America had two basic "natures" for the Pilgrims that were expressed in different contexts in their records. The land at times seemed to them a conveniently "empty" refuge, a "wild" place totally unlike the English farm-counties, deer parks and moors of their homeland; and one of great "potential for improvement," in later years of ample harvest or trade even a Biblical "promised land" come true. But at first, and later whenever the land and its "creatures" seemed "uncooperative," it was "a hideous and desolate wilderness, full of wild beasts and wild men"---the "desert" home of Satan and "his." (See Cave's *The Pequot War* for recent study of these Biblical and American linkages, which troubled "even" colonists from Morton to Roger Williams.)

Economically, the Plimothers had begun life a mixed array of farmers, yeomen, craftsmen and lower-middle-class English villagers: in time they became proto-capitalists, traders in unknown country, "merchant-adventurers," part of Europe's reachings-out into the "unknown" world, into which men "invested" resources and labor, and from it, expected profit. Amid the demand for dependably-disciplined colonists who could expand Europe's Early Modern economic system, the Plimothers reached America and a place for their exiled religious practices by becoming "undertakers" of contracts and (by 1627) financial debts to "incorporated" groups of English businessmen---their "backers." To meet *their* expectations of timely profit, to pay their debts and sustain the future growth of their colony, Plimothers had to expand their control over American lands and resources. These were quite different "reasons for existence" than those of Native Americans already on the land. There were also great differences in their social structures, for Plimoth was like its mother country and continent: virtually all affairs except the household's were decided, controlled and conducted by adult men.[15]

The remaining chief participants in this story were Thomas Weston and the "lusty young men" indentured to him for the building of his own plantation at Wessagusset/Weymouth. Weston, a "citizen and ironmonger of London" had met the "Saints" in The Netherlands and become a go-between for them in their effort to arrange the American passage. According to Bradford's *History* and letters, Weston was an opportunistic businessman who did not hesitate to "help" the Pilgrims into labor-contracts for their American passage, nor to trade cast-iron guns to the French against the rules of ongoing war: he was literally a "merchant adventurer" in the accelerating race for the profits of planting in "the Massachusetts,"[16] and more than once Weston vowed help for Plimoth, only to prove "but wind."

---

[15] "Touching our government you are mistaken if you think we admit women and children to have to do in the same, for they are excluded, as both reason and nature teacheth they should be; neither do we admit any but such as are above the age of 21 years, and they also but only in some weighty matters, when we think good...." Gov. Wm. Bradford, "A Letter," 1623.

"Before landing the leaders of the Pilgrims drew up the famous Mayflower Compact to serve as the basis of government. There was no intention of making a new departure in the direction of a democratic constitution, and the short document was merely a modification of the customary form of church covenant to meet a temporary crisis in an unfamiliar situation" (*Encyclopedia Britannica* entry by "J.A.T"; who adds of 1630's Boston Puritans: "The intention of [King Charles I] was evidently to create a merely commercial company with...stockholders, officers, and directors, but by a shrewd and legally questionable move [John Winthrop's] patentees decided to transfer the entire management and the charter itself to Massachusetts, thus paving the way...for the unwarranted assumption, pregnant with most important consequences, that the charter for a commercial company was in reality a political constitution for a new government with only indefinable dependence upon the imperial one at home."

Captain Myles Standish, one of many English soldiers sent by Queen Elizabeth to help fight the Spanish, met the Plimoth "Saints" in The Netherlands and became their "chief man at arms" for the intended colony. Unlike gentleman Edward Winslow, Standish never joined the official church congregation at Plimoth Plantation.

[16] "If God had seen it good we should have been right glad it [a 'large and liberall supply'] had come sooner, both for our good and your profit; for we have both been in a languishing state...so as we have little or nothing to send you ['the New Plimoth Adventurers dwelling on London Bridge'], for which we are not a little sorry....yet those [small profits] are nothing to those we have lost for want of means to gather them when the time was, which I fear will scarce ever be again, seeing [that] the Dutch on one side and the French on the other side and the fishermen and other plantations between both have, and do furnish the savages, not with toys and trifles, but with good and substantial commodities...." Bradford, "A Letter," 1623.

In the end---in Virginia, that is, when he'd quit Massachusetts---Weston did find success; but Bradford summed him up as "a bitter enimie unto [Plimoth] upon all occasions" (FBH1:299). On American shores, the parties' enmities acquired mortal consequences starting in 1622-23. Drawing men from promotional calls for "young Youths from Parishes, that have not been tainted with any villainies or misdemeanors to be sent to New England" (Deane ed., Council Records 31), Weston shipped groups totaling almost 100 persons without experience or supplies into the already-tight situation at Plimoth. To send so many implied his means to compete against Plimoth as a planter; and yet, to send them without "vittels, nor hope of any" almost had to be seen as direct intent to erect his own Weymouth on the ruins of an overburdened Plimoth. The dispiriting impact of such "help from home" on the surviving Plimoth colonists---who had only just seen more than half of their company die of cold, hunger, and fever on these frozen shores---can hardly be imagined. On that basis it can be said that, until 1621-23, colonists of New England had never faced such a moment that seemed to demand the adoption of "survival values."[17]

Weston's young indentured men, anonymous to history except Phinehas Pratt, played central parts in these events and chronicles. Like many of Plimoth's "Strangers," they did not care for the religious mission of "the Saints," and mocked it. The Weymouth men must have cared even less for Native New Englanders, for immediately they became known as incompetent and unwilling students to the skills of survival here, as "desperate" stealers of Native foodstores and abusers of Native women. At the same time, at least one man did, apparently, "turn savage" and join Massachusetts peoples, while others earned a

---

[17] How much "necessity" was behind this tragedy? We begin to ask what real *options* seemed to exist for those involved. Contrast two notes from Young's edition of *Good News*. On the Native side, the much-confirmed observation that "Their Sachems have not their men in such subjection but that very frequently their men will leave them upon distaste or harsh dealing, and go and live under other sachems that can protect them; so that their princes endeavor to carry it obligingly and lovingly unto their people, lest they should desert them" (Gookin qtd. on 360). On the Plimoth side, in the words of their pastor John Robinson, "No man to whom England is known can be ignorant that all the natives there, and subjects of the kingdom...are without difference compelled and enforced by most severe laws, civil and ecclesiastical, into the body of that church [of England]....Every subject of the kingdom, dwelling in this or that parish, is bound, will he, nil he, fit or unfit, as with iron bonds, to participate in all holy things, and some unholy also" (390).

share of Native food as many shipwrecked sailors had earned it before, fetching water and wood: here they also began to build boats for their hosts. Still more Weymouth men (much to Captain Standish's annoyance) ranged the area for ground-nuts without weapons or fear for their lives. To Weston and these planters, survival and business were, in Morton's words, as much as they needed to care for, "aiming at Beaver principally."

"Disorderly" as the Weymouth newcomers seemed, that policy (or the lack of one) had characterized the transatlantic well into the 1600s.

3) The Transatlantic

> The advancement of the King's dominions, with the advancement of religion in those desert parts, are matters of highest consequence, and far exceeding a simple and disorderly course of fishing...for that so goodly a coast could not be long left unpeopled [*sic*] by the French, Spanish or Dutch....
>
> [The] mischief already sustained by those disorderly persons, are inhumane and intolerable; for first, in their manners and behavior they are worse than the very savages, impudently and openly lying with their women, teaching their men to drink drunk, to swear and blaspheme the name of God, and in their drunken humor to fall together by the ears [argue], thereby giving them occasion to seek revenge. Besides, they cozen and abuse the savages in trading and trafficking, selling them salt covered with butter instead of so much butter, and the like
>
> ....[And] they sell unto the savages muskets, fowling pieces, powder, shot, swords, arrow-heads, and other arms, wherewith the savages slew many of those fishermen, and are grown so able and so apt [that] they become dangerous to the planters....

This was the region's leading colonial proponent, Sir Ferdinando Gorges, describing the transatlantic Northeast before the increasingly-Puritan members of Parliament (*Narration* 38) just as Weymouth was launched and unfolding. Indeed, the peoples of the transatlantic had been behaving just like the rest of humanity: warily intermixing, trading, reveling, cheating, fighting, murdering and "making it up" through their human bonds; and, in another sense, "making it up" as they lived with each other day by day. These decades offer no record of *ideological* or (in that sense) "cultural struggle," only the random encounters of exploration and trade, of peoples in cautious pursuit of an edge in the bargain, which leads here and there to spontaneous scuffling. The small fortunes so far made by Gorges and other merchant adventurers had been built on the discovery---no doubt shared by Native Americans---that these "strange" new peoples were, as Gorges put it, "tractable [as long as] discreet courses be taken with them" (qtd. in Rowse 99). Fishermen salting cod or mending a boat on a beach found Native peoples orchestrating "first encounters" that traded furs for cloth or manufactured goods; goods which in time became liquors, too, broken swords, then knives, then guns. Clearly, Native people realized early that the strangers did not offer their best things first, and learned to drive a bargain for their incomparably-profitable beaver.

One of the defining traits of this period---put to an end as a defining part of the Puritan order---is the fact that during the transatlantic, the two sides traded *what the other asked for* in exchange for their own wealth. Europeans were glad to trade a 2-shilling iron "trade axe" or garden-hoe for a single beaver-pelt that yielded as much as 16 shillings' profit at home (about 800%: Eddy Snow 100-01); while Native people, who offered "six and seven [pelts] for one" gun likely traded by Morton (*Canaan* 155), gained in the bargain not a more reliable or accurate weapon for their needs, but a share of the "thunders" they feared so much (citations below) and, thus, a sense of power-backed *options*---the right to a *say* in how these unprecedented relationships would affect their lives and country. As often, a sailor wanted "our daughters" as a Canarsee sachem put it. These "courses" had begun well before the 1580s voyages of Captain Davis in search for a Northwest Passage;[18] and they were still in action when in 1622 Weston's Plimoth-bound ship arrived at Damaris Cove fishing-station, where

---

[18] "The people of the country, having espied us, made a lamentable noise, as we thought, with great outcries and screeching: we hearing them thought it had been the howling of wolves.... We brought our musicians, purposing by force to rescue us, if need should so require, or with courtesy to allure the people. When they came unto us, we caused our musicians to play, ourselves dancing and making many signs of friendship....[We] were in so great credit with them upon this single acquaintance that we could have anything they had. We bought five canoes...the clothes from their backs....They are very tractable people, void of craft or double-dealing, and easy to be brought to any civility and good order...." (Capt. John Davis, 1585 *First Voyage*; rpt. in David, ed. Hakluyt 336-8)

people had "newly set up a maypole and were very merry" (Pratt, also qtd. in FBH1:256).

It was no utopia. Since the first contacts between Early Modern Englishmen and Native (Beothuk) peoples of Newfoundland, Native Americans had at times faced bigotry and violence that reduced them to the status of game-animals "in the way" of trade (Brasser 83). At times, they no doubt tested the strangers' mettle or responded with mortal aim. But it is seldom recognized that, more often, different kinds of practical protocols prevented or at least inhibited offensive behaviors:

> ....The second day after our comming from the [sea], we
> espied 9 canowes or boats, with fiftie Indians in them, coming
> toward us...and being loth they should discover our fortification,
> we went out on the sea side to meet them; and comming somewhat
> neere them, they all sate down upon the stones, calling aloud to
> us (as we rightly guessed) to doe the like, a little distance from
> them. Having sate awhile in this order, Captaine Gosnold willed
> me to go unto them...but as soon as I came up unto them, one of them
> ...knew me (whom I also very well remembred) and smiling upon
> me, spake somewhat unto their lord or captaine, which sat in the
> midst of them, who presently rose up and tooke a large Beaver
> skin...and gave it unto me, which I requited....While we were
> thus merry...the rest of the day we spent in trading....(John
> Brereton, *Relation* 1602: rpt. in Levermore 37)

It followed that later (1623) the Wampanoag Sachem Corbitant, as part of a community with "transatlantic experience," remained adamant against the *in*experienced Plimother Edward Winslow's protest that Plimoth's guns trained upon Native visitors were "the most honorable and respect[ful] entertainment we could give." "[S]haking the head [Corbitant] answered that he liked not such salutations" (45).

There were contacts among groups of males such as Brereton's above, and as well, multiple forms of English male/Native female contact: acts of intercultural diplomacy, of spontaneous hospitality and trade, of cohabitation and at least quasi-marriage leading to offspring.[19] As French planter Marc

---

[19] All these practices are visible in Gorges' narratives assembled from the reports of his own ships' captains: see also *Mourt's Relation*'s multiple Native women suddenly met, traded with and/or working as guides and interpreters; Wm. Morrell's poem *New-England* (1622) on Native women's function as diplomats between feuding factions; the voyages of Pring and Morton each with their contacts with Native females; and continuing examples in Winslow's *News* and Pratt's

Lescarbot sketched it in 1610, relations were made up (not surprisingly) of equal portions of genuine liking and subtle manipulation, to gain for each side both a sense of control in novel circumstances, and the benefits of trade:

> Anxious about their old friends, [Native people]
> asked how they were all getting along, calling each
> individual by his name, and asking why such and
> such a one had not come back. This shows the great
> amiability of these people....And consequently by
> a certain gentleness and courtesy, which are as well
> known to them as to us, it is easy to make them pliant
> to all our wishes.   ("Conversion" 69)

Music, feasts and maypole dances, shared technologies and medical cures, wrestling, cooperative hunts for venison---these contingency-pleasures became known in French, English and Dutch records as the "fair means" of commerce-fostering contact, and the same blend of intentions informed a Native family's offer of *weeg-waman* or "welcome" to food and shelter, the gesture of "a large Beaver skin" spontaneously handed over, the hint that perhaps midshipman Y would like to marry Native daughter X. In a sense, kindness and generosity were ways to (hopefully) impose expectations of good behavior upon unknown and unpredictable strangers. There were norms built upon mutual recognition and, at times, pilfering, small tests of the other's attention, toleration and strength. As everywhere, there was treachery and expectation of it: there were "means" to justice, and that expectation too.

"The Weymouth Affair" must be understood in terms of the assumptions held by the people on all sides. According to a comprehensive study by (once again!) Karen Ordahl Kupperman (her 1977 "English Perceptions of Treachery, 1583-1640: The Case of the American 'Savages'"), the English in this period saw Native peoples as "inherently treacherous" not because they were supposedly "savage": rather, "they must be treacherous given their circumstances because they were men....Treachery was simply an important fact of life" (278).

"Declaration." Plimoth itself sends Hobbomock's wife on more than one diplomatic errand, and so does Sachem Chikatawbak/Obdakiest/Abdercest send his. Historian Colin Calloway has estimated that "thousands" of children were born of the early transatlantic.

Given their circumstances. As in Europe, "treachery" had been part of Native New England's ongoing human world of feuds, traditions of individual dueling, and territorial rivalries.[20] But the transatlantic period had forced new "circumstances" upon the peoples of the Atlantic coast as a whole; and as Kupperman details in her study of both early Virginia and New England, there was "from the earliest writers on" a "genuine recognition that English mistreatment had been largely responsible for attacks by Indians" (274). In Kupperman's clear anatomy of this complicated circle of causes and effects, it was one thing "to keep one's guard up" against the chance of treachery; but sometimes, as the English managed these affairs, "keeping one's guard up included overawing one's potential enemy if possible" (278).

Too often missed is the "mistreatment" inflicted in this "overawing." Europeans without knowledge of Native ways were often "misled by their own assumptions" (266) into following "a policy of intimidation, certainly insofar as it meant requisitioning food for the colonists and using the methods [*believed to be*] necessary to ensure this food supply" (267).[21] This has crucial relevance to the

---

[20] While Morton's *Canaan* details traditions of the duel that all sides seemed to respect, and Wood (76) mentions a second-hand report of cannibalistic, though non-fatal torment of a Native "stranger" as part of larger feuds, there are few early-recorded New England Native examples that suggest "treachery" in the classic sense of an unexpected violation of shared norms or "rules." For examples, see the late Williams letter that mentions the Narragansetts' pushing Massasoit's Wampanoags territorially back over the Seekonk River just before the Pilgrims' arrival, taking advantage (it was said) of the Wampanoags' loss of numbers due to "plague." The Massachusetts under Chikatawbak also practiced a "treachery" in creating a "visual threat" that armored English would assault the Narragansetts for intrusions in Massachusett back-country (*Canaan* Book 3). Third, we have the Native view recorded by Bradford that Wampanoag sachem Corbitant of Nemasket, often Massasoit's rival, was "too conversant" with Narragansetts. His destabilization of Plimoth's early relations could be called "treacherous." Yet, none of these acts is recorded as having cost a life. As 1610 comes and goes, more European "visits" result in either robbery, abduction or killing of Native people.

[21] If we want multicultural understanding of these events, we need to ask what it might have meant had the Plimothers given any weight to "Native ways" such as the following, as they held their crucial March 1623 meeting that commissioned Captain Standish's attack:
1) They find ceremony important between groups: for example the Pemaquids who responded with rare "discourtesy" when ritual protocols were neglected: they began to behave in a "devious" half-hostile manner "though doing [the English] no harm" (Rosier's 1605 report in Quinn ENEV 108, 412n1). **2) They do not "respond well" to compulsion:** 1625's Captain Levett, who told some hesitant Abenaki "If they did not truck it was no matter, I would be good friends with them," found that "they smiled and talked one to the other, saying that I had the right fashion of the Abenaki Sagamores" (in Levermore 2:623). **3) In matters of war, they do not kill**

events of that winter of starvation at Plimoth in 1622-23. In the words of the late
Wampanoag Sachem Slow Turtle,

> The Europeans were all controlled people, you know,
> they had a monarch, or a dictator, or a king, or a church that
> *ran their life*, and told them exactly what they were to do and
> what they weren't to do. And that was something that was
> totally...never heard of here....People that had a mind that
> had been abused by where they come from, they...came over and
> behaved in ways that weren't necessary here....
>   (Interview in Dempsey documentary
>   *Thomas Morton* 1992)

Unfortunately, with time, the dual expectations of treachery and justice
came apart: there were both more incidents of treachery, and ever-fewer
opportunities to address them by familiar methods. This was at Wemouth:

> "Ask Pecksuot why they come thus armed."
> He answered, "Our Sachem is angry with you."
> I said, "Tell him if he be angry with us, we are angry with
> him."
> Then said their Sachem, "English men, when you come into the
> Country, we gave you gifts and you gave us gifts; we bought and sold
> with you, and we were friends. And now tell me if I or any of my men
> have done you wrong....Some of you steal our corn, and I have sent
> you word times without number, and yet our corn is stole. I come to see
> what you will do."
> We answered, "It is one man which hath done it. Your men
> have seen us whip him divers times, besides other manner of punish-
> ments, and now here he is, bound. We give him unto you...."
> He answered, "It is not just dealing. If my men wrong my
> neighbor Sachem, or his men, he sends me word, and I beat or kill

---

women and children: There was *brinksmanship*, threat as the left hand of diplomacy; but there is
no non-Puritan record of even anticipation of such an act against anyone.
   Early histories of "New France" are full of regret over Champlain's bungled intervention
(with his guns) in a Huron-Iroquois "feud," which led to generations of "needless" Iroquois hate
for colonists. Studies by Feest and Lewis/Loomie demonstrate that Spanish intrusions in 1570s
"Virginia" were by no means forgotten when Englishmen began to arrive. Early Virginia
governor Ralph Lane, there before Captain (*"vide est vincere"*) John Smith, "kidnapped a chief's
son in advance of entering an Indian village in order to gain the cooperation of the inhabitants"
(Quinn ed. of *Roanoke Voyages* I:262, qtd. in Kupperman). This is one of dozens of examples cited
by Kupperman of sources showing that "In most cases...it was the English who attacked first"
(273), that "the reasons for Indian attacks were recognized from the beginning" (274). English
behavior "had been the cause of a change in the Indians' regard": in Thomas Hariot's words,
colonists had "shewed themselves too fierce...upon causes that on our part, might easily enough
have bene borne withall."

> my men according to the offense....All Sachems do justice by their
> own men. If not, we say They are all [conspiring], and then we fight;
> and now I say you all steal my corn."
>   At this time some of them, seeing some of our men upon our fort,
> begun to start...then....went away in a great rage.
>   At this time we strengthened our watch until we had no food
> left.   (Pratt, "Declaration" 116)

As the chances for resolution faded, explosion on one or both sides became inevitable.[22] In 1622-23, neither Plimoth's families nor Weymouth's men could assume anything about their survival. Hunger forced their small boats out into the teeth of Atlantic winter to find food; and as they searched for villages willing to trade their own food-supplies, the colonists found themselves intolerably exposed, to Native anger and their own position:

> When English writers observed that the Indians were
> treacherous by nature, they were really saying, 'We are extremely
> vulnerable, because we have put ourselves into a situation over
> which we do not have sufficient control.' Such statements were,
> in this sense, statements about the English, not the Indians....In
> fact, there were many clear statements of the knowledge that the
> Indians held the colonies' continued existence in their hands....
> This general feeling of insecurity reflected the objective situation.
>   ("Treachery" 270-1)

Again, the transatlantic had been not utopia (only Europeans thought so), but "cautious coexistence." Study of events before and after 1620 suggests that the driving causes of 1623's "conspiracy" were functions of "new," different or more intensely-practiced values coming into the region.

Several deadly encounters before the 1620s occurred during "visits" by French vessels. Between July 1605 and October 1606, two different ships under respective commands of Champlain and Poutrincourt made landings and contact with Native Americans of Nauset, Seaquanset and Monomoy, all of which began in trade and ended in killings by both sides.[23] But the result amid

---

[22] Why is the offer of the prisoner "not just" to the Sachem above? The English know the "real" thieves; but *this* man might be somebody they want to lose for their *own* reasons. See Note 239 herein---it is far from clear that this is *really* what Morton's *Canaan* charged vs. Weymouth (most historians say Morton reported an old man hanged in place of a youth).

[23] Here is Cape Cod historian Frederick Sears Nickerson's summary of accounts by Champlain and Lescarbot: "We do not know how the Native Americans felt when a company from the ship, armed to the teeth, marched through the village and circled into the back country...[as]

these Native communities of families was no wholesale, unexceptioned defensive hostility or unresolvable grievance against the strangers.[24]

Not long after the serious harms of 1605-6, in 1614, another French ship foundered off Cape Cod. When many crewmen made it to shore, the Nausets "never left watching and dogging" the new intruders "till they got advantage" and, according to Bradford (*History* 1:119), killed "all but 3 or 4." If we consider those "explorers" from the view of the Nausets on their own ancient land, we see people unable to feel secure until they had compelled some new arrangement from these quite unpredictable people roving their country. The French dug in what supplies they had saved, and somehow, the Nausets "made them tell" its location and "made them our servants," "parting" them among Native groups, and feeding them (if with less than royal menu). Some, as at later Weymouth, became "gatherers of wood and water." In time, at least one became the spouse of a Nauset woman (Smith *General History* 204, Dermer qtd. in Bradford). Some did not live long, but at least one managed passage home with fishing ships. And the fellow who "married in," when he died, left "a son alive" (Pratt 112).

To that same year, we must add the infamous Captain Hunt's mass abduction of nearly 30 more New England people (of Plimoth, Nauset, Capawac and elsewhere) for the slavemarkets of Malaga (on which, more below). Within two years of this atrocity, Native New England heard a 1616 "prophecy" from another French castaway (below) that they would soon be swept *en masse* from New England---a frightening prediction already visibly commenced by Hunt. And yet, among so many villages with personal, family losses to count, they act

---

Poutrincourt sent his soldiers among them brandishing their swords....It is probable that [he] would have gotten away without an open break had not some Indian tried to hide a French hatchet. Instead of reporting the loss to the Head Men of the tribe who undoubtedly would have brought the offender to justice according to Indian custom, the soldiers opened fire into a group of Natives among whom the thief had taken refuge" (*Early Encounters* 62).

[24] De Rasieres (72): "They reckon [blood relation] to the eighth degree, and revenge an injury from generation to generation *unless it be atoned for*" (emph. added). Of these same peoples, Pory (11-12) noted that "Notwithstanding that those of...Capawac [the Vineyard] are mortal enemies to all other English, ever since Hunt [below] stole away their people... yet they are in good terms with them of Plymouth, because as [the Pilgrims] never did wrong to any Indians, so will [the Indians] put up [with] no injury at their hands." Pory adds to this a detail and contrast significant to later events here: "And though [the Indians] gave [Plimothers] kindly entertainment, yet stand [the latter] day and night precisely on their guard."

in the records without a uniform hostility toward European strangers. Record by record, trace by trace of events, we see them "keeping their guard up" against treachery, keeping their desire for trade alive, and dealing more or less afresh with each separate European group: "they [did] not...take one for another," as *Canaan* remarked (110).

Indeed, they kept initiating new contacts.[25] As "late" as Spring 1621, the newcome Plimothers "marvelled" at the coming of English-speakers such as Samoset and Tisquantum. And yet, in one of their own first digs into Native stores and graves on Cape Cod, Plimothers had already found an elaborate Native burial full of honorific goods, "a great quantity of fine and perfect red [ochre]," "and in it the bones and skull of a man. The skull had fine yellow hair still on it," and with this man were "the bones and head of a little child" (*Mourt's Relation* 27).

4) "Conspiracy": Atmosphere, Evidences, and Aftermath

The signs of a Native conspiracy that Plimoth and Weymouth colonies found most compelling were sudden outbursts of Native anger, demands for justice, and/or implicit threats to impose it (as all peoples do) themselves. If the

---

[25] "When I was a kid I used to wonder about Massasoit, and one of the things I wondered was, Why would he welcome the English, why would he be so kind to them? Because everybody said that he was such an humanitarian, that he felt sorry for the Pilgrims so they gave them corn and all this stuff, you know. That's a big self-serving American myth. It's just justifying their presence here, legitimizing the taking-over of territory by saying the Natives welcomed them. The Native peoples that made alliance with Plimoth Colony, Massasoit's people, Pokanoket, of the Wampanoag nation, made it basically because---Why would they want to have two enemies? The Narragansetts, whom they probably considered to be their biggest threat; *and* these gnat-like English people, that kept coming around the country but who'd never seemed to stay before? Now all of a sudden they had a group of them building houses, who have brought their families with them, and women (first time that English women had been in New England) --- Native logic would say, Well, you don't bring your families where you're going to make war. So let's make friends with these people, use them as allies, they've got their strange weapons, and if we make peace with them first before anybody else does, then we'll have them on our side and we won't have to face their guns. To me that's the logic of it....You had to somehow come to terms with them, because they were there...." Nanepashemet (Anthony E. Pollard), late Director of Plimoth Plantation's Wampanoag Indian Programs; interview in Dempsey videodocumentary *Nani: A Native New England Story* (1998).

English-colonial texts of this book try to explain most of all their side, how would Native peoples tell theirs? How had Native New Englanders come to those atypically-blunt expressions, just as Europeans planted themselves in "permanent" terms on Massachusetts Bay? What points of view lie scattered among the lines of evidence? Given previous transatlantic norms, we can better comprehend new collisions with them, and so the changes that at last brought on "massacre." It matters because 1623 was the first year when blood was used to "permanently" rewrite the future of this "new England" according to ideological, programmatic "reformist" assumptions.[26] Texts born in support of those newcoming "actors themselves" distorted as they rewrote New England's intercultural past. The reshaping and reform made visible in this book became, in time, part of national-scale, mainstream, monological myth.[27] As a dramatic watershed-moment, The Weymouth Affair became a building-block, a reference-point for the way colonizers decided to behave toward Native peoples.

The higher frequency and more purposeful intent of European voyages to New England were a chief cause of 1620s intensification, the international competition driven by nascent capitalist economies. By 1618 the English (namely most of the time Sir Ferdinando Gorges for The Council of New England), still floundering, found "Hollanders" intruding northward from 1603's "New Amsterdam" to "trade with the natives...in the right of our patent" (*Narration* 40). As seen above, a state of war existed with the French, who would soon lose Quebec to English fishermen-turned-corsairs, and they returned such favors by hijacking English vessels, such as Plimoth's own *Fortune* in 1622---the French

---

[26] "Reform" made "The Pilgrims" pilgrims and landed them in New England. At home they had been reformers of *Old* England's religion(s) and culture(s). When that effort had caused their mockery as "puritans" and "saints," and their political exile, and when they had found The Netherlands also preoccupied, they made their way to "empty" America rather than give up the plan to reform humanity. The "conversion" of New England was only the beginning. Even Boston's "Saints" wished to distinguish themselves from Plimothers' ideological ardor. Winslow (4) dubbed the Weymouthers "rather the Image of men endued with bestial, yea, diabolical affections, than the Image of God, endued with reason...and holiness."

[27] For example, the tightly-coherent body of incoherent works on King Philip's War: by that time, we find "merciless savages" descending for no apparent reason upon white "frontier families" such as Mary Rowlandson's (who just happen to be the cutting edge of a new empire annihilating Native peoples). A modern monological synonym would be "terrorist."

perhaps armed with guns from English "merchant adventurers" like Thomas
Weston himself.

Amid this disorder, Gorges' ambitions drove many men's share of the
work that built toward lasting colonies. The main rewards he laid out to attract
men like himself were blunt enough: profit, and its best insurance in what
amounted to political control for chief investors:

> ...To descend from those generals to more particulars.
> What can be more pleasing to a generous nature than to be exercised
> in doing public good? especially when his labor and industry tends
> to the private good and reputation of himself and posterity: and
> what monument so durable, as erecting of houses, villages and
> towns? and what more pious than advancing of Christian
> religion amongst people who have not known the excellency
> thereof? But, seeing works of piety and public good are in this age
> rather commended by all than acted by any, let us come a little
> nearer to that which all hearken unto, and that forsooth is profit.
> Be it so....
>   But art thou of a greater fortune and more gloriously
> spirited? I have told thee before what thou mayst be assured
> of, whereby it may appear thou shalt not want means nor
> opportunity to exercise the excellency of thine own justice,
> and ingenuity to govern and act the best things, whether
> it be for thyself or such as live under thee, or have their
> dependency or hopes of happiness upon thy worth and virtue
> as their chief....   (*Brief Narration* 64)

In a sense this was exactly what the Plimothers needed as they struggled
to decide where to go next from The Netherlands: an economic framework that
allowed, and whose profits paid for, their intended "public covenant" or new
political lives based on their Christian beliefs.[28] Despite the dangers and

---

[28] Actually the Plimothers's arrangements were with Robert Cushman and other businessmen,
but the attractions were the same in contracts to which Plimoth (with Weston's help) agreed.

According to Harris' *Saga of the Pilgrims*, Plimoth's "true Christians" felt compelled to
deny a church (and so at that time in England, a state) that failed to exclude persons deemed
irreligious: as noted, their Protestant church-authority under their readings of The Bible was
meant to become (somewhere, at last America) a civil authority, a political order for living, as
they "united by a public covenant" ("Separatist" Robert Browne qtd. in Harris 10).

It seems impossible to study The Pilgrim families' "saga"---their religious idealism, their
persecutions and ordeals in emigrating to Holland, years of poverty and community-in-exile,
their courage and persistent determination---without granting them full measure of human
sympathy. Nevertheless, "history" has rarely confessed one simple "scientific" fact: even given
their ideals, story and pathos, Native American New England "owed" them not one thing. The
only factors that made Native Americans "answerable" were, as C.F. Adams, Jr. notes here (133),
the microbe, "the knife and the shotgun."

challenges, the attractions were too many to decline. By 1621 they were in New England trying their hands at this combination of trade and evangelism, "hoping" as Winslow said (84) "that...Religion and profit jump together (which is rare)."

But Massachusetts seemed disappointingly preoccupied.

> One thing was very grievous unto us at this place
> [Sachem Iyanough's village at Cummaquid/Barnstable].
> There was an old woman, whom we judged to be no less than
> a hundred years old, which came to see us because she never
> saw English, yet could not behold us without breaking forth
> into great passion, weeping and crying excessively....[They]
> told us she had three sons who, when [Captain] Hunt was
> in these parts [in 1614], went aboard his ship to trade with
> him, and he carried them captives into Spain (for Squanto
> at that time was carried away also) by which means she
> was deprived of the comfort of her children in her old age.
> We told them...that all the English that heard of it
> condemned him for the same....   (*Mourt's Relation* 70)

Native people wanted back what had been theirs. By that day in June 1621, Native New Englanders---their country full of game, their beans, squash and corn yielding easily 50-60 bushels an acre (Young 123)---were holding on for their collective lives, after five years and more of unprecedented stress. There was little in their world to make them either the needy consumers or salvation-hungry souls Plimoth had hoped for; but, when the colonists listened, they were told in the ways and words of two leading Massachusetts men the sources of Native New England's increasingly "bad attitude." It was a collective stance full of complexity, a dangerous patience pushed to its limits.

Two of the most important Native actors in Weymouth's story had come of age and come to terms with those stresses among close communities: Neponset Massachusett Sachem Chikatawbak and the (apparently) Massachusett pneise named Pecksuot.[29] Both men had grown up within the region-wide

---

[29] The Sachem called Chikatawbak in both Morton's *Canaan* and Winthrop's *Journals* is the same man---"House Afire"---called Obdakiest, Abdercest or Abordikees by Winslow and Pratt. A **pneise**, as Winslow explains, is both a Sachem and Powah, recognized as both a political and shamanistic leader in the community. Wituwamat, another apparently-Massachusett pneise often with Pecksuot, became an adult under similar influences.

recognition and authority accorded to "the Massasoit" or "Supreme Sachem" Nanepashemet, who had dwelt just north of the Bay on the Mystic River. His intertribal powers, like those of his "Squa Sachem" who survived him at least till 1623 (Altham 30), would have been much like the next man's in office, Ousamequin/Yellow Feather of the Wampanoags, in time known by that *title* "Massasoit."

As young men, Chikatawbak and Pecksuot shared their gender's "forest trials" and vision-questing rituals, whose teachers taught them "to be "eager and free in speech, fierce in countenance" (71) and to temper this with "courage and wisdom" (73).[30] And they had shared, witnessed, or heard of some of the earliest directly-recorded incidents with Europeans: 1605 would have brought them fearful warning about their elders abducted from beaches by "Captain Waymouth"; outraged complaints from the families harmed by "Captain Harlow's" similar crimes in 1611; and from their kin of Capawac, including those of one Epenow. (He was going to make it back---below.) The two men's words and deeds were some of the most informed of their (recorded) peoples'. Pecksuot as well as Chikatawbak "applied himself to learn English" (Pratt 112), Pecksuot saying that he "loved them very well," though he disliked that in hunger they hoarded corn from each other (114).

Because Chikatawbak grew up to become the leading Sachem in Weymouth's vicinity, he must have been a young man who naturally kept apprised of new events and information, a man "ingenious and observative" (*Good News* 60). Pecksuot, "a subtle man" (Pratt 123) was as vigorous, learning the Powah's arts of divination and healing, pursuing connections with nature

---

[30] De Rasieres recorded that "The savages [of New England] practice their youth in labor...the young girls in sowing maize, the young men in hunting; they teach them to endure privation in the field in a singular manner, to wit: when there is a youth who begins to approach manhood, he is taken by his father, uncle, or nearest friend, and is conducted blindfolded into a wilderness, in order that he may not know the way, and is left there by night...with a bow and arrows, and a hatchet and a knife.

"He must support himself there a whole winter, with what the scanty earth furnishes at this season, and by hunting. Towards the spring they come again, and fetch him out of it, take him home and feed him up again until May. He must then go out again every morning with the person who is ordered to take him in hand...to seek wild herbs and roots....[After further trials] he comes home, and is brought by the men and women, all singing and dancing, before the Sackima; and if he has been able to stand it all out well, and if he is fat and sleek, a wife is given to him" (in Morton *Memorial* 499).

and visions from it to learn and work with its powers. On record Pecksuot speaks of strange new visitors:

> ...How long it was ago since they first see ships?
> [Pecksuot answered], they could not tell, but they had heard
> men say [that] ye first ship that they saw, seemed to be a
> floating Island, as they supposed broken off from the main
> land, wrapped together with the roots of trees, with some
> trees upon it. They went to it with their canoes, but seeing
> men and hearing guns, they made haste to be gone....
>   (qtd. in Pratt 113)

How soon did the Massachusetts' curiosity overcome their fear, and cost them? Soon, they faced "unprovoked and wholesale killing" (Adams' phrase, *Three Episodes* 5) aboard an English or French ship---"who having many of them on board, made a great slaughter with their murderers [cannon] and small shot, when as (they say) they [had] offered no injurie on their part" (c.1614: Dermer qtd. in Bradford 1:117).

If Chikatawbak could show his explosive side later over the desecration of his mother's grave at Passonagessit (*Canaan* Book 3), he was also disciplining himself to become the patient, often-sly man we find across the records. But Pecksuot grew into a man of dark periods, artfully-boasting language, and fearsome revenge. As a pneise and leader active in far-flung villages, Pecksuot bore with him both the stabilizing presence and authority of his status, and a troubling memory he repeated, a disturbing "prophecy" from a French castaway in 1614 (qtd. in Pratt 12):

> ...They weept much....One of them had a book he
> would often read in. We asked him what his book said. He
> answered, 'It saith, there will be a people, like French men,
> come into this Country and drive you all away....'

Bold words in the Frenchman's situation, and so remarkable ones; and Pecksuot, whose people placed "heavy emphasis" on language, gave it the weight of a "protocol of war preparation" (see Bragdon's study "'Emphaticall

Speech'" 103). Men like these were expected to take an overview approach to the interests of all their kin, and he made the prediction a watchword.³¹

Yet, though these villages dealt each their way with the newcomers, times grew worse that very year. Now came Captain John Smith's New England visit: on the same journey that made him declare Massachusetts "the paradise of those parts," his Virginia-hardened shore parties---what Gorges' *Narration* called "land soldiers" (27)---killed Native people at both Cohasset and Patuxet (future Plimoth: Arber ed. *Works* 719; Barbour ed. 2: 418). Directly in their wake, Smith's fellow-officer Captain Hunt put in at the same place plus others, and carried off as many as 30 more individuals for the profits of Malaga slavery, this time including the resourceful Tisquantum (Ceci, Dunn). Connections are intimate and obvious between these events preceding Plimoth Colony and the very soil and people where they came to build it.

Since it is likely that "Supreme Sachem" Nanepashemet of Mystic was consulted with about such crimes and importuned for Native justice, what was his response before the clans, the *pneise* of his councils, the angry young? We know only that (as treated below) Nanepashemet's manpower was deployed protecting the Bay region from corn-stealing raiders out of northern Micmac ("Tarratine") territories, who coasted New England in fearsome 30-man canoes (WJH1: 66). Chikatawbak as a local Sachem, *pneise* such as Pecksuot and Wituwamat were expected to *do something*---even, if such was the world now, to "overawe" these ferocious strangers. So it came about in the same year that, off Peddock's Island in Massachusetts Bay,

> ...Another ship came into the bay with much goods to truck. And I [Pecksuot] said to the Sachem, 'I will tell you how you shall have all for nothing.'....Thus we killed them all....[The] ship went ashore and lay upon her side and slept there....Then our Sachem divided their goods and fired their ship and it made a very great fire.
> (qtd. in Pratt 113)

---

³¹ Winslow and Pratt record both Native men spending time in villages across "the Massa-chusetts." Tisquantum, Hobbamock (also a pneise) and Tokamahamon ("a special friend") are also regarded across the land in all "Pilgrim" histories, and these villages have enough regular contact to know (for ex.) in Cummaquid when a lost English boy has been found in Manomet (Bradford *History* 1:124), taken to Nauset on the lower Cape (*Mourt* 69) and reported to Massasoit at Sowams. Tragically, such connections must have borne "plague" so far and wide.

This happened in sight of the bay's richest shellfish beds, where today the Massachusetts' shellmounds still bear witness to generations who lived and entertained themselves "many days together." Pecksuot kept "as a moniment" (Pratt 115) a Frenchman's knife, and he was rarely hesitant to let it be seen. Perhaps they cheered and sang beneath the moon as the great boat burned and, with it they hoped, the last of these marauders in their country.

At this moment came the thunderclap, the *Wesauash-aumitch* or great plague; which, in two or three years, killed nearly 9 of 10 Native people from Maine to Rhode Island.[32] We can scarcely imagine the carnage except through Morton's image of Massachusetts as "a newfound Golgotha," of villages filled with "heaps" of unburied corpses. This was a mass cultural death, obliteration of countless family lines each with its share of the deep American past. Virtually overnight, generations young and old vanished, the survivors were shattered in their most basic assumptions about the universe, and found their "medicines" helpless against a European microbe. The people who survived were forced to cope with utterly unfamiliar situations now without huge parts of their past, and without most of the elders who taught them how to live or imagine tomorrow. Social structure, technologies of tools and music and art, spiritual memory itself---few peoples have survived such loss at all.

The Massachusetts and their kinsmen responded in their own terms. Before the Plimothers' arrival "they got all the Powahs of the country, for three days together, in a horrid and devilish manner to curse and execrate [the English] with their conjurations, which assembly and service they held in a dark and dismal swamp," Bradford reported (1:119). Chikatawbak, Pecksuot, even perhaps the regional "master" Passaconaway were likely present. The "devilish"

---

[32] Smith's *History* and Bradford use the "scarcely one-tenth of them remain" estimate: Cushman (in Young 258) said 19 out of 20. Morton's *Canaan* conflates the 1614 French prophecy with men of the "second" French ship burned in 1616; though in Dexter's time line (57), Richard Vines "discovered fatal plague among Indians" at Saco Bay, Maine a year earlier. Wherever the first outbreak, intertribal traffic was the carrier, and a general population of at least 100,000 dropped to less than 15,000 in Mass. Bay by the 1630s. The name of the Weymouth river *Monatoquit* means "river of many villages" (Horner 2), and Winslow estimates "thousands" based on their cleared lands; but they are "desert" places in these records. Another wave struck in 1633 and killed Chikatawbak himself.

gathering's location in a swamp reflected classic Native retreat-tactics used when people felt threatened, the region's wetlands with its groves of cedar a refuge of safety, and spiritual power. Salisbury (114) sees a "ritual purge" of anger in this.

Even so, the English kept coming, and to Plimoth visitor Robert Cushman "those that are left" seemed to "have their courage much abated, and their countenance...dejected, and they seem as a people affrighted" (in Young 258). It was an image of complete trauma, that included further terror as survivors were told, one way or another, that the English "God...at his pleasure" could send more epidemic against his "enemies" (Winslow 15).

The epidemic burned itself out in 1618 when people became too few and far-between to sustain it. As it did so, at least two kidnapped Native men made unexpected returns to their home villages. One was Tisquantum, soon to be Plimoth's "Squanto," the only one who somehow made his way to England from Captain Hunt's sale of many into slavery: he arrived back assisting the first voyage of Captain Thomas Dermer, here "for discovery and other designs in these parts" (Bradford 1:116). Tisquantum, finding his entire home-village of Patuxet annihilated, spent time coasting "Virginia" with traders and worked up north for John Mason's short governorship: he seems to have kept returning to his home region. At one point, he guided Dermer about in his "designs," and saved his life.

At both Nemasket and Monomoy, because of the "French" and other incidents on Native minds, Dermer was either threatened or held: at the latter he escaped by "seizing" some of them till the people sent him away with a canoe-full of corn (qtd. in Bradford 1:118). Bad blood would still be the reason Native people "kept aloof and were so long before they came" to Plimoth. It was worsening when Dermer returned to Capawac/Martha's Vineyard waters in June 1620, the summer before *Mayflower*. This time, even with "Squanto" there, "he going ashore amongst the Indians to trade, as he used to do, was betrayed and assaulted by them, and all his men slain, but one that kept the boat [and] himself...very sore wounded" (1:118). Dermer died that autumn, and the New England transatlantic went from bad to worse in front of the coming Plimothers.

The second captive returned in 1618 had been one Epenow, apparently kidnapped from a Nauset village by one Captain Harlowe, and a man to rival Chikatawbak for patient sagacity. We learn something of his spirit in Gorges' report (*Narration* 25) that, as "Americans," Epenow and his fellows were "found to be unapt for their uses" as slaves; and that Epenow had been "showed in London for a wonder." Surviving seven years of this, and in the homes of Englishmen being probed for information for their colonies, Epenow surmised that promises of "gold" and wealth had narcotic effect on his hosts, and he suggested that he could guide them. Back in New England, he jumped overboard to his freedom. One clue suggests that Epenow went on to become the Sachem "Aspinet" (the 1621 treaty among Plimoth and many Native groups includes "Appanow" of Nauset; in Young 232).

But Epenow, speaking in 1618 before gathered groups of his dispirited, frightened, angry people, cannot have had much to say for these English or their home-country ways. He was no "overawed" survivor and had told the English plainly when he showed himself to Captain Dermer on Capawac. "This savage, speaking some English, laughed at his own escape, and reported the story of it" (Gorges *Narration* 31).

Interestingly, in the details of the "treacherous attack" that cost Dermer's life, we find that Epenow and his men had not attacked him, but "conspired...to take the Captain." Given the words that describe this "so cunning" man, Epenow may have meant to return the good captain his London favor and "show" Dermer in *his* villages. "Thereupon they laid hands upon him; but he being a brave, stout gentleman, drew his sword and freed himself, but not without fourteen wounds." (It is not recorded how many his men inflicted). If it was Native "treachery" that killed Dermer's party on the beach at Capawac, it was their second violation of things as they'd "used to do."[33]

Plague had other effects that destabilized Native New England even more as it became the host-country of Plimoth and Weymouth. In 1619, the region's above-noted Supreme Sachem Nanepashemet was killed by Micmac intruders: it may be that Mystic's numbers were slashed by epidemic. At the same time, the Narragansetts (even more numerous because less affected by plague) found the

---

[33] Including the early colony attempt at Sagadahoc (1608-9), where at first the parties "got on remarkably well," until a new-come English officer "changed their tactics. They drove the Savages away without ceremony; they beat, maltreated and misused them outrageously"; and according to historian Vaughan, Native people "determined to kill the whelp before its teeth and claws became stronger" (*Frontier* 24).

same new lack of numbers in the Wampanoags under Ousamequin or "Massasoit": New England's center of "supreme" power was shifting as Wampanoag influence was pushed back east over the Seekonk River. Ousamequin's very assumption of the title "Massasoit" testifies to his *claim* of "Supreme" status: Nanepashemet's widow-Sachem was still "a player" in many documents, and Narragansett concerns brought "Massasoit" to orchestrate his alliance with Plimoth's "permanent" intentions and guns. A chief treaty-condition for *both* his and Plimoth's security dictated that Massasoit "should send to his neighbor confederates, to certify them of this, that they...might be likewise comprised in the conditions of peace" (*Mourt* 57). Even so, and with grave consequences, Ousamequin's Narragansett rivals kept dogging him through years recorded by Plimoth.[34]

Within these ongoing disturbances, Chikatawbak, Pecksuot, Wituwamat and others labored to hold their worlds together. If Massasoit was already in back-country retreat when (March 1621) he came to meet the Plimothers, he may have called in obligations from Chikatawbak plus others now in the Wampanoag sphere, to add to the "brave show" they needed to make before the houses a-building on the site of their Patuxet. "After an hour the king came to the top of a hill over against us, and had in his train sixty men, that we could well behold them and they us....all strong, tall, all men in appearance" (*Mourt* 54-7).

Could this sickly handful of people with their "good news" of The Gospel be the destined beneficiaries of Native American dispossession? (Pratt 92 noted that Plimothers were then "so distressed with sickness that they, fearing the salvages should know it, had set up their sick men with their muskets upon their rests and their backs leaning against trees.") If New England's leaders wondered thus, their response was a kind of defiant optimism. For by turning out this

---

[34] "...[The] Narragansett Sachems...declared that Ousamequin was their subject, and had solemnly himself, in person, with ten men, subjected himself and his lands unto them at the Narragansett; only now [c.1620] he seemed to revolt from his loyalties under the shelter of the English at Plimoth." Ousamequin further, "without any stick, acknowledged it to be true that he had so subjected [himself]...but withal, he affirmed that he was not subdued by war, which himself and his father had maintained against the Narragansetts, but God, he said, subdued me by a plague, which swept away my people, and forced me to yield." Letter of Roger Williams, Dec. 13, 1661; in Bartlett ed., Vol. 7: 316). For Salisbury (115), many Native groups did not appreciate Massasoit as would-be "Indian agent" orchestrating any "submission."

show of strength at Plimoth, they were presenting themselves as the worthy "ally" of a power that, in fact, they feared almost as much as epidemic---the strangers' guns and muskets.[35] They had not given up vigorous diplomacy as a way to solve problems. The two sides appropriated each other's needs to their own, and the Plimothers---struggling to recover from that first dreadful winter on the shore---were just as deeply relieved by the achievement of early good terms.

This "local" treaty of Spring 1621 had promising results that testify to the comparatively good intentions of Plimoth *as* a colony of Europeans on Native New England soil, as well as to Native peoples' eager embrace of what forms of stability they could improvise. Both sides built peace in which to trade and plant crops, and by Fall, Massasoit delivered that wider-ranging treaty including his "confederates"---even the "much incensed and provoked" Nausets (*Mourt* 52).

1621's summer of "no want" was followed by "the first Thanksgiving" plenty; and it is important to remember that the list of Native villages and Sachems who marked that wider September treaty (in *Mourt* 83) were virtually the same list of people and places later accused (by Hobbamock) of the "Conspiracy" itself. Noting that parties to the treaty range from "Chikkatabak" to "an Isle at sea" called Capawac, we find one year between the islanders' confrontation with Captain Dermer's crew (summer 1620) and their "yield[ing] willingly to be under the protection, and subjects to our sovereign lord King James."[36]

But within a year, promise turned to a hardening "frown." And out of the months that followed came "conspiracy" and bloodshed.

---

[35] At this March 1621 treaty Massasoit's brother Quadequina made it clear that he was "very fearful of our pieces, and made signs of dislike, that they should be carried away"; "he hath a potent adversary the Narragansetts, that are at war with him, against whom he thinks we may be some strength to him, for our pieces are terrible unto them" (*Mourt* 58).

[36] *Mourt* suggests how Plimothers understood the moment: "We have found the Indians very faithful in their covenant of peace with us, very loving....Yea, it hath pleased God so to possess the Indians with a fear of us, and love unto us, that not only the greatest king amongst them, called Massasoit, but also all the princes and peoples round about us have either made suit unto us, or been glad of any occasion to make peace....So that there is now great peace amongst the Indians themselves, which was not formerly, neither would have been but for us" (83).

Winslow begins the story of his *Good News* in November 1621, as the ship *Fortune* brought 35 new men (Weston's) to Plimoth without supplies. Given Plimoth's good 1621 harvest, there is no mention of a "crisis" of food-supplies (not till the following summer[37]). The turn toward disaster came in two main phases. The first phase showed itself somewhere between the high points of September-October's 1621's treaty with "Thanksgiving," and the worrying crisis that begins *Good News*; that "the common talk [already that November 1621] of our neighbor Indians on all sides was of the preparation [the Narragansetts] made to come against us" (7).[38]

This was the return, as it were, of the larger Native American world around the relations between Plimoth and the "Wampanoag Confederacy"; and the "sole survivor" Tisquantum was the means. Having made it back to New England in time to be of service between these parties, Tisquantum had directly helped to create the plenty of 1621 by teaching Plimothers the skills of obtaining food and fur-trade connections here. But everything he did to strengthen Massasoit's alliance with Plimoth made him less popular with those Native rivals affiliated with the Narragansetts---including Nemasket's Sachem Corbitant. Salisbury clearly traces many small-band "intrigues" here (119-122.)

What Winslow's anxious opening pages do not include or explain, then, are the Narragansetts' and others' *reasons* for making it "common talk" (if they did so) that they were "against" the presence and/or the effects of Plimoth upon the balances of Native power.

Indeed, during that first treaty-month of September, word had come to Plimoth that Nemasket's Corbitant ("too conversant" with Narragansetts, we recall) "took" Tisquantum prisoner and threatened his doings: "if he were dead the English had lost their tongue" (*Mourt* 74).[39] Plimoth now assumed that its

---

[37] It is June/July 1622 (as yet another "fifty or sixty men" arrive with the *Charity* and *Swan*) when Winslow describes "That little store of corn we had...exceedingly wasted by the unjust and dishonest walking of these strangers" (21 herein).

[38] Wood (1636, 81): "Although [the Narragansetts] be...the most numerous people in those parts," "yet I never heard they were desirous to take in hand any martial enterprise or expose themselves to the uncertain events of war, wherefore the Pequots call them women-like men."

[39] Winslow himself (44) knows Massasoit's rival Corbitant as "a notable politician, yet full of merry jests and squibs, and never better pleased than when the like are returned upon him." The

treaty obligations required them to send armed men to rescue Tisquantum; and not surprisingly, several Nemasket "women and children" were wounded ("we were sorry for it though [they] themselves procured it in not staying in the house, at our command," 76). Sachem Corbitant, surely not pleased as he fled in front of his own people, was loudly warned that "any insurrection" or violence would bring "the overthrow of him and his."

And it was *this* bloodshed and threat that brought to Plimoth---by late November 1621---the infamous "bundle of new arrows lapped in a Rattlesnake's skin," which summed up this first phase of events on the path to Weymouth. Yet, something crucial was missed again: the messenger from Narragansett Sachem Canonicus---would-be ally of Nemasket's Corbitant--- had sent the snakeskin *"for him"*---for *Tisquantum, not for Plimoth itself.*

The best support for giving weight to those crucial two words is the fact that the messenger *for Tisquantum* had also a greater mission: to clear up with *Plimoth* a "diplomatic snafu" of deep concern to the Narragansetts, which had occurred "in the fore-going summer" of 1621 (Winslow 7). The Narragansetts, Winslow himself says, had early-on sent their *own* diplomat to Plimoth for "their desired and obtained peace." But that *original* messenger had gone back from to Canonicus and, for some reason, "persuaded [Canonicus] rather to war" (9). We will never know the reason, but the original diplomat had proceeded to "scorn the meanness" of Plimoth's well-meant gifts, and told Canonicus that Plimoth had likewise scorned "his own person." *Even so,* Canonicus had detected the problem, punished that "former Messenger," and sent this second one (his name was Tokamahamon); who clearly "assured" Plimoth that "he [Canonicus of Narragansett] would be friends with us."

Bradford, persuaded by Tisquantum that *his own* problem was "no better than a challenge" to Plimoth itself, decided to "stuff the skin with powder and shot" and sent it back *"returning no less defiance* to Canonicus" (10) and with it, "no small terror." Even though Winslow himself makes clear that Tisquantum had blurred the two messages into one threat against them all, the perception had no

---

"taking" of Tisquantum was well within the code of *brinksmanship* shown earlier, for he *would* have been dead if that were Corbitant's real intention. Unfortunately, instead of first inquiring into Corbitant's complaint, Plimoth sent the famously undiplomatic Standish.

effect. The result was a needless, major wrong turn in Plimoth policy, and another in history.[40]

It may be that Plimothers were further confused just now by more manipulative feints and shadows from Hobbamock, another Wampanoag who "still lived" in the area and had become a regular friend; for given his reports of whispered threats from Narragansetts and Massachusetts, a great deal of anxiety at Plimoth was resolved only when Hobbamock's "wife" went abroad; and she revealed "the right state of things....all things quiet, and...no such matter...intended" (12).

Nonetheless, this "hardening" phase continued. For "in the meane time" of that period between November 1621-February 1622, the Plimothers deemed it "needful to impale our Towne...with all expedition" (10). Bradford says this huge labor was taken up "cheerfully," meaning that there was agreement about it; but it did not stop when Hobbamock's wife had delivered the facts. (Recall Pory [12] writing in January 1622 that though Native peoples gave Plimothers "kind entertainment, yet stand they day and night precisely upon their guard.") If, through the above misjudgments, Plimoth had found a reason to fortify themselves against their surroundings, they were now---it appears, needlessly--- *becoming* the reason behind their own rising fears.

Other events just now suggest this. Massasoit, just like Canonicus with his faulty messenger, had decided to put his unreliable Tisquantum to death, and he sent braves to Plimoth "to cut off his head and hands" (17). But just when Bradford was "ready to deliver him," a minor unrelated incident interrupted proceedings. When that "delay" became (in Native eyes, if nowhere in Plimoth's records) a full "forgetting" and refusal of their justice, Massasoit's Wampanoags

---

[40] Robinson's "Lost Opportunities" suggests that the snakeskin was sent as a "gift" to "create a mutual relationship of gift-giving interdependence," but that it became, somehow, a "mutual refusal to submit to the other" (19). Given that the Narragansetts were "well situated" between Plimoth English and the south's Dutch "merchants protecting their own nascent wampum market," he speculates that Dutchmen convinced Canonicus to consider the weaker Wampanoags their "clients" and the Pilgrims as "meddling in that relationship." But this is to speculate on external reasons for the snafu: diplomatic confusions were enough to mislead both the Plimothers and historians, including Kupperman, who in *Facing Off* (226-7) concludes that "Canonicus intended war." His recorded message (above) in fact states exactly the opposite.

grew "mad with rage, and impatient at delay...[they] departed in great heat" (17).

Clearly, Plimoth desired to make itself a player, even a leader, in this complicated ongoing world, and now, whether they knew it or not, they had "told" Native New Englanders (already wary of their own dispossession) that their justice was no longer a serious priority. Whatever their intent, the Plimothers kept building their palisade through February 1622, and it did not help. Nor did the coming of a ship that unloaded "six or seven" hungry mouths, like heralds of the next two years of hunger and searches for food-assistance (Winslow 18-19).

So began a new phase on the path to Weymouth:

> In the time of these straits...the Indians began again to cast forth many insulting speeches, glorying in our weakness, and giving out how easy it would be ere long to cut us off. Now also Massassowat seemed to frown on us, and neither came nor sent to us as formerly. These things occasioned further thoughts of fortification; and...we resolved to erect a fort....And, though it took the greatest part of our strength from dressing our corn, yet...we hoped God would raise some means instead therof....
> *(Good News* 20)

At just this moment "before the harvest" of 1622, Plimothers got word of the Powhatan "Conspiracy" against the Virginia colonies, and heard its one-day toll of 322 English people killed in coordinated surprise-attacks.[41] But Native New Englanders, watching closely all spring and summer, did not know of this far-off reason for Plimoth's fear. All they could see was their own justice denied, refused or forgotten, apparently as a function of Plimoth's protecting its own interests; and with that, a palisade being raised up against them, followed by a fort mounted with cannon and "murtherers."

---

[41] As noted in FBH1:275, Smith's *General History* (236) includes an "abstract of letters" sent from Plimoth with the date July 16, 1622; and it says that "Since the news of the massacre in Virginia, though the Indians continue their wonted friendship, yet are we more wary of them than before; for their hands hath been embrued in much English blood, only by too much confidence, but not by force." (See final notes to *Good News* and the passage from historian Bancroft cited with Adams here for more information.) Smith added that Plimoth was building "a strong fort, they hope shortly to finish," and that they were pleased with the endowments of the country.

Fence, fort, and "frowns" now comprised a stalemate of misunderstandings between would-be allies. Straight into this very uncertain situation, in midsummer 1622, came "fifty or sixty" more of Weston's Englishmen. And amid growing food-shortages, their quasi-criminal contributions commenced the second phase in earnest: the breakdown of "civility" itself.

Their offenses began at Plimoth and spread outward with the ravenous search for food. The Weymouth men "seem[ed] to help" with Plimoth's corn but then stole any edible green ears, and added insults to injuries (Winslow 21). As Plimoth was quickly learning, good stores of corn could mean life itself through New England's winters---but this had long been a fact to Native people. Especially now in the wake of so many killings, traumatized by epidemic, they could hardly be asked to see the pilferage (and before long, plunder) of their careful food-supplies as anything but another mortal threat against them on their own lands. Almost as soon as the Weymouth men left Plimoth for their own building-site at Wessagusset (on the edge of Chikatawbak's and Pecksuot's Massachusett territory), the Plimothers began to hear "clamours against them, for stealing their corn, and other abuses" (22). Plimoth's response was: "we knew no means to redress those abuses, save reproof, and advising them to better walking, as occasion served."[42]

The evidence leaves no doubt that Weymouth's men, compared with Plimoth's people, brought great appetite and "great disorder" to the fragile region. They pilfered corn, "traded" some of it back for "keeping Indian women" (Bradford 157), and shifted between doing village-chores for food and "plain stealing...night and day." As 1621 faded into deep winter, they began to die, one "so weak as he stuck fast in the mud" while gathering shellfish. Desperate, some of them stumbled upon the honored grave of Chikatawbak's mother, and "defaced" it looking for food-stores (*Canaan* 107).

Plimoth's Bradford rued that "famine must still ensue...if not some way prevented....Markets there was none to go to, but only the Indians" (152-3). Once

---

[42] Morton in 1624-27 knew what was called for under the old transatlantic code of "humors": "a privy knife or string of beads would well enough have qualified" to deal with such a "huge complaint" (*Canaan* 108). Here at Plimoth and Weymouth it was not the knife or beads lacking but the knowledge that some direct *gesture* of respectful concern was the most needful thing to avoiding a mortal crisis. But there is little recorded effort to understand preexisting norms.

forced by starvation to face this, Plimothers began a series of uneasy voyages in search of Native corn. But---in keeping with other broadly-supported findings--- the reason for English unease lay precisely in their "semi-awareness" of Native American anger. Plimoth and Weymouth knew there were many reasons for it. Though they wished to become "players" or even controllers of the region, they assumed no sense of responsibility for any previous wrongs committed by fellow Europeans, even as a gesture to reciprocate the food being given from "all they could spare." These very different parties of English both felt Native anger increase each time they "decided by default" not to respond, or even to restrain themselves.

In this "hardening" period, with the means of truly interpersonal contact dying off, and little if any willingness to learn, accept, or make use of the earlier transatlantic code between cultures, this "new English" failure to respond became, in the face of Native forbearance, the nerve to ignore.

Instead, as Plimoth's Bradford, Winslow and Standish made their voyages, it was their own interpersonal behaviors---their concern for nothing *but* obtaining food-supplies---that in a "final" way drove Native people to the blunt expressions of their feelings recorded in 1622-23. Now we understand how these expressions came home as the main "evidences of conspiracy."[43]

As the Weymouth men struggled to build against the winter, Plimoth was already "worn out of all trucking stuff" by late August. A small re-supply (in October: Winslow 23) was insufficient, "partly, because we [had been] enforced to neglect our corn, and spend much time in fortification." So began Bradford's and others' voyages, the first to Monomoy (Winslow 25); where there was still enough fear to make people "loath their dwellings should be known." "[T]hey would all be gone, bag and baggage" (26). Nevertheless the parties managed

---

[43] Winslow and Bradford denounce the Weymouth men's behavior, and show how they "became contemned and scorned of the Indians, [who] began greatly to insult over them in a most insolent manner." But as noted, Native people were not satisfied about these issues, nor by the hanging of one thief among almost 100 men robbing them. No Plimother criticizes their *own* behavior across the region just now. Nor could their best guiding lights and elders help with these matters. Plimoth's beloved minister Robinson (who did at last rebuke Standish-like policies---see Adams) had not been allowed to emigrate. First governor Carver had collapsed planting corn and died in April 1621; and Elder Brewster, "the postmaster of Scrooby," was an eminent divine but no frontiersman. Though consulted at all times, his views are not recorded. Governor Bradford was now in his early 30s.

trade, "about 26 or 28 hogsheads of corn and beans...more than the Indians could well spare in these parts" (Bradford 155).

No discussion of relations was recorded (Winslow 26). Instead,

> From thence they departed...for the Massachusetts...
> When they came thither, they found a great sickness to be
> amongst the Indians, not unlike the plague, if not the same.
> They renewed their complaints to our Governor, against that
> other plantation seated by them, for their injurious walking.
> But indeed, the trade both for Furs and corn was overthrown
> in that place...so that little good could be there done.
> From thence they returned to the bottom of the Bay....

Native people---Chikatawbak's and Pecksuot's and Wituwamat's people--- were dying again. After five years of epidemic death, they could not have been expecting the English to cure them. Trade for hoes, kettles and pretty cloth was probably not a great village-priority just now. Yet, as the Massachusetts mustered their attention and handed over more corn, they took the moment to demand some gesture toward justice from their now-hungry "allies" of last September. The response was that little "good"---little action toward Plimoth's aim---could there be done. In their hungry preoccupation, the Plimothers neglected *gestures* of concern being sought.[44]

What the Massachusetts felt when Bradford had gone, we do not know. But Plimothers soon discovered a frosty change in the region about to "rise in conspiracy." Bradford, having managed to secure more food at Mattakiest (Winslow 28), was forced by boat-damage to leave it there: in time, he sent Captain Myles Standish, lately recovered from sickness, to retrieve it.

Apparently this had been long enough for new shades of feeling to circulate among Native people. First, someone at Mattakiest allegedly "stole certain beads, scissors and other trifles" from Standish's shallop. Standish, there

---

[44] The trade is "spoiled" because starving Weymouth men have paid "high" prices for Native food. In the 1623 "Letter" cited above, as well as five years later, Bradford still believed it was others' place to accept less and so offer his "Pilgrims" profit and success in their godly aims: others "went and filled the Indians with corn, and beat down the prise, giving them twice as much as [Plimoth] had done" (FBH1:449). Other support for this impression they must have left behind comes from their farewells to Tisquantum, who died "struck...with sickness" on this journey between Monomoy and Massachusetts. Bradford most remarked Tisquantum's last wish "that he might go to the Englishman's God in Heaven." Winslow's style was plainer (26): "this crossed their Southern trading."

to collect food traded out of generosity, made not the slightest inquiry as to what this might be about. Was it a bit of the transatlantic's typically-trivial larceny? A deliberate tease, a parody of the theft going on all over the country? An insult as a demand for a hearing? (Recall the French hatchet "filched" in 1605-06.) Standish, "refusing whatsoever kindness they offered" (29), "swore he would revenge it on them before his departure."

Now that they had their guests' attention, the Native men attempted to address matters. The response to them marked the parting of the ways.

> On the morrow, the Sachem came to their rendezvous,
> accompanied with many men in a stately manner. He saluted
> the Captain in this wise: He thrust out his tongue...and there-
> with licked his hand from the wrist to the fingers' end, withall
> bowing the knee, striving to imitate the English gesture....His
> men did the like, but in so rude and savage a manner as our men
> could scarce forbear to break out in open laughter. (Winslow 29)

We are not told the Native people's response to this. Instead we learn the Plimothers': the Sachem "delivered the Beads, and other things to the Captain, saying he had much beaten the party for doing it, [and] causing the women to make bread...seeming to be very sorry for the fact, but glad to be reconciled."[45]

Glad to be reconciled. Not likely. Either these Native people made smiling impostors of themselves that day, or the phrase is pure colonial monologic. For Winslow's point is that from here on, Plimoth began to make surprising discoveries about the peoples all around them. Immediately they are back at Mattakiest for more food: "Here they *pretended* their wonted love," even as the village "spared them a good quantity of corn to confirm the same." As the lives of their own families were measured out in barrels of Native families' food, the Plimothers warily noticed that "Strangers [to Plimoth] also came to this place." But these "strange" Native people now seemed to be somehow "*pretending* only to see [the Sachem] and his company..." (Winslow 31). The English of Plimoth

---

[45] Wood (88) wrote that because "they are love-linked thus in common courtesy, so they are no way sooner disjointed than by ingratitude, accounting an ungrateful person a double robber of a man." He adds (93): "Laughter in them is not common, seldom exceeding a smile, never breaking out into such a loud laughter as do many of our English. Of all things they love not to be laughed at upon any occasion." Open weeping was also rare in his observations, except at "the death of friends, for whom they lament most exceedingly."

and Weymouth were sensing now, wherever they went, that some critical mass had been reached in the feelings against them.

From just this point their "evidences of conspiracy" begin to build, seasoned with details such as the "lusty Indian of Paomet or Cape Cod then present," who---as we know, despite all odds---had been "very affable, courteous, and loving, especially toward the Captain." "This savage [*sic*] was now entered into confederacy with the rest" (34).

It would be hard to maintain that Native people were *not* beginning to conceive some common action. In the words from "the Sachem" above, custom dictated that if one group believed that even their opponents' leaders were involved in an injustice, the tradition was that then "we fight."

There were three main "revelations of conspiracy" that interested readers must examine for themselves: the speeches by Wituwamat and Pecksuot, in Standish's presence and to Pratt; the statement by Hobbamock that most villages party to the 1621 treaty were now hatching a "conspiracy" against both plantations (43); and the incidents at Weymouth itself detailed by Pratt (also Winslow 52).[46]

---

[46] More than one evidence of "plot" runs the other way. Just when Plimoth was finishing its fortifications, "in February a [Weymouth] messenger came...who brought a letter showing the great wants they were fallen into; and...[the Indians] would lend him [no more corn]. He desired advice whether he might not take it from them by force to succor his men." Bradford, well-knowing that Native people were "much incensed," used "all means" to dissuade. But "so base" were "some of their own company as they went and told the Indians....The which *with other things* made them enter into a conspiracy against the English" (156). Now, especially since there was no deliberate diplomacy, *no one* could feel secure.

This is not to say that nobody tried. Pecksuot, quite directly when the time came, announced that he "understood that the Captain was come to kill himself and the rest of the Salvages" (Winslow 55). In fact he had "understood" it at least as soon as he'd been told, by "a young man, wanting wit" (in Pratt 118), that the English were now sure of a "treacherous plot." Pecksuot went straight to Pratt himself and tried to drag all this into plain sight by offering to *help* Pratt find his way to Plimoth---mockingly or not---"because I love you"; and with an offer of supplies, and no less than his son Nahamit as a guide---who amounted to a hostage. Pratt's response? An utter denial of the intrigues, even phrased as a mockery of truth: "Who told you so great a lie [of my intended flight to Plimoth], that I may kill him." "It is no lie, " Pecksuot answered, refusing to name his (not surprisingly, English) informant. And with that "response" of denial and threat from Pratt, Pecksuot gave up and "went home to his house" (119).

It is remarkable how much the records reveal that the English "knew" and yet denied crucial things: they seem to be full of perceptions that are "not allowed" to bear themselves out in either their acts or their writings. The reader has several examples above of this "selective emphasis." Perhaps Susan Griffin's definition of "denial" can help: "the means by which the mind forgets part of itself." Salisbury 124: "the role of their own conduct was beyond..grasp or interest."

However, as we attempt fresh understanding of this affair through its contexts and complexities, we must actively work to include in consideration two further things: these records' greatest silence, and their greatest "encouragement" toward tragedy; both of which can only have come from what this book must call "selective emphasis" on the part of "the actors themselves" and by the scholars writing history.

Again, it would be surprising---given all that passed from late summer of 1622, through the winter, to the last week of March 1623, when the killings happened---if Native people were *not* in fact considering some coordinated strike against the starving, inept yet would-be permanent planters on their lands. What we find upon second examination is that that is an understatement. For exactly at this time, into the midst of all these complaints came the "voyage" of one Captain Thomas Jones.

Jones had sailed for English investors in the East Indies of 1617, and was accused by that Company of adopting at-least-irregular methods, perhaps attempted piracy. Awaiting trial, he was despatched on a new business-voyage to help assure English pockets (against French and Dutch ones in this newly-competitive decade) of "a most certain and beneficial trade of Furs to be had with the Indians" (Jones' commission in FBH1: 276-7). According to record, Jones reached Jamestown in April 1622, and was in New England waters at Plimoth by August. As glibly recorded, "So active was he in carrying out his instructions" that by midwinter 1622-23, Jones stood charged as follows in the records of the Council for New England (modernized minutes of its meeting Tuesday December 17, 1622):

> Whereas the Council are informed by Leo Peddock that Captain Jones, who was employed by the Company of Virginia to fish upon the coasts of New England, hath this last year robbed the Natives there of their furs, and offered [sic] to carry some of them away prisoners, but being grounded upon the sands near Cape Cod, the savages escaped and made great exclamation against the present planters of New England.
> For punishment whereof, Sir Ferdinando Gorges is desired to signify this abuse by letter from the Council....
> (Deane ed., "An Order for a Letter against Capt. Jones," *Records of the Council for New England*, 30)

How could yet-another crime like this fall, just now, into the midst of Cape Cod peoples and *not* bring outright attack, let alone conspiracy? The insignificant "early comer" Leo Peddock was to be the only agent through whom Native New Englanders managed to make themselves heard about this---*across the Atlantic*---while not a word was relayed or even recorded of Jones' crimes by "those present planters," Native New England's "allies."[47]

Across 300 years of history the illusion persists: Native people are irrationally "plotting" an attack of annihilation, and the struggling, baffled, well-meaning Christian colonists are "forced to survive."[48] In dutiful footnotes that do mention Jones' crimes in the Massachusetts Historical Society edition of Bradford's *History*---a severely myopic yet imposingly annotated two volumes that have indoctrinated generations of historians and teachers---the Plimothers in the shadow of this "crisis" are defended yet held to no account whatsoever for their behaviors. "Small" examples of gaping lacks of interest in Plimoth "morality" underwrite larger ones. Plimoth's minor "backer" Captain Emmanuel Altham, for some reason, "craved a boy of [Massasoit]" for his brother Sir Edward: refused, he promised to "bring you one hereafter" (29). We learn that Chikatawbak's son "Papawhinnet" was in fact taken to England. As a hostage, a convert, an exotic houseboy? For "showing"? As a catamite? The editors note without "uncomfortable" explanation that Peddock was ordered to return the boy; that the Council ordered Captain Jones punished. There is no record or

---

[47] Leo or Leonard Peddock was one of the earliest "old comers/lone planters" on Massachusetts Bay, and his name was attached to that island. Morton says he "landed there" (19), and by Nov. 1622 Peddock was ordered by the Council to oversee return, from the unexplained company of Thomas Weston's brother Andrew, of a son of Chikatawbak's named Papawhinnet, taken to England in autumn 1622 aboard the *Charity* (FBH1: 264). No more is known of Peddock but this positions him as an outsider between Native people, Plimoth and Weymouth.

[48] Hence what Roy Harvey Pearce would term the "complementary" idea and image of Native people "lurking" everywhere in the "wilderness," to use two of Adams' favorite terms. The attack seems "imminent" over and over again, but (we are told), the warriors must wait "till the snow is gone." Why? If they intend to kill every English man, woman and child, who would be tracking them? They also "must wait" for three starving English "servants" in Chikatawbak's village to finish building them a boat so that they can simultaneously attack the pinnace *Swan*. Why New England's commonly sea-going and -trading peoples (who, as noted, build canoes seating 30 men) seem to lack boats is not recorded or questioned.

evaluation of any of these acts, and none of them exert any influence upon historians' other "moral evaluations" lacing the work.

Jones' crimes may be the events of most magnitude "silenced" in the midst of these records. Ironically, perhaps *only* a retaliatory attack by Native braves would have brought the crimes to notice. There was no attack. This too, once surrounded by silence, speaks.

At the same time, one of the most crucial "encouragements" to the massacre came from Weymouth colonist Phinehas Pratt himself. Pratt's lost-in-the-backyard "wilderness journey" to Plimoth in early spring 1623, to provide a crucial warning of "Native conspiracy," became a decisive part of Plimoth's anxious idea of its position. And, though Pratt's "Declaration" helped bolster both Plimoth's actions and the accounts of them, it remained unanalyzed and in its wretched textual state until the edition in this book.

"Their plot was to kill all English people in one day when the snow was gone" (118): that was what Pratt reported. In all the detail based around and upon it, we find only Pratt's own "selectively emphasized" explanation of *how* he discovered the "conspiracy."

Typical of Pecksuot's upbringing, he had told Pratt directly of the Massachusetts' willingness to kill, in defense and/or revenge, with his tale of the burning French ship of 1616: they made no secret of it. Then Pratt, also criticized for hoarding food ("You have much corn and English men die for want," 114), recorded his first "warning sign": "...intent to make war they removed some of their houses to th...a great swamp near...our plantation." Starving, because keeping too much within his "pale," Pratt had it exactly backwards. For across the records we find Native people *retreating* to "swamps" when threatened or sensing danger themselves.[49]

---

[49] After Weymouth's collapse, Pratt found new colonial work and told his story to Captain Christopher Levett in 1625. As Levett saw "the whole business," "when they came there, they neither applied themselves to planting of corn nor taking of fish, more than for their present use, but went about to build Castles in the Aire, and making of Forts, neglecting the plentiful time of fishing. When winter came their Forts would not keep out hunger, and they having no provision beforehand, and wanting both powder and shot to kill deer and fowl, many were starved to death, and the rest hardly escaped" (633).

This is the same "formula" by which the Plimothers began to see "pretending" and plots behind a sudden new lack of civility. At this same point, Pratt "saw" and helped to create the "conspiracy."

> After this [New year, late March?], a morning
> I see a man going into one of their houses, weary with
> traveling and Galded on his feet. Then I said to Mr. Sals-
> bery, our Chirurgeon, surely their Sachem hath employed
> him for some intent to make war upon us.

Pratt did not explain why he marked a weary man with a cankered foot for a Sachem's agent of war. He fashioned himself a billy-club, tucked it into his pants, and went into the house where the man, not unlike a patient, was "laid upon a mat" (14):

> The woman of the house took hold of the bag,
> saying, "What is this so big?"
> I said, "It is good for savages to eat," and struck
> her on the arm as hard as I could.
> Then she said, "Matchet powder English men,
> much Matchit. By and by, [Chikatawbak] bring Mouch
> Mans, Mouch Sannups, and kill you and all English...."

And, not surprisingly,

> The man that lay upon the mats, seeing this, was
> angry and in a great rage, and the woman seemed to be sore
> afraid. Then I went out of the house....

The crucial question: What *exactly* put the man in his "rage"? Was it the violent answer to the woman's saucy inquiry (perhaps as she tugged at those funny English trousers)? Pratt answered her with words ironic for a starving man---equivalent to "*Eat* it"---and struck her with his strength. Or, was the patient enraged that the woman had thoughtlessly spilled a plot? She clutched at her arm and screamed for her men to teach Pratt "and all" a lesson, "by and by."

But Pratt---unmolested for this act---moved to confirm his "suspicion" (or now, expectation) by way of a subtle ploy: he asked Native people to inform on each other for his benefit. "Go ask ye woman, but not in ye man's hearing...." The reader must interpret the Native answer of a "conspiracy" about to fall (115): "...he and all Indians will be angry...."

lxx   *Introduction*

This incident---what Vaughan calls the complaint of "a loquacious squaw"---was followed directly by Massachusetts braves' demand to see justice at Weymouth; and their tearing away "in a great rage" (117). Now, Pratt began to "notice" them "creep[ing] upon the snow, starting behind bushes and trees to see whether we kept watch or not." He discovered starved-dead Englishmen along his exhausting security-rounds, and looked back to counsel "all ye people of New England" to "put your trust in God." At this point, Pecksuot made his effort against the worsening trouble (see note above); and in answer, Pratt blazed his harrowing trail for Plimoth with "intelligence."

It could not have come at a worse time into the midst of other "evidences." Plimoth had no accurate idea of the Native rules of war. They gave "commission" to resolve this not to a diplomat, but to Standish and "10 or 11" men at arms (Pratt 123). Plimoth also had to suppose that Weymouth would find its strength soon. They resolved on a "preemptive" massacre where there was both means to justice and plenty for them all.

Bradford reports "we killed seven" Native men ("Letter"); Winslow totals seven; Altham (31) says "five or six" besides "our chief enemy" Wituwamat and/or Pecksuot; Morton claims three Natives killed; and Pratt says two, "with others where they could find them" (123). Pratt also adds two English killed, "took in their houses at an advantage" (123) to the three English counted by the others.[50]

From Bradford and Winslow we also learn of at least three Native "collateral" deaths, men whose descriptions mark them as the flower of Native New England, "affable, courteous, and loving": Canacum, Sachem of Manomet, Aspinet of Nauset, Iyanough of Mattakiest. They died of "fevers" when, at news

---

[50] Contrast Winslow's suddenly not-plain-style sentences on the ambush with those of Pratt; who says (123) that Standish's party "first gave warning to the master of the [*Swan*] and then contrived how to make sure of the lives of two of their chief men." Winslow says Standish "could not get many of them together at once" (56); but waited till "about as many of his own" were "in a room" with a total of four Native men. Historian McWade, noting that Pecksuot had spoken directly to Standish's purposes, believes that the Native men were made drunk and bleary (Morton's *Canaan* describes a "feast" of pork) before Standish "began" with Pecksuot's own knife. That they had let themselves be hemmed in by the Weymouth block-house also suggests that they felt no "fear" at the moment; and if we "turn around" Winslow's words, we see that the Native leaders had not themselves gathered "many of them together at once" for their own "attack" or defense.

of the killings, they sought refuge in swamps. "[V]ery many" others died too (FBH1: 296); though changes of name/abode might account for some.

While many historians note that at least one Native man's severed head, Wituwamat's, was stuck on a pike atop Plimoth's fort and church, visitors to today's Plimoth (where "it's always 1627") will not see human heads there. Nor will they see---and no historian has ever shown---the further sign of victory posted, proudly noted by "outsider" Altham (31): "instead of an ancient [a flag], we have a piece of linen cloth dyed in the same Indian's blood, which was hung out upon the fort when Massasoit was here" (for Governor Bradford's later wedding).[51]

By all accounts, the "preemptive" action devastated Plimoth's trade. It took years to recover. "There where we had most skins the Indians are run away...and set no corn" (FBH1: 296). That same 1623 the Narragansetts *rejected* Plimoth's offer of a trading-visit (Robinson 20), while new alliances were forged around them: for example, Chikatawbak's Massachusetts eventually "went with many men" to aid their "enemy" Narragansetts under Canonicus in his 1632-35 struggle with the Pequots (Drake 43). Bradford mentioned no "Indians" until 1625, when Plimoth's first surplus of corn was bartered at Kennebec (1: 439). Still "raw and weak," they faced "great sums" of debt. Morton, when he came to the same country and (by transatlantic methods) produced different results, dubbed them "Princes of Limbo." Resorting to wampum in 1627 (exactly as Morton prospered through trade of guns), Plimoth took two further years to trade away its first supply of it (FBH2: 43).

Resentments, and killings, continued after the massacre.[52] In time Pratt joined Plimoth, but became destitute. In asking a pension from Massachusetts

---

[51] Samuel Eliot Morison's 1963 introduction to James' *Three Visitors to Early Plymouth* attested that Altham's unvarying restatement of Winslow's story "corroborates" it. "Detractors of the Pilgrim colony will find no ammunition" in the letters therein. "[N]othing to disparage. They have given us fresh reason to respect the faith and fortitude of that little band in its struggle to maintain a toe hold on the edge of the American wilderness."

[52] Winslow (58) states that just after the killings, a Weymouth man "saved his [own] life" by hurrying from a Massachusett village where there were "none but women left, and the other [Weymouth Englishman] that was turned salvage." Hopefully the reader will contrast the above period of "marriage" and children with a new cultural period begun with the massacre. The facts below reveal new "policy" toward persons who amounted, in fact, to transatlantic family:

Bay, Pratt spoke proudly of his youth spent as a ground-breaker. He told of working at the "first plantation at Piscataqua" (124), where he met "Two of [Chikatawbak's] men." Seeing Pratt, they mocked that the slain English had "cried and made ill-favored faces." Pratt mocked back that at least "torment" had not been part of killing Native people. (Morton says the three English had been "asleep" when "knocked in the head.")

But mockery did not end the matter. After his stay with Levett, "Then," Pratt records, "we went with our ship into the bay [of Massachusetts] and took from them two shallops' loading of corn, and of their men, prisoners." Their fates are not recorded.

We know of no Native response in kind. Winslow noted (63) that "from one of these places" a Native "boat was sent with presents to the Governour, hoping thereby to work their peace. But the boat was cast away, and three of the persons drowned" not far from Plimoth.

Trade grew scarce, and "an English living" had to be made. Pratt 102:

> The third and last time was in the bay of Agawam
> [in the "Cape Anne/Ipswich" area]. At this time they took for
> their castle a thick swamp. At this time one of our ablest men
> was shot in the shoulder. Whether any of them were killed or
> wounded, we could not tell.[53]

Nobody tried to find out. Not the distinguished Court of Massachusetts Bay, nor the historians schooled under its "Native" motto, "Come Over and Help Us." No historian has investigated exactly how or why, as Adams said (134 here), "extermination....saved the Anglo-Saxon stock" from *marrying into* Native

---

Jack Frost's Weymouth history *Immortal Voyage* (75: see Illustrations) includes notes and photos from archaeologist G. Stinson Lord on the 1930s discovery of multiple human remains near the colony site. (See Illustrations.) Injuries to the skeletons matched descriptions of Pecksuot and the others killed, beheaded, hanged and (by someone) buried. Not far from them was also found "a papoose skeleton [with] its head bashed in. Later enlargement of diggings brought to light [a] Squaw with her head in the same condition. One wonders," Lord wrote, "if this could be the child of the man who married an Indian Squaw at Weston's Colony. No doubt he suffered a worse fate in the game of tit-for-tat, typical of these rough (?) times."

[53] The "Sachem of Agawam" or "Ipswich" was then Masconomo or Masconomo (Drake 47), who still "welcomed" the later 1630 colonists of Boston Bay to "his shores," and whose "squaw for some time [after 1643] survived him and had a piece of land that she could not [*sic*] dispose of, or that none were allowed to purchase."

societies and becoming "a nation of half-breeds." "New England," like the Pilgrims---whose "dearest country" was not of this world---faced early-on with a Native American speaking "excessively," turned away from what the people of the land had to teach, not least about themselves; turned away, back to an errand in the wilderness. For all these reasons, "The Pilgrims" too have more to teach us than perhaps they or we ourselves imagined.[54]

Stoneham, Massachusetts
Spring 2001

---

[54] Adams, *Three Episodes* (12): "And in this way, as that eminent Christian divine and close student of the precepts of his Master, the Rev. Cotton Mather, charitably observed eighty years later [in his *Magnalia Christi Americana*, 1:2: 6], 'the woods were almost cleared of those pernicious creatures, to make room for a better growth.'" "Massacre thus completed the work of pestilence. It may have been necessary,---almost certainly it was best...." (104). The *good news* of Winslow's account did not concern the progress of The Gospel.

Sanctification of genocide as the "just reward" of a people for "conspiracy" by a few of them is the most serious consequence of these "selective emphases." "Another Indian... escaped [the Massacre] and spread the alarm, thus preventing the full accomplishment of Standish's purpose...the indiscriminate killing of all the males of the [Massachusetts] tribe" (93-4). Killing "all the males" of a group results in genocide. Historical neglect and/or erasure continue the "work." The fate of Pecksuot's son Nahamit is not known. Chikatawbak's sons were called Papawhinnet and Josias (the latter's life and "considerable knowledge in the Christian religion" recounted in Drake 43-6). As a matter of "official" notice, Massachusett people were "not fifty" by the 1630s under Boston's "protection" (WPF3: 172). See end of the Chronology.

"Yet," Adams continued at the edge of the 20th century (100), "admitting everything which in harshest language modern philanthropy could assert, there is still no reasonable doubt that, in the practical working of human events, the course approved in advance by the Plimoth magistrates, and ruthlessly put in execution by Standish, was in this case the most merciful, the wisest and, consequently, the most justifiable course. The essential fact was, and is, that the settlers were surrounded by Indians and had to deal with them; and Indians were not Europeans....[they were] partially developed, savage human beings."

EDWARD WINSLOW,
GOOD NEWS from NEW ENGLAND (1624)

Edward Winslow (1595-1655) was born the son of Edward Winslow, Esquire, in Draughtwich (Droitwich) in the county of Worcester, and was the family's first son, with four brothers and three sisters to follow. Young's short biography (274-5) includes documents concerning Winslow's family origins. In a region "celebrated for its salt springs" the family prospered under the father's trade as a salt victualler. He was able to send Edward to the King's School, one of the best Elizabethan "public" grammar schools, and the son---in time a "printer's apprentice"---completed his studies from Latin to The Bible and Classical Literature.

Brief-biographers Hutchinson, Morton and Morison describe Winslow as "traveling into the low countries" by the 1610s. Many young Englishmen "finished" their educations this way, while others took up common law or soldiering against the Spanish (such as Plimoth compatriot Myles Standish). Sources agree that by 1617 Winslow had begun "living three years under Mr. Robinson's ministry before we began the work of plantation" in 1620. Morton says he "fell into acquaintance with the church of Leyden, in Holland, unto whom he joined" (169); and by 1620 he and wife Elizabeth had two children (who according to Young, "died young").

Thus Winslow, 25 and six years William Bradford's junior, arrived with *Mayflower* in November 1620 on Cape Cod. Within two years he and other planters had assembled records of their first explorations and Native relationships in *Mourt's Relation*, and *Good News from New England* became Winslow's next work, combining observations with an unfolding narrative of Plimoth's purposes---as a colony, and as a Christian-evangelical enterprise of "Saints" intent on the many-sided "reform" of their own "congregation," fellow English, and Native Americans.

Winslow's and Bradford's writings describe each other's parts in the "Affair" of 1621-23. After it, Winslow voyaged to England both to defend Plimoth before The Council for New England and to extend its effort for a patent to rights of trade. Meanwhile the Massachusetts Bay Company under John Winthrop landed in force at nearby Boston in 1630. With Plimoth both helped and frustrated by their presence (Willison), by 1633 Winslow was chosen to relieve Bradford as Governor: he served again in 1636 and 1644. In legal battle against attorney and rival planter Thomas Morton, Winslow landed briefly in The Fleet prison due to Anglican Bishop William Laud's hostility to Puritans and his then-close control of The Council for New England.

Winslow's later children included Josiah, a Massachusetts governor from 1673-1680. In 1637 the family acquired lands at Marshfield. Winslow served the colonies in England ("buttonholing members of Parliament," Vaughan *Frontier* 254) as of 1646; and then amid the breakout of hostilities in the English Civil War, was chosen by Cromwell to help superintend English forces against the Spanish in the West Indies. There, at sea off Hispaniola on May 8th, Winslow died at age 60.

After *Good News* Winslow did not publish again until 1646. (Some of his letters are in Winthrop's *Papers*). In his last years came the rest of his works, intense involvements in colonial disputes over questions of religious doctrine and so (in Puritan New England) with questions of civil authority and order. In *Hypocrisie Unmasked* (1646) and *New England's Salamander* (1647), as well as in English courts, Winslow condemned the cantankerous critic of Boston Bay, Samuel Gorton (his story in Willison, rpt. in Young). Winslow's *A Platform of Church-Discipline* (London 1653) was important to the "Cambridge Synod" of evolving Puritanism; and in 1648-9 he assisted with pamphlets *The Clear Sun-shine* and *The Glorious Progress of the Gospel Among the Indians of New England*, including texts by John Eliot and Thomas Mayhew. His final *The Danger of Tolerating Levellers in a Civil State* (1649) was part of the extraordinary political and social debates that followed the final victories of Cromwell against King Charles I. Jennings' *Invasion* and Petegorsky offer detailed and broad related perspectives.

The copy-text for *Good News from New England* (London 1624) is the original copy in the John Carter Brown Library at Brown University, Providence RI USA. Later editions of *Good News* appeared (with *Mourt's Relation*) in Samuel Purchas' 4th volume of *Purchas His Pilgrims* in 1625: in an abridged 1802 printing by Massachusetts Historical Society, with "omissions" appearing in 1822; and Alexander Young's, from the Harvard Library copy in 1841. Edward Arber published an edition in 1897's *Story of the Pilgrim Fathers*: Young's was reprinted by Little Brown in 1941.

GOOD NEWS

from NEW ENGLAND, *or*

A True Relation of Things Very Remarkable
at the Plantation of Plimoth
in New England

Shewing the wondrous providence & goodness
of GOD, in their preservation & continuance,
being delivered from many apparent deaths and dangers.

Together with a Relation
of religious and civil Laws & Customs in practice amongst
the Indians, adjoyning to them at this day.
As also what Commodities are there to be raised
for the maintenance of that and other
Plantations in the said Country.

Written by **E. W.**, who hath borne a part
in the fore-named troubles, and there lived
since their first Arrival.
Whereunto is added by him a brief Relation
of a credible intelligence of the present estate of Virginia.

LONDON

Printed by I.D. for *William Bladen* and *Iohn Bellamie*, and are to be sold
at their Shops, at the *Bible* in *Paul's* Churchyard,
and at the Three Golden Lyons in Corn Hill,
near the *Royal Exchange.*
1624.

The Epistle Dedicatory
To
ALL WELL-WILLERS and
FURTHERERS of PLANTATIONS
in NEW ENGLAND:
especially to such as ever have or desire to assist
the people of Plimoth in their just proceedings---
Grace, and Peace Be Multiplied[55]

RIGHT Honorable and Worshipful Gentlemen, or whatsoever:

Since it hath pleased God to stir you up to be instruments of his glory, in so honorable an enterprise as the enlarging of his Majesty's Dominions by planting his loyal subjects in so healthful and hopeful a Country as *New England* is, where the Church of God being seated in sincerity, there is no less hope of convincing the Heathen of their evil ways, and converting them to the true knowledge and worship of the living God, and so consequently the salvation of their souls by the merits of Iesus Christ, than elsewhere, though it be much talked on, and lightly [A/2] or lamely prosecuted.

I therefore think it but my duty to offer the view of our proceedings to your worthy considerations, having to that end composed them together thus briefly, as you see; wherein, to your great encouragement, you may behold the good providence of God working with you, in our preservation from so many dangerous plots and treacheries as have been intended against us; as also in giving his blessing so powerfully upon the weak means we had, enabling us with health and ability beyond expectation in

---

[55] **Note:** Spacing required deletion of two words from the title page 3rd paragraph (words cut shown here in *italics*): "Together with a Relation of *such* religious and civil Laws & Customs *as are* in practice amongst the Indians..."

our greatest scarcities, and possessing the hearts of the Salvages with astonishment and fear of us; whereas if God had let them loose, they might easily have swallowed us up, scarce being an handful in comparison of those forces they might have gathered together against us, which now by God's blessing will be more hard and difficult, in regard our number of men is increased, our town better fortified, and our store better victualed. Blessed therefore be his name, that hath done so great things for us, and hath wrought so great a change amongst us.

Accept, I pray you, my weak endeavors, pardon my unskillfulness, and bear with my plainness in the things I have handled. Be not discouraged by our former necessities, but rather encouraged with us, hoping that as God hath wrought with us in the beginning of this worthy Work, undertaken in his name and fear, so he will by us accomplish the same to his glory and our comfort, if we neglect not the means. I confess, it hath not been much less chargeable to some of you[56] than hard and difficult to us, that have endured the brunt of the battle, and yet small profits returned. Only by God's mercy we are safely seated, housed, and fortified, by which means a great step is made unto gain, and a more direct course taken for the same than if at first we had rashly and covetously fallen upon it.

Indeed, three things are the overthrow and bane (as I may term it) of Plantations.

1. The vain expectation of present profit, which too too commonly taketh a principal seat in the heart and affection; though God's glory, etc., is preferred before it in the mouth with protestation.

2. Ambition in their Governours and Commanders, seeking only to make themselves great, and slaves of all that are under them, to maintain a

---

[56] **some of you**   Plimoth's financial backers/suppliers, The Merchant Adventurers or Plymouth Company. Like many men incl. Weston, Cushman, and The Council's aristocrat-investors, their "joint stock" or "corporations" financed fishing and trade voyages. John Smith (*General Hi-story* 251): "about seventy [of them], some gentlemen, some merchants, some handicraftsmen, some venturing great sums, some small." Their letters, contract terms etc. FBH1: 52-136.

    Textual note   Young positions the "Brief Relation...of Virginia" between Winslow's note "To the Reader" and the start of *Good News*. In the original copy used for this edition, that "Relation" followed the "Postscript."

transitory base honour in themselves, which God oft punisheth with contempt.

3. The carelessness of those that send over supplies of men unto them, not caring how they be qualified, so that oft times they are rather the Image of men endued with bestial, yea, diabolical affections, than the Image of God, endued with reason, understanding, and holiness. I prayse God I speak not these things experimentally, by way of complaint of our own condition, but having great cause on the contrary part to be thankful to God for his mercies towards us. But rather, if there be any too desirous of gain, to entreat them to moderate their affections, and consider that no man expecteth fruit before the tree be grown; advising all men, that as they tender their own well-fare, [A3] so to make choice of such to manage and govern their affairs, as are approved not to be seekers of themselves, but the common good of all for whom they are employed; and beseeching such as have the care of transporting men for the supply and furnishing of Plantations, to be truly careful in sending such as may further and not hinder so good an action.

There is no godly honest man but will be helpful in his kind, and adorn his profession with an upright life and conversation; which Doctrine of manners ought first to be Preached by giving good example to the poor Savage Heathens amongst whom they live. On the contrary part, what great offense hath been given by many profane men, who being but seeming Christians, have made Christ and Christianity stink in the nostrils of the poor Infidels, and so laid a stumbling block before them; *but woe be to them by whom such offenses come.*

These things I offer to your Christian considerations, beseeching you to make a good construction of my simple meaning, and take in good part this ensuing Relation, dedicating my selfe and it ever more unto your service; beseeching God to crown our Christian and faithful endeavors with his blessings temporal and eternal.

Yours in service, ever to be commanded: **E. W.**

To the Reader

GOOD READER, *when I first penned this discourse, I intended it chiefly for the satisfaction of my private friends, but since that time, have been persuaded to publish the same. And the rather, because of a disorderly colony that are dispersed, and most of them returned, to the great prejudice and damage of him that set them forth; who as they were a stain to old England that bred them, in respect of their lives and manners amongst the Indians: So it is to be feared, will be no less to New-England in their vile and clamorous reports, because she would not foster them in their desired idle courses. I would not be understood to think there were no well-deserving persons amongst them; for of mine own knowledge it was a grief to some that they were so yoked; whose deserts as they were then suitable to their honest protestations, so I desire still may be, in respect of their just and true Relations.*

Peradventure, thou wilt rather marvel that I deal so plainly, than any way doubt of the truth of this my Relation; yea, it may be, tax me therewith, as seeming rather to discourage men than any way to further so noble an action? If any honest mind be discouraged, I am sorry, sure I am, I have given no just cause; and am so far from being discouraged my selfe, as I purpose to return fortwith. And for other light and vain persons, if they stumble hereat, I have my desire, accounting it better for them and us that they keep where they are, as being unfit and unable to perform so great a task.

Some faults have escaped because I could not attend on the Press, which I pray thee correct as thou findest, and I shall account it as a favor unto me.

Thine E. W.

GOOD NEWS
from
NEW ENGLAND

The Good Ship called the *Fortune*, which in the month of November 1621 (blessed be God) brought us a new supply of 35 persons, was not long departed our Coast, ere the Great people of *Nanohigganset*, which are reported to be many thousands strong, began to breathe forth many threats against us, notwithstanding their desired and obtained peace with us in the fore-going summer.[57] Insomuch as the common talk of our neighbour *Indians* on all sides was of the preparation they made to come against us, in reason a man would think they should have now more cause to fear us than before our supply came. But, though none of them were present[58], yet un- **[B]** derstanding by others that they neither brought Arms nor other provisions with them, but wholly relied on us, it occasioned them to sleight and brave us with so many threats as they did.

At length came one of them to us, who was sent by *Conanacus* their chief *Sachem* or King,[59] accompanied with one *Tokamahamon* a friendly

---

[57] **Nanohigganset**   more commonly **Narragansett**---Acc. to Wood (1636: 80) "the most numerous people in those parts," relatives and traditional rivals of the Wampanoag, with territories from Rhode Island to eastern Connecticutt. "[T]hese be populous, yet I never heard they were desirous to take in hand any martial enterprise or expose themselves to the uncertain events of war, wherefore the Pequots call them women-like men." Acc. to Winslow (73) and FBH1: 220 they had been spared other peoples' heavy losses in the 1616-18 "plague." On "the fore-going summer" see Introduction Part 4

[58] **none of them were present**   at the *Fortune*'s arrival

[59] **Conanacus**   Canonicus (?--1647), Sachem of perhaps 30,000, was grandson of the "very powerful" Tashtussuck (Hutchinson 1: 458), eldest of 4 sons, and father of several important leaders (FBH2: 364). **Tokamahamom**   little is known of him: in *Mourt's Relation* (68, 73) he seems associated with Nemasket. **Tisquantum**   A Wampanoag *pneise* (73) kidnapped by Hunt from Patuxet in 1616 (Chronology *xii*; Introduction): later finding his village decimated by "plague," he worked with many English before serving, like **Hobbamock** (11: "a Wampanoag"

Indian. This messenger inquired for *Tisquantum* our Interpreter, who not being at home seemed rather to be glad than sorry; and, leaving for him[60] a bundle of new arrows lapped in a rattle Snakes skin, desired to depart with all expedition. But our Governours[61], not knowing what to make of this strange carriage, and comparing it with that we had formerly heard, committed him to the custody of Captain *Standish*,[62] hoping now to know some certainty of that we so often heard, either by his own relation to us, or to *Tisquantum* at his return; [and] desiring myself, having special familiarity with the other fore-named *Indian*, to see if I could learn any thing from him; whose answer was sparingly to this effect, that he could not certainly tell, but thought they were enemies to us.

That night, Captain *Standish* gave me and another charge of him, and gave us order to use him kindly, and that he should not want any thing he desired, and to take all occasions to talk and inquire of the reasons of those reports we heard, and withall to signify that upon his true relation he should be sure of his own freedom. At first, fear so possest him that he could scarce say any thing; but in the end became more familiar, and told

---

acc. to FBH1: 225), as go-between for Ousamequin or "Massasoit" and Plimoth Colony. (Hobbamock appears in no record later than 1623 [FBH1: 346] when "Hobamacks ground" is listed in land allotments. Tisquantum (with Samoset, likely of Monhegan origin) had come to Plimoth in March 1621 (FBH1: 202-3) and his help in planting, fishing and trade made him seem "a spetiall instrument sent of God for their good beyond their expectation"

[60] **him**   Tisquantum

[61] **our Governours**   after the April 1621 death of first governor John Carver (FBH1: 194), William Bradford took office with Assistant Isaac Allerton (1: 216)

[62] **Captain [Myles] Standish**   (1583?-1656) Morton's *Memorial* (170) says Standish was born "a gentleman...in Lancashire, and was heir apparent unto a great estate of lands and livings....In his younger time he went over into the Low Countries, and was a soldier there, and came acquainted with the ["Pilgrim"] church at Leyden...." A Standish family-descendant's article on this "question" published in *Smithsonian Magazine* (March 2000) confessed no "gentle" lineage.
Hobbamock first remarked his "little chimney" height and temperament. Standish's wife Rose died in the harsh winter of 1620. Though he never joined the Plimoth church he became one "undertaker" of its debts in 1626. After this decade of actions enforcing law and/or policy, he functioned more as a sheriff and tax collector (2: 354) and resided at "Duxburrow" north of Plimoth. He had skirmished with Nausets ("First Encounter" 1620) and at Nemasket in August 1621 (FBH1: 226; *Mourt* 76), there wounding "women and children" while "rescuing" Tisquantum from Sachem Corbitant, "too conversant" (*Mourt* 73) with Narragansett rivals

us that the messenger which his Master sent in Summer to treat of peace, at his return persuaded him rather to war; and to the end he might provoke him thereunto, (as appeared to him by our reports) de*ained[63] many of the things were sent him by our Governour, scorning the meanness of them both in respect of what himself had formerly sent, & also of the greatness of his own person; so that he much blamed the former Messenger, saying, that upon the knowledge of this his false carriage, it would cost him his **[2]** life. But [he] assured us that upon his relation of our speech then with him to his Master, he would be friends with us.

Of this we informed the Governour and his Assistant, and Captain *Standish*, who after consultation considered him howsoever but in the state of a messenger, and it being as well against the Law of Arms amongst them as us in *Europe* to lay violent hands on any such, set him at liberty, the Governour giving him order to certify his Master that he had heard of his large and many threatenings, at which he was much offended; daring him in those respects to the utmost, if he would not be reconciled to live peaceably as other his neighbours; manifesting withall (as ever) his desire of peace, but his fearless resolution if he could not so live amongst them. After which he caused meat to be offered him, but he refused to eat, making all speed to return, and giving many thanks for his liberty. But requesting the other *Indian* again to return, the weather being violent, he used many words to persuade him to stay longer, but could not. Whereupon he left him, and said he was with his friends, and would not take a journey in such extremity.

After this, when *Tisquantum* returned, and the arrows were delivered, and the manner of the messenger's carriage related, he signified to the Governour that to send the rattle Snakes skin in that manner, imported enmitie, and that it was no better than a challenge. Hereupon after some deliberation, the Governour stuffed the skin with powder and shot, and sent it back, returning no less defiance to *Conanacus*, assuring him if he had shipping now present thereby to send his men to

---

[63] **de*ained**   a letter (*) was missing from this word in the original, whatever word may have been intended. Young (282) makes it "detained," as in "held back"

Nanohigganset (the place of his abode): they should not need to come so far by land to us, yet withall shewing that they should never come unwelcome or unlooked for. This message was sent by an *Indian*, and delivered in such sort as it was no small terrour to this savage [3/B2] King; insomuch as he would not once touch the powder and shot, or suffer it to stay in his house or Country. Whereupon the Messenger refusing it, another took it up, and having been posted from place to place a long time, at length came whole back again.

In the meane time, knowing our own weakness, notwithstanding our high words and loftie looks towards them, and still lying open to all casualty, having as yet (under God) no other defense than our Arms, we thought it most needful to impale our Towne, which with all expedition we accomplished in the month of February and some few days; taking in the top of the Hill under which our Towne is seated, making four bulwarks or jetties without the ordinary circuit of the pale, from whence we could defend the whole Towne; in three whereof are gates, and the fourth in time to be. This being done, Captain *Standish* divided our strength into four squadrons or companies, appointing whom he thought most fit to have command of each; and at a general Muster or Trayning, appointed each his place, gave each his Companie, giving them charge upon every alarum to resort to their Leaders to their appointed place, and in his absence, to be commanded and directed by them. That done according to his order, each drew his Companie to his appointed place for defense, and there together discharged their muskets. After which they brought their new Commanders to their houses, where again they graced them with their shot, and so departed.

Fearing also lest the enemie at any time should take any advantage by firing our houses, Captain *Standish* appointed a certain Companie, that whensoever they saw or heard fire to be cryed in the Towne, should only betake themselves to their Arms, and should [4] inclose the house or place so indangered, and stand aloof on their guard, with their backs towards the fire, to prevent treachery, if any were in that kind intended. If the fire were in any of the houses of this guard, they were then freed from it, but not otherwise, without special command.

Long before this time we promised the people of *Massachuset* in the beginning of March to come unto them, and trade for their Furs; which being then come, we began to make preparation for that voyage.[64] In the meane time, an *Indian* called *Hobbamock*, who still lived in the Towne, told us that he feared the *Massachusets* or *Massachuseucks* (for they so called the people of that place) were joyned in confederacy with the *Nanohigganneucks*, or people of *Nanohigganset*; and that they therefore would take this opportunity to cut off Captain *Standish* and his company abroad. But howsoever in the meane time, it was to be feared that the *Nanohigganeuks* would assault the Towne at home; giving many reasons for his jealousie[65]; as also that *Tisquantum* was in the confederacie, who, we should find, would use many perswasions to draw us from our shallops to the *Indians* houses for their better advantage. To confirm this his jealousie, he told us of many secret passages that passed between him and others, having their meetings ordinarily abroad in the woods; but if at home howsoever, he was excluded from their secrecie, saying it was the manner of the *Indians* when they meant plainly to deal openly. But in this his practice[66] there was no shew of honesty.

Hereupon the Governour, together with his Assistant and Captain *Standish*, called together such as by them were thought most meet for advice in so weighty a business; who, after consideration hereof, came to this resolution; That as hitherto upon all occasions between them and us, we had ever manifested undaunted courage and reso- **[5/B3]** lution, so it would not now stand with our safety to mew up our selves in our new-enclosed town; partly because our Store was almost empty, and therefore must seek out for our daily food, without which we could not long subsist; but especially for that thereby they would see us dismayed, and be encouraged to prosecute their malicious purposes with more eagerness

---

[64] In September 1621 the Plimoth shallop under Standish had explored Massachusetts Bay (*Mourt* 77-9) incl. the Mystic River and Squantum areas, "to procure...truck"

[65] **jealousie** suspicion

[66] **in this his practice** in Tisquantum's alleged secret "confederacy"

than ever they intended. Whereas on the contrary, by the blessing of God, our fearless carriage might be a means to discourage and weaken their proceedings. And therefore thought best to proceed in our trading voyage, making this use of that we heard, to go the better provided, and use the more carefulness both at home and abroad, leaving the event to the disposing of the Almighty, whose providence as it had hitherto been over us for good; so we had now no cause (save our sins) to despair of his mercy in our preservation and continuance, where we desired rather to be instruments of good to the Heathens about us, than to give them the least measure of just offense.

All things being now in readiness, the forenamed Captain with ten men, accompanied with *Tisquantum* and *Hobbamock*, set forwards for the *Massachusetts*. But we had no sooner turned the point of the harbour called the *Gurnets nose*[67] (where being becalmed we let fall our grapnel, to set things to rights, and prepared to row), but there came an Indian of *Tisquantum*'s family, running to certain of our people that were from home with all eagerness, having his face wounded, and the bloud still fresh on the same, calling to them to repair home; oft looking behind him, as if some others had him in chase, saying that at *Namaschet* (a town some fifteen miles from us[68]) there were many of the *Nanohigganseis*, *Massassowat* our supposed friend, and *Conbatant* our feared enemy, with many others, with a resolution to take advantage on the present opportunity to assault the town in the Captain's absence; affirming that he received the wound on his face for **[6]** speaking in our behalf, and by sleight escaped, looking oft backward as if he suspected them to be at hand.[69]

---

[67] **Gurnet's Nose**   a small peninsula on Plimoth Harbor named after "several places on the coast of England" (sources in Young 287)

[68] **Namaschet**   Nemasket (today's Middleboro), village of Sachem **Corbitant**

[69] **Massasowat**   after the death of Nanepashemet c.1619 (*Mourt* 78), Ousamequin (Yellow Feather) of the Pokanoket Wampanoag became "Massasoit" or "High Sachem" of the region. **Sachem** (in Proto-Algonquian *Sa-kima-wa*) means "leader" of many groups and their "subchiefs" or **Sagamores. Conbatant**   usually Corbitant, Sachem of the Nemasket Wampanoag

This he affirmed again to the Governour, whereupon he gave command that three piece of Ordnance should be made ready and discharged, to the end that if we were not out of hearing, we might return thereat. Which we no sooner heard, but we repaired homeward with all convenient speed, arming our selves, and making all in readiness to fight. When we entered the harbour, we saw the Towne likewise on their guard; whither we hasted with all convenient speed. The news being made known unto us, *Hobbamock* said flatly that it was false, assuring us of *Massassowat's* faithfulness; howsoever, he presumed he would never have undertaken any such act without his privitie[70], himself being a Pinse[71], that is, one of his chiefest champions or men of valour, it being the manner amongst them not to undertake such enterprises without the advice and furtherance of men of that rank. To this the Governour answered, he should be sorry that any just and necessary occasions of war should arise between him and any of the Savages, but especially *Massassowat*; not that he feared him more than the rest, but because his love more exceeded towards him than any. Whereunto *Hobbamock* replied: There was no cause wherefore he should distrust him, and therefore should do well to continue his affections.

But to the end things might be made more manifest, the Governour caused *Hobbamock* to send his wife with all privacy to *Puckanokick*, the chief place of *Massassowat's* residence[72] (pretending other occasions), there to inform herself, and so us, of the right state of things. When she came thither, and saw all things quiet, and that no such matter was or had been intended, [she] told *Massassowat* what had happened at *Plimoth* (by them called *Patuxet);* which, when he understood, he [7] was much offended at the carriage of *Tisquantum,* returning many thanks to the Governour for his good thoughts of him; and assuring him that according to their first

---

[70] **privitie**   without Hobbamock's being privy to or aware of it

[71] **Pinse**   usually spelled **pneise**: a "man of notable spirit" (55), "of great courage and wisdom" (73), with qualities of both a Sachem and a Powah (see 70-75)

[72] **Puckanokick**   Pokanoket, near Sowams and Montop, residences of Massasoit's people

Articles of peace, he would send word and give warning when any such business was towards.[73]

Thus by degrees we began to discover *Tisquantum*, whose ends were only to make himself great in the eyes of this Countrymen, by means of his nearness and favour with us, not caring who fell so he stood. In the general, his course was to persuade them he could lead us to peace or war at his pleasure, and would oft threaten the *Indians*, sending them word in a private manner [that] we were intended shortly to kill them; that thereby he might get gifts to himself to work their peace, insomuch as they had him in greater esteem than many of their *Sachims*; yea, they themselves sought to him, who promised them peace in respect of us; yea and protection also, so as[74] they would resort to him. So that whereas divers were wont to rely on *Massassowat* for protection, and resort to his abode, now they began to leave him, and seek after *Tisquantum*.

Now, though he could not make good these his large promises, especially because of the continued peace between *Massassowat* and us, he therefore raised this false alarum, hoping whilst things were hot in the heat of bloud to provoke us to march into his Country against him; whereby he hoped to kindle such a flame as would not easily be quenched, and hoping if that block were once removed, there were no other between him and honor; which he loved as his life, and preferred before his peace. For these and the like abuses, the Governour sharply reproved him; yet was he so necessary and profitable an instrument, as at that time we could not miss him.

But, when we understood his dealings, we certified all the *Indians* of our ignorance and innocence therein, assuring **[8]** them [that] till they begun with us, they should have no cause to fear. And if any hereafter should raise any such reports, they should punish them as liars and

---

[73] **first Articles of peace**   Plimoth's first (March 1621) formal treaty with Massasoit is recorded in FBH1: 199-202, and in *Mourt's Relation* (56-7)

[74] **so as**   if

seekers of their and our disturbance, which gave the *Indians* good satisfaction on all sides.

After this, we proceeded in our voyage to the *Massachusets*, where we had good store of Trade, and (blessed be God) returned in safety, though driven from before our Towne in great danger and extremity of weather.

At our return, we found *Massassowat* at the Plantation, who made his seeming just Apology for all former matters of accusation, being much offended and enraged against *Tisquantum*, whom the Governour pacified as much as he could for the present. But, not long after his departure, he sent a messenger to the Governour, entreating him to give way to the death of *Tisquantum*, who had so much abused him. But the Governour answered: Although he had deserved to die both in respect of him and us, yet for our sakes he desired he would spare him, and the rather because without him he knew not well how to understand himself, or any other [of] the *Indians*.

With this answer the messenger returned, but came again not long after, accompanied with divers others demanding him from[75] *Massassowat* their Master, as being one of his subjects, whom by our first Articles of peace we could not retain. Yet, because he would not willingly do it without the Governour's approbation, [*Massassowat*] offered him many Beavers skins for his content thereto; saying that according to their manner, their *Sachim* had sent his own knife, and them therewith, to cut off his head and hands, and bring them to him. To which the Governour answered, It was not the manner of the *English* to sell men's lives at a price, but **[9]** when they had deserved justly to die, to give them their reward, and therefore refused their Beavers as a gift; but sent for *Tisquantum*, who, though he knew their intent, yet offered not to fly, but came and accused *Hobbamock* as the author and worker of his overthrow; yielding himself to the Governour to be sent according as he thought meet. But at the instant when our Governour was ready to deliver him into the hands of his

---

[75] **from** on behalf of

Executioners, a boat was seen at sea to cross before our Towne, and fall behind a head-land not far off; whereupon, having heard many rumors of the *French*[76], and not knowing whether there were any combination betwen the Savages and them, the Governour told the *Indians* he would first know what boat that was, ere he would deliver him into their custody. But, being mad with rage, and impatient at delay, they departed in great heat.

Here let me not omit one notable (though wicked) practice of this *Tisquantum*, who to the end he might possess his Countrymen with the greater fear of us, and so consequently of himself, told them we had the plague buried in our store-house[77]; which, at our pleasure, we could send forth to what place or people we would, and destroy them therewith, though we stirred not from home. Being upon the fore-named brabbles[78] sent for by the Governour to this place, where *Hobbamock* was and some other of us, the ground being broke in the middest of the house, (whereunder certain barrels of powder were buried, though unknown to him), *Hobbamock* asked what it meant? To whom he readily answered: That was the place wherein the plague was buried, whereof he formerly told him and others. After this, *Hobbamock* asked one of our people whether such a thing were, and whether he had such **[10]** command of it? Who answered, No; but the God of the English had it in store, and could send it at his pleasure to the destruction of his and our enemies.

This was, as I take it, about the end of May 1622. At which time our store of victuals was wholly spent, having lived long before with a bare and short allowance. The reason was that supply of men before mentioned[79], which came so unprovided, not landing so much as a barrel of bread or meal for their whole company, but contrarywise received from

---

[76] **French**   Though English and French privateers hijacked each other's American shipping (for ex., the *Fortune* in 1622), war was not openly declared until 1627

[77] **The plague**   Morton's *Canaan* (104) also relates this belief. On the 1616-18 "plague" see Introduction Parts 2 and 4

[78] **brabbles**   disputes (Young, "clamors" 292)

[79] **supply of men**   the 35 men who arrived off the *Fortune* at the start of *Good News*

us for their ship's store homeward. Neither were the setters-forth thereof altogether to be blamed therein, but rather certain amongst our selves, who were too prodigal in their writing and reporting of that plenty we enjoyed. But that I may return---

This Boat[80] proved to be a Shallop that belonged to a fishing ship called the *Sparrow*, set forth by Master *Thomas Weston*, late Merchant and Citizen of London, which brought six or seven passengers at his charge, that should before have been landed at our Plantation.[81] Who also brought no more provision for the present than served the Boat's gang for their return to the ship; which made her voyage at a place called *Damarins Cove* near *Munhiggen* some forty leagues from us Northeastward[82], about which place there fished about thirty sail of ships. And whither my self was employed by our Governour, with orders to take up such victuals as the ships could spare; where I found kind entertainment and good respect, with a willingness to supply our wants.

But being not able to spare that quantity I desired, by reason of the necessity of some amongst themselves whom they supplied before my coming, [they] would not take any Bils[83] for the same, but did what they could freely, wishing their store had been such as they might [11/C2] in greater measure have expressed their own love, and supplied our necessities, for which they sorrowed, provoking one another to the utmost of their abilities. Which, although it were not much amongst so many people as were at the Plantation, yet through the provident and discreet

---

[80] **This Boat**   the possibly-"French" vessel seen passing Plimoth (17)

[81] **Thomas Weston**   a "citizen and ironmonger" as well as Merchant Adventurer, he met Plimothers in Holland (FBH1: 99) and helped arrange *Mayflower*'s 1620 voyage (Introduction Part 2). Morton's *Canaan*: "his people were no chosen Separatists, but men made choice of at all adventures, fit to have served...Weston's undertaking; and that was as much as he need to care for, aiming at Beaver principally."

[82] **Damarins Cove, Munhiggen**   These "thirty sail" reflect the average 250 ships per year reaching Damariscove, Monhegan Island and other fishing/trade stations by 1615 along the coasts from Newfoundland to New England (Biggar *Early* 23; Duncan)

[83] **Bils**   documents undertaking legal debt: given lack of cash in coin, an "I.O.U."

care of the Governours, recovered and preserved strength till our own crop on the ground was ready.

Having dispatched there, I returned home with all speed convenient, where I found the state of the Colony much weaker than when I left it; for, till now, we were never without some bread, the want whereof much abated the strength and flesh of some, and swelled others. But here it may be said, if the country abound with Fish and Fowl in such measure as is reported, how could men undergo such measure of hardness, except through their own negligence? I answer: Everything must be expected in its proper season. No man, as one saith, will go into an Orchard in the Winter to gather Cherries: so he that looks for Fowl there in the Summer will be deceived in his expectation. The time they continue in plenty with us is from the beginning of October to the end of March; but these extremities befell us in May and June.[84]

I confess that as the Fowl decrease, so Fish increase. And indeed their exceeding abundance was a great cause of increasing our wants. For though our Bay and Creeks were full of Bass, and other fish, yet for want of fit and strong Saynes[85] and other netting: they for the most part broke through and carried all away before them. And, though the Sea were full of Cod, yet we had neither tackling nor harfeis[86] for our Shallops. And indeed we had not been in a place where divers sorts of shellfish are that may be taken with the hand, we must have perished, unless God had rai-[12] sed some unknown or extraordinary means for our preservation.

In the time of these straits (indeed before my going to *Munhiggen*), the *Indians* began again to cast forth many insulting speeches, glorying in our weakness, and giving out how easy it would be ere long to cut us off. Now also *Massassowat* seemed to frown on us, and neither came or sent to

---

[84] **as is reported**   As Young (292) points out, "Winslow himself" with *Mourt's Relation* had written of great abundance

[85] **Saynes**   fishing nets

[86] **harfeis**   original text. Young (294) and Arber (530) make the word "hawsers," heavy-gauge rope for fishing

us as formerly.[87] These things occasioned further thoughts of Fortification; and whereas we have a Hill called the Mount enclosed within our pale, under which our Towne is seated, we resolved to erect a Fort thereon, from whence a few might easily secure the Towne from any assault the *Indians* can make, whilst the rest might be employed as occasion served. This work was begun with great eagerness, and with the approbation of all men, hoping that this being once finished, and a continual guard there kept, it would utterly discourage the Savages from having any hopes or thoughts of rising against us. And, though it took the greatest part of our strength from dressing our corn, yet (life being continued) we hoped God would raise some means instead thereof for our further preservation.

In the end of June, or beginning of July [1622], came into our harbour two ships of Master *Weston's* aforesaid, the one called the *Charity*, the other the *Swan*, having in them some fifty or sixty men sent over at his own charge to plant for him.[88] These we received into our Towne, affording them whatsoever curtesie our mean condition could afford. There the *Charity*, being the bigger ship, left them, having many passengers which she was to land in *Virginia*. In the meane time, the body of them refreshed themselves at *Plimoth*, whilst some most fit sought out a place for them.

That little store of corn we had [13/C3] was exceedingly wasted by the unjust and dishonest walking of these strangers; who though they would sometimes seem to help us in our labour about our corn, yet spared not day and night to steal the same, it being then eatable, and pleasant to taste, though green and unprofitable. And though they received much kindness, set light both by it and us; not sparing to requite the love we showed them with secret backbitings, revilings, &c., the chief of them being forestalled and made against us before they came, as after appeared.

---

[87] **insulting speeches, etc.**   The narrative including Native people here resumes from 15 above: they were last mentioned leaving Plimoth "mad with rage, and impatient at delay" when their demand for Tisquantum's life had been deferred

[88] **Charity** and **Swan**   As told in FBH1: 256, 262, *Sparrow* was "a vessel of thirty tons," while *Swan* was "a pinnace of Mr. Weston's": "a small, light, 2-masted vessel"

Nevertheless for their Master's sake, who formerly had deserved well from us, we continued to do them whatsoever good or furtherance we could, attributing these things to the want of conscience and discretion; expecting[89] each day, when God and his providence would disburden us of them, sorrowing that their Over-seers were not of more ability and fitness for their places, and much fearing what would be the issue of such raw and unconscionable beginnings.

At length their Coasters returned, having found in their judgment a place fit for plantation, within the Bay of the *Massachusets*, at a place called by the Indians *Wichaguscusset*. To which place the body of them went with all convenient speed, leaving still with us such as were sick and lame; by the Governour's permission, though on their parts undeserved, whom our Surgeon[90] by the help of God recovered gratis for them, and they fetched home, as occasion served.

They had not been long from us, ere the Indians filled our ears with clamours against them, for stealing their corn, and other abuses conceived by them. At which we grieved the more, because the same men, in mine own hearing, had been earnest in persuading Captain *Standish*, before their coming to solicit our [14] Governour to send some of his men to plant by them, alledging many reasons how it might be commodious for us. But we knew no means to redress those abuses, save reproof, and advising them to better walking, as occasion served.

In the end of *August* came other two ships into our harbour, the one (as I take it) was called the *Discoverie*, Captain *Jones* having the command thereof[91]; the other was that ship of Mr. *Weston's* called the *Sparrow*, which had now made her voyage of fish, and was consorted with the other, being

---

[89] **expecting**   "wondering hopefully"

[90] **Surgeon**   colonist Samuel Fuller

[91] **Captain Jones**   Acc. to Young (298), this is the same Jones who captained the 1620 *Mayflower*. In FBH1: 276-7, this is the (same?) Captain Jones "employed by the Company of Virginia to fish upon the coasts of New England" who, by year's end, stood accused by The Council for New England of "robb[ing] the Natives there [on Cape Cod] of their furs, and offer[ing] to carry some of them away prisoners" (Introduction Part 4)

both bound for *Virginia*. Of Captain *Jones* we furnished our selves of such provisions as we most needed, and he could best spare, who as he used us kindly, so made us pay largely for the things we had. And had not the Almighty, in his All-ordering Providence, directed him to us, it would have gone worse with us than ever it had been or after was; for, as we had now but small store of corn for the year following: so for want of supply, we were worn out of all manner of trucking-stuffe, not having any means left to help our selves by trade; but, through God's good mercy toward us, he had wherewith, and did supply our wants on that kind competently [.]

In the end of *September*, or beginning of *October* [1622], Mr. *Weston's* biggest ship called the *Charitie* returned for England, and left their Colony sufficiently victualled, as some of most credit amongst them reported. The lesser, called the *Swan*, remained with his Colony for their further help, at which time they desired to join in partnerships with us to trade for corn; to which our Governour and his Assistant agreed, upon such equal conditions as were drawn and confimed between them and us. The chief places aimed at were to the Southward of *Cape Cod*, and the more because *Tisquantum*, whose peace before this time **[15]** was wrought with *Massassowat*, undertook to discover unto us that supposed and still hoped passage within the Sholes.[92]

Both Colonies being thus agreed, and their companies fitted and joined together, were resolved to set forward, but were oft crossed in our purposes; as first, Master *Richard Greene* brother in Law to Master *Weston*, who from him had a charge in the oversight and government of his Colony, died suddenly at our Plantation, to whom we gave burial befitting his place, in the best manner we could. Afterward, having further order to proceed by letter from their other Governour at the *Massachusets*, twice

---

[92] **...to discover unto us...the Sholes**   *i.e.*, Plimoth hoped to build trade by sea with Native peoples of Cape Cod and the region, by passing safely through or "within" the shifting shoals and breakers southeast of the Cape. These include Great and Little Round Shoals, Bass Rip, Point Care (Monomoy Point) and "Tucker's Terror," now Pollock Rip, whose "roaring" Bradford described (in Young 102)

Captain *Standish* set forth with them, but were driven in again by cross and violent winds: himself the second time being sick of a violent fever.[93]

Our own wants were like to be now greater than formerly; partly, because we were enforced to neglect our corn, and spend much time in fortification; but especially because such havoc was made of that little we had, through the unjust and dishonest carriage of those people before mentioned, at our first entertainment of them. By reason whereof, our Governour in his own person supplied the Captain's place, and in the month of *November* again set forth, having *Tisquantum* for his Interpreter and Pilot; who affirmed he had twice passed within the Sholes of *Cape Cod*, both with *English* and *French*. Nevertheless, they went so far with him, as the Master of the ship saw no hope of passage; but being (as he thought) in danger, bare up, and according to *Tisquantum's* directions, made for an harbour not far from them, at a place called *Manamoycke*, which they found. And sounding it with their shallop, [they] found the channel, though but narrow and crooked, where at length they harboured the ship.

Here they perceived that the tide set in and out with more violence [than] at some **[16]** other place more Southerly, which they had not seen nor could discover, by reason of the violence of the season all the time of their abode there. Some judged the entrance thereof might be beyond the Sholes, but there is no certainty thereof as yet known.

That night, the Governour, accompanied with others, having *Tisquantum* for his Interpreter, went ashore. At first the Inhabitants[94] played least in sight, because none of our people had ever been there before; but understanding the ends of their coming, at length came to them, welcoming our Governour according to their Savage manner, refreshing them very well with store of venison and other victuals which they brought them in great abundance, promising to trade with them, with a seeming gladness of the occasion. Yet their joy was mixed with much

---

[93] Textual Note: The next original paragraph began, "By reason whereof..."; but I have moved that phrase as shown, and deleted one pair of parentheses, to improve clarity

[94] **Inhabitants**　　at Monomoy/Manamoycke

jealousy,[95] as appeared by their after practices. For at first, they were loath their dwellings should be known; but, when they saw our Governour's resolution to stay on the shore all night, they brought him to their houses, having first conveyed all their stuff to a remote place not far from the same, which one of our men walking forth occasionally espied.

Whereupon, neither it nor them could be found. And so many times after, upon conceived occasions, they would be all gone, bag and baggage. But, being afterwards (by *Tisquantum*'s means) better persuaded, they left their jealousy and traded with them; where they got eight hogsheads of corn and beans, though the people were but few.

This gave our Governour and the company good encouragement. *Tisquantum* being still confident in the passage, and the Inhabitants affirming, they had seen ships of good burthen pass within the Sholes aforesaid. But here, though they had determined to make a second assay, yet God had other ways disposed, who struck *Tisquantum* with sickness, in so much as he **[17/D]** there died; which crossed their Southward trading, and the more because the Master's sufficiency was much doubted, and the season very tempestuous, and not fit to go upon discovery, having no guide to direct them.[96]

From thence they departed, and the wind being fair for the *Massachusets* went thither; and the rather because the Savages upon our motion had planted much corn for us, which they promised not long before that time. When they came thither, they found a great sickness to be amongst the *Indians*, not unlike the plague, if not the same. They renewed their complaints to our Governour, against that other plantation seated by them, for their injurious walking. But indeed, the trade both for Furs and

---

[95] **jealousy**   as used above and just below, "fear" or "suspicion"

[96] Young (191): "The beautiful promontory in Dorchester, near Thomson's Island, will perpetuate the name of this early friend of the Pilgrims. They probably called it after him in their first expedition to the Massachusetts in 1621, when he accompanied them as an interpreter." In fact, there is no memorial to Tisquantum. That place-name (and more likely, his name *from* it) derive "from Musquantum, a place of awesome significance" connected with "a most awesome male/female spirit" there. See Horner, and Dempsey *Morton* 233

corn was overthrown in that place, they giving as much for a quart of corn as we used to do for a Beaver's skin; so that little good could be there done.

From thence they returned into the bottom of the Bay of Cape Cod, to a place called *Nauset*, where the *Sachim* used the Governour very kindly, and where they bought eight or ten hogsheads of corn and beans; also, at a place called *Mattackiest*, where they had like kind entertainment and corn.[97] During the time of their trade in these places, there were so great and violent storms as the ship was much endangered, and our shallop cast away; so that they had now no means to carry the corn aboard that they had bought; the ship riding, by their report, well near two leagues from the same, [and] her own Boat being small, and so leaky (having no Carpenter with them) as they durst scarce fetch wood or water in her.

Hereupon, the Governour caused the corn to be made in a round stack, and bought mats and cut sedge to cover it, and gave charge to the *Indians* not to meddle with it; promising him that dwelt next to it a reward if he would keep vermin also from it; which he undertook and the [19] *Sachim* promised to make good. In the meane time, according to the Governour's request, the *Sachim* sent men to seek the shallop, which they found buried almost in sand at a high-water mark, having many things remaining in her, but unserviceable for the present; whereof the Governour gave the *Sachim* special charge that it should not be further broken, promising ere long to fetch both it and the corn; assuring them [that] if neither were diminished, he would take it as a sign of their honest and true friendship, which they so much made show of. But if they were [diminished], they should certainly smart for their unjust and dishonest dealing, and further make good whatsoever they had so taken.

So he did likewise at *Mattachiest*, and took leave of them, being resolved to leave the ship and take his journey home by land with our own company; sending word to the ship that they should take their first opportunity to go for *Plimoth*, where he determined by the permission of

---

[97] A redundant second "also" was deleted here. **Nauset**   the Sachem's name was Aspinet: he also appears in *Mourt* (71) where in 1621 with "not less than a hundred" people he returned a lost English boy

God to meet them. And having procured a Guide, it being no less than fifty miles to our Plantation, set forward, receiving all respect that could be from the *Indians* in his journey, and came safely home, though weary and furbated;[98] whither some three days after the ship also came. The corn being divided which they had got, Master *Weston*'s company went to their own Plantation, it being further agreed that they should return with all convenient speed and bring their Carpenter; that they might fetch the rest of the corn, and save the shallop.

At their return, Captain *Standish* being recovered and in health, took another shallop, and went with them to the corn, which they found in safety as they left it. Also they mended the other shallop, and got all their corn aboard the ship. This was in January [1623], as I take it, it being very cold and stormy, insomuch as (the harbor being none of the best) they were constrained to cut both the shallops from the ship's stern, **[19/D2]** and so lost them both a second time. But the storm being over, and seeking out, they found them both, not having received any great hurt. Whilst they were at *Nauset*, having occasion to lie on the shore, laying their shallop in a Creek not far from them, an *Indian* came into the same, and stole certain beads, scissors and other trifles out of the same, which when the Captain missed, he took certain of his company with him, and went to the *Sachim*[99], telling him what had happened, and requiring the same again, or the party that stole them (who was known to certain of the *Indians*), or else he would revenge it on them before his departure; and so took leave for that night, being late, refusing whatsoever kindness they offered.

On the morrow, the *Sachim* came to their rendezvous, accompanied with many men in a stately manner, saluting[100] the Captain in this wise:

---

[98] **furbated**   Young (213n2): "surbated, bruised, wearied"

[99] **Mattackiest**   As Young notes (215), this community is closely connected with Cummaquid's, given that Sachem Iyanough is identified with both here and in *Mourt* (69). He was "not exceeding twenty-six years of age, but very personable, gentle, courteous and fair conditioned, indeed not like a savage, save for his attire. His entertainment was answerable to his parts, and his cheer plentiful and various"

[100] Original text read: " who saluting." Young (304) renders it "who saluted"

He thrust out his tongue, that one might see the root thereof, and therewith licked his hand from the wrist to the fingers' end, withall bowing the knee, striving to imitate the English gesture, being instructed therein formerly by *Tisquantum*. His men did the like, but in so rude and savage a manner as our men could scarce forbear to break out in open laughter.

After salutation, he delivered the Beads, and other things to the Captain, saying he had much beaten the party for doing it; [and] causing the women to make bread, and bring them, according to their desire, seeming to be very sorry for the fact, but glad to be reconciled. So they departed, and came home in safety; where the corn was equally divided as before.[101]

After this the Governour went to two other inland Townes, with another company, and bought corn likewise of them: the one is called *Namasket*, the other *Manomet*.[102] That from *Namasket* was brought home partly by *Indian* women; but a great sickness arising amongst them, our own men were enforced to fetch **[20]** home the rest.

That at *Manomet* the Governour left in the *Sachim*'s custody: this Towne lieth from us South well near twenty miles, and stands upon a fresh river which runneth into the Bay of *Nanohigganset*,[103] and cannot be less than sixty miles from thence. It will bear a boat of eight or ten ton to this place. Hither the Dutch or French or both use[d] to come. It is from hence to the Bay of Cape Cod about eight miles; out of which Bay it floweth into a Creek some six miles almost direct towards the Towne. The heads of the River and this Creek are not far distant. This River yieldeth thus high, Oysters, Mussels, Clams, and other shellfish, one in shape like a bean,

---

[101] **bread**   poss. the nourishing traditional food "nocake" (corn meal, cranberries etc.)

[102] **Manomet**   village along the Manomet River south of Plimoth, its Sachem named Canacum (also Cawnacome, Conecoman): a signer of the Sept. 1621 treaty (FBH1: 227), as Winslow notes below

[103] As both Arber (540) and Young (305) agree, Winslow "intended" to say Manomet or Buzzards Bay; for the distance is "from hence to the Bay of Cape Cod [at Scusset] about eight miles" overland

another like a Clam, both good meat, and great abundance at all times; besides it aboundeth with divers sorts of fresh fish in their seasons.

The Governour or *Sachim* of this place was called *Canacum*, who had formerly (as well as many others, yea all with whom as yet we had to do) acknowledged themselves the subjects of our Sovereign Lord the King. This *Sachim* used the Governour very kindly, and it seemed was of good respect and authority amongst the *Indians*. For whilst the Governour was there within night in bitter weather, came two men from *Manamoick* before spoken of. And having set aside their bows and quivers, according to their manner, sat down by the fire and took a pipe of Tobacco, not using any words in that time, nor any other to them, but all remained silent, expecting when they would speak. At length, they looked toward *Canacum*, and one of them made a short speech, and delivered a present to him from his *Sachim*, which was a basket of Tobacco, and many Beads, which the other received thankfully. After which he made a long speech to him: the contents hereof was related to us by *Hobbamock* (who then accompanied the Governour for his guide) to be as followeth:

It happened that two of their men fell out as they were in game (for they **[21/D3]** use gaming as much as any where, and will play away all, even their skin from their backs, yea and for their wives' skins also, though it may be they are many miles distant from them, as my selfe have seen). And growing to great heat, the one killed the other. The actor of this fact was a *Powah*, one of special note amongst them, and such an one as they could not well miss. Yet, another people greater than themselves threatened them with war, if they would not put him to death. The party offending was in hold, neither would their *Sachim* do one way or other till their return, resting upon him[104] for advice and furtherance in so weighty a matter. After this there was silence a short time: at length, men gave their judgment what they thought best. Amongst others, he asked *Hobbamock* what he thought? Who answered, He was but a stranger to them, but thought it was better that one should die than many, since he had

---

[104] **him**   that is, Canacum

deserved it, and the rest were innocent; whereupon he passed the sentence of death upon him.

Not long after, having no great quantity of corn left, Captain *Standish* went again with a shallop to *Mattachiest*, meeting also with the like extremity of weather, both of wind, snow, and frost, insomuch as they were frozen in the harbour the first night they entered the same.

Here they pretended their wonted love, and spared them a good quantity of corn to confirm the same. Strangers also came to this place, pretending only to see him and his company, whom they never saw before that time, but intending to join with the rest to kill them, as after appeared. But being forced through extremity to lodge in their houses, which they much pressed, God possessed the heart of the Captain with just jealousy, giving straight command that as one part of his company slept, the rest should wake; declaring some things to them which he understood, whereof he could make no **[22]** good construction.

Some of the *Indians* spying a fit opportunity, stole some beads also from him; which he no sooner perceived, having not above six men with him, [than he] drew them all from the Boat, and set them on their guard about the *Sachim's* house, where the most of the people were; threatening to fall upon them without further delay if they would not fortwith restore them; signifying to the *Sachim* especially, and so to them all, that as he would not offer the least injury, so he would not receive any at their hands, which should escape without punishment or due satisfaction.

Hereupon the *Sachim* bestirred him to find out the party; which, when he had done, caused him to return them again to the shallop, and came to the Captain, desiring him to search whether they were not about the Boat. Who, suspecting their knavery, sent one, who found them lying openly upon the Boat's cuddy.[105] Yet, to appease his anger they brought corn afresh to trade, insomuch as he laded his shallop, and so departed.

This accident so daunted their courage, as they durst not attempt any thing against him; so that through the good mercy and providence of

---

[105] **cuddy**   a small enclosed cabin

God, they returned in safety. At this place the *Indians* get abundance of Bass both summer and winter: for it being now February, they abounded with them.

In the beginning of March [1623], having refreshed himself, [Captain Standish] took a shallop and went to *Manomet*, to fetch home that which the Governour had formerly bought, hoping also to get more from them; but was deceived in his expectation, not finding that entertainment he found elsewhere, and the Governour had there received. The reason whereof, and of the treachery intended in the place before spoken of, was not then known unto us, but afterwards; wherein may be observed the abundant mercies of God working with his providence for our good.

Captain *Standish* being now far **[23]** from the Boat, and not above two or three of our men with him, and as many with the shallop, was not long at *Canacum* the *Sachim*'s house, but in came two fof the *Massachuset* men: the chief of them was called *Wituwamat*,[106] a notable insulting villain, one who had formerly imbrued his hands in the bloud of *English* and *French*, and had oft boasted of his own valor, and derided their weakness, especially because (as he said) they died crying, making sowre faces, more like children than men. This villain took a dagger from about his neck which he had gotten of Master *Weston*'s people, and presented it to the *Sachim*; and after, made a long speech in an audacious manner, framing it in such sort as the Captain (though he be the best Linguist amongst us) could not gather any thing from it. The end of it was afterward discovered to be as followeth:

The *Massacheuseucks* had formerly concluded to ruinate Master *Weston*'s Colony, and thought themselves, being about thirty or forty men strong, enough to execute the same. Yet they durst not attempt it, till such time as they had gathered more strength to themselves to make their party good against us at *Plimoth*; con-cluding that if we remained (though they had no other Arguments to use against us), yet we would never leave the death of our Countrymen unrevenged; and therefore, their safety could not

---

[106] **Wituwamat**   like Pecksuot below, a *pneise* probably of the Massachusetts: see Introduction Parts 3 and 4. He appears again on page 50 and afterward

be without the overthrow of both Plantations. To this end, they had formally solicited this *Sachim*, as also the other called *Ianough* at *Mattachiest*, and many others to assist them, and now again came to prosecute the same. And, since there was so fair an opportunity offered by the Captain's presence, they thought best to make sure him and his company.

After this his message was delivered, his entertainment much exceeded the Captain's, insomuch as he scorned at their behavior, and told them of it; after which they would have persuaded him, be- **[24]** cause the weather was cold, to have sent to the Boat for the rest of his company. But he would not, desiring according to promise that the corn might be carried down, and he would content the women for their labour; which they did.

At the same time there was a lusty *Indian* of *Paomet* or *Cape Cod* then present, who had ever demeaned himself well towards us, being in his general carriage very affable, courteous, and loving, especially towards the Captain. This Savage was now entered into confederacy with the rest; yet to avoid suspicion, made many signs of his continued affections, and would needs bestow a kettle of some six or seven gallons on him, and would not accept of any thing in lieu thereof, saying he was rich, and could afford to bestow such favours on his friends whom he loved. Also, he would freely help to carry some of the corn, affirming he had never done the like in his life before; and, the wind being bad, would needs lodge with him and their Rendezvous; having indeed undertaken to kill him before they parted, which done, they intended to fall upon the rest.

The night proved exceeding cold, insomuch as the Captain could not take any rest, but either walked or turned himself to and fro at the fire. This the other observed, and asked wherefore he did not sleep as at other times; who answered, He knew not well, but had no desire at all to rest; so that he then missed his opportunity.

The wind serving on the next day, they returned home, accompanied with the other *Indian*, who used many arguments to persuade them to go to *Paomet*, where himself had much corn, and many other, the most whereof he would procure for us, seeming to sorrow for our wants. Once the Captain put forth with him, and was forced back by contrary wind, which wind, serving for the *Massachuset*, was fitted to go thither. But on a sudden it altered again.[107]

During the time that the Captain was at *Manomet*, news came to *Plimoth* that *Massassowat* was like to die, and that at the same time there was a Dutch ship driven so **[25/E]** high on the shore by stress of weather, right before his dwelling, that till the tides increased she could not be got off.[108]

Now, it being a commendable manner of the Indians, when any (especially of note) are dangerously sick, for all that profess friendship to them to visit them in their extremity, either in their persons or else to send some acceptable persons to them; therefore it was thought meet, being a good and warrantable action, that as we had ever professed friendship, so we should now maintain the same, by observing this their laudable custom. And the rather, because we desired to have some conference with the Dutch, not knowing when we should have so fit an oppportunity.

To that end, my self having formerly been there, and understanding in some measure the Dutch tongue, the Governour again laid this service upon my self, and fitted me with some cordials to administer to him, having one Master *Iohn Hamden* a Gentleman of *London* (who then wintered with us and desired much to see the Country[109]) for my comfort, and *Hobbamock* for our guide. So we set forward, and lodged the first night at *Namasket*, where we had friendly entertainment. The next day, about one of the clock, we came to a ferry in *Conbatant*'s Country, where upon discharge of my piece, divers Indians came to us from a house not far off.

There, they told us that *Massassowat* was dead, and that day buried; and that the Dutch would be gone before we could get thither, having hove off their ship already. This news struck us blank; but especially

---

[107] The narrative of Standish's journey resumes on page 45

[108] Young (313) supplies the date "March 1623" at this point

[109] **Master John Hamden**   Young (314) shows that this is not "the celebrated English patriot" and 1621 member of Parliament, but an "ordinary" colonist. The **ferry** over the Taunton River was known later as Slade's Ferry in Swansea. Mattapuyst/Mattapoiset lay within the territory of Sachem Corbitant of Nemasket

Hobbamock, who desired we might return with all speed. I told him I would first think of it, considering now that he being dead, *Conbatant* was the most like to succeed him, and that we were not above three miles from *Mattapuyst* his dwelling place. Although he were but a hollow-hearted friend toward us, I thought no time so fit as this to enter into more friendly terms with him, and the rest of the *Sachims* thereabout, hoping (through the blessing of God) it would be a means in that unsettled state to settle their affections toward us.

And though it were **[26]** somewhat dangerous, in respect of our personal safety, because my self and *Hobbamock* had been employed upon a service against him, which he might now fitly revenge; yet esteeming it the best means, leaving the event to God in his mercy, I resolved to put it in practice if Master *Hamden* and *Hobbamock* durst attempt it with me; whom I found willing to that, or any other course might tend to the general good. So we went toward *Mattapuyst*.

In the way, *Hobbamock*, manifesting a troubled spirit, brake forth into these speeches: *Neen womasu Sagimus, Neen womasu Sagimus,* &c---My loving *Sachim*, My loving *Sachim*, Many have I known, but never any like thee. And turning him to me, said: Whilst I lived, I should never see his like among the *Indians*. Saying, He was no liar, He was not bloody and cruel like other *Indians*: In anger and passion he was soon reclaimed, easy to be reconciled toward such as had offended him, ruled by reason in such measure as he would not scorn the advice of mean men, and that he governed his men better with few strokes than others did with many; truly loving where he loved. Yea, [*Hobbamock*] feared we had not a faithful friend left among the *Indians*, showing how he oft-times restrained their malice, &c., continuing a long speech with such signs of lamentation and unfeigned sorrow as it would have made the hardest heart relent.

At length we came to *Mattapuyst*, and went to the *Sachemo Comaco* (for so they call the *Sachim*'s place, though they call an ordinary house *Witeo*); but *Conbatant* the *Sachim* was not at home, but at *Puckanokick*, which was some five or six miles off. The *Squa Sachim* (for so they call the *Sachim*'s wife) gave us friendly entertainment. Here we inquired again concerning *Massassowat*: they thought him dead, but knew no certainty;

whereupon I hired one to go with all expedition to *Puckanokick*, that we might know the certainty thereof, and withall to acquaint *Conbatant* with our there being.

About half an hour before Sun-setting, the messenger returned, and told us that he was not yet dead, though there was no hope **[27/E2]** we should find him living. Upon this we were much revived, and set forward with all speed though it was late within night ere we got thither.

About two of the clock that afternoon the Dutchmen [had] departed, so that in that respect our journey was frustrate. When we came thither, we found the house so full of men that we could scarce get in, though they used their best diligence to make way for us.

There were they in the middest of their charms for him, making such a hellish noise as it distempered us that were well, and therefore unlike to ease him that were sick. About him were six or eight women, who chafed his arms, legs, and thighs to keep heat in him: when they had made an end of their charming, one told him that his friends the *English* were come to see him. Having understanding left, but his sight was wholly gone, he asked who was come: they told him *Winsnow* (for they cannot pronounce the letter *l*, but ordinarily *n* in the place thereof), he desired to speak with me. When I came to him, and they told him of it, he put forth his hand to me, which I took: then he said twice, though very inwardly, *Keen Winsnow*, which is to say, Art thou *Winslow*? I answered, *ahhe*, that is, Yes. Then he doubled these words: *Matta neen wonckanet namen Winsnow*: that is to say, *O Winslow, I shall never see thee again.*

Then I called *Hobbamock*, and desired him to tell *Massassowat* that the Governour, hearing of his sickness, was sorry for the same, and though by reason of many businesses he could not come himself, yet he [had] sent me with such things for him as he thought most likely to do him good in this his extremity. And whereof, if he pleased to take, I would presently give him; which he desired. And having a confection of many comfortable conserves, &c., on the point of my knife, I gave him some, which I could scarce get through his teeth. When it was dissolved in his mouth, he swallowed the juice of it; whereat those that were about him much rejoiced, saying he had not swallowed anything in two days before.

Then I desired to see his mouth, which was exceedingly furred, and
[28] his tongue swelled in such manner as it was not possible for him to eat
such meat as they had, his passage being stopped up. Then I washed his
mouth, and scraped his tongue, and got abundance of corruption out of
the same. After which, I gave him more of the confection, which he
swallowed with more readiness: then, he desiring to drink, I dissolved
some of it in water, and gave him thereof. Within half an hour this
wrought a great alteration in him in the eyes of all that beheld him:
presently after, his sight began to come to him, which gave him and us
good encouragement. In the mean time I inquired how he slept, and when
he went to the stool? They said he [had] slept not in two days before, and
had not had a stool in five. Then I gave him more, and told him of a
mishap we [had] had by the way in breaking a bottle of drink which the
Governour also sent him, saying [that] if he would send any of his men to
Patuxet, I would send for more of the same; also for chickens to make him
broth, and for other things which I knew were good for him; and would
stay the return of the messenger if he desired.

This he took marvelous kindly, and appointed some who were
ready to go by two of the clock in the morning; against which time I made
ready a letter, declaring therein our good success, the state of his body,
&c., desiring [Plimoth] to send me such things as I sent for, and such
physic as the Surgeon durst administer to him. [*Massassowat*] requested me
that the day following, I would take my Piece and kill him some Fowl, and
make him some English pottage such as he had eaten at *Plimoth*, which I
promised; after his stomach coming to him, I must needs make him some
without Fowl before I went abroad, which much troubled me, being
unaccustomed and unacquainted in such businesses, especially having
nothing to make it comfortable, my Consort being as ignorant as my self.
But, being we must do somewhat, I caused a woman to bruise some corn
and take the flour from it, and set over the grut or broken corn in a pipkin
(for they have earthen pots of all sizes). [29/E3]

When the day broke, we went out (it being now March) to seek
herbs, but could not find any but strawberry leaves, of which I gathered a
handful and put it into the same. And because I had nothing to relish it, I

went forth again and pulled up a Saxafras root, and sliced a piece thereof and boiled it till it had a good relish, and then took it out again. The broth being boiled, I strained it through my handkerchief, and gave him at least a pint, which he drank and liked it very well. After this, his sight mended more and more: also he had three moderate stools, and took some rest.

Insomuch as we with admiration blessed God for giving his blessing to such raw and ignorant means, making no doubt of his recovery, himself and all of them acknowledging us the instruments of his preservation. That morning he caused me to spend in going from one to another amongst those that were sick in the Town, requesting me to wash their mouths also, and give to each of them some of the same I gave him, saying, They were good folk. This pains I took with willingness, though it were much offensive to me, not being accustomed with such poisonous savours.

After dinner he desired me to get him a Goose or Duck, and make him some pottage therewith, with as much speed as I could; so I took a man with me and made a shot at a couple of Ducks, some six score paces off, and killed one, at which he wondered. So we returned fortwith, and dressed it, making more broth therewith, which he much desired. Never did I see a man, so low brought, recover in that measure in so short a time.

The Fowl being extraordinary fat, I told *Hobbamock* I must take off the top thereof, saying it would make him very sick again if he did eat it.[110] This he acquainted *Massassowat* therewith, who would not be persuaded to it, though I pressed it very much, showing the strength thereof, and the weakness of his stomach, which could not possibly bear it. Notwithstanding, he made a gross meal of it, and ate as much as would well have satisfied a man in health. About **[30]** an hour after, he began to be very sick, and straining very much, cast up the broth again, and in overstraining himself began to bleed at the nose, and so continued the space of four hours. Then they all wished he had been ruled, concluding now he would die, which we much feared also. They asked me what I thought of

---

[110] **top**   probably meaning the fatty outer layer of the duck's skin

him: I answered, His case was desperate, yet it might be it would save[111] his life; for if it ceased in time, he would fortwith sleep and take rest, which was the principal thing he wanted. Not long after, his blood staied[112], and he slept at least six or eight hours: when he waked I washed his face, and bathed and suppled his beard and nose with a linen cloth. But on a sudden he chopt his nose in the water, and drew up some therein, and sent it forth again with such violence [that] he began to bleed afresh. Then they thought there was no hope; but we perceived it was but the tenderness of his nostril, and therefore told them I thought it would stay presently, as indeed it did.

The messengers were now returned. But finding his stomach come to him, he would not have the chickens killed, but kept them for breed. Neither durst we give him any physic which was then sent, because his body was so much altered since our instructions: neither saw we any need, not doubting now of his recovery if he were careful. Many, whilst we were there, came to see him, some by their report from a place not less than an hundred miles. To all that came, one of his chief men related the manner of his sickness, how near he was spent, how amongst others his friends the *English* came to see him; and how suddenly they [had] recovered him to this strength, they saw, he being now able to sit upright of himself.

The day before our coming, another *Sachim* being there, told him, that now he might see how hollow-hearted the *English* were; saying if we had been such friends in deed as we were in shew, we would have visited him in this his sickness; using many arguments to withdraw his affections, and to persuade him to give way to some things against us which were motioned to him not long before. But upon **[31]** this his recovery, he brake forth into these speeches: Now I see the *English* are my friends and love me, and whilst I live I will never forget this kindness they have showed me. Whilst we were there, our entertainment exceeded all other strangers'.

---

[111] **save**   spare

[112] **staied**   original text: Young (322) makes it "stayed" (coagulated, stopped)

Divers other things were worthy the noting, but I fear I have been too tedious.

At our coming away, he called *Hobbamock* to him; and, none hearing save two or three other of his *Pneeses* who are of his Council, privately revealed the plot of the *Massacheuseucks* before spoken of, against Master *Weston*'s Colony, and so against us; saying that the people of *Nauset, Paomet, Succonet, Mattachiest, Manomet, Agowaywam,* and the Isle of *Capawack*[113] were joined with them; himself also in his sickness was earnestly solicited, but he would neither join therein, nor give way to any of his. Therefore, as we respected the lives of our Countrymen, and our own after-safety, he advised us to kill the men of *Massachuset* who were the authors of this intended mischief.

And whereas we were wont to say we would not strike a stroke till they first begun---If, said he, upon this intelligence they make that answer, tell them [that] when their Countrymen at *Wicha-guscusset* are killed, they being not able to defend themselves, then it will be too late to recover their lives; nay through the multitude of adversaries they shall with great difficulty preserve their own, and therefore he counseled without delay to take away the principals, and then the plot would cease. With this [*Massassowat*] charged [*Hobbamock*] thoroughly to acquaint me by the way, that I might inform the Governour thereof at my first coming home.

Being fitted for our return, we took our leave of him, who returned many thanks to our Governour, and also to our selves for our labor and love: the like did all that were about him. So we departed.

That night through the earnest request of *Cobatant,* who till now remained at *Sawaams* or *Puckanukick,* we lodged with him at *Mattapuyst.* By the way I had much conference with him; so likewise at his house, he being a notable politician, yet full of merry jests and squibs, and never better pleased than when **[32]** the like are returned again upon him. Amongst other things, he asked me, If in case he were thus dangerously

[113] **Capawac(k),** later known as Martha's Vineyard   **Agawam**   Young (323) locates it as "part of [the later] Wareham" near the Agawam River; but there is another "definite" place (and river) of that name in the Ipswich/"Cape Anne" area. See end of Introduction Part 4

sick, as *Massassowat* had been, and should send word thereof to *Patuxet* for *Maskiet*, that is Physic, whether Mr. Governour would send it? And if he would, whether I would come therewith to him? To both which I answered Yea, whereat he gave me many joyful thanks.

After that, being at his house, [*Corbitant*] demanded further, How we durst, being but two, come so far into the Country? I answered, Where was true love there was no fear, and my heart was so upright towards them that for mine own part I was fearless to come amongst them. But, said he, if your love be such, and it bring forth such fruits, how cometh it to pass that when we come to *Patuxet*, you stand upon your guard, with the mouths of your Pieces presented towards us? Whereunto I answered, It was the most honorable and respective entertainment we could give them, it being an order amongst us to receive our best respected friends; and as it was used on the Land, so the ships observed it also at Sea, which *Hobbamock* knew, and had seen observed. But shaking the head he answered that he liked not such salutations.

Further, observing us to crave a blessing on our meat before we did eat, and after to give thanks for the same, he asked us What was the meaning of that ordinary custom? Hereupon I took occasion to tell them of God's workes of Creation, and Preservation, of his Laws and Ordinances, especially of the Ten Commandments, all which they hearkened unto with great attention, and liked well of. Only the seventh Commandment they excepted against, thinking there were many inconveniences in it, that a man should be tied to one woman; about which we reasoned a good time.

Also I told them that whatsoever good things we had, we received from God, as the Author and giver thereof; and therefore craved his blessing upon that we had, and were about to eat, that it might nourish and strengthen our bodies, and having eaten suf- **[33/F]** ficient, being satisfied therewith, we again returned thanks to the same our God for that our refreshing, &c. This all of them concluded to be very well, and said they believed almost all the same things; and that the same power that we called God, they called *Kiet: tan*. Much profitable co[n]ference was occasioned hereby, which would be too tedious to relate, yet was no less delightful to them, than comfortable to us. Here we remained only that night, but never had better entertainment amongst any of them.

The day following,[114] in our journey, *Hobbamock* told me of the private conference he had with *Massassowat*, and how he [had] charged him perfectly to acquaint me therewith (as I shewed before); which, having done, he used many arguments himself to move us thereunto. That night we lodged at *Namasket*, and the day following about the mid-way between it and home, we met two *Indians*, who told us that Captain *Standish* was that day gone to the *Massachusets*; but contrary winds again drive[115] him back, so that we found him at home; where the *Indian* of *Paomet* still was, being very importunate that the Captain should take the first opportunity of a fair wind to go with him; but their secret and villainous purposes being through God's mercy now made known, the Governour caused Captain *Standish* to send him away without any distaste or manifestation of anger, that we might the better effect and bring to pass that which should be thought most necessary.

Before this journey we heard many complaints both by the *Indians* and some others of best desert amongst Master *Weston*'s Colony, how exceedingly their Company abased themselves by indirect means, to get victuals from the *Indians*, who dwelt not far from them, fetching them wood and water, &c. and all for a meal's meat, whereas in the meane time, they might with diligence have gotten enough to have served them three or four times. Other by night brake the earth, and robbed the *Indians*' store, **[34]** for which they had been publicly stocked and whipt; and yet was there small amendment.

This was about the end of February, at which time they had spent all their bread and corn, not leaving any for seed; neither would the *Indians* lend or sell them any more upon any terms. Hereupon they had thoughts to take it by violence, and to that spiked up every entrance into the Towne

---

[114] The narrative resumes from page 30, when "contrary" winds had kept Standish from either Paomet or Massachusetts

[115] **drive**   original text: Young (326) makes it "drove"

(being well impaled) save one, with a full resolution to proceed. But some more honestly minded, advised *Iohn Sanders* their Over-seer first to write to *Plimoth,* and if the Governour advised him thereunto, he might the better do it.[116] This course was well liked, and an *Indian* was sent with all speed with a letter to our Governour, the contents whereof were to this effect:

That being in great want, and their people daily falling down, he intended to go to *Munhiggen,* where was a Plantation of Sir *Ferd*[*inando*] *Gorges,*[117] to buy bread from the Ships that came thither a-fishing, with the first opportunity of wind; but [he] knew not how the Colony would be preserved till his return. He had used all means both to buy and borrow of *Indians* whom he knew to be stored and, he thought, maliciously withheld it, and therefore was resolved to take it by violence; and only waited the return of the Messenger, which he desired should be hastened, craving his advice therein, [and] promising also to make restitution afterward.

The Governour upon the receipt hereof, asked the Messenger what store of corn they had, as if he had intended to buy of them; who answered, Very little more than that they reserved for seed, having already spared all they could. Fortwith the Governour and his Assistant sent for many of us to advise with them herein, who after serious consideration, no way approving of this intended course, the Governour answered [with] his Letter; and [he] caused many of us to set our hands thereto, the contents whereof were to this purpose:

We altogether disliked their intendment, as being against the law of God and Nature, shewing how it would cross the worthy ends and

---

[116] **Iohn Sanders**   Acc. to FBH1: 281, 284, Sanders was "left cheefe" and gained "some charge in the oversight and government" of Thomas Weston's Weymouth Colony when "Master Richard Greene, [Weston's] brother in law" died suddenly while at Plimoth

[117] **Gorges**   Monhegan (Island) had long been a way-station for Europe's fishing fleets rather than a "plantation" of Gorges' (1560-1647). Under Kings James I and Charles I, Gorges was a leading organizer of English colonial efforts, "a simple man of modest means and no great intellectual ability or business acumen" (biographer Preston 3: see also Adams *Three Episodes* and Dempsey *Canaan* and *Morton*). Gorges was also head of the King's Council for New England mentioned just below

proceedings of the King's Majesty, and **[35/F2]** his honorable Council for
this place; both in respect of the the peaceable enlarging of his Majesty's
Dominions, and also of the propagation of the knowledge and Law of God,
and the glad tydings of salvation, which we and they were bound to seek,
and were not to use such means as would breed a distaste in the Savages
against our persons and professions; assuring them their Master would
incur much blame hereby.

Neither could they answer the same. For our own parts our case was
almost the same with theirs, having but a small quantity of Corn left, and
were enforced to live upon ground nuts,[118] clams, mussels, and such other
things as naturally the Country afforded, and which did and would
maintain strength, and were easy to be gotten; all which things they had in
great abundance, yea, Oysters also which we wanted; and therefore
necessity could not be said to constrain them thereunto.

Moreover, that they should consider, [that] if they proceeded
therein, all they could so get would maintain them but a small time, and
then they must perforce seek their food abroad, which having made the
Indians their enemies, would be very difficult for them; and therefore
much better to begin a little the sooner, and so continue their peace; upon
which course they might with good conscience desire and expect the
blessing of God, whereas on the contrary they could not.

Also that they should consider their own weakness, being most
swelled, and diseased in their bodies, and therefore the more unlikely to
make their party good against them; and that they should not expect help
from us in that or any the like unlawful actions. Lastly, that howsoever
some of them might escape, yet the principal Agents should expect no
better than the Gallows whensoever any special Officer should be sent
over by his Majesty, or his Council for *New England*, which we expected,
and who would undoubtedly call them to account for the same.

---

[118] FBH1: 290 offers a researched discussion of what species of "ground nut" is meant. Citing
Slafter's edition of Champlain's chronicles, editor Ford believed this was the Jerusalem
Artichoke (*Helianthus tuberosus*); though other kinds, *Arachis hypogaea* and *Apios tuberosa* were
also available. *Mourt* (58) does not specify species

These were the contents of our Answer, which was directed to their whole Colony. Another particular **[36]** Letter our Governour sent ot *Iohn Sanders*, shewing how dangerous it would be for him above all others, being he was their leader and commander; and therefore in friendly manner advised him to desist.

With these Letters we dispatched the Messenger; upon the receipt whereof they altered their determination, resolving to shift as they could till the return of *Iohn Sanders* from *Munhiggen*; who first coming to *Plimoth*, notwithstanding our own necessities, the Governour spared him some Corn to carry them to *Munhiggen*. But not having sufficient for the Ship's store, he took a Shallop, and leaving others with instructions to oversee things till his return, set forward about the end of February; for that he knew not of this conspiracy of the *Indians'* before his going; neither was it known to any of us till our return from *Sawaams* or *Puckanakick*. At which time also another *Sachim* called *Wassapinewat*, brother to *Obtakiest* the *Sachim* of the *Massachusets*, who had formerly smarted for partaking with *Coubatant*, and fearing the like again, to purge himself revealed the same thing.[119]

The three and twentieth of March [was] now come, which is a yearly Court day. The Governour---having a double testimony, and many circumstances agreeing with the truth thereof, not being [[120]]to undertake war without the consent of the body of the Company---made known the same in public Court, offering it to the consideration of the Company; it

---

[119] **Wassapinewat**   This seems to be the only primary-source mention of this "brother" of Neponset Massachusett Sachem Chikatawbak/Obdakiest/Abdercest. He did not sign the Sept. 1621 treaty (in Young 232). Another perhaps-related man, Obbatinewat, Sachem of Shawmut (future site of Boston), is named in *Mourt* (78: Sept. 1621) as Sachem "in the bottom of the Massachusetts Bay, yet he is under Massasoit." At that time, "It seemed good to the [Plimoth] company in general, that though the Massachusetts had often threatened us (as we were informed), yet we should go amongst them, partly to see the country, partly to make peace with them, and partly to secure their truck." Obbatinewat "used us very kindly." See Salisbury 121

[120] As in Young's copy-text and edition (330), an original word seems to be missing at this point. "The word *inclined* or *disposed* seems to have been accidentally omitted," he notes; while *empowered* might also work. This editor has inserted two dashes in an attempt to clarify while changing no text of this complex sentence

being high time to come to resolution, how sudden soever it seemed to them, fearing it would be put in execution before we could give any intelligence thereof. This business was no less troublesome than grievous; and the more, because it is so ordinary in these times for men to measure things by the events thereof; but especially for that we knew no means to deliver our Countrymen and preserve our selves, than by returning their malicious and cruel purposes upon their own heads, and causing them to fall into the same pit [37/F3] they had digged for others; though it much grieved us to shed the blood of those whose good we ever intended and aimed at, as a principall[121] in all our proceedings.

But in the end we came to this public conclusion, that because it was a matter of such weight as every man was not of sufficiency to judge, nor fitness to know because of many other *Indians* which daily as occasion serveth converse with us; therefore the Governour, his Assistant, and the Captain, should take such to themselves as they thought most meet, and conclude thereof; which done, we came to this conclusion:

That Captain *Standish* should take so many men as he thought sufficient to make his party good against all the *Indians* in the *Massachuset bay*; and because (as all men know that have had to do in that kind) it is impossible to deal with them upon open defiance, but to take them in such traps as they lay for others. Therefore he should pretend trade as at other times; but first go to the *English* and acquaint them with the plot, and the end of his own coming; that comparing it with their carriages towards them[122] he might the better judge of the certainty of it, and more fitly take opportunity to revenge the same; but should forbear if it were possible till such time as he could make sure *Wituwamat* [were there],[123] that bloody and bold villain before spoken of; whose head he had order to bring with him, that he might be a warning and terrour to all of that disposition.

---

[121] **principall** original text: poss. "principle"

[122] **their** (Native people's) **carriages** (behavior) **toward them** (Weymouth colonists)

[123] Apparently some original text was missing. Young (332) renders it: "...till such time as he could make sure [of] Wituwamat, that...." **Before spoken of** on page 33

Upon this Captain *Standish* made choice of eight men, and would not take more because he would prevent jealousy,[124] knowing their guilty consciences would soon be provoked thereto. But on the next day before he could go, came one of Mr. *Weston*'s Company by land unto us, with his pack at his back,[125] who made a pitiful narration of their lamentable and weak estate, and of the *Indians'* carriages, whose boldness increased abundantly, insomuch as the victuals they got, they would take it out of their pots and eat before their faces; yea if any thing they gain-sayd them, they were ready to hold a knife at their breasts. That to give **[38]** them content, since *Iohn Sanders* went to *Munhiggen*, they had hanged one of them that stole their corn, and yet they regarded it not. That another of their Company was turned Salvage, that their people had most forsaken the town, and made their rendezvous where they got their victuals, because they would not take pains to bring it home. That they had sold their clothes for corn, and were ready to starve both with cold and hunger also, because they could not endure to get victuals by reason of their nakedness; and that they were dispersed into three Companies scarce having any powder and shot left.

What would be the event of these things (he said) he much feared; and therefore not daring to stay any longer among them, though he knew not the way, yet adventured to come to us, partly to make known their weak and dangerous estate, as he conceived, and partly to desire he might there remain till things were better settled at the other plantation. As this relation was grievous to us, so it gave us good encouragement to proceed in our intendments; for which Captain *Standish* was now fitted, and the wind coming fair, the next day set forth for the *Massachusets*.

The *Indians* at the *Massachusets* missed this man, and suspecting his coming, to us as we conceive, sent one after him and gave out there that he would never come to *Patuxet*, but that some Wolves or Bears would eat him; but we know both by our own experience, and the report of others,

---

[124] **jealousy**   suspicion

[125] Phinehas Pratt (see his own "Declaration" here; and Introduction Parts 3 and 4)

that though they find a man sleeping, yet so soon as there is life discerned they fear and shun him.

This *Indian* missed him but very little, and missing him passed by the town and went to *Manomet*, whom we hoped to take at his return, as afterward we did. Now was our Fort made fit for service and some Ordnance mounted; and though it may seem long work it being ten months since it begun with such small means, a little time cannot bring [it][126] to perfection. Beside those works which **[39]** tend to the preservation of man, the enemy of mankind will hinder what in him heth[127], sometimes blinding the judgment and causing reasonable men to reason against their own safety; as amongst us, divers, seeing the work prove tedious, would have dissuaded from proceeding, flattering themselves with peace and security, and accounting it a work of superfluity and vaine-glory, than simple necessity. But God (whose providence hath waked and as I may say, watched for us whilst we slept), having determined to preserve us from these intended treacheries, undoubtedly ordained this as a special means to advantage us and discourage our adversaries; and therefore so stirred up the hearts of the Governours and other forward instruments, as the work was just made serviceable against this needful and dangerous time, though we ignorant of the same.

But that I may proceed, the *Indian* last mentioned in his return from *Monomet*, came through the town pretending still friendship and in love to see us. But as formerly others,[128] so his end was to see whether we continued still in health and strength, or fell into weakness like their neighbors, which they hoped and looked for (though God in mercy provided better for us), and [which] he knew would be glad tidings to his Countrymen.

---

[126] Both Young (335) and Arber (565) add this apparently-missing word

[127] **heth**   Young (335) and Arber (565) render this original text as "lieth"

[128] **others**   original phrase---poss. "as at other times"

But here the Governour stayd him, and sending for him[129] to the Fort, there gave the Guard charge of him as their prisoner, where he told him he must be contented to remain till the return of Captain *Standish* from the *Massachusets*, so he was locked in a chain to a staple in the Court of guard, and there kept. Thus was our fort hanselled,[130] this being the first day, as I take it, that ever any watch was there kept.

The Captain being now come to the *Massachusets*, went first to the ship, but found neither man, or so much as a dog therein. Upon the discharge of a Musket, the Master and some others of the plantation shewed themselves, who were on the shore gathering ground-nuts, and getting other food. After salutation, Captain *Standish* **[40]** asked them how they durst so leave the ship and live in such security, who answered like men senseless of their own misery: they feared not the *Indians*, but lived and suffered them to lodge with them, not having sword, or gun, or needing the same.

To which the Captain answered, If there were no cause, he was the gladder; but upon further inquiry, understanding that those in whom *Iohn Sanders* had received most special confidence and left in his stead to govern the rest were at the Plantation, thither he went. And, to be brief, [he] made known the *Indians'* purpose and the end of his own coming; as also (which formerly I omitted) that if, afterward, they durst not there stay, it was the intendment of the Governours and people of *Plimoth* there to receive them till they could be better provided. But if they conceived of any other course that might be more likely for their good, that himself should further them therein to the uttermost of his power.

These men, comparing other circumstances with that they now heard, answered [that] they could expect no better, and [that] it was God's mercy that they were not killed before his coming, desiring therefore that he would neglect no opportunity to proceed. Hereupon he advised them to secrecy, yet withall to send special command to one third of their

---

[129] **for him**   poss. he "sent" for guards to take the Native man in custody

[130] **a staple**   an iron anchoring-ring or cleat   **hanselled**   used for the first time

Company that were farthest off to come home, and there enjoyne them on pain of death to keep [to] the town; himself allowing them a pint of *Indian* corn to a man for a day (though that store he had was spared out of our seed). The weather proving very wet and stormy, it was the longer before he could do anything.

In the meane time an *Indian* came to him and brought some furs, but rather to gather what he could from the Captains coming then for trade[131]; and, though the Captain carried things as smoothly as possibly he could, yet at his return he reported he saw by his eyes that he was angry in his heart, and therefore began to suspect themselves discovered. This caused one *Pecksuot*, who was a *Pinese*, being a man of notable spirit, to come to [41/G] *Hobbamock*, who was then with them. And [*Pecksuot*] told him he understood that the Captain was come to kill himself and the rest of the Salvages there. Tell him, said he, we know it, but fear him not, neither will we shun him; but let him begin when he dare, he shall not take us at unawares.

Many times after, divers of them severally, or few together, came to the Plantation to him[132], where they would whet and sharpen the points of their knives before his face, and use many other insulting gestures and speeches. Amongst the rest, *Wituwamat* bragged of the excellency of his knife: on the end of the handle there was pictured a woman's face. But, said he, I have another at home wherewith I have killed both *French* and *English*, and that hath a man's face on it; and by and by, these two must marry. Further, he said of that knife he there had: *Hinnaim namen, hinnaim michen, matta cuts*: that is to say, By and by it should see, and by and by it should eat, but not speak.

Also, *Pecksuot*, being a man of greater stature than the Captain, told him [that] though he were a great Captain, yet he was but a little man; and, said he, though I be no Sachim, yet I am a man of great strength and courage.

---

[131] A second redundant "then" is deleted from this sentence

[132] **him** Standish

These things the Captain observed, yet bare with patience for the present.

On the next day, seeing he could not get many of them together at once, and this *Pecksuot* and *Wituwamat* both together with another man, and a youth of some eighteen years of age which was brother to *Wituwamat* and villain-like trode in his steps, daily putting many tricks upon the weaker sort of men.[133] And, having about as many of his own Company in a room with them, [Captain *Standish*] gave the word to his men; and the door being fast shut, began himself with *Pecksuot*. And snatching his own knife from his neck, though with much struggling, [*Standish*] killed him therewith, the point whereof he had made as sharp as a needle, and ground the back also to an edge.

Wituwamat and the other man, the rest killed; and took the youth, whom the Captain caused to be hanged. But it is incredible how many **[42]** wounds these two Pueefes[134] received before they died, not making any fearful noise, but catching at their weapons and striving to the last.

Hobbamock stood by all this time as a spectator and meddled not, observing how our men demeaned themselves in this action. All being here ended, smiling he brake forth into these speeches to the Captain: Yesterday *Pecksuot*, bragging of his own strength and stature, said [that] though you were a great Captain, yet you were but a little man. But today I see you are big enough to lay him on the ground.

But to proceed. There being some women at the same time, Captain *Standish* left them in the custody of Mr. *Weston*'s people at the town, and sent word to another Company that had intelligence of things, to kill those *Indian* men that were amongst them. These killed two more. Himself also with some of his own men went to another place, where they killed another; and through the negligence of one man an *Indian* escaped, who discovered and crossed their proceedings.

---

[133] The only change to this important but awkward original text is this period and new sentence beginning "And...." The entire passage was originally one sentence

[134] **Pueefes** most likely a printer's inverted "n" causes this error for "pneise(s)"

Not long before this execution, three of Mr. *Weston's* men which more regarded their bellies than any command or Commander, having formerly fared well with the *Indians* for making them Clanoes,[135] went again to the *Sachim* to offer their service, and had entertainment. The first night they came thither within night late came a Messenger with all speed, and delivered a sad and short message; whereupon all the men[136] gathered together, put on their boots and breeches, trussed up themselves, and took their bows and arrows and went forth, telling them they went a-hunting, and that at their return they should have venison enough.

[They] being now gone, one [man]---being more ancient and wise than the rest, calling former things to mind, especially the Captain's presence, and the strait charge that on pain of death none should go a Musket-shot from the plantation, and comparing this sudden departure of theirs therewith---began to dislike and wish himself at home again, which was further of[f] than divers other dwelt.[137] Hereupon he moved his fellows to [43/C2] return, but could not persuade them. So, there being none but women left, and the other that was turned salvage, about midnight came away, forsaking the paths lest he should be pursued, and by this means saved his life.

Captain *Standish* took the one half of his men, and one or two of Mr. *Weston's*, and *Hobbamock*, still seeking to make spoyle of them and theirs. At length they espied a file of *Indians* which made towards them amaine,[138] and there being a small advantage in the ground by reason of a hill near them, both Companies strove for it. Captain *Standish* got it, whereupon they retreated and took each man his tree, letting fly their arrows amaine, especially at himself and *Hobbamock*. Whereupon *Hobbamock* cast off his coat, and being a known *Pinese* (theirs being now killed), chased them so

---

[135] original text: most likely "canoes" (or in this region, dugout boats or *mishoon*)

[136] **men**   that is, the Native men

[137] Again, dashes added to this sentence may improve clarity without changing original text

[138] Pratt and Morton agree that these braves were led by Chikatawbak/Obdakiest/ Abdercest of the Neponset Massachusetts

fast as our people were not able to hold way with him; insomuch as our men could have but one certain mark and then but the arm and half face of a notable villain[139] as he drew at Captain *Standish*. Who, together with another, both discharged at once at him, and brake his arm; whereupon they fled into a swamp.

When they were in the thicket they parlyed,[140] but to small purpose, getting nothing but foul language. So our Captain dared the Sachim to come out and fight like a man, shewing how base and woman-like he was in tonguing it as he did; but he refused and fled.

So the Captain returned to the Plantation, where he released the women, and would not take their beaver coats from them, nor suffer the least discourtesy to be offered them.

Now were Mr. *Weston*'s people resolved to leave their Plantation and go for *Munhiggen*, hoping to get passage and return with the fishing ships. The Captain told them that for his own part, he durst there live with fewer men than they were. Yet since they were otherways minded, according to his order from the Governours and people of *Plimoth*, he would help them with corn competent for their pro- **[44]** vision by the way; which he did, scarce leaving himself more than brought them home.

Some of them disliked the choice of the body to go to *Munhiggen*, and therefore desiring to go with him to *Plimouth*, he took them into the shallop. And seeing them set sail and clear of the *Massachuset bay*, he took leave and returned to *Plimouth*, whither he came in safety (blessed be God) and brought the head of *Wituwamat* with him.

Amongst the rest there was an *Indian* youth that was ever of a courteous and loving disposition towards us. He notwithstanding the death of his Countrymen came to the Captain without fear, saying his good conscience and love towards us emboldened him so to do. This youth confessed that the *Indians* intended to kill Mr. *Weston*'s people, and not to delay any longer than till they [had] had two more Canoes or Boats, which

---

[139] that is, they could not get a good musket-shot at people behind the trees

[140] **parlyed**   poss. "they" (the Plimothers?) "tried to negotiate"

Mr. *Weston*'s men would have finished by this time (having made them three already), had not the Captain prevented them, and the end of stay for those Boats, was to take their Ship therewith.[141]

Now was the Captain returned and received with joy: the head being brought to the fort and there set up, the Governours and Captains with divers others went up the same further,[142] to examine the prisoner, who looked pitiously on the head,[143] being asked whether he knew it, he answered, yea. Then he confessed the plot, and that all the people provoked *Obtakiest* their *Sachim* thereunto, being drawn to it by their importunity. Five there were (he said) that prosecuted it with more eagerness than the rest: the two principall were killed, being *Pecksuot* and *Wituwamat*, whose head was there: the other three were *Powahs*, being yet living, and known unto us, though one of them was wounded, as aforesaid. For himself he would not acknowledge that he had [had] any hand therein, begging earnestly for his life, saying, He was not a *Massachuset* man, but as a stranger lived with them. *Hobbamock* also gave a good report of him, and besought for him, but was bribed so **[45/G3]** to do: Nevertheless, that we might shew mercy as well as extremity, the Governour released him; and the rather because we desired he might carry a message to *Obtakiest* his Master.

No sooner were the irons from his legs, but he would have been gone. But the Governour bid him stay and fear not, for he should receive no hurt; and by *Hobbamock* commanded him to deliver this message to his Master: That for our parts, it never entered into our hearts to take such a course with them, till their own treachery enforced us thereunto. And therefore [they] might thank themselves for their own overthrow. Yet since he had begun, if again by any the like courses he did provoke him, his

---

[141] Perhaps this means that the finished dugout-canoes were taken aboard the home-bound English vessel

[142] **up the same further**   poss. meaning they went higher up the Fort Hill to where the Native prisoner was being held

[143] **looked pitiously on the head**   original text: this editor unable to clarify

Country should not hold him, for he would never suffer him or his to rest in peace, till he had utterly consumed them; and therefore should take this as a warning. Further, that he should send to *Patuxet* the three Englishmen he had and not kill them; also that he should not spoyle the pale and houses at *Wichaguscusset*, and that this Messenger should either bring the English, or an answer, or both, promising his safe return.

This message was delivered, and the party would have returned with answer, but was at first dissuaded by them whom, afterward, they would but could not persuade to come to us. At length (though long) a Woman came and told us that *Obtakiest* was sorry that the English were killed before he [had] heard from the Governour; otherwise he would have sent them. Also she said, He would fain make his peace again with us, but none of his men durst come to treat about it, having forsaken his dwelling, and daily removed from place to place, expecting when we would take further vengeance on him.

Concerning those other people that intended to join with the *Massachuseucks* against us, though we never went against any of them: yet this sudden and unexpected execution, together with the just judgment of God upon their guilty consciences, hath so terrified and amazed them, [that] in like manner they forsook their houses, running **[46]** to and fro like men distracted, living in swamps and other desert places, and so brought manifold diseases amongst themselves, whereof very many are dead: as *Canacum* the *Sachim* of *Manomet*, *Aspinet*, the *Sachim* of *Nauset*, and *Ianowh*, *Sachim* of *Mattachuest*. This *Sachim* in his life, in the middest of these distractions, said the God of the English was offended with them, and would destroy them in his anger; and certainly it is strange to hear how many of late have [died], and still daily die amongst them; neither is there any likelihood it will easily cease, because through fear they set little or no Corn, which is the staff of life, and without which they cannot long preserve health and strength.

From one of these places a boat was sent with presents to the Governour, hoping thereby to work their peace. But the boat was cast away, and three of the persons drowned, not far from our plantation. Only one escaped, who durst not come to us, but returned, so as none of them dare come amongst us.

I fear I have been too tedious both in this and other things. Yet when I consider how necessary a thing it is that the truth and grounds of this action especially should be made known, and the several dispositions of that dissolved Colony, whose reports undoubtedly will be as various, I could not but enlarge my self where I thought to be most brief; neither durst I be too brief, lest I should eclipse and rob God of that honour, glory, and prayse which belongeth to him for preserving us from falling, when we were at the pit's brim, and yet feared nor knew not that we were in danger.

The month of April [1623] being now come, on all hands we began to prepare for Corn. And because there was no Corn left before this time, save that was preserved for seed, being also hopeless of relief by supply, we thought best to leave off all other works, and prosecute that as most necessary. And because there was no small hope of doing good in that common course of labor that formerly we were in, for that the Governours that followed men to their **[47]** labours had nothing to give men for their necessities; and therefore could not so well exercise that command over them therein as formerly they had done; especially considering that self-love wherewith every man (in a measure more or less) loveth and preferreth his own good before his neighbour[']s, and also the base disposition of some drones, that as at other times, so now especially would be most burdenous to the rest.

It was therefore thought best that every man should use the best diligence he could for his own preservation, both in respect of the time present, and to prepare his own Corn for the year following; and [to] bring in a competent portion for the maintenance of public Officers, Fishermen, &c., which could not be freed from their calling without greater inconveniences. This course was to continue till harvest, and then the Governours to gather in the appointed portion for the maintenance of themselves and such others as necessity constrained to exempt from this condition.

Only if occasion served upon any special service they might employ such as they thought most fit to execute the same, during this appointed time, and at the end thereof all men to be employed by them in such service as they thought most necessary for the general good. And because there is great difference in the ground, that therefore a set quantity should be set down for a person, and each man to have his fall by lot, as being most just and equal, and against which no man could except.

At a general meeting of the Company, many courses were propounded, but this approved and followed as being the most likely for the present and future good of the Company. And therefore before this month began to prepare our ground against seed-time. In the middest of April [1623] we began to set, the weather being then seasonable, which much encouraged us, giving us good hopes of after plenty: the setting season is good till the latter end of May. But it pleased God for our further chastisement, to send a great drowth, insomuch as in six weeks after the **[48]** latter setting there scarce fell any rain; so that the stalk of that [which] was first set began to send forth the ear before it came to half growth, and that which was later, not like to yield any at all, both blade and stalk hanging the head, and changing the color in such manner as we judged it utterly dead. Our Beans also ran not up according to their wonted manner, but stood at a stay, many being parched away as though they had been scorched before the fire. Now were our hopes overthrown, and we discouraged, our joy being turned into mourning.

To add also to this sorrowful estate in which we were, we heard of a supply [ship] that was sent unto us many months since, which having two repulses before, was a third time in company of another ship three hundred Leagues at Sea, and now in three months' time heard no further of her; only the signs of a wrack were seen on the coast which could not be judged to be any other than the same. So that at once God seemed to deprive us of all future hopes. The most courageous were now discouraged, because God which hitherto had been our only Shield and Supporter, now seemed in his anger to arm himself against us; and who can withstand the fierceness of his wrath[?]

These, and the like considerations moved not only every good man privately to enter into examination with his own estate between God and his conscience, and so to humiliation before him; but also more solemnly to humble our selves together before the Lord by fasting and prayer. To that end a day was appointed by public authority, and set apart from all other employments, hoping that the same God which had stirred us up hereunto, would be moved hereby in mercy to look down upon us, and grant the request of our dejected souls, if our continuance there might any way stand with his glory and our good.

But oh the mercy of God[144] Who was as ready to hear as we to ask. For though in the morning when we assembled together, the heavens were as clear and the drought as like to continue as ever it was; yet (our exer- **[49/H]** cise continuing some eight or nine hours) before our departure the weather was over-cast, the clouds gathered together on all sides, and on the next morning distilled such soft, sweet, and moderate showers of rain, continuing some fourteen days, and mixed with such seasonable weather, as it was hard to say whether our withered Corn, or [our] drooping affections were most quickened or revived. Such was the bounty and goodness of our God.

Of this the *Indians* by means of *Hobbamock* took notice; who being then in the Towne, and this exercise in the midst of the week, said, It was but three days since Sunday, and therefore demanded of a boy what was the reason thereof? Which, when he knew and saw what effects followed thereupon, he and all of them admired the goodness of our God towards us, that wrought so great a change in so short a time; shewing the difference between their conjuration, and our invocation on the name of God for rain; theirs being mixed with such storms and tempests as sometimes instead of doing them good, it layeth the Corn flat on the

---

[144] Slippage of type has obscured the original end-punctuation, but a faint vertical line between *God* and *Who* may suggest that an exclamation mark was intended. Young (349) inserts that punctuation

ground, to their prejudice; but ours in so gentle and seasonable a manner, as they never observed the like.[145]

At the same time Captain *Standish*, being formerly employed by the Governour to buy provisions for the refreshing of the Colony, returned with the same, accompanied with one Mr. *David Tompson*, a Scotchman, who also that Spring began a Plantation twenty-five leagues north-east from us, near *Smith*['s] Isles, at a place called *Pascatoquack*, where he liketh well.[146] Now also heard we of the third repulse that our supply had, of their safe though dangerous return into *England*, and of their preparation to come to us. So that having these many signs of God's favour and acceptation, we thought it would be great ingratitude if secretly we should smoother up the same, or content our selves with private thanksgiving for that which by private prayer could not be obtained. And therefore another solemn day was set apart and appointed for that end, **[50]** wherein we returned glory, honour, and prayse, with all thankfulness to our good God, which dealt so graciously with us, whose name for these and all other his mercies towards his Church and chosen ones, by them be blessed and praysed now and evermore, Amen.

In the latter end of July and the beginning of August [1623] came two Ships with supply unto us, who brought all their passengers except one in health, who recovered in short time; who also notwithstanding, all our wants and hardship (blessed be God) found not any one sick person amongst us at the Plantation. The bigger ship called the *Anne* was hired, and there fraighed[147] back, from whence we set sail the tenth of September

---

[145] As Young (350) notes, this is the last mention of Hobbamock in Plimoth's records except for the 1623 noting of "Hobamack's ground" lying "betwene" lands assigned to colonists John Howland and Stephen Hopkins (FBH1: 346)

[146] **Tompson**   Acc. to Gorges (*Relation* and *Narration*) and Morton's *Canaan*, Tompson was a Scot, an attorney or land agent in Gorges' and other transatlantic merchants' employ. With family, he lived first at Little Harbor on the Piscataqua River ("New Hampshire"), and then by 1626 "between" Squantum and the (Thompson's) island named for him in Mass. Bay, dying there in 1628 (FBH1: 418; Adams *Three Episodes* 191). **Smith's Isles**   In 1614 Capt. John Smith had thus named the Isles of Shoals

[147] **fraighed**   original text: Young (353) renders it "freighted" (sent back with freight)

[1623]. The lesser, called the *Little James*, was built for the Company at their charge. She was now also fitted for Trade and discovery to the South-ward of Cape *Cod*, and almost ready to set sail, whom I pray God to bless in her good and lawful proceedings.

Thus have I made a true and full Narration of the state of our Plantation, and such things as were most remarkable therein since December 1621. If I have omitted any thing, it is either through weakness of memory or because I judged it not material. I confess my style rude, and unskillfulness in the task I undertook, being urged thereunto by opportunity, which I knew to be wanting in others, and but for which I would not have undertaken the same. Yet as it is rude so it is plain, and therefore the easier to be understood; wherein others may see that which we are bound to acknowledge, *viz*:

That if ever any people in these later ages were upheld by the providence of God after a more special manner than others, then we; and therefore the more bound to celebrate the memory of his goodness, with everlasting thankfulness. For in these forenamed strayts, such was our state, as in the morning we had often our food to seek before the day, and yet performed the duties of our Callings, I mean other daily labours, to provide for after time; and though at some [51/H2] times in some seasons at noon I have seen men stagger by reason of faintness for want of food, yet ere night by the good providence and blessing of God, we have enjoyed such plenty as though the windows of heaven had been opened unto us.

How few, weak, and raw were we at our first beginning, and there settling, and in the middest of barbarous enemies? Yet God wrought our peace for us. How often have we been at the pit's brim, and in danger to be swallowed up, yea, not knowing till afterward that we were in peril? And yet God preserved us; yea, and from how many that we yet know not of, he that knoweth all things can best tell. So that when I seriously consider of things, I cannot but think that God hath a purpose to give that Land as

---

NOTE: Arber (580) here dates Winslow's writing of *Good News* between Dec. 13, 1621, and Sept. 10, 1623

an inheritance to our Nation; and great pity it were that it should long lie in so desolate a state, considering it agreeth so well with the constitution of our bodies, being both fertile, and so temperate for heat and cold, as in that respect one can scarce distinguish *New-England* from *Old*.

A few things I thought meet to add hereunto which I have observed amongst the *Indians*, both touching their Religion, and sundry other Customs amongst them.

And first, whereas my selfe and others, in former Letters (which came to the Press against my will and knowledge) wrote, that the *Indians* about us are a people without any Religion, or knowledge of any God; therein I erred, though we could then gather no better. For as they conceive of many divine powers, so of one whom they call *Kiehtan*, to be the principall and maker of all the rest, and to [have been] made by none.[148] He (they say) created the heavens, earth, sea, and all creatures contained therein. Also that he made one man and one woman, of whom they and we and all mankind came; but how they became so far dispersed, that they know not.[149]

At first they say, there was no *Sachim*, or *King*, but *Kiehtan*, who dwelleth above in the Heavens, whither all good men go when **[52]** they die, to see their friends, and have their fill of all things. This his habitation lyeth far West-ward in the heavens, they say: thither the bad men go also, and knock at his door, but he bids them *Quatchet*, that is to say, Walk abroad, for there is no place for such; so that they wander in restless want and penury.

Never man saw this *Kiehtan*, only old men tell them of him, and bid them tell their children, yea, to charge them to teach their posterities the same, and lay the like charge upon them. This power they acknowledge to be good, and when they would obtain any great matter, meet together, and cry unto him, and so likewise for plenty, victory, &c., sing, daunce, feast,

---

[148] A gloss printed at the lower left corner of this page reads: "The meaning of the word, *Kiehtan*, I think hath reference to Antiquity, for *Chife* is an old man, and *Kiehchife*, a man that exceedeth in age"

[149] **dispersed**   see Introduction Part 1

give thanks, and hang up Garlands and other things in memory of the same.

Another power they worship, whom they call *Hobbamock*, and to the Norward of us *Hobbamoqui*: this as far as we can conceive is the Devill, him they call upon to cure their wounds and diseases. When they are curable, he persuades them he sends the same[150] for some conceived anger against them, but upon their calling upon him[,] can and doth help them. But when they are mortall, and not curable in nature, then he persuades them *Kiehtan* is angry and sends them, whom none can cure: insomuch, as in that respect only they somewhat doubt whether he be simply good, and therefore in sickness never call upon him.

This *Hobbamock* appears in sundry forms unto them, as in the shape of a Man, a Deer, a Fawn, an Eagle, &c., but most ordinarily a Snake. He appears not to all but to the chiefest and most judicious amongst them, though all of them strive to attain to that hellish height of honour.

He appeareth most ordinary and is most conversant with three sorts of people: one I confess I neither know by name nor office directly. Of these they [53/H3] have few but esteem highly of them, and think that no weapon can kill them. Another they call by the name of *Powah*, and the third *Pniese*.

The office and duty of the *Powah* is to be exercised principally in calling upon the Divell, and curing diseases of the sick or wounded.[151] The common people join with him in the exercise of invocation, but do but only assent, or as we term it, say *Amen* to that [which] he sayeth; yet sometimes break out into a short musical note with him. The *Powah* is eager and free in speech, fierce in countenance, and joineth many anticke[152]

---

[150] **he persuades them he sends**   poss. "he" (a Powah) persuades "them" (people) that "he" (the spirit-power Hobbamock) "sends" afflictions. The same question applies below concerning Kiehtan

[151] For an overview of the *Powah* in New England Native cultures see Simmons, "Southern New England Shamanism: An Ethnographic Reconstruction"

[152] **anticke**   that is, "antic" (as in ancient "antic hey" dance traditions of magic); or "antique." The word derives from terms used for long-forgotten kinds of imagery, of "human, animal and floral forms, incongruously [*sic*] running into one another," found by Early Modern "archaeo-

and labourious gestures with the same over the party diseased. If the party be wounded he will also seem to suck the wound, but if they be curable (as they say) he toucheth it not, but a Skooke, that is the Snake,[153] or Wobsacuck, that is the Eagle, sitteth on his shoulder and licks the same. This none see but the *Powah*, who tells them he doth it himself. If the party be otherwise diseased, it is accounted sufficient if in any shape he but come into the house, taking it for an undoubted sign of recovery.

And as in former ages *Apollo* had his temple at *Delphos*,[154] and *Diana* at *Ephesus*; so have I heard them call upon some as if they had their residence in some certain places, or because they appeared in those forms in the same. In the *Powah*'s speech he promiseth to sacrifice many skins of beasts, kettles, hatchets, beads, knives, and other the best things they have to the fiend, if he will come to help the party diseased; but whether they perform it I know not.

The other practices I have seen, being necessarily called at some times to be with their sick, and have used the best arguments I could to make them understand against the same. They have told me I should see the Divell at those times come to the party, but I assured my selfe and them of the contrary, which so proved: yea, themselves have confessed they never saw him when any of us were present. In desperate and extraordinary hard travell[155] in childbirth, when the party cannot be delivered by the **[54]** ordinary means, they send for this *Powah*,[156] though ordinarily their travell is not so extreme as in our parts of the world, they

---

logical" digs into the past. Hence "grotesque, bizarre, uncouthly ludicrous," because "hopelessly out of place or date" (*Oxford English Dictionary*). The etymology also informs the use of the word "*dis*figure" below

[153] *Canaan* (77) records the word *ascowke*: Williams' *Key* Ch. 17, *askug*, "a snake"

[154] **Delphos**   Winslow conflates the Greek-mainland oracle Del*phi* with the oracular Cycladic island Del*os*, though both were associated in part with god Apollo

[155] **travell**   *travail* or labor

[156] **this *Powah***   poss. "such a" Powah, one skilled in midwifery: perhaps a rare reference to Native *women* bearing the title of Powah

being of a more hardy nature; for on the third day after childbirth I have seen the mother with the infant upon a small occasion in cold weather in a boat upon the Sea.

Many sacrifices the *Indians* use, and in some cases kill children.[157] It seemeth they are various in their religious worship in a little distance, and grow more and more cold in their worship to *Kiehtan*; saying in their memory he was much more called upon. The *Nanohiggansets* exceed in their blind devotion, and have a great spacious house wherein only some few (that are as we may term them Priests) come: thither at certain known times resort all their people, and offer almost all the riches they have to their gods, as kettles, skins, hatchets, beads, knives, &c., all which are cast by the Priests into a great fire that they make in the midst of the house, and there consumed to ashes. To this offering every man bringeth freely, and the more he is known to bring, hath the better esteem of all men. This the other *Indians* about us approve of as good, and with their *Sachims* would appoint the like; and because the plague hath not reigned at *Nanohigganset* as at other places about them, they attribute to this custom there used.

The *Pnieses* are men of great courage and wisdom; and to these also the Divell appeareth more familiarly than to others, and, as we conceive, maketh covenant with them to preserve them from death, by wounds, with arrows, knives, hatchets, &c.; or at least, both themselves and especially the people think themselves to be freed from the same. And though against their battles all of them by painting disfigure themselves, yet they are known by their courage and boldness; by reason whereof[158] one of them will chase almost an hundred men, for they account it death for whomsoever stand in their way. These are highly esteemed of all sorts of people, and are of the *Sachims'* [55] Council, without whom they will not war or undertake any weighty business. In war, their *Sachims* for their

---

[157] Likely refers to the use of abortifacents. See Cave's *Pequot War* study of the Puritans' Biblical rhetoric against such practices

[158] **by reason whereof**   for example

more safety go in the midst of them. They are commonly men of the greatest stature and strength, and such as will endure most hardness, and yet are more discreet, courteous, and humane in their carriages than any amongst them, scorning theft, lying, and the like base dealings, and stand as much upon their reputation as any men.

And to the end they may have store of these, they train up the most forward and likeliest boys from their childhood in great hardness, and make them abstain from dainty meat, observing divers orders prescribed. To the end that when they are of age, the Divell may appear to them, causing [them] to drink the juyce of Sentry or other bitter herbs[159] till they cast, which they must disgorge into the platter, and drink again, and again, till at length through extraordinary oppressing of nature it will seem to be all blood; and this the boys will do with eagerness at the first, and so continue till by reason of faintness they can scarce stand on their legs, and then must go forth into the cold. Also they beat their shins with sticks, and cause them to run through bushes, stumps, and brambles, to make them hardy and acceptable to the Divell, that in time he may appear unto them.

Their *Sachims* cannot be all called Kings, but only some few of them, to whom the rest resort for protection, and pay homage unto them. Neither may they war without their knowledge and approbation, yet to be commanded by the greater as occasion serveth. Of this sort is *Massassowat* our friend, and *Conanacus* of *Nanohigganset* our supposed enemy.

Every *Sachim* taketh care for the widow and fatherless, also for such as are aged and any way maimed, if their friends be dead or not able to provide for them.

A *Sachim* will not take any to wife but such an one as is equal to him in birth; otherwise they say their seed would in time become ignoble. And though they have **[56]** many other wives, yet are they no other than concubines or servants, and yield a kind of obedience to the principall, who ordereth the family, and them in it. The like their men observe also,

---

[159] The herb "centaury" may be *sabbatia chloroides*, "found in great abundance on the margin of the ponds in Plymouth. It belongs to the natural order of Gentians...an intense bitterness residing both in the stems and roots" (Young 360)

and will adhere to the first during their lives; but put away the other at their pleasure.

This government is successive and not by choice. If the father die before the son or daughter be of age, then the child is committed to the protection and tuition of some one amongst them, who ruleth in his stead till he be of age, but when that is I know not.

Every *Sachim* knoweth how far the bounds and limits of his own Country extendeth, and that is his own proper inheritance. Out of that, if any of his men desire land to set their corn, he giveth them as much as they can use, and sets them their bounds. In this circuit, whosoever hunteth, if they kill any venison, bring him his fee, which is the foreparts of the same if it be killed on the land; but if in the water, then the skin thereof. The great *Sachims* or Kings know their own bounds or limits of land as well as the rest.

All travelers or strangers for the most part lodge at the *Sachim's*, when they come they tell him how long they will stay and to what place they go, during which time they receive entertainment according to their persons, but want not.

Once a year the *Pnieses* use to provoke the people to bestow much corn on the *Sachim*. To that end they appoint a certain time and place near the *Sachim's* dwelling, where the people bring many baskets of corn, and make a great stack thereof. There the *Pnieses* stand ready to give thanks to the people on the *Sachim's* behalf, and after acquainteth the *Sachim* therewith, who fetcheth the same, and is no less thankful, bestowing many gifts on them.

When any are visited with sickness, their friends resort unto them for their comfort, and continue with them oft- **[57/I]** times till their death or recovery. If they die, they stay a certain time to mourn for them. Night and morning they perform this duty many days after the burial in a most doleful manner, insomuch as though it be ordinary and the note musical, which they take one from another, and all together, yet it will draw tears from their eyes, and almost from ours also. But if they recover then because their sickness was chargeable,[160] they send corn and other gifts unto them at a certain appointed time, whereat they feast and dance; which they call *Commoco*.

When they bury the dead they sew up the corpse in a mat and so put it in the earth. If the party be a *Sachim* they cover him with many curious mats, and bury all his riches with him, and enclose the grave with a pale. If it be a child the father will also put his own most special jewels and ornaments in the earth with it, also will cut his hair and disfigure himself very much in token of sorrow. If it be the man or woman of the house, they will pull down the mats and leave the frame standing, and bury them in or near the same, and either remove their dwelling or give over house-keeping.

The men employ themselves wholly in hunting, and other exercises of the bow, except at some times they take some pains in fishing.

The women live a most slavish life, they carry all their burdens, set and dress their corn, gather it in, seek out for much of their food, beat and make ready the corn to eat, and have all household care lying upon them.

The younger sort reverence the elder, and do all mean offices whilst they are together, although they be strangers.[161] Boys and girls may not wear their hair like men and women, but are distinguished thereby.

A man is not accounted a man till he do some notable act, or show forth such courage and resolution as becometh his place. The men take much tobacco, but for boys so to do they account it odious.

All their names are significant and variable; for when **[58]** they come to the [e]state of men and women, they alter them according to their deeds or dispositions.[162]

---

[160] **chargeable**   curable

[161] **although**   possibly meaning *even when* they are strangers

[162] **significant and variable**   poss. meaning that each name signifies actual personal traits, which can change with age and circumstance. Morton's *Canaan* says "the Salvages are significiant in their denomination of any thing" (77)

When a maid is taken in marriage she first cutteth her hair, and after weareth a covering on her head till her hair be grown out. Their women are diversely disposed, some as modest as they will scarce talk one with another in the company of men, being very chaste also; yet other some light, lascivious and wanton.

If a woman have a bad husband, or cannot affect[163] him, and there be war or opposition between that and any other people, she will run away from him to the contrary party and there live, where they never come unwelcome; for where are most women, there is greatest plenty.

When a woman hath her monthly terms, she separateth herself from all other company, and liveth certain days in a house alone; after which she washeth her self and all that she hath touched or used, and is again received to her husband's bed or family.

For adultery the husband will beat his wife and put her away, if he please. Some common strumpets there are as well as in other places, but they are such as either never married, or widows, or put away for adultery; for no man will keep such an one to wife.

In matters of unjust and dishonest dealing, the *Sachim* examineth and punisheth the same. In case of thefts, for the first offense he is disgracefully rebuked; for the second, beaten by the *Sachim* with a cudgell on the naked back; for the third, he is beaten with many strokes, and hath his nose slit upward, that thereby all men may both know and shun him. If any man kill another, he must likewise die for the same.

The *Sachim* not only passeth the sentence upon malefactors, but executeth the same with his own hands, if the party be then present; if not, [he] sendeth his own knife in case of death, in the hands of others to perform the same. But if the offender be to receive other punishment, he will not receive the same but from the **[59/12]** *Sachim* himself; before whom being naked he kneeleth, and will not offer to run away though he beat him never so much, it being a greater disparagement for a man to cry during the time of his correction, than is his offense and punishment.

---

[163] **affect**   poss. meaning "cannot move, change, or appeal to" his "affections"

As for their apparel, they wear breeches and stockings in one like some *Irish*, which is made of Deer skins, and have shoes of the same leather. They wear also a Deer's skin loose about them like a cloak, which they will turn to the weather side. In this habit they travel, but when they are at home or come to their journey's end, presently they pull off their breeches, stockings and shoes, wring out the water if they be wet, and dry them, and rub or chafe the same. Though these be off, yet have they another small garment that covereth their secrets. The men wear also, when they go abroad in cold weather, an Otter or Fox skin on their right arm, but only their bracer[164] on the left. Women and all of that sex wear strings[165] about their legs, which the men never do.

The people are very ingenious and observative. They keep account of time by the moon, and winters or summers: they know divers of the stars by name: in particular, they know the North-star and call it *Maske*, which is to say The Bear. Also they have many names for the winds. They will guess very well at the wind and weather beforehand, by observations in the heavens. They report also that some of them can cause the wind to blow in what part they list, can raise storms and tempests which they usually do when they intend the death or destruction of other people, that by reason of the unseasonable weather they may take advantage of their enemies in their houses. At such times they perform their greatest exploits, and in such seasons when they are at enmity with any, they keep more careful watch than at other times.

As for the language, it is very copious, large, and difficult. As yet we cannot attain to any great measure thereof, **[60]** but can understand them, and explain our selves to their understanding, by the help of those that daily converse with us. And though there be difference in an hundred miles distance of place, both in language and manners, yet not so much but that they very well understand each other.

And thus much of their lives and manners.

---

[164] **bracer**   a small cloaking fur

[165] **strings**   poss. "bracelets"

Instead of Records and Chronicles, they take this course: where any remarkable act is done, in memory of it, either in the place, or by some pathway near adjoining, they make a round hole in the ground about a foot deep, and as much over[166]; which when others passing by behold, they inquire the cause and occasion of the same, which being once known, they are careful to acquaint all men, as occasion serveth therewith. And lest such holes should be filled, or grown up by any accident, as men pass by they will oft renew the same; by which means many things of great Antiquity are fresh in memory. So that as a man traveleth, if he can understand his guide, his journey will be the less tedious by reason of the many historical Discourses [that] will be related unto him.

In all this it may be said, I have neither praysed nor dispraysed the Country; and since I lived so long therein, my judgment thereof will give no less satisfaction to them that know me, than the Relation of our proceedings. To which I answer, that as in one so of the other: I will speak as sparingly as I can, yet will make known what I conceive thereof.

And first for that Continent, on which we are called *New England*. Although it hath ever been conceived by the English to be a part of that main Land adjoining to *Virginia*, yet by relation of the *Indians* it should appear to be otherwise. For they affirm confidently that it is an Island, and that either the *Dutch* or *French* pass through from Sea to Sea, between us and *Virginia*, and drive a great Trade in the same. The name of that inlet of the Sea they call *Mohegon*; which I take to be the same which we call *Hudson's* River, up which Master *Hudson* went many **[61/I3]** Leagues, and for want of means (as I hear) left it undiscovered.[167] For confirmation of this, their opinion is thus much: Though *Virginia* be not above an hundred and fifty Leagues from us, yet they never heard of *Powhatan*,[168] or knew that any English were planted in his Country, save only by us and

---

[166] **over**   across

[167] A boat from Henry Hudson's 1609 ship *Half Moon* explored as far as "Albany"

[168] **Powhatan**   see Winslow's final pages concerning the Powhatan peoples' attacks on Virginia's English plantations (1622)

Tisquantum, who went in an English ship thither. And therefore it is the more probable, because the water is not passable for them, who are very adventurous in their Boats.

Then for the temperature of the air: in almost three years' experience, I can scarce distinguish *New-England* from *Old England*, in respect of heat, and cold, frost, snow, rain, winds, &c. Some object, because our Plantation lieth in the latitude of 42 it must needs be much hotter. I confess, I cannot give the reason of the contrary: only experience teacheth us that if it do exceed *England*, it is so little as must require better judgments to discern it. And for the winter, I rather think (if there be difference) it is both sharper and longer in *New England* than *Old*; and yet the want of those comforts in the one which I have enjoyed in the other, may deceive my judgment also.

But in my best observation, comparing our own condition with the Relations of other parts of America, I cannot conceive of any to agree better with the constitution of the English, not being oppressed with extremity of heat, nor nipped with biting cold; by which means, blessed be God, we enjoy our health, notwithstanding those difficulties we have undergone, in such a measure as would have been admired if we had lived in *England* with the like means.

The day is two hours longer than here when it is at the shortest, and as much shorter there, when it is at the longest.

The soil is variable, in some places mould, in some clay, others a mixed sand, &c. The chiefest grain is the *Indian* [Maize], or *Ginny*-Wheat; the seed-time beginneth in midst of April, and continueth good till the midst of **[62]** May. Our harvest beginneth with September.

This corn increaseth in great measure, but is inferior in quantity to the same in *Virginia*. The reason, I conceive, is because *Virginia* is far hotter than it is with us, [maize] requiring great heat to ripen. But whereas it is objected against *New-England* that corn will not there grow except the ground be manured with fish? I answer that where men set with fish (as with us), it is more easy so to do than to clear ground and set without some five or six years, and so begin anew, as in *Virginia* and elsewhere.

Not but that in some places, where they[169] cannot be taken with ease in such abundance, the *Indians* set four years together without, and have as good Corn or better than we have that set with them; though indeed I think if we had Cattle to till the ground, it would be more profitable and better agreeable to the soil, to sow Wheat, Rye, Barley, Peas, and Oats, than to set [Maize], which our *Indians* call *Ewachim*. For we have had experience that they like and thrive well; and the other will not be procured without good labour and diligence, especially at seed time, when it must also be watched by night to keep the Wolves from the fish till it be rotten, which will be in fourteen days. Yet, men agreeing together, and taking their turns, it is not so much.

Much might be spoken of the benefit that may come to such as shall here plant by Trade with the *Indians* for Furs, if men take a right course for obtaining the same. For I dare presume upon that small experience I have had, to affirm that the *English, Dutch,* and *French* return yearly many thousand pounds' profits by Trade only from that *Island* on which we are seated.

Tobacco may be there planted, but not with that profit as in some other places. Neither were it profitable there to follow it,[170] though the increase were equal, because fish is a better and richer Commodity, and more necessary; which may be and are there had in as great abundance as in any other part of the world. Witness the West Coun- **[63]** try Merchants of *England,* which return incredible gains yearly from thence.

And if they can so do [who] here buy their salt at a great charge, and transport more Company to make their voyage than will sail their Ships, what may the planters expect when once they are seated, and make the most of their salt there, and employ themselves at least eight months in fishing? Whereas the other fish but four, and have their ship lie dead in the harbour all the time. Whereas such shipping as belong to plantations may

---

[169] **they**   that is, menhaden, herring and other fish that spawn up New England's streams every year

[170] **follow it**   that is, spend time developing it as a commodity or trade

take freight of passengers or cattle thither, and have their lading provided against they come.[171]

I confess, we have come so far short of the means to raise such returns, as with great difficulty we have preserved our lives; insomuch, as when I look back upon our condition and weak means to preserve the same, I rather admire at God's mercy and providence in our preservation than that no greater things have been effected by us.

But though our beginning have been thus raw, small, and difficult, as thou hast seen, yet the same God that hath hitherto led us through the former, I hope will raise means to accomplish the latter. Not that we altogether or principally propound profit to be the main end of that we have undertaken, but the glory of God, and the honour of our Country, in the enlarging of His Majesty's dominions. Yet wanting outward means to set things in that forwardness we desire, and to further the latter by the former, I thought meet to offer both to consideration, hoping that where Religion and profit jump together (which is rare) in so honourable an action, it will encourage every honest man, either in person or purse, to set forward the same; or at least-wise, to commend the well-fare thereof in his daily prayers to the blessing of the blessed God.

I will not again speak of the abundance of fowl, store of Venison, and variety of Fish, in their seasons, which might encourage many to go in their persons. Only I advise all such beforehand to consider, that as they hear of Countries that abound with the good creatures of **[64]** God, so means must be used for the taking of every one in his kind; and therefore not only to content themselves that there is sufficient, but to foresee how they shall be able to obtain the same. Otherwise, as he that walketh *London* streets, though he be in the middest of plenty, yet if he want means, is not the better but hath rather his sorrow increased by the sight of that he wanteth, and cannot enjoy it. So also there, if thou want art and other necessaries thereunto belonging, thou mayest see that thou wantest, and thy heart desireth, and yet be never the better for the same.

---

[171] **lading provided**   after leaving passengers in America, they can load up with fish before returning to England, and thus pay their voyage expenses

Therefore if thou see thine own insufficiency of thy self, then join to some others, where thou mayest in some measure enjoy the same. Otherwise assure thy self, thou art better where thou art. Some there be that, thinking altogether of their present wants they enjoy here, and not dreaming of any there, through indiscretion plunge themselves into a deeper sea of misery. As for example, it may be here, rent and firing are so chargeable,[172] as without great difficulty a man cannot accomplish the same; never considering, that as he shall have no rent to pay, so he must build his house before he have it, and peradventure may with more ease pay for his fuel here, than cut and fetch it home, if he have not cattle to draw it there; though there is no scarcity but rather too great plenty.

I write not these things to dissuade any that shall seriously upon due examination set themselves to further the glory of God, and the honour of our Country, in so worthy an Enterprise; but rather, to discourage such as with too great lightness undertake such courses; who peradventure strain themselves and their friends for their passage thither, and are no sooner there, than seeing their foolish imagination made void, are at their wit's end, and would give ten times so much for their return if they could procure it; and, out of such discontented passions **[65/K]** and humors, spare not to lay that imputation upon the Country, and others, which [they] themselves deserve.

As for example, I have heard some complain of others for their large reports of *New England*, and yet because they must drink water and want many delicates they here enjoyed, could presently return with their mouths full of clamors. And can any be so simple as to conceive that the fountains should stream forth Wine, or Beer, or the woods and rivers be like Butchers' shops, or Fishmongers' stalls, where they might have things taken to their hands[?]

If thou canst not live without such things, and hast no means to procure the one, and wilt not take pains for the other, nor hast ability to employ others for thee, rest where thou art. For as a proud heart, a dainty

---

[172] **rent and firing**   that is, housing and firewood for warmth, cooking etc.---a far more scarce and controlled commodity in England and Europe than in America at this time

tooth, a beggar's purse, and an idle hand be here intolerable, so that person that hath these qualities there is much more abominable.

If therefore God hath given thee a heart to undertake such courses, upon such grounds as bear thee out in all difficulties, *viz.* his glory as a principall, and all other outward good things but as accessories, which peradventure thou shalt enjoy, and it may be not: then thou wilt with true comfort and thankfulness receive the least of his mercies. Whereas on the contrary, men deprive themselves of much happiness, being senseless of greater blessings, and through prejudice smoother up the love and bounty of God, whose name be ever glorified in us, and by us, now and evermore. *Amen.*

FINIS.

[66]

A Postscript.

If any man desire a more ample relation of the State of this Country, before such time as this present relation taketh place, I refer them to the two former printed books: the one published by the President and Council for New England, and the other gathered by the Inhabitants of this present Plantation at Plimouth in New England: Both which books are to be sold by Iohn Bellamy, at his shop at the three golden Lions in Corn Hill near the Royal Exchange.[173]

[59][174]

---

[173] These works are most likely "President" Ferdinando Gorges' 1622 *A Brief Relation of the Discovery and Plantation of New England*; and the collection of Plimoth writings called *Mourt's Relation*

[174] The pagination of the copy-text gave this inexplicable number here without explanation or any apparently-missing material. A blank left-hand page followed between this one and "A Brief Relation"

A Brief Relation
of a Credible Intelligence
of the Present Estate
of Virginia

At the earnest entreaty of some of my much respected friends, I have added to the former Discourse, a Relation of such things as were credibly reported at *Plimoth* in *New England* in *September* last past [1623], concerning the present estate of *Virginia*. And because men may doubt how we should have intelligence of their Affairs, being we are so far distant, I will therefore satisfy the doubtful therein.

Captain *Francis West* being in *New England* about the latter end of May past, sailed from thence to *Virginia*, and returned in *August*. In *September* the same Ship and Company being discharged by him at *Damarins*-Cove, came to *New Plimoth*; where, upon our earnest inquiry after of the state of *Virginia* since that bloudy slaughter committed by the *Indians* upon our friends and Countrymen,[175] the whole ship's Company agreed in this, *Viz*.:

That upon all occasions as they chased the *Indians* to and fro, insomuch as they sued daily unto the *English* for peace, who for the present would not admit of any; That Sir *George Early*, &c. was at that

---

[175] **Slaughter**   As noted, Young's *Good News* positions this addendum at the front of Winslow's text. This news reached Plimoth in early summer 1622 (FBH 1: 273; and Introduction Part 4).

In March 1622 the so-called Powhatan Confederacy "rose up" in a day and killed 347 colonists. An overview and bibliograpy are in Trigger, ed., Vol. 15, *Handbook*. Young (279): "a war of extermination immediately ensued." See Bancroft quoted in Adams (144 here), and Jennings' *Invasion* (79), which cites a rarely-seen 1622 "complaint" by Virginian "Captain Butler," "The Unmasked Face of Our Colony...." Butler attested that "not fewer than Tenn thousand soules [were] transported thither," and that through "abuses and neglects" by Virginia Company, there remained "above Two thousand of them att the present to be found alive." Jennings: "If Indians deserved a bad name because of the 347, what might the Virginia Company's gentlemen deserve to be called for the other 7,600?"

present employed upon service against them; That amongst many others, *Opachancano* the chief Emperour [ )(2]¹⁷⁶ <u>was supposed to</u> be slain, his son also was killed at the <u>same time</u>.

And though by reason of these forenamed <u>broiles in</u> the fore-part of the year, the *English* had under<u>gone</u> great want of food; yet through God's mercy there <u>was</u> n<u>e</u>ver more shew of plenty, having as much and as good Corn on the ground as ever they had; neither was the hopes of their *Tobacco* crop inferior to that of their Corn. So that the Planters were never more full of encouragement; which I pray God long to continue, and so to direct both them and us, as his glory may be the principall aim and end of all our Actions, and that for his mercy's sake, AMEN.

FINIS.

---

¹⁷⁶ These reversed parentheses and number "2" between the boldface brackets were the only pagination provided for the two pages of this addendum. **NOTE:** The <u>underscored</u> words and letters in the remaining text were *written in by hand* in the copy text

WILLIAM BRADFORD, from
OF PLIMOTH PLANTATION (1630-1647)

William Bradford (1589-1657) was born at Austerfield in England's Yorkshire county, the son of "a prosperous yeoman" (Willison 45) who farmed his own lands to a "considerable" inheritance (Young 486). But William's father grew ill and died, so the youth was brought up by aunts, uncles and grandparents in their village ways based in farming and husbandry. Bradford himself was often unwell as a child, though his adult years were increasingly robust. Without formal schooling, he had a lifelong interest in languages: as a colonist he needed French and Dutch, but he early took up Latin, Greek and Hebrew to enrich his readings in The Bible and matters of religion.

By age 12, these interests had cost Bradford some criticism for his "reformist" affiliations. They also drew him to the ministry of Richard Clyfton, whose comments on Anglican Church policies and "Old England's" folk-culture (such as "sports on the green" on Sundays, Whitsun Ales, maypoles, saints' days, etc.) inspired listeners with his call for change. This demand to "purify" official Church and English life of Catholic and "pagan" influences, and to "reverte" churches to "anciente puritie...order, libertie, and bewtie" [FBH1:3], had inspired the pejorative "puritan." Through Clyfton, Bradford met intellectual and "postmaster of Scrooby" William Brewster, already dissenting voice; and from here on, while they shared fortunes, Bradford always consulted his elder for advice.

Elizabeth I died in 1603, and successor King James I held the Hampton Court Conference the next year to address disputes growing worse across the realm. But James I's ideas did not include the more democratic demands of church participants. His famous outburst---"I will make them conform, or I will harry them out of the land"---set the tone of years to come. According to Westbrook and others, Bradford found inspiration in the eloquent John Robinson (and he was influenced by them in turn). And as they all became identified with what the Crown called the "very dangerous" Brownists (followers of Robert Browne), they found themselves facing arrests, fines, imprisonment or exile. Together, Bradford and "the Scrooby Congregation" chose the latter by 1608, and escaped to Amsterdam to shelter in its more liberal environment.

Though Bradford's group found the Continent "godly...and strongly flowing with abundance," their lives had not prepared them for urban life and labor, and as their group evolved ideologically, they saw "the grimme and grisly face of povertie coming upon them," as well as their children coming to practical terms with the Low Countries. Moving to Leyden, where Bradford married Dorothy May, Bradford and Brewster, newcomer Winslow and others managed to set up a press. In time, their publications brought legal pursuit of Brewster; and at last the "Pilgrims" began to look abroad. Whatever sources they consulted about "Virginia"---and at the time, English conceptions of "Indians" were still generally "optimistic" (Pennington)---they came to imagine peoples there as "cruell, barbarous, and most trecherous...furious in their rage, and merciles wher they overcome; not being contente only to kill...but delight[ing] in torment" (FBH1: 57).

They found passage via the struggling Virginia Company and its circle of "merchant-adventurers" including church-friend Robert Cushman. Investors wanted disciplined colonists. Negotiations were intense over harsh terms, breaking off several times and causing delays with tragic consequences. Merchant Thomas Weston proved instrumental, yet this became "the ground of discontent between them." By departure in September 1620, a larger company of "Strangers" joined the voyage---secular-minded planters without "The Pilgrims'" Christian ardor. Pastor John Robinson was not allowed to emigrate, and died (1625) before it could be arranged. With 102 passengers crowded aboard, and far less supply because *Mayflower*'s sister-ship *Speedwell* had proven unseaworthy, they reached Cape Cod only to face the worst of New England winter. Half of their number had died by Spring 1621; and both Bradford's and Winslow's narratives commence from that time. The Introduction provides more detail on Bradford's and Plimothers' next experiences.

Bradford served Plimoth for 30 years as governor. According to Westbrook, he began his *History* in 1630. At his death he was "the richest...in the colony" (Willison 338). Bradford also wrote "sundrie verses" in his late years; two "Dialogues" on religious issues, a "Memoir" on Brewster (rpts. in Young); and scores of letters gathered in his *Letter Book* and other collections.

OF PLIMOTH PLANTATION

[c. August 1621][177] Soon...ye great people of ye Narigansets, in a braving manner, sent a messenger unto [Plimoth] with a bundle of arrows tied about with a great snake-skin; which their interpreters told them was a threatening and a challenge. Upon which ye Governour, with the advice of others, sent them a round answer; That if they had rather have war than peace, they might begin when they would: neither did they fear them, nor should they find them unprovided. And, by another messenger, [they] sent ye snake-skin back with bullets in it; but they would not receive it, but sent it back again. But **[133]** these things I do but mention, because they are more at large already put forth in print by Mr. Winslow, at ye request of some friends.

And it is like[ly] the reason was their own ambition, who, since the death of so many of the Indians, thought to domineer and lord it over the rest, and conceived the English would be a bar in their way; and saw that Massasoit took shelter already under their[178] wings.

But this made them the more carefully look to themselves, so as they agreed to enclose their dwellings with a good strong pale, and make flankers in convenient places, with gates to shut, which were every night locked, and a watch kept, and when need required there was also warding

---

[177] The copy-text for these excerpts from the *History* is the transcription of Bradford's manuscript published in 1898 (Boston: Wright & Potter) for the Massachusetts Secretary of State. I have compared this with the edition by Ford *et als* and Massachusetts Historical Society (Boston: Houghton Mifflin 1912, 2 vols.) and the excerpt begins at FBH1:240. These pages are modernized according to the Introduction's General Editing Note. Because Bradford's narrative is sometimes interspersed with letters from friends and other documents irrelevant to "The Weymouth Affair," those are the *only* passages omitted, as indicated below

[178] **their**   Plimoth's

in the daytime. And the company was by the Captain and the Governour's advise, divided into 4 squadrons, and every one had their quarter appointed them, unto which they were to repair upon any sudden alarm. And if there should be any cry of fire, a company were appointed for a guard, with muskets, whilst others quenched the same, to prevent Indian treachery. This was accomplished very cheerfully, and the town impaled round by the beginning of March [1621], in which every family had a pretty garden plot secured....

[1622]   At ye spring of the year they had appointed ye Massachusets to come again and trade with them, and began now to prepare for that voyage about ye latter end of March. But upon some rumors heard, Hobamak, their Indian, told them upon some jealousies he had: he feared [the Massachusets] were joined with ye Narighansets and might betray them if they were not careful. He intimated also some jealousy of Squanto [Tisquantum], by what he gathered from some private whisperings between him and other Indians. But they resolved to proceed, and sent out their shallop with 10 of their chief men about the beginning of April, and both Squanto [135] and Hobamak with them, in regard of ye jealousy between them.

But they had not been gone long, when an Indian belonging to Squanto's family came running in seeming great fear, and told them that many of ye Narihgansets, with Corbytant, and he thought also Massasoyte, were coming against them; and he got away to tell them, not without danger. And being examined by ye Governour, he made as if they were at hand, and would still be looking back, as if they were at his heels. At which the Governour caused them to take arms and stand on their guard; and supposing the boat to be still within hearing (by reason it was calm), caused a warning piece or two to be shot off, the which they heard and came in.

But no Indians appeared: watch was kept all night, but nothing was seen. Hobamak was confident for Massasoyt, and thought all was false; yet ye Governour caused him to send his wife privately, to see what she could observe (pretending other occasions). But there was nothing found, but all was quiet.

After this they proceeded on their voyage to ye Massachusets, and had good trade, and returned in safety, blessed be God.

But by the former passages, and other things of like nature, they began to see that Squanto sought his own ends, and played his own game, by putting the Indians in fear, and drawing gifts from them to enrich him self; making them believe he could stir up war against whom he would, and make peace for whom [136] he would. Yea, he made them believe they kept ye plague buried in the ground, and could send it amongst whom they would, which did much terrify the Indians, and made them depend more on him, and seek more to him than to Massasoyte. Which procured him envy, and had like to have cost him his life. For, after the discovery of his practices, Massasoyt sought it, both privately and openly; which caused him to stick close to the English, and [he] never durst go from them till he died.

They also made good use of the emulation that grew between Hobamack and him, which made them carry more squarely. And the Governour seemed to countenance the one, and the Captain the other, by which they had better intelligence, and made them both more diligent.

Now in a manner their provisions were wholly spent, and they looked hard for supply, but none came....[137]....[179]

Thus all their hopes in regard of Mr. Weston were layed in ye dust, and all his promised help turned into an empty advice, which they apprehended was neither lawful nor profitable for them to follow. And they were not only thus left destitute of help in their extreme wants, having neither vittles, nor any thing to trade with; but others prepared and ready to glean up what ye country might have afforded for their relief.

As for those harsh censures and suspicions intimated in ye former and the following letters, they desired to judge as charitably and wisely of them as they could, weighing them in the balance of love and reason; and

---

[179] At this point Bradford inserts a number of letters from their financial backers, the Merchant Adventurers; whose "parsimonie" and expectation of immediate profits, Weston reports, is the reason that they will send no supplies. "They will do great matters when they hear great news [and] Nothing before," Weston reports as their policy [138]. This excerpt resumes immediately after the last Weston letter given by Bradford [146]

though they (in part) came from godly and loving friends, yet they
conceived many things might arise from over deep jealousy and fear,
together with unmeet provocations. Though they well saw Mr. Weston
pursued his own ends, and was embittered in spirit. For after the receipt of
the former letters, the Governour received one from Mr. Cushman[180]:

> *Beloved Sir:*
>
> *I heartily salute you, with trust of your health, and*
> *many thanks for your love....*
>
> *I purpose by God's grace to see your shortly, I hope in June*
> *next, or before. In ye mean space, know these things, and I pray you*
> *be advertised a little:*
>
> *Mr. Weston hath quite broken off from our company,*
> *through some discontents that arose betwixt him and some of our*
> *Adventurers; and hath sold all his adventures, and hath now sent*
> *3 small ships for his perticuler plantation. The greatest whereof,*
> *being 100 ton, Mr. Reynolds goeth [as] Master, and [Weston] with*
> *the rest purposeth to come him self; for what end I know not.*
>
> *The people which they carry are no men for us, wherefore*
> *I pray you entertain them not, neither exchange man for*
> *man with them, except it be some of your worst. [Weston]*
> *hath taken out a patent for him self.*
>
> *If they offer to buy anything of you, let it be such as you*
> *can spare, and let them give ye worth of it. If they borrow any*
> *thing of you, [147] let them leave a good pawn, &c. It is like*
> *he will plant to ye southward of ye Cape, for William Trevore*
> *hath lavishly told but what he knew or imagined of Capawack, Mohiggen,*
> *and ye Narigansets.*

---

[180] **Robert Cushman**   one of the earliest Merchant Adventurer friends of Robinson's,
Brewster's and Bradford's group of "Pilgrims," who met them in Leyden and sailed with them in
1620 but was turned back with the leaking ship *Speedwell*. As an agent of the Adventurers he
came on the 1621 *Fortune* (see Winslow's first page), and returned with that ship, intending
return in 1624; but he died that December. At Plimoth, he wrote "Of the State of the Colony, and
the Need of Public Spirit in the Colonists" and "The Sin and Danger of Self-Love" (rpts. in
Young)

I fear these people will hardly deal so well with ye
savages as they should. I pray you therefore signify to Squanto
that they are a distinct body from us, and we have nothing to do
with them, neither must be blamed for their faults, much less can
warrant their fidelity....

I hope all will turn to ye best, wherefore I pray you
be not discouraged, but gather up yourself to go through
these difficulties cheerfully and with courage in that place
wherein God hath set you, until ye day of refreshing come.
And the Lord God of sea and land bring us comfortably
together again, if it may stand with his glory.
Yours, Robert Cushman[181]

All these things they pondered and well considered, yet concluded
to give his men friendly entertainment; partly in regard of Mr. Weston him
self, considering what he had been unto them, and done for them, and to
some, more especially; and partly in compassion to ye people, who were
now come into a wilderness (as them selves were), and were by the ship to
be presently put ashore (for she was to carry other passengers to Virginia,
who lay at great charge); and they were altogether unacquainted and knew
not what to do.

So as they had received [Weston's] former company of 7 men, and
vittled them as their own hitherto, so they also received these, being about
60 lusty men; and gave housing for them selves and their goods; and many
being sick, they had the best means the place could afford them. They
stayed here the most part of the summer [1622], till the ship came back
again from Virginia. Then, by his direction, or those whom he set over
them, they removed into ye Massachusset Bay, he having got a patent for

---

[181] Elided is a second letter [148-9] from John Pierce (associate of the Virginia Company)
concerned with the Pierce Patent; through which Plimoth hoped to restore their right to plant,
made "void and useless" when they landed in New England instead of "Southern Virginia"
(documents in FBH1: 234, 246). Pierce noted that "as for Mr. Weston's company, I think them so
base in condition (for ye most part) as in all appearance not fit for an honest man's company. I
wish they prove otherwise...." Bradford's text resumes directly after the letter [149]

some part there (by light of some former discovery in letters sent home). Yet they left all their sick folk here till they were settled and housed. But of their victuals they had not **[149]** any, though they were in great want, nor any thing else in recompense of any courtesy done them; neither did they desire it, for they saw they were an unruly company, and had no good government over them, and by disorder would soon fall into wants if Mr. Weston came not the sooner amongst them; and therefore, to prevent all after occasion, would have nothing of them....[182]

This summer [1622] they built a fort with good timber, both strong and comely, which was of good defense, made with a flat roof and battlements, on which their ordnance were mounted, and where they kept constant watch, especially in time of danger. It served them also for a meeting house, and was fitted accordingly for that use. It was a great work for them in this weakness and time of wants; but the danger of ye time required it, and both the continual rumours of ye fears from ye Indians here, especially ye Narigansets, and also the hearing of that great massacre in Virginia, made all hands willing to despatch the same.

Now ye welcome time of harvest approached, in which all had their hungry bellies filled. But it arose but to a little, in comparison of a full year's supply; partly by reason they were not yet well acquainted with ye manner of Indian corn (and they had no other), also their many other employments; but chiefly their weakness for want of food, to tend it as they should have done.

Also much was stolen both by night and day, before it became scarce eatable, and much more afterward. And though many were well whipped (when they were taken) for a few ears of corn, yet hunger made others (whom conscience did not restrain) to venture. So as it well

---

[182] Bradford's next 1½ pages describe the arrival of a small supply boat that "upheld them till harvest. It arose but to a quarter of a pound of bread a day to each person...." It also brought a short letter "from a stranger" John Huddleston, captain of a fishing vessel; which told of the Native "Powhatan Confederacy" uprising against English plantations in Virginia. In March 1622 one day's attacks killed 347 colonists (in this letter, "such a blow that 400 persons large will not make good our losses"). "Happy is he whom other men's harms doth make to beware." Bradford's narrative resumes from [152] with more events of 1622

appeared that famine must still ensue ye next year also, if not some way prevented, or supply should fail, to which they durst not trust. Markets there were none to go to, but **[153]** only ye Indians, and they had no trading commodities.

Behold now another providence of God: a ship comes into ye harbor, one Captain Jones being chief therein.[183] They were set out by some merchants to discover all ye harbors between this and Virginia, and ye shoulds of Cape Cod, and to trade along ye coast where they could. This ship had store of English-beads (which were then good trade) and some knives, but would sell none but at dear rates, and also a good quantity together. Yet they were glad of the occasion, and fain to buy at any rate: they were fain to give after ye rate of cento per cento, if not more, and yet pay away coat-beaver at 3s. per, which in a few years after yielded 20s. By this means they were fitted again to trade for beaver and other things, and intended to buy what corn they could....[184]

Shortly after harvest, Mr. Weston's people, who were now seated at ye Massachusets, and by disorder (as it seems) had made havoc of their provisions, began now to perceive that want would come upon them. And hearing that they here had bought trading commodities and intended to trade for corn, they write to ye Governour and desired they might join with them, and they would employ their small ship in ye service; and further requested either to lend or sell them so much of their trading commodities as their part might come to, and they would undertake to make payment when Mr. Weston, or their supply, should come.

The Governour condescended upon equal terms of agreement, thinking to go about ye Cape to ye southward with ye ship, where some store of corn might be got. All things being provided, Captain Standish

---

[183] **Captain Jones**   This is the Jones in Winslow's *Good News* (Note 91) who according to Council For New England records, by December 1621 stood accused of robbing and attempting to kidnap Nauset Native Americans. While adding citations on Jones' full career, editors of FBH1: 276-7 note that the Nausets "fortunately escaped"

[184] Bradford's page 153 "take[s] liberty to make a little digression" to include a friend's unrelated, short personal letter. Then on [154] he resumes as follows

was **[155]** appointed to go with them, and Squanto for a guide and interpreter, about ye latter end of September [1622]. But ye winds put them in again, and putting out the second time, he fell sick of a fever; so ye Governour went him self.

But they could not get about ye shoals of Cape Cod, for flats and breakers; neither could Squanto direct them better, nor ye Master durst venture any further. So they put into Manamoyack Bay and got what they could there. In this place Squanto fell sick of an Indian fever, bleeding much at the nose (which ye Indians take for a symptom of death), and within a few days, died there; desiring ye Governour to pray for him, that he might go to ye Englishmen's God in heaven; and bequeathed sundry of his things to sundry of his English friends, as remembrances of his love; of whom they had a great loss.

They got in this voyage, in one place and other, about 26 or 28 hogsheads of corn and beans, which was more than ye Indians could well spare in these parts; for they set but a little till they got English hoes. And so were fain to return, being sorry they could not get about the Cape, to have been better laden. Afterward ye Governour took a few men and went to ye inland places, to get what he could, and to fetch it home at ye spring, which did help them something.

After these things, in February [1623], a messenger came from John Sanders, who was left chief over Mr. Weston's men in ye bay of Massachusets; who brought a **[155]** letter shewing the great wants they were fallen into; and he would have borrowed a hogshead of corn of ye Indians, but they would lend him none. He desired advice whether he might not take it from them by force to succor his men till he came from ye eastward, whither he was going.[185]

The Governour and rest dissuaded him by all means from it, for it might so exasperate the Indians as might endanger their safety, and all of us might smart for it; for they had already heard how they had so wronged the Indians by stealing their corn, &c. as they were much incensed against

---

[185] **eastward**   that is, to Monhegan or other customary anchorages for fishing vessels

them. Yea, so base were some of their own company, as they went and told the Indians that their Governour was purposed to come and take their corn by force. The which with other things made them enter into a conspiracy against ye English, of which more in ye next. Herewith I end this year.

Anno Dom: 1623

It may be thought strange that these people should fall to these extremities in so short a time, being left, competently provided when ye ship left them, and had an addition by that moiety of corn that was got by trade, besides much they got of ye Indians where they lived, by one means and other. It must needs be their great disorder, for they spent excessively whilst they had, or could get it; and, it may be, wasted part away among ye Indians (for he that was their chief [157] was taxed by some amongst them for keeping Indian women, how truly I know not).

And after they began to come into wants, many sold away their clothes and bed coverings: others (so base were they) became servants to ye Indians, and would cut them wood and fetch them water, for a cap full of corn. Others fell to plain stealing, both night and day, from ye Indians, of which they grievously complained. In the end, they came to that misery that some starved and died with cold and hunger. One, in gathering shellfish, was so weak as he stuck fast in ye mud, and was found dead in ye place.

At last most of them left their dwellings and scattered up and down in ye woods, and by ye watersides, where they could find ground nuts and clams, here six and there ten. By which their carriages they became contemned and scorned of ye Indians, and they began greatly to insult over them in a most insolent manner: insomuch, many times as they lay thus scattered abroad, and had set on a pot with ground nuts or shellfish, when it was ready the Indians would come and eat it up; and when night came, whereas some of them had a sorry blanket, or such like, to lappe themselves in, the Indians would take it and let ye other lie all night in the cold; so as their condition was very lamentable.

Yea, in the end they were fain to hang one of their men, whom they could not reclaim from stealing, to give ye Indians content. **[157]**

Whilst things went in this manner with them, ye Governour and people here had notice that Massasoyte their friend was sick and near unto death. They sent to visit him, and withall sent him such comfortalbe things as gave him great content, and was a means of his recovery; upon which occasion he discovers ye conspiracy of these Indians, how they were resolved to cut off[186] Mr. Weston's people, for the continual injuries they did them, and would now take opportunity of their weakness to do it; and for that end had conspired with other Indians their neighbors thereabout. And thinking the people here would revenge their death, they therefore thought to do ye like by them, and had solicited him to join with them. He advised them therefore to prevent it, and that speedily by taking of some of ye chief of them, before it was too late, for he assured them of ye truth hereof.

This did much trouble them, and they took it into serious deliberation, and found upon examination other evidence to give light hereunto, too long here to relate. In ye mean time, came one of them from ye Massachucts,[187] with a small pack at his back; and though he knew not a foot of ye way, yet he got safe hither, but lost his way, which was well for him, for he was pursued, and so was missed. He told them here how all things stood amongst them, and that he durst stay no longer, he apprehended they (by what he observed) would be all knocked in ye head shortly. **[158]**

This made them make ye more haste, and dispatched a boat away with Captain Standish and some men, who found them in a miserable condition, out of which he rescued them, and helped them to some relief; cut off some few of ye chief conspirators, and, according to his order, offered to bring them all hither if they thought good; and they should fare no worse than them selves, till Mr. Weston or some supply came to them.

---

[186] **cut off**   kill

[187] **one of them**   most likely, Phineas Pratt. Introduction Part 4

Or, if any other course liked them better, he was to do them any helpfulness he could.

They thanked him and ye rest. But most of them desired he would help them with some corn, and they would go with their small ship to ye eastward, where haply they might hear of Mr. Weston, or some supply from him, seeing ye time of the year was for fishing ships to be in ye land. If not, they would work among ye fishermen for their living, and get their passage into England, if they heard nothing from Mr. Weston in time.

So they shipped what they had of any worth, and he got them all ye corn he could (scarce leaving to bring him home), and saw them well out of ye bay, under sail at sea. And so [Captain Standish] came home, not taking ye worth of a penny of any thing that was theirs. I have but touched these things briefly, because they have already been published in print more at large.

This was ye end of these that some time boasted of their strength (being all able lusty men), and what **[159]** they would do and bring to pass, in comparison of ye people here, who had many women and children and weak ones amongst them; and said at their first arrival, when they saw the wants here, that they would take an other course, and not to fall into such a condition as this simple people were come to.

But a man's way is not in his own power: God can make ye weak to stand. Let him also that standeth take heed lest he fall.

PHINEHAS PRATT (1662),
A DECLARATION OF THE AFFAIRS
OF THE ENGLISH PEOPLE
THAT FIRST INHABITED NEW ENGLAND

[*Introduction from Mass. Historical Society Collections*][188]

Phinehas [*a.k.a.* Phineas] Pratt was one of a company of about sixty, who were sent to Massachusetts to found a Colony by Thomas Weston, a London merchant, who was first a friend, and then a rival, of the Plymouth Colony. His patent is not known to be extant.

Pratt, with nine others, sailed from England in the *Sparrow*, which arrived at Damariscove Islands, in May, 1622. Here he, with others, left the vessel, in a shallop, and, after touching at several places on the coast, landed, in the latter part of May, at Plymouth. About the first of July, the *Charity* and the *Swan*, two other vessels sent out by Weston, also arrived; and subsequently a party left Plymouth in the *Swan*, and commenced the settlement at Wessaguscus, in the present town of Weymouth. Pratt was one of this company.

The head man of this Colony was Richard Greene, a brother-in-law of Weston; but he, dying on a subsequent visit to Plymouth, was succeeded by John Sanders. These settlers began "with little provision." [According to Capt. Christopher Levett's 1628 *Voyage into New England*, Chap. 5], "They neither applied themselves to planting of corn, nor taking of fish, more than for their present use; but went about to build castles in the air, and making of forts, neglecting the plentiful time of fishing. When winter came, their forts would not keep out hunger, and they, having no provision before hand, and

---

[188] The copy-text of this Introduction, its citations, and of Pratt's narrative are in *Massachusetts Historical Society Collections*, 4 ser. IV (1858), 474-487. That constitutes the only known complete printing of Pratt's narrative. This Introduction's author is identified only as "R. F., Jr." and this editor has been unable to identify the person by this printing

wanting both powder and shot, to kill deer and fowl, many were starved to death, and the rest hardly escaped."

The survivors of this Colony were then really in the power of the natives; and they were indebted to the courage, adroitness and endurance of Phinehas Pratt, for their deliverance and their lives. In the winter of 1623, the Indians matured a plan to cut off the English, both at Wessaguscus and Plymouth, in one day. Pratt, then about thirty-two years of age, had seen some of his companions die of starvation; and learning, in his intercourse with the Indians, of this scheme of massacre for the rest, resolved to send intelligence of it to Plymouth. When all refused to go, he determined to go himself; and by deceiving the savages, effected his escape. Though closely pursued, and suffering much in body and mind, he made good his way to Plymouth, which he reached on the 24th of March, 1623. His story corresponded with intelligence already received from Massasoit [according to "Deane's Bradford, p. 131"]; and hence Standish and his party, on the next day, started on the expedition which resulted in inflicting on Pecksuot and Wittewamut the doom which they had in store for the English, and in saving the remnant of the Colony.

Pratt was too much exhausted to accompany Standish. On regaining strength, he went to Piscataqua, and was in skirmishes with the natives at Agawam and at Dorchester.[189] Hence he sums up his early perils by saying: "Three times we fought with them; thirty miles I was pursued for my life, in a time of frost and snow, as a deer chased by wolves."

Pratt settled at Plymouth, and is termed "a joiner." In 1630 he married...and his name, as inhabitant, occurs in the records as a freeman, rate payer, and grantee of lands, for many years. He is classed with the "Old Comers" and "Purchasers."

[As New England historian Mike McWade points out, Pratt's petition and narrative come to light in the years just after the deaths of "The Weymouth Affair's" other main participants: Winslow died in 1655, Standish in 1656, and Bradford in 1657.---Dempsey ed.]

....The same records have the following grant, under the date of June 5, 1658:---"Liberty was granted by the Court, unto Phinehas Pratt, or any for him, to look out a parcel or tract of land and to accommodate him and his posterity withal, together with other freemen or alone, as he shall think meet, and to make report of the same unto the

---

[189] On these "skirmishes" see the end of Introduction Part 4

Court, that so a considerable proportion thereof may be confirmed unto him." [*Plymouth Records* 3:145]

Before this date, Pratt left Plymouth. In 1648, he purchased the place in Charlestown on which probably he subsequently lived and died. In 1658, his name appears, with other inhabitants, in a division of lands. Four years later, in 1662, he presented to the General Court of Massachusetts what he terms "An History," called [title above]. Under the date of May 7, is the following record:

"In answer to the petition of Phinehas Pratt, of Charlestown, who presented this Court with a narrative of the straits and hardships that the first planters of this Colony underwent, in their endeavors to plant themselves at Plymouth and since, whereof he was one, the Court judge it meet to grant him three hundred acres of land, where it is to be had, not hindering a plantation." This land was laid out "in the wilderness, on the East of Merrimack river, near the upper end of Nacooke Brook."

[Young 332 includes the Court Order describing Pratt's land-grant "near the upper end of Nacook Brook, on the southeast of it."---Dempsey, ed.]

....[Pratt] died in Charlestown, April 19, 1680, where he was buried.

....The manuscript of Pratt's "Declaration"...consists of three folio sheets, sewn together, one half of which appear to have been torn off after they were thus arranged. Hence a portion is lost. The MS. is torn at the edges, and portions of the writing are obliterated. It is printed [in the *Collections*] as it is written, except as to punctuation, and where this required capital letters....

R. F., Jr.[190]

---

[190] This editor has deleted several passages from Court records included by "R.F. Jr." concerning Pratt's affairs from house-servants to land petitions; transcription of his inscribed tombstone, his "Petition of 1668" and a 3 1/2-page version of his story by Increase Mather.

Pratt's 1658 "Petition" includes this statement: "I am one of that little number, ten men that arrived in Massachusetts Bay for the settling of a Plantation, and am the remainder of the forlorn hope sixty men [*sic*]. We bought the south part of the Bay of Aberdecest their Sachem. Ten of our company died of famine. Then said the Natives of the Country, Let us kill them, whilst they are weak, or they will possess our Country, and drive us away. Three times we fought with them, thirty miles I was pursued for my life, in time of frost, and snow, as a deer chased with wolves. Two of our men were killed in war, one shot in the shoulder. It was not by the wit of man, nor by the strength of the arm of flesh, that we prevailed against them. But God, that overrules all power, put fear in their hearts....Now in times of prosperity, I beseech you consider the day of small things; for I was almost frozen in time of our weak beginnings, and now am lame. My humble request is for that may be for my subsistance, the remaining time of my life. And I shall be obliged, Your thankful servant...."

TEXTUAL NOTE: I have modernized Pratt's very erratic and difficult spellings and syntax according to the Introduction's General Editing Note. Ellipses (...) indicate precisely what

A Declaration of the Affairs
of the English People
that First Inhabited New England

In the Time of Spiritual darkness, when the State Ecclesiastic...Rome ruled and over ruled most of the nations of Europe, it plea...to give wisdom to many, kings and people, in breaking that spiritual yo...; yet, notwithstanding, there arose great strife among such people that are known by the name of Protestants[191], in many cases concerning the worship of God; but the greatest and strongest number of men commonly prevailed against the smaller and lesser number. At this time the honored States of Holland gave more liberty in cases of Religion than could be enjoyed in some other places. Upon which diverse good Christians removed the...dwellings into the Low Countries. **[476]**

Then one Company dwelt in the city of Leyden, being not well able outwardly to subsist, took counsel and agreed to remove into America, into some port northward of Virginia. Ye Dutch people offered them divers conditions to supply them with things necessary if they would live under the government of their State, but they refused it. This they did that all men might know the Intier[192] Love they bore to their King and Country; for in them their was never found any lack of Lifill obedience. They sent to their friends in England to let them understand what they intended to do. Then divers ffr...Disbursed some moneys for the furthering of so good a work.

---

the *Collections* editor term "obliterated" words and phrases in the original manuscript. Boldface numbers refer to pages of the *Collection's* edition

[191] **Protestants** original spelling of this word was "prodastonce"

[192] **Intier** poss. an error for "entire." In the next line, **Lifill** may signify "lawful" or "loyal"

It is ff...to be understood that, in the year 1618, there appeared a blazing star over Germany that made the wise men of Europe astonished there...

Speedily after, near about that time, these people begun to propose Removal. They agreed that their strongest and ablest men should go...to provide for their wives and children. Then coming into England, they set forward in two ships, but their lesser ship sprung a leak and returned ...England; the bigger ship arrived at Cape Cod, 1620, it being winter, then called New England but formerly called Canidy.[193]

They sent forth their boat upon discovery. Their boat being returned to their ship, they removed into the bay of Plimoth and begun their planta ...by the River of Patuxet. Their ship being returned and safely arrived in England, those Gentlemen and Merchants that had undertaken to supply them with things necessary, understanding that many of them were sick and some dead, made haste to send a ship with many things necessary; but some indiscreet men, hoping to encourage their friends to come to them, wrote letters concerning the great plenty of fish, fowl and deer, not considering that ye wild Salvages were many times hungry, that have a better skill to catch such things than English men have. The Adventurers, willing to save their moneys, sent them weekly provided of victuals, as many more after them did the like; and that was the great cause of famine.

At the same time, Mr. Thomas Weston, a merchant of good credit in London that was then their treasurer, which had disbursed much of his money for the good of New England, sent forth a ship for the settling a plantation in the Massa- 477] chusetts Bay. But wanting a pilot, we arrived at Damoralls Cove. The men that belong[ed] to the ship, there fishing, had newly set up a may pole and were very merry.

We made haste to prepare a boat fit for coasting. Then said Mr. Rodgers, Master of our ship, "Here are many ships, and at Munhigin, but no man that doth undertake to be your pilot; for they say that an Indian called Runhigin undertook to pilot a boat to Plimoth, but they all lost their

---

[193] **Canidy**   an English rendering of "Canada"

lives."[194] Then said Mr. Gibbs, Master's Mate of our ship, "I will venture my life with them." At this time of our discovery, we first arrived at Smith's Islands, first so called by Captain Smith at the time of his discovery of New England,...fterwards called [The] Isles of Shoals; from thence to Cape Anne, so called by Captain Mason[195]; from thence to ye Mathechusits Bay. There we continued 4 or 5 days.

Then we perceived that on the south part of the Bay were fewest of the natives of the Country dwelling there. We thought best to begin our plantation, but fearing a great Company of Salvages, we being but 10 men, thought it best to see if our friends were living at Plimoth. Then sailing along the coast, not knowing the harbor, they shot off a piece of ordnance, and at our coming ashore, they entertained us with 3 volley of shots.

Their second ship was returned to England before we came to them.[196] We asked them where the rest of our friends were that came in the first ship. They said that God had taken them away by death, and that before their second ship came, they were so distressed with sickness that they, fearing the salvages should know it, had set up their sick men with their muskets upon their rests and their backs leaning against trees.

At this time, one or two of them went with us in our vessel to ye place of fishing to buy victuals. 8 or 9 weeks after this, two of our ships arrived at Plimoth---the lesser of our 3 ships **[478]** continued in the Country with us.[197] Then we made haste to settle our plantation in the Massachusets bay---our number being near sixty men.

At the same time there was a great Plague among the salvages, and, as themselves told us, half their people died thereof. The Natives called

---

[194] This seems to be the only recorded mention of "Runhigin" and this minor voyage

[195] **Captain John Mason**   a colleague of The Council for New England's leading investor Sir Ferdinando Gorges. He served as "governor" of the "swarming fishermen" c. 1620-21 and continued to promote colonies till his death in 1636. See Demsey, *Canaan* 96

[196] Refers (like the following) to Plimoth's first year (1620-21)

[197] *The Sparrow*

the place of our plantation Wesaguscasit. Near unto it is a town of later time called Weymouth.

The Salvages seemed to be good friends with us while they feared us, but when they saw famine prevail, they begun to insult, as appeareth by the sequel. For one of their Pennesses or Chief men, called Pexsouth, applied himself to learn to speak English, observing all things for his bloody ends.[198]

He told me he loved English men very well, but he loved me best of all. Then he said, "You say French men do not love you, but I will tell you what we have done to them.

"There was a ship broken by a storm. They saved most of their goods and hid it in the ground. We made them tell us where it was. Then we made them our servants. They weept much. When we parted[199] them, we gave them such meat as our dogs eat.

"One of them had a book he would often read in. We asked him, 'What his book said.' He answered, 'It saith, there will a people, like French men, come into this Country and drive you all away, and now we think you are they.[200] We took away their clothes. They lived but a little while. One of them lived longer than the rest, for he had a good master and [he?] gave him a wife. He is now dead, but hath a son alive.

"Another ship came into the bay with much goods to truck. And I said to the Sachem, 'I will tell you how you shall have all for nothing. Bring all our canoes and all our Beaver and a great many men, but no bow

---

[198] **Pexsouth** is original text: likely **Pecksuot.** a *pneise* of the Massachusetts

[199] **parted**   poss. "when we distributed them among our own groups" (*Canaan* 19 for ex.)

[200] This confusion is not helped by the fact that Pratt and/or *Collections* editor "R.F. Jr." failed to mark the exact end of the Frenchman's words and the resumption of Pecksuot's. (The only provided pair of double-quotation-marks do not close until [480].) As is, the passage may mean that the Frenchman speaking within Pecksuot's story "now" thinks the Massachusetts are the Native people to be driven away. Or, the Frenchman's prediction that people "like" himself will drive them away causes *them* to respond: "Now we think you [the French speaking, must be] they [the very ones you predict]." A third possibility is that Pecksuot, the Native speaker of this whole passage, told *Pratt himself* that the Massachusetts believed the English planters were come to fulfill the earlier French prediction of their own disposession

nor arrow, clubs nor hatchets, but knives under ye skins that about our loins. Throw up much Beaver upon their deck; sell it very cheap, and when I give the word, thrust your knives in the French men's bellies.'

"Thus we killed them all. But Monsieur Finch, Master of their ship, being wounded, leaped into the hold. **[479]** We bid him come up, but he would not. Then we cut their cable and the ship went ashore and lay upon her side and slept there. Finch came up and we killed him. Then our Sachem divided their goods and fired their ship and it made a very great fire."

Some of our Company asked them, "How long it was ago since they first see ships?" They said they could not tell, but they had heard men say [that] ye first ship that they saw, seemed to be a floating Island, as they supposed broken off from the mainland, wrapped together with the roots of trees, with some trees upon it. They went to it with their canoes, but seeing men and hearing guns, they made haste to be gone.[201]

But after this, when they saw famine prevail, Peckworth[202] said, "Why do your men and your dogs die?"

I said, "I had corn for a time of need.[203]Then I filled a chest, but not with corn, and spread corn on...him come, opened the cover and when I was sure he see it, I put dow...as if I would not have him see it."[204]

Then he said "No Indian soe...You have much corn and English men die for want."

---

[201] Another New England tradition records that "some ages past, a number of white men arrived in the [Taunton] river, in a bird; that the white men took Indians into the bird, as hostages; that they took fresh water...at a neighboring spring; that the Indians fell upon and slaughtered the white men at the spring; that, during the affray, thunder and lightning issued from the bird; that the hostages escaped from the bird; and that a spring, now called White Spring...has its name from this event." Qtd. in Simmons, *Spirit* 70

[202] **Peckworth**   likely a mistake for **Pecksuot**, and "corrected" thus below

[203] Editor "R.F. Jr." may have neglected to close the quotation marks at this point, although the next note indicates where the *Collections* text closed them

[204] This and what follows represent the *Collections* ' original use of quotation marks

Then they h...intent to make war they removed some of their houses to th...a great swamp near to the pale of our plantation.

After this yer...a morning I see a man going into one of their houses, weary with traveling and Galded on his feet.[205] Then I said to Mr. Salsbery, our Chirurgeon, surely their Sachem hath employed him for some intent to make war upon us.

Then I took a bag with gunpowder and put it in my pocket, with the top of the bag hanging out,[206] and went to the house where the man was laid upon a mat. The woman of the house took hold of the bag, saying, "What is this so big?"

I said, "It is good for Salvages to eat," and struck her on the arm as hard as I could.

Then she said, "Matchet powder English men, much Matchit.[207] By and by, Abordicis bring Mouch Mans, Mouch Sannups, and kill you and all English men at Wessaguscus and Patuxet."

The man that lay upon the mats, seeing this, was angry and in a great rage, and the woman seemed to be sore afraid. Then I went out of the house, **[480]** and said to a young man that could best understand their language, "Go ask ye woman, but not in ye man's hearing, why the man was angry, and she afraid?"

Our interpreter, coming to me, said, "These are the words of the woman---ye man will...Abordicis what I said and he and all Indians will be angry with me...

This Pecksuot said, "I love you."

I said, "I love you." I said, "I love you as well as you love me."

---

[205] **Galded**   poss. "swollen" as with chancre or "gall"

[206] According to Pratt's use of it below, a small bag with a few musket-balls added makes a weapon something like a blackjack

[207] **Matchet powder...Matchit**   In Captain Levett's "Narrative" (1628: 622), the word *matchett* means "naughtie [or evil] and rebellious"; and *mouch* or *mouchick* means "very," as in *mouchick hoggery*, "very angry." A **sannup** is an "ordinary" man as distinct from a Sachem, Sagamore, or *winnaytue* (a "man of estimation" in *Canaan*).
   Abordicis   likely Pratt's version of the Neponset Massachusett Sachem's name **Aberdecest**, in Winslow called Obtakiest; *a.k.a.*, Chikatawbak/but. (Bowman, McWade)

Then he said, in broken English, "Me hear you can make the likeness of men and women, dogs and deers, in wood and stone. Can you make...[.]"

I said, "I can see a knife in your hand, with an ill-favored face upon the haft."

Then he gave it into my hand to see his workmanship, and said, "This knife cannot see, it cannot hear, it cannot speak, but by and by it can eat. I have another knife at home with a face upon the haft as like a man as this is like a woman. That knife cannot see, it cannot hear, it cannot speak, but it can eat. It hath killed much, French men, and by and by this knife and that knife shall marry and you shall be there...knife at home he had kept for a moniment, from the time they had killed Monsieur Finch;"[208] but as the word went out of his mouth, I had a good will to thrust it in his belly.

He said, "I see you are much angry."

I said, "Guns are longer than knives."

Some time after this their Sachem came suddenly upon us with a great number of armed men; but their spies seeing us in a readiness, he and some of his chief men turned into one of their houses a quarter of an hour. Then we met them without the pale of our plantation and brought them in. Then said I to a young man that could best speak their language, "Ask Pecksuot why they come thus armed."

He answered, "Our Sachem is angry with you."

I said, "Tell him if he be angry with us, we are angry with him."

Then said their Sachem, "English men, when you come into the Country, we gave you gifts and you gave us gifts; we bought and sold with you, and we were friends. And now tell me if I or any of my men have done you wrong."

We answered, "First tell us if we have done you any wrong." **[481]**

---

[208] This use of quotation-marks is as the *Collections* editor provides: perhaps they "should" close after Pecksuot's word *there* in the previous line. Here an *MHSC* footnote refers readers to this same conversation in Winslow's *Good News*

He answered, "Some of you steal our corn, and I have sent you word times without number, and yet our corn is stole. I come to see what you will do."

We answered, "It is one man which hath done it. Your men have seen us whip him divers times, besides other manner of punishments, and now here he is, bound. We give him unto you to do with him what you please."

He answered, "It is not just dealing. If my men wrong my neighbor Sachem, or his men, he sends me word, and I beat or kill my men according to the offense. If his men wrong me or my men, I send him word, and he beats or kills his men according to the offense. All Sachems do justice by their own men. If not, we say They are all agreed,[209] and then we fight; and now I say you all steal my corn."

At this time some of them, seeing some of our men upon our fort, begun to start, saying, "Machit Pesconk," that is, "Naughty guns"---then, looking round about them, went away in a great rage.

At this time we strengthened our watch until we had no food left.

In these times the Salvages oftentime did creep upon the snow, starting behind bushes and trees to see whether we keep watch or not...times I having rounded our plantation until I had no longer...nth; then in the night, going into our court of guard, I see one man dead before me and another at my right hand and another at my left for want of food. O, all ye people of New England that shall hear of these times of our weak beginning, Consider what was the strength of the arm of flesh or the wit of man; therefore, in the times of your greatest distress, put your trust in God.

The offender being bound, we let him loose, because we had no food to give him; charging him to gather ground nuts, clams, and mussels, as other men did, and steal no more. One or two days after this, the salvages brought him, leading him by the arms, saying, "Here is the corn. Come see the place where he stole it."

---

[209] **agreed**   that is, in a scheme together

Then we keep him bound some few days. After this, two of our Company said, "We have been at the Sachem's house, and they have near finished their last canoe, [so] that they may encounter with our ship. Their greatest care is how to send their armies to Plimoth because of the snow."

Then we prepared to meet them there. One of our Company said, "They have killed one of our hogs."**[482]** Another said, "One of them striked (?) at me with his knife"; and others say, "They threw dust in our faces."

Then said Pecksuot to me, "Give me powder and guns and I will give you much corn."

I said, "By and by men bring ships and vittles."

But when we understood that their plot was to kill all English people in one day when the snow was gone, I would have sent a man to Plimoth, but none were willing to go. Then I said, "If Plimoth men know not of this treacherous plot, they and we are all dead men: therefore if God willing, tomorrow I will go."

That night a young man, wanting wit, told Pecksuot, early in the morning.[210] Pecksuot came to me and said in English, "Me hear you go to Patuxet. You will lose yourself. The bears and the wolves will eat you; but, because I love you, I will send my boy Nahamit with you. And I will give you victuals to eat by the way and to be merry with your friends when you come there."

I said, "Who told you so great a lie, that I may kill him."

He said, "It is no lie. You shall not know." Then he went home to his house.

Then came five men armed. We said, "Why come you thus armed."

They said, "We are friends. You carry guns where we dwell, and we carry bow and arrows where you dwell."

These attended me seven or eight days and nights. Then, they supposing it was a lie, were careless of their watch near two hours on the morning. Then said I to our Company, "Now is the time to run to Plimoth.

---

[210] This original sentence may mean, "during the wee hours of night" he was told; or that the man told Pecksuot that Pratt would be leaving "early in the morning"

Is there any compass to be found." They said, "None but them that belong to the ship."

I said, "They are too big. I have borne no arms of defense this seven or eight days. Now if I take my arms they will mistrust me."

Then they said, "The salvages will pursue after you and kill you and we shall never see you again." Thus with other words of great lamentation, we parted.

Then I took a hoe, and went to ye Long Swamp nearby their houses, and digged on the edge thereof, as if I had been looking for ground nuts. But seeing no man, I went in and run through it. Then, looking roundabout me, I run southward till 3 of ye clock, but the snow being in many places, I was the more distressed because of my footsteps. The sun being beclouded, I wandered, not knowing my way; but at the going down of the sun, it appeared red.

Then, hearing a great howling of wolves, I came to a river. The water being deep and cold and many rocks, I passed **[483]** through with much ado. Then was I in great distress---for want of food, weary with running, fearing to make a fire because of them that pursued me.[211] Then I came to a deep dell or hole, there being much wood fallen into it. Then I said in my thoughts, this is God's providence that here I may make a fire. Then, having made a fire, the stars began to appear and I saw Ursa Major and the...pole yet fearing...beclouded.

The day following, I began to travel...but being unable, I went back to the fire the day fall...sun shined and about 3 of the clock I came to that part...Plimoth bay where there is a town of later time...Duxbury. Then passing by the water on my left hand...came to a brook, and there was a path.

Having but a short time to consider...fearing to go beyond the plantation, I kept running in the path. Then passing through James River,[212] I said in my thoughts, Now am I as a deer chased...the wolves. If I

---

[211] It is not clear what or whom this refers to

[212] **James River**   difficult to identify given the number of these between Weymouth and Plimoth: see maps

perish, what will be the condish...of distressed English men. Then finding a piece of a...I took it up and carried it in my hand. Then finding a...of a Jurkin,[213] I carried them under my arm. Then said I in my...God hath given me these two tokens for my comfort; that now he will give me my life for a pray.

Then running down a hill J...an English man coming in the path before me. Then I sat down on a tree and rising up to salute him said, "Mr. Hamdin[214], I am glad to see you alive."

He said, "I am glad and full of wonder to see you alive. Let us sit down, I see you are weary."

I said, "Let...eat some parched corn."

Then he said, "I know the Caus...Come. Massasoit hath sent word to the Governor to let him ( )[215] that Aberdikees[216] and his confederates have contrived a plot hoping...all English people in one day here as men hard by (ma)king canoe...stay and we will go with you."[217]

The next day a young...named Hugh Stacye went forth to fell a tree and see two...rising from the ground. They said, Aberdikees had sent...the **[484]** governor that he might send men to truck for much Beaver; but they would not go. But said,[218] "Was not there an English...come from Wessaguscus." He answered, "He came"...They said he was their friend[219],

---

[213] **Jurkin** a "jerkin" or outer-garment of either heavy cloth or tanned hide

[214] a *Collections* footnote identifies this as the John Hamden with Winslow on his visit to the ailing Massasoit (*Good News*)

[215] this and the following use of parentheses [in the word "(ma)king"] are as in the *Collections* original text

[216] **Aberdikees** presumably Aberdecest/Abordicis/Obtakiest/Chikatawbak

[217] The *Collections* edition does not close the quotation marks: they are inserted here

[218] **but said** poss. this means, "The Native people then further enquired,..."

[219] presumably, The Massachusetts here said that *Pratt* was their "friend"...

and said come and see who...But they turned another way. He said, "You come to let us..."[220]

Providence to us was great in those times as appeareth...after the time of the arrival of the first ship at Pl...fornamed Massasoit came to Plimoth and there made a co...peace, for an Indian called Tisquantum came to them and speak English...They asked him, How he learned to speak English? He said that an Englishman called Captain Hunt came into the harbor pretending to trade for beaver and stole 24 men and their beaver, and carried and sold them in Spain. And from thence with much ado he went into England and from England with much ado he got into his own country. This man told Massasoit what wonders he had seen in England and if he could make English his friends then...Enemies that were too strong for him would be constrained to bow to him; but being prevented by some that came in the first ship that[221]...Recorded that which concerned them I leave it.

Two or three days after my coming to Plimoth, 10 or 11 men went in a boat to our plantation, but I being fanted was not able to go with them. They first gave warning to the master of the ship[222] and then contrived how to make sure of the lives of two of their chief men, Wittiwomitt, of whom they boasted no gun would kill, and Pecksuot, a subtle man. These being slain they fell upon others where they could find them.

Then Abordikees, hearing that some of this men were killed, came to try his manhood. But as they were starting behind bushes and trees, one of them was shot in the arm. At this time an Indian called Hobermack, that formerly had fled from his life from his Sachem to Plimoth, approved himself a valiant man in fighting and pursuing after them.

---

[220] Here the *Collections* original becomes particularly fragmentary and obscure. The text seems to suddenly turn back to earlier New England history (on "Captain Hunt" and others, and to Tisquantum's life, etc.). Pratt's narrative resumes in the following paragraph

[221] Appears to refer to Massasoit's rivalries with Narragansett people just before that "first ship" *Mayflower*. May also suggest that Pratt knew Winslow's and Bradford's writings

[222] **ship** presumably, the *Swan*

Two of our men were killed that they took in their houses at an advantage...this **[485]**time pl...were instruments in the...nds of God for...their own lives and ours. They took the head of...and set it on their fort at Plimoth at...9 (?)[223] of our men were dead with famine and one died in the ship before they came to the place where at that time of year ships came to fish---it being in March. At this time, ships began to fish at ye Islands of Shoals, and I having recovered a little of my...th[224] went to my Company near about this time...

The first plantation at Piscataqua[225] the...thereof was Mr. David Tompson at the time of my arrival (?) at Piscataqua.

Two of Abordikees' men came thither, and seeing me, said, "When we killed your men, they cried and made ill-favored faces."

I said, "When we killed your men, we did not torment them to make ourself (?) merry."

Then we went with our ship into the bay and took from them two shallops' loading of corn, and of their men, prisoners.

There is a town of later time called Dorchester.

The third and last time was in the bay of Agawam. At this time they took for their castle a thick swamp. At this time one of our ablest men was shot in the shoulder. Whether any of them were killed or wounded, we could not tell. There is a town of later time near unto the place, called Ipswich.

Thus...plantation being deserted, Captain Robert Gore cam..the country with six gentlemen attending him and divers men to do his labor, and other men with their families. They took possession of our plantation,

---

[223] the numeral 9 and figure (?) are as in the *Collections* original

[224] again, this is as original; as are the next two examples of (?) within the text

[225] **Piscataqua**   As noted (Introduction), Captain Levett ("Louitt" below) recorded his impressions of Pratt and others at this fishing and trade station just north of Massachusetts. No other record mentions the following actions at "Dorchester" and Agawam

but their ship supply from England came too late. Thus was famine their final overthrow. Most of them that lived returned for England.[226]

The overseers of the third plantation in the bay was Captain Wooliston and Mr. Rosdell. These, seeing the Ruing of the former plantation, said, We will not pitch our tents here, lest we should do as they have done. Notwithstanding these gentlemen were wise men, they seemed to blame the overseers of the former Companies, not considering that God plants and pulls up, builds and pulls down, and turns the wisdom of wise men into foolishness.

These called the name of their place Mount Wooliston. They continued near a year as others had done before them; but famine was their final overthrow.[227] Near unto that place is a town of later time called Brantry [Braintree].

Not long after the overthrow of the **[486]** first plantation in the bay, Captain Louit cam to ye Country. At the time of his being at Pascataway, a Sachem or Sagamore gave two of his men, on to Captain Louit, and another to Mr. Tompson; but on[e] that was there said, "How can you trust these Salvages. Call the name of one, Watt Tylor, and the other, Jack Straw, after the names of the two greatest Rebills that ever were in England."[228]

Watt Tylor said, "When he was a boy, Captain Dormer found him upon an Island in great distress."[229] **[487]**

---

[226] **Captain Robert Gorges**   Pratt now turns to the post-massacre history of Weymouth, when this son of Sir Ferdinando brought in more would-be settlers. They departed within a year, "having scarcely saluted the country" (more in Dempsey, *Thomas Morton*)

[227] A further record of this settlement under Captain Wollaston and Mr. Rasdall, omitted by Pratt, is told in *Canaan* (next)

[228] **Watt Tylor, Jack Straw, English rebels**   These historical/legendary figures date from at least the 1400s; when, as Young 126 notes in his biography of Captain Myles Standish, "a squire" of King Richard II's named "John Standysshe...drewe out his sword, and put [it] into Wat Tyler's belye, and so he dyed"

[229] As noted in Introduction Part 4, Chikatawbak reportedly "gave" a son named Papawhinnet into the care of Andrew (brother of Thomas) Weston, and Council for New England orders dictated his (uncertain) return via trader Leonard Peddock. This "boy" may somehow be confused with Papawhinnet, and the "Captain Dermer" with Peddock

THOMAS MORTON,
from *NEW ENGLISH CANAAN* (1637)

Thomas Morton (1576?-1647?) left behind almost no certain records about himself. Clues suggest that his family came of middling gentry in England's West Country (likely Devonshire), where he received excellent Elizabethan educations in both field sports (such as hunting) and in rhetoric and Classics. Like many gentlemen who had to work for a living, Morton apparently spent time at and/or received a law degree at Clifford's Inn, one of London's Inns of Court, and there took some interest in the intense literary and cultural life that (c. 1590) included Thomas Lodge, young Shakespeare and Ben Jonson.

For about the next 20 years Morton worked as a West Country lawyer and, like many Devon men, become interested in American commercial ventures financed by courtiers such as Sir Ferdinando Gorges. By 1623 Morton had wed a Berkshire widow and then become embroiled in a lawsuit against her stepson: he first appears in New England c. June 1624, under one Captain Wollaston and others (including Humphrey Rasdall, a "manager" of indentured servants) aboard the *Unity*, who came to trade and develop English colonial ventures (records in Holly). When that company dispersed, Morton and a few indentured servants reorganized and renamed their hilltop "Ma-re Mount" (or Merrymount). There in 1627 they staged a MayDay Revel to celebrate and promote their trade (probably including guns) and other relations with Native American peoples and nonPuritan planters; and this, according to Morton, marked the beginning of his long conflict with Plimoth Plantation and, in time, Massachusetts Bay (Boston).

By late 1628 Plimoth had arrested and deported Morton, but no legal action kept him from returning to New England affairs. Meanwhile, more Puritan planters founded Salem and Boston (1628-30), and together they banished him (this time he was hoisted aboard ship under protest). After a perilous winter voyage home, Morton began to seek redress through Gorges and The Council for New England. By the time the attorney had prevailed in court against Mass. Bay's Puritans (c. 1637) the beleaguered English government could do little to enforce decisions about America.

Morton bided his time and composed *New English Canaan* (Amsterdam 1637), a subtle and spirited 3-part prose-and-poetry portrait of Native New England cultures, of the landscape and its "commodities," and of the various planters in the region, each with their different ways of "complying" (or not) with the New World. But the book's secularism and satire were reviled by its few Puritan readers: *Canaan* was also mistakenly confiscated by Royalist censors. As the English Civil War commenced, Morton found his own way back to New England by 1645, to end his days in "the land which he loveth," as his will stated. He was immediately arrested and imprisoned through the winter in Boston, where (for lack of legal charges) he was released "to go out of the jurisdiction" next spring. Apparently Morton journeyed to Agamenticus (York), Maine, where he joined West Country English settlers; Samuel Maverick wrote that he "died soon after," while Winthrop's journal claimed he lived another "two years."

Morton was not present during "The Wessagusset Conspiracy" but arrived the following spring (1624). Several possibly-former Weymouthers, now "Old Comers" or "Lone Planters" round the bay---William Jeffreys, Maverick, William Blackstone--- became Morton's friends and likely sources of information. In time these "indifferent-minded planters" would all face the Puritan "new creed," as the transatlantic Morton calls it. But in 1630s exile, Morton assembled his Book 3 much like a lawyer's brief, and his first six chapters used the "Conspiracy" as first evidence of Puritan-colonial abuses of chartered (and unchartered) powers, and of their misguidedness toward Native Americans. With its dedication to the "thorough" anti-Puritan Archbishop Laud, made head of the Council by King Charles I to set New England affairs in "better" order, *Canaan* was as successful as it had to be against the Puritans' charter to New England.

Hence *Canaan*'s unique Macchiavellian reputation and "outside the canon" status. "I need make no comments upon the authority, or warn the reader concerning the stories of *Morton*, as this is done in almost every book, early and late, about New England," commented Samuel Drake (43). But this neglects the lack of any evidence that Morton "knew" Weston: they simply shared earlier secular ways of colonizing, and "that was as much as [Weston] need to care for, aiming at Beaver principally" (109). Morton had a qualified admiration for Plimoth's early achievements, and soundly criticized Weymouthers even well after this "Affair" (Book 3, Ch. 11).

The copy-text for these chapters is this editor's 2000 edition of *Canaan* (Scituate MA: Digital Scanning Inc.), which is the only *Canaan* collated with all 16 original copies in the world. Boldface-numbers refer to original copies.

NEW ENGLISH CANAAN
or, New Canaan
The Third Book

**Containing a Description of the People that are Planted There,
What Remarkable Accidents have happened There
Since They were Settled, and what Tenets They Hold,
Together with the Practice of Their Church.**

CHAPTER I.
*Of a Great League made
with the Plimoth Planters after Their Arrival,
by the Sachem of Those Territories.*

The Sachem of the Territories where the Planters of New England are settled (that are the first of the now Inhabitants of New Canaan), not knowing what they were, or whether they would be friends or foes, and **[103]** being desirous to purchase their friendship, that he might have the better assurance of quiet trading with them (which he conceived would be very advantageous to him), was desirous to prepare an Ambassador with commission to treat on his behalf, to that purpose.[230]

And having one that had been in England (taken by a worthless man out of other parts, and after left there by accident), this Salvage he instructed how to behave himself in the treaty of peace. And the more to give him encouragement to adventure his person amongst these newcome inhabitants, which was a thing he durst not himself attempt

---

[230] The **Sachem**   Ousamequin/Massasoit of the Wampanoags. His "ambassador" is either **Samoset** of Morattiggon/Monhegan (*Mourt* 51) who first came to Plimoth in March 1621; or **Tisquantum**, one of many "taken" by Captain Hunt in 1614 (the "worthless man" referred to here). The question about "plague" below comes from **Hobbamock** in Winslow's *Good News*

without security or hostage, promised that Salvage freedom who had been detained there as their captive.

Which offer he accepted, and accordingly came to the Planters, saluting them with welcome in the English phrase; which was of them admired, to hear a Salvage there speak in their own language. And they used him with great courtesy to whom he declared the cause of his coming, and contrived the business so that he brought the Sachem and the English together, between whom was a firm league concluded, which yet continueth.

After which league, the Sachem, being in company with the other whom he had freed and suffered to live with the English, espying a place where a hole had been made in the ground (where was their store of powder laid to be preserved from danger of fire, underground), demanded of the Salvage what the English had hid there underground; who answered, *The plague*, at which he startled, because of the great mortality lately [104] happened by means of the plague (as it is conceived). And the Salvage, the more to increase his fear, told the Sachem that if he should give offence to the English party, they would let out the plague to destroy them all, which kept him in great awe.

Not long after, being at variance with another Sachem bordering upon his territories, he came in solemn manner and entreated the governor that he would let out the plague to destroy the Sachem and his men who were his enemies, promising that he himself and all his posterity would be their everlasting friends; so great an opinion he had of the English.

CHAPTER II.
Of the Entertainment of Mr. Weston's People,
Sent to Settle a Plantation There.

Master Thomas Weston, a Merchant of London that had been at some cost to further the Brethren of New Plimoth in their designs for these parts, shipped a company of servants fitted with provision of all sorts for the undertaking of a plantation to be settled there, with an intent to follow after them in parson.[231] These servants at first arrived at New Plimoth, where they were entertained with court holy bread by the Brethren[232]: they were made very welcome, in show at least. There these servants' goods were landed, with promises to be assisted in the choice of a convenient place, and still the good cheer went forward, and the strong liquors walked. In the meantime the Brethren were in consultation what was best for their advantage, singing the song *Frustra sapit, qui sibi non sapit*.[233] **[105/O]**

This plantation would hinder the present practice and future profit, and Master Weston, an able man, would want for no supplies upon the return of Beaver, and so might be a plantation that might keep them under who had a hope to be the greatest. Besides, his people were no chosen Separatists, but men made choice of at all adventures, fit to have served for the furtherance of Master Weston's undertakings; and that was as much as he need to care for, aiming at Beaver principally, for the better effecting of his purpose.

Now, when the Plimoth men began to find that Master Weston's men's store of provision grew short with feasting, then they hasted them in a weak case to a place called Wessaguscus, and there left them fasting.

---

[231] **parson**   original text: poss. "person"

[232] **Brethren**   poss. borrowed from Morton's Inns of Court contemporary Ben Jonson, whose 1610 *The Alchemist* (II, 4, l. 30) mentions "the holy Brethren of Amsterdam, the exiled saints"   **no chosen...**   The Bible, *Exodus* 19:5 (for ex.): "Ye shall be a peculiar treasure unto Me above all people"   **marginal glosses to this page:** "Court holy bread at Plimmouth" (*i.e.,* the elite's communion-bread and/or, the best they had)

[233] *Frustra...sapit*   Latin, source unknown: poss. "Discretion gossips not about deception"

CHAPTER III.

Of a Battle Fought at the Massachusetts,
between the English and the Indians.[234]

The Planters of Plimoth, at their last being in those parts having defaced the monument of the dead at Passonagessit (by taking away the hearsecloth which was two great bearskins sowed together at full length and propped up over the grave of Chikatawbak's mother[235])---The Sachem of those territories, being enraged at the same, stirred up his men in his behalf to take revenge; and having gathered his men together, he began to make an oration in this manner.[236]

"When last the glorious light of all the [106] sky was underneath this globe, and birds grew silent, I began to settle (as my custom is) to take repose. Before mine eyes were fast closed, methought I saw a vision, at which my spirit was much troubled and trembling at that doleful sight. A spirit cried aloud, 'Behold, my son, whom I have cherisht, see the paps that gave thee suck, the hands that lapped thee warm, and fed thee oft. Canst thou forget to take revenge of those wild people, that hath my monument defaced in despiteful manner, disdaining our ancient antiquities and honorable customs? See now, the Sachem's grave lies like unto the common people's, of ignoble race

---

[234] Adams' 1883 *Canaan* (247) reprints the error found here in Force's (1836 *Tracts* 2: 72). There, the word "Indians" here reads "French." But no known *original* copy contains this error. It appears that though Adams claimed (101) to be working from an original copy, he inserted Force's error, only to correct Morton for it as evidence of "confused and misleading" statements

[235] **Chikatawbak's mother**   This is the only primary-source reference to this incident. Adams says starving Wessagusset planters were the "far more probable" offenders, though noting (his *Canaan* 247n2) that Plimothers "may have despoiled the grave...during one of their earlier visits to Boston Bay."   **Passonagessit** refers to "the little neck of land" (now Hough's Neck" and its vicinity, close by today's Merrymount Park in Quincy, Mass.

[236] **glosses to original pps. [106-7]:** "The Sachem's Oration. A spirit moving the Sachem to War. The grand Captain makes a speech." Major *Diss.* 223: This passage is "certainly distinct from Morton's normal style and indicates some feeling for Indian mannerisms"

defaced: thy mother doth complain, implores thy aid against this theevish people, newcome hither. If this be suffered, I shall not rest in quiet within my everlasting habitation.'

"This said, the spirit vanished, and I all in a sweat, not able scarce to speak, began to get some strength, and to recollect my spirits that were fled. All which I thought to let you understand, to have your counsel, and your aid likewise."

This being spoken, straightway arose the grand captain, and cried aloud, *Come, let us to arms, it doth concern us all, let us bid them battle*; so to arms they went, and laid weight for the Plimoth boat, and forcing them to forsake their landing-place,[237] they sought another best for their convenience. Thither the Salvages repaired in hope to have like success, but all in vain, for the English captain warily foresaw, and perceiving their plot, knew the better how to order his men fit for battle in that place. He boldly leading his men on, ranged about the field to and fro, [107/O2] and taking his best advantage, let fly, and made the Salvages give ground. The English followed them fiercely on and made them take trees for their shelter (as their custom is), from whence their captain let fly amain, yet no man was hurt. At last, lifting up his right arm to draw a fatal shaft (as he then thought) to end this difference, he received a shot upon his elbow, and straightway fled; by whose example all the army followed the same way, and yielded up the honor of the day to the English party. Who were such a terror to them after, that the Salvages durst never make to a head against them anymore.

---

[237] Morton may have confused this skirmish with accounts of the post-"massacre" fight between Standish's men and Obdakiest/Chikatawbak's, told in *Good News*, Bradford and Pratt **glosses:** [107] "The main Battle. [108] The field won by the English"

CHAPTER IV.
Of a Parliament Held at Wessaguscus, and the Acts.

Master Weston's plantation being settled at Wessaguscus, his servants (many of them lazy persons that would use no endeavor to take the benefit of the country), some of them fell sick and died.[238]

One amongst the rest an able-bodied man, that ranged the woods to see what it would afford, lighted by accident on an Indian barn, and from thence did take a capful of corn. The Salvage owner of it, finding by the foot some English had been there, came to the plantation, and made complaint after this manner. [108]

The chief Commander of the company on this occasion called a Parliament of all his people but those that were sick and ill at ease. And wisely now they must consult upon this huge complaint, that a privy knife or string of beads would well enough have qualified; and Edward Iohnson was a special judge of this business.[239] The fact was there in repetition, construction made[240] that it was a felony, and by the laws of England punished with death. And this in execution must be put for an example, and likewise to appease the Salvage; when straightway one arose, moved as it were with some compassion, and said he could not well gainsay the former sentence, yet he had conceived within the compass of his brain an Embrion[241] that was of special consequence to be delivered.

---

[238] **glosses:** here "Some lazy people." Below: "A lusty fellow"

[239] Banks (*York* 89) describes Johnson as a "gentleman by birth" who settled in Maine rather than be a "freeman" in later Mass. Bay Colony. **glosses:** "A poor complaint. Edward Johnson a chief judge. Made a hainous fact."

Young (334): "It will be observed that Morton mentions this substitution merely as the suggestion of an individual, which was rejected by the company. Even had it been adopted by them, and put into execution, it would not have implicated the Plymouth people at all, nor cast the least slur on their characters or principles."

[240] **repetition...**   terms from trial law, "recitation and interpretation of the facts"

[241] **Embrion** from medieval Latin: a "germ," still an idea rather than a fact (OED)

And cherished,[242] he said that it would most aptly serve to pacify the Salvage's complaint, and save the life of one that might (if need should be) stand them in some good stead, being young and strong, fit for resistance against an enemy which might come unexpected for anything they knew. The Oration made was liked of everyone, and he entreated to proceed to show the means how this might be performed. Says he, "You all agree that one must die, and one shall die: this young man's clothes we will take off, and put upon one that is old and impotent, a sickly person that cannot escape death, such is the disease on him. Confirmed that die he must, put the young man's clothes on this man, and let the sick person be hanged in the other's stead." *Amen* says one, and so say many more. [109/O3]

And this had like to have proved their final sentence, and there confirmed by Act of Parliament to after ages, for a precedent. But one with a ravenous voice began to croak and bellow for revenge, and put by that conclusive motion, alleging such deceits might be a means hereafter to exasperate the minds of the complaining Salvages; and that by his[243] death, the Salvages should see their zeal to Justice, and therefore he should die.

This was concluded; yet nevertheless a scruple now to countermand this act did represent itself unto their minds. Which was, how they should do to get the man's goodwill: this was indeed a special obstacle, for without that, they all agreed, it would be dangerous for any man to attempt the execution of it, lest mischief should befall them every man. He was a person that in his wrath did seem to be a second Samson, able to beat out their brains with the jawbone of an ass.[244]

---

[242] **cherished** cheered on, encouraged

[243] **his** the real thief's? "This" just below suggests the "real" thief *was* the one hanged **glosses:** "A fine device. A wise Sentence. To hang a sick man in the other's stead"

[244] **jawbone...** In The Bible (*Judges* 15:15) this "Danite" hero slew his enemies thus **non plus** Latin, "No more" to express a state of helplessness **glosses:** "Very fit justice. A dangerous attempt. Jesting turned to earnest"

Therefore they called the man, and by persuasion, got him fast-bound in jest; and then hanged him up hard by in good earnest, who with a weapon, and at liberty, would have put all those wise judges of this Parliament to a pitiful *non plus*, as it hath been credibly reported; and have made the chief Judge of them all buckle to him. [110]

CHAPTER V.
Of a Massacre
Made upon the Salvages at Wessaguscus.

After the end of that Parliament, some of the plantation there, about three persons, went to live with Chikatawbak and his company, and had very good quarter, for all the former quarrel with the Plimoth planters: they are not like Will Sommers,[245] to take one for another.

There they purposed to stay until Master Weston's arrival; but the Plimoth men intending no good to him (as appeared by the consequence) came in the meantime to Wessaguscus, and there pretended to feast the Salvages of those parts, bringing with them pork and things for the purpose, which they set before the Salvages. They ate thereof without suspicion of any mischief, and were taken upon a watchword given, and with their own knives hanging about their necks were by the Plimoth planters stabbed and slain: one of which was hanged up there, after the slaughter.

In the meantime the Sachem had knowledge of this accident, by one that ran to his countrymen at the Massachusetts and gave them intelligence of the news; after which time the Salvages there, consulting of the matter, in the night when the other English, fearless of danger, were asleep, knocked them all in the head, in revenge of the death of their [111] countrymen.

---

[245] **Will Sommers**   Court Fool to Henry VIII: AC253 recounts an anecdote of Sommers to which Morton may refer; and suggests sources incl. Armin's 1608 *Nest of Ninnies*, Doran's *Court Fools*   **glosses:** "Good quarter with the Salvages. A plot from Plimmouth. Salvages killed with their own weapons. News carried. A revenge"

But if the Plimoth Planters had really intended good to Master Weston or those men, why had they not kept the Salvages alive in custody until they had secured the other English? Who, by means of this evil managing of the business, lost their lives, and the whole plantation was dissolved thereupon, as was likely for fear of a revenge to follow, as a relation to this cruel antecedent. And when Master Weston came over, he found things at an evil exigent by means thereof; but could not tell how it was brought about.

The Salvages of the Massachusetts, that could not imagine from whence these men should come, or to what end, seeing them perform such unexpected actions, neither could tell by what name properly to distinguish them; and did from that time afterwards call the English Planters *Wotawquenange*, which in their language signifieth *Stabbers*, or *Cutthroats*.

And this name was received by those that came there after for good, being then unacquainted with the signification of it for many years following; until from a southerly Indian that understood English well, I was by demonstration made to conceive the interpretation of it, and rebuked these other, that it was not forborne. The other called us by the name of *Wotoquansawge*: what that doth signify, he said he was not able by any demonstration to express. And my neighbors durst no more in my hearing call us by the name formerly used, for fear of my displeasure.[246] **[112]**

---

[246] **Wotawquenange**   Adams (and here, linguist Jonathan Trumbull in AC254) fault Morton on these Eastern Algonquian words. But Adams knew how "imperfectly if at all" Morton's typesetter knew English (102). Adams had also noted numerous letters (especially **n** and **u**) set upside-down in original *Canaan* copies, as in "muit" for "mint." If the reader "sets right" the apparent second "n" in the supposedly incorrect *Wotawquenange* above, the result— Wotawque*nauge*—*is* the word recorded by Williams (*Key* Ch. 8, 137) for "Englishman, men. *That is*, coat-men, *or* clothed." This, Adams and Trumbull say, is "the correct word." But *their* correction of Morton is hasty; for, given what *Morton* is saying about English "cutthroats," the correct word he was after (if Williams was right) was closer to "chauquaqock": "Englishmen, *properly* sword-men." The second word above, **Wotoquansawge**, does not appear in other sources

CHAPTER VI.

Of the Surprizing of a Merchant's Ship in Plimoth Harbor.[247]

This Merchant a man of worth, arriving in the parts of New Canaan and finding that his plantation was dissolved, some of his men slain, some dead with sickness and the rest at Plimoth; he was perplexed in his mind about the matter, coming as he did with supply, and means to have raised their fortunes and his own exceedingly. And seeing what had happened, he resolved to make some stay in the Plimoth harbor; and this suited to their purpose.

Wherefore the Brethren did congratulate with him at his safe arrival, and their best of entertainment for a sweetening cast, deploring the disaster of his plantation and glozing[248] upon the text, alleging the mischievous intent of the Salvages there, which by friendly intelligence of their neighbors[249] was discovered before it came to be full summed; so that they lost not all, although they saved not all. And this they pretended to proceed from the fountain of love and zeal to him, and Christianity; and they chastised the insolency of the Salvages, of which that part had some dangerous persons.

And this, as an article of the new creed of Canaan, would they have received of every newcomer there to inhabit; that the Salvages are a dangerous people, subtle, secret, and mischievous, and that it is dangerous to live separated, but [113/P] rather together, and so be under their lee; that none might trade for Beaver but at their pleasure, as none do or shall do there. Nay, they will not be reduced to any other song yet of the Salvages to the southward of Plimoth, because they would have

---

[247] **Merchant**   Thomas Weston   **gloss:** "A gloss upon the false text"

[248] **glozing**   adding a "gloss" or "explanatory information" to "the facts" or text; but also, "flattery, deceit"; "pretense...disguise"; "to deceive with smooth talk" (OED)

[249] **intelligence...neighbors**   poss. Phinehas Pratt, and/or Hobbamock's "intelligence"

none come there; saying that he that will sit down there, must come strong.[250]

But I have found the Massachusetts Indians more full of humanity than the Christians, and have had much better quarter with them; yet I observed not their humors,[251] but they mine, although my great number that I landed were dissolved, and my company as few as might be.[252] For I know that this falls out infallibly where two nations meet: one must rule, and the other be ruled, before a peace can be hoped for.[253] And for a Christian to submit to the rule of a Salvage, you will say, is both shame and dishonor: at least, it is my opinion, and my practice was accordingly, and I have the better quarter by the means thereof. The more Salvages, the better quarter: the more Christians, the worser quarter, I found, as all the indifferent-minded planters can testify.

Now, while the Merchant[254] was ruminating on this mishap, the Plimoth planters perceiving that he had furnished himself with excellent commodities fit for the merchandise of the country (and holding it good to fish in troubled waters, and so get a snatch[255] unseen), practiced in secret with some other in the land whom they thought apt to embrace the benefit of such a cheat; and it was concluded and resolved upon that

---

[250] Capt. John Smith charged that men such as kidnapper Capt. Thos. Hunt antagonized Natives "to keepe this abounding Countrey still in obscuritie, that onely he and some few Merchants...might enjoy wholly the benefit of the Trade" (*Gen. History*: Arber ed. 2:698)

[251] **humors** idiosyncrasies, habits, cultural ways

[252] **few** most of Morton's original company of "30 servants" were taken to Virginia c.1625-6, leaving "nine persons, besides dogs" (86) or a "seven-headed Hydra" (150)

[253] **gloss:** "Where two nations meet, one must rule, the other must be ruled, or no quietness." (*Quietness* was a social value of "peace between neighbors with differences," practiced in Morton's West Country England: see Dempsey, *Thomas Morton*)

[254] **Merchant** Thomas Weston

[255] **snatch** "a hasty meal or morsel" (OED)   **glosses:** "A Machivell plot"; "The Vaile" (a trick/device to obscure vision)

all his ship and goods should be confiscated, for business done by him
the Lord knows when, or where. **[114]**

A letter must be framed to them, and hands unto it, to be their
warrant: this should shadow them. That is the first practice: they will
insane[256] a man, and then pretend that Justice must be done. They cause
the Merchant (secure) to come ashore, and then take him in hold,
showing they are compelled unto it legally[257]; and enter straight aboard,
peruse the cargazowne,[258] and then deliver up the charge of her to their
confederates. And how much less this is than Piraty, let any practice in
the Admiralty be judge.

The Merchant, his ship and goods confiscated, himself a prisoner,
and threatened so to be sent and conveyed to England, there to receive
the sum of all that did belong to him, a malefactor (and a great one
too).[259] This the good man endured with patience, a long time, until the
best of all his goods were quite dispersed, and every actor his
proportion. The Merchant, enlarged,[260] his ship a burden to the owner
now, his undertakings in these parts being quite overthrown, was
redelivered, and bonds of him were taken not to prosecute. He being
grieved hereat, betakes him to drive a trade between that and Virginia
many years.

---

[256] **shadow**   fig., give protective "darkness" to work with   **insane a man**   poss. misprint
for "defame." Also, as Morton composed this, his court-witness before The Coucil for New
England, Philip Ratcliffe, was being called "mad" by Mass. Bay Puritan legal opponents

[257] **legally**   Bradford described a "very formal"-looking warrant (FBH1:335)

[258] **Cargazowne**   Spanish *cargazon*, "cargo"

[259] **malefactor**   Weston was apparently "wanted" for trading guns to the French before his
arrival in New England (FBH1:331). See also Introduction

[260] **enlarged**   granted a time-extension, or a "release" to convert one legal status to another; for
ex., from defendant to "redelivered" merchant. Weston and Robt. Gorges reached "some sort" of
agreement (Adams' *Canaan* 258).   **glosses:** "When every Conspirator had his share the ship
delivered again. Bonds taken not to prosecute. Report Mr. Weston was mad in New England.
Honest men in particular"

The Brethren (sharp-witted) had it spread by and by amongst his friends in England that the man was mad. So thought his wife, so thought his other friends, that had it from a planter of the town.[261] So was it thought by those that did not know the Brethren could dissemble: "Why, thus they are all of them honest men in their particular, and every man being bound to seek another's good shall in the general do the best he can to effect it." And so they may be excused, I think. **[115/P2]**

---

[261] According to FBH1: 298, 330-335, soon after the Weymouth killings, Weston came over "in disguise" to see "how things were"; but was shipwrecked, stripped to his shirt by Merrimack Natives, and reached Plimoth showing "strang[e] alteration" and "things boyling in his mind." He was loaned supply and went thanklessly on his way. But by Sept. 1623, Sir Ferdinando Gorges sent son Robert to take over Weymouth (331); and *he* called Weston to answer for both Weymouth and alleged weapons-trade with France. With Plimoth's aid, Robert Gorges briefly impounded Weston's ship; but released, Weston laid hands on the *Sparrow* then fishing northern waters, and began his latter years' prosperity as a Virginia trader till 1644. He died of "plague" at Bristol in 1647

HENRY WADSWORTH LONGFELLOW, from
THE COURTSHIP OF MILES STANDISH (1856)

Born in 1807 in Portland, Maine and educated at Bowdoin College, Longfellow studied languages and literature before fame made him putative leader of America's "Fireside Poets." His career as a professor took him to France, Germany, Spain and Italy for extended visits, and he began as a writer with his textbooks published in those tongues. (His commencement oration "Our Native Writers" vowed that, in a society with little or no place for writers, he would give himself with "a noble self-devotion to the cause of literature.") Soon his voyages had inspired a travel book, *Outre-Mer: A Pilgrimage Beyond the Sea*, which some critics saw as his imitation of Washinton Irving's popular *Sketch Book*. In 1834 he accepted a professorship at Harvard.

During a stay in Europe, Longfellow's wife Mary died of a miscarriage. A year later, Longfellow met Fanny Appleton, and after seven years they wed. They took up life at Harvard, and there Longfellow remained until 1854. His recognition increased, he was compared to Tennyson and Wordsworth; and his 75th birthday was celebrated across the country. After his death in 1882 Longfellow became the only American poet whose bust stands in Poets' Corner in England's Westminster Abbey.

Courtship manifest continuities between colonial America and the Republic's post-Revolution quest for a national "origin myth." As Cleanth Brooks put it, "Against the expansion of the new country and the centrifugal pull of the West, the sea, and the wicked city, there was 'home'---the glowing fireside with the windows shut against the old fear of the forest and the new challenge of [national] destiny" (*Makers* 384: hence "fireside poets," with the "window... most tightly shut" against "the darkness of the self"). Though "Many writers den[ied] that the English language [was] capable of being moulded into tolerable verse" (1859: Harris ed. 478), Longfellow took up the task, and used Bradford's *History* (published 1856) much as Dwight had used "Pequot War" sources in *The Conquest of Canaan* (1785) and *Greenfield Hill* (1794), to define the "new America" between "savages" and "civilization." (See Pearce, and Barrett's *Ignoble Savage*.)

Other such influences surrounded the maturing Longfellow. Back in 1769, "well to do families" of Plymouth had founded The Old Colony Club to create "a social environ-ment of a more refined nature" (Deetz 17), which brought about Forefathers'

Day (Dec. 22), the designation of Plymouth Rock, Thanksgiving and today's "living history" museum, Plimoth Plantation. By 1808 (Eddy-Snow 25), public pageants and *tableaux vivant* began to "ritualize" emerging concepts of "Pilgrims" and "Indians." But, while the 1830s saw Native Removal(s) and The Mashpee Revolt (see O'Connell's edition of Apess' writings), Fireside writers "ritualized and refined presentation of accepted attitudes and feelings" (Brooks *Makers* 385). Even "frontier romances" (Childe's *Hobomok*, Sedgwick's *Hope Leslie*, Cooper's novels, plus poems of Bryant and others) included "Indians" only to pronounce "doom" upon them. Instead, events such as Edward Everett's 1839 Address at Cape Cod's Centennial Celebration described "the fated vessel [*Mayflower*]...almost sinking...with all her treasures, not of silver and gold...but of courage, of patience, of zeal, of high spiritual daring....freighted with the destinies of a continent....Yes, the everlasting God Himself...gather[ed] the meek company of his worshippers as in the hollow of His hand" (qtd. in Young 104).

In the year before *Courtship*, "good, inoffensive, comforting Longfellow" (Henry James Sr.) did make a "bold plunge...into untrodden tracts" (Harris ed. 476) with his long poem *Hiawatha*. Published the same year as *Leaves of Grass* by Walt Whitman--- to whom Longfellow attributed a "total want of both education and delicacy" (Kaplan 353)---*Hiawatha* was both popular and attacked in the same continuity of "reasons" expressed by one of the first American anthologists, Moses Coit Tyler; who in the late 1870s termed Native peoples "fierce dull bipeds standing in our way" (1:10). "The only really Indian thing about the poem is the Indian summer haze that softens all its outlines, but even this...was borrowed from German Romantic poets" (Pattee in Matthiessen 174).

> ...The essential characteristic of Indian life, and so of
> Indian literature, is that it is childlike....He cannot graduate
> at a classical college. He cannot fight in an English regiment.
> He cannot make his bow at a French court. And for all these
> reasons, he cannot be sung about in an epic poem.
>
> (Edward Everett Hale, 1856: in *19th Century* 477)

While *Hiawatha* tried for a "spoken" poetic line, *Courtship* returned to Homeric hexameters, complete with "heroic inversions" and dangling gerunds. "No man...has bestowed more pains upon poetry," wrote *Blackwood's* in 1852. Poe claimed that Longfellow done "violent wrong to his own high powers." Ironically, while Emerson called Longfellow "trivial and vulgar," he included him in his 1874 collection *Parnassus* and omitted Whitman. Yet, at Longfellow's funeral Emerson remarked: "The gentleman we have just been burying was a sweet and beautiful soul; but I forget his name."

The Courtship of Miles Standish
from Part I[262]

In the Old Colony days, in Plymouth the land of the Pilgrims,
To and fro in a room of his simple and primitive dwelling,
Clad in doublet and hose, and boots of Cordovan leather,
Strode, with a martial air, Miles Standish the Puritan Captain.
    Buried in thought he seemed, with his hands behind him,
        and pausing
Ever and anon to behold his glittering weapons of warfare,
Hanging in shining array along the walls of the chamber,---
Cutlass and corselet of steel, and his trusty sword of Damascus,
Curved at the point and inscribed with its mystical Arabic sentence,
While underneath, in a corner, were fowling-piece, musket,
    and matchlock.
    Short of stature he was, but strongly built and athletic,
Broad in the shoulders, deep-chested, with muscles and sinews
        of iron;
Brown as a nut was his face, but his russet beard was already
Flaked with patches of snow, as hedges sometimes in November.

Near him was seated John Alden, his friend and
        household companion,
Writing with diligent speed at a table of pine by the window;

---

[262] The copy-text is *The Complete Poetical Works of Henry Wadsworth Longfellow* (1841: rpt. 1899). Original line-breaks are marked by capital letters: the short remaining phrases here are caused by spacing limitations. For a brief biography of Myles Standish see Note 5, page 7. On Longfellow see Edward Wagenknecht, *Portrait of an American Humanist* (1966) and *His Poetry and Prose* (1986); also Louis Untermeyer, *The Poems of* (1961) and Kenneth W. Cameron, *Among His Contemporaries* (1978)

Fair-haired, azure-eyed, with delicate Saxon complexion,
Having the dew of his youth, and the beauty thereof, as the captives
Whom Saint Gregory saw, and exclaimed, "Not Angles, but Angels."
Youngest of all was he of the men who came in the *Mayflower*.

      Suddenly breaking the silence, the diligent scribe interrupting,
Spake, in the pride of his heart, Miles Standish
        the Captain of Plymouth.
"Look at these arms," he said, "the warlike weapons that hang here
Burnished and bright and clean, as if for parade or inspection!
This is the sword of Damascus I fought with in Flanders;
        this breastplate,
Well I remember the day! once saved my life in a skirmish;
Here in front you can see the very dint of the bullet
Fired point-blank at my heart by a Spanish arcabucero.
Had it not been of sheer steel, the forgotten bones of Miles Standish
Would at this moment be mould, in their grave
        in the Flemish morasses."

Thereupon answered John Alden, but looked not up
        from his writing:
"Truly the breath of the Lord hath slackened the speed of the bullet;
He in his mercy preserved you, to be our shield and our weapon!"

      Still, the Captain continued, unheeding the words
        of the stripling:
"See, how bright they are burnished, as if in an arsenal hanging;
That is because I have done it myself, and not left it to others.
Serve yourself, would you be well served, is an excellent adage;
So I take care of my arms, as you of your pens and your inkhorn.
Then, too, there are my soldiers, my great, invincible army,
Twelve men, all equipped, having each his rest and his matchlock,
Eighteen shillings a month, together with diet and pillage,
And, like Caesar, I know the name of each of my soldiers!"

This he said with a smile, that danced in his eyes,
            as the sunbeams
Dance on the waves of the sea, and vanish again in a moment.
Alden laughed as he wrote, and still the Captain continued:
"Look! You can see from this window my brazen howitzer planted
High on the roof of the church, a preacher who speaks
            to the purpose,
Steady, straightforward, and strong, with irresistible logic,
Orthodox, flashing conviction right into the hearts of the heathen.
Now we are ready, I think, for any assault of the Indians;
Let them come, if they like, and the sooner they try it the better,---
Let them come, if they like, be it sagamore, sachem, or pow-wow,
Aspinet, Samoset, Corbitant, Squanto, or Tokamahamon!"

            Long at the window he stood, and wistfully gazed
            on the landscape,
Washed with a cold gray mist, the vapory breath of the east-wind,
Forest and meadow and hill, and the steel-blue rim of the ocean,
Lying silent and sad, in the afternoon shadows and sunshine.
Over his countenance flitted a shadow like those on the landscape,
Gloom intermingled with light; and his voice was subdued
            with emotion,
Tenderness, pity, regret, as after a pause he proceeded:

            "Yonder there, on the hill by the sea, lies buried
            Rose Standish,
Beautiful rose of love, that bloomed for me by the wayside!
She was the first to die of all who came in the *Mayflower*!
Green above her is growing the field of wheat we have sown there,
Better to hide from the Indian scouts the graves of our people,
Lest they should count them and see how many already
            have perished!"
Sadly his face he averted, and strode up and down,

and was thoughtful.

Fixed to the opposite wall was a shelf of books, and
          among them
Prominent three, distinguished alike for bulk and for binding;
Bariffe's Artillery Guide, and the Commentaries of Caesar
Out of the Latin translated by Arthur Goldinge of London,
And, as if guarded by these, between them was standing the Bible.
Musing a moment before them, Miles Standish paused,
          as if doubtful
Which of the three he should choose for his consolation
          and comfort,
Whether the wars of the Hebrews, the famous campaigns
          of the Romans,
Or the Artillery practice, designed for belligerent Christians.

Finally down from its shelf he dragged
          the ponderous Roman,
Seated himself at the window, and opened the book, and in silence
Turned o'er the well-worn leaves, where thumb-marks
          thick on the margin,
Like the trample of feet, proclaimed the battle was hottest.

Nothing was heard in the room but the hurrying pen
          of the stripling,
Busily writing epistles important, to go by the *Mayflower*,
Ready to sail on the morrow, or next day at latest, God willing!
Homeward bound with the tidings of all that terrible winter,
Letters written by Alden, and full of the name of Priscilla!
Full of the name and the fame of the Puritan maiden Priscilla![263]

---

[263] This is the end of Part I. In Parts II through IV, John Alden takes on the role of emissary from Standish to Priscilla ("I can march up to a fortress and summon the place to surrender,/But march up to a woman with such a proposal, I dare not" he tells Alden). When Alden completes his speech to her in Standish's favor, she responds: "Why don't you speak for yourself, John?" When Standish hears this, he angrily assumes himself "supplanted, defrauded, betrayed"; and

...Meanwhile the choleric Captain strode wrathful away
          to the council,
Found it already assembled, impatiently waiting his coming;
Men in the middle of life, austere and grave in deportment,
Only one of them old, the hill that was nearest to heaven,
Covered with snow, but erect, the excellent Elder of Plymouth.
God had sifted three kingdoms to find the wheat for this planting,
Then had sifted the wheat, as the living seed of a nation;
So say the chronicles old, and such is the faith of the people!

          Near them was standing an Indian, in attitude stern
          and defiant,
Naked down to the waist, and grim and ferocious in aspect;
While on the table before them was lying unopened a Bible,
Ponderous, bound in leather, brass-studded, printed in Holland,
And beside it outstretched the skin of a rattlesnake glittered,
Filled, like a quiver, with arrows: a signal and challenge of warfare,
Brought by the Indian, and speaking with arrowy tongues
          of defiance.

          This Miles Standish beheld, as he entered, and
          heard them debating
What were an answer befitting the hostile message and menace,
Talking of this and of that, contriving, suggesting, objecting;
One voice only for peace, and that the voice of the Elder,
Judging it wise and well that some at least were converted,
Rather than any were slain, for this was but Christian behavior!
          Then out spake Miles Standish, the stalwart
          Captain of Plymouth,
Muttering deep in his throat, for his voice was husky with anger,
"What! do you mean to make war with milk and the water

---

departs "frowning fiercely," with "his sword with its scabbard of iron." The excerpt resumes in
Part IV as Alden is "left alone" and "Pray[s] in the silence of night."

of roses?
Is it to shoot red squirrels you have your howitzer planted
There on the roof of the church, or is it to shoot red devils?
Truly the only tongue that is understood by a savage
Must be the tongue of fire that speaks from the mouth
      of the cannon!"

Thereupon answered and said the excellent
      Elder of Plymouth,
Somewhat amazed and alarmed at this irreverent language:
"Not so thought St. Paul, nor yet the other Apostles;
Not from the cannon's mouth were the tongues of fire they
      spake with!"
But unheeded fell this mild rebuke on the Captain,
Who had advanced to the table, and thus continued discoursing:
"Leave this matter to me, for to me by right it pertaineth.
War is a terrible trade; but if the cause is righteous,
Sweet is the smell of powder; and thus I answer the challenge!"

Then from the rattlesnake's skin, with a sudden,
      contemptuous gesture,
Jerking the Indian arrows, he filled it with powder and bullets
Full to the very jaws, and handed it back to the savage,
Saying, in thundering tones: "Here, take it! this is your answer!"

Silently out of the room then glided the glistening savage,
Bearing the serpent's skin, and seeming himself like a serpent,
Winding his sinuous way in the dark to the depths of the forest.

from V

Just in the gray of the dawn, as the mists uprose
      from the meadows,
There was a stir and a sound in the slumbering village of Plymouth:

Clanging and clicking of arms, and the order imperative, "Forward!"
Given in tone suppressed, a tramp of feet, and then silence.
Figures ten, in the mist, marched slowly out of the village.
Standish the stalwart it was, with eight of his valorous army,
Led by their Indian guide, by Hobomok, friend of the white men,
Northward marching to quell the sudden revolt of the savage.
Giants they seemed in the mist, or the mighty men of King David;
Giants in heart they were, who believed in God and the Bible,---
Ay, who believed in the smiting of Midianites and Philistines.
Over them gleamed far off the crimson banners of morning;
Under them loud on the sands, the serried billows, advancing,
Fired along the line, and in regular order retreated....[264]

VII
The March of Miles Standish

Meanwhile the stalwart Miles Standish was marching
        steadily northward,
Winding through forest and swamp, and along the trend
                of the seashore,
All day long, with hardly a halt, the fire of his anger
Burning and crackling within, and the sulphurous odor of powder
Seeming more sweet to his nostrils than all the scents of the forest.
Silent and moody he went, and much he revolved his discomfort;
He who was used to success, and to easy victories always,
Thus to be flouted, rejected, and laughed to scorn by a maiden,
Thus to be mocked and betrayed by the friend whom most
                he had trusted!
Ah! 't was too much to be borne, and he fretted and chafed
                in his armor!

---

[264] Parts V ("The Sailing [Home] of the *Mayflower*"), and VI now take up relations between Priscilla and John Alden. Part VII begins as given here

"I alone am to blame," he muttered, "for mine was the folly.
What has a rough old soldier, grown grim and gray in the harness,
Used to the camp and its ways, to do with the wooing of maidens?
'T was but a dream,---let it pass,---let it vanish like so many others!
What I thought was a flower, is only a weed, and is worthless;
Out of my heart I will pluck it, and throw it away,
            and henceforward
Be but a fighter of battles, a lover and wooer of dangers!"
Thus he revolved in his mind his sorry defeat and discomfort,
While he was marching by day or lying at night in the forest,
Looking up at the trees, and the constellations beyond them.

        After a three days' march he came to an Indian encampment
Pitched on the edge of a meadow, between the sea and the forest;
Women at work by the tents, and warriors, horrid with war-paint,
Seated about a fire, and smoking and talking together;
Who, when they saw from afar the sudden approach
            of the white men,
Saw the flash of the sun on breastplate and sabre and musket,
Straightway leaped to their feet, and two,
            from among them advancing,
Came to parley with Standish, and offer him furs as a present;
Friendship was in their looks, but in their hearts there was hatred.

        Braves of the tribe were these, and brothers,
            gigantic in stature,
Huge as Goliath of Gath, or the terrible Og, king of Bashan;
One was Pecksuot named, and the other was called Wattawamat.
Round their necks were suspended their knives in scabbards
            of wampum,
Two-edged, trenchant knives, with points as sharp as a needle.
Other arms had they none, for they were cunning and crafty.

"Welcome, English!" they said,---these words they had
          learned from the traders
Touching at times on the coast, to barter and chaffer for peltries.
Then in their native tongue they began to parley with Standish,
Through his guide and interpreter, Hobomok, friend
               of the white man,
Begging for blankets and knives, but mostly for muskets
               and powder,
Kept by the white man, they said, concealed, with the plague,
               in his cellars,
Ready to be let loose, and destroy his brother the red man!

     But when Standish refused, and said he would give them
          the Bible,
Suddenly changing their tone, they began to boast and to bluster.
Then Wattawamat advanced with a stride in front of the other,
And with a lofty demeanor, thus vauntingly spake to the Captain:
     "Now Wattawamat can see, by the fiery eyes of the Captain,
Angry is he in his heart; but the heart of the brave Wattawamat
Is not afraid at the sight. He was not born of a woman,
But on a mountain at night, from an oak tree riven by lightning.
Forth he sprang at a bound, with all his weapons about him,
Shouting, 'Who is there here to fight with the brave Wattawamat?'"

     Then he unsheathed his knife, and, whetting the blade on his
          left hand,
Held it aloft and displayed a woman's face on the handle;
Saying, with bitter expression and look of sinister meaning:
"I have another at home, with the face of a man on the handle;
By and by they shall marry; and there will be plenty of children!"

     Then stood Pecksuot forth, self-vaunting, insulting
          Miles Standish,
While with his fingers he patted the knife that hung at his bosom,

Drawing it half from its sheath, and plunging it back,
          as he muttered,
"By and by it shall see; it shall eat; ah, ha! but shall speak not!
This is the mighty Captain the white men have sent to destroy us!
He is a little man; let him go and work with the women!"

          Meanwhile Standish had noted the faces and figures
               of Indians
Peeping and creeping about from bush to tree in the forest,
Feigning to look for game, with arrows set on their bow-strings,
Drawing about him still closer and closer the net of their ambush.
But undaunted he stood, and dissembled, and
          treated them smoothly;
So the old chronicles say, that were writ in the days of the fathers.
But when he heard their defiance, the boast, the taunt, and
          the insult,
All the hot blood of his race, of Sir Hugh and of Thurston de
     Standish,
Boiled and beat in his heart, and swelled in the veins of his temples.

          Headlong he leaped on the boaster, and, snatching his knife
               from its scabbard,
Plunged it into his heart, and, reeling backward, the savage
Fell with his face to the sky, and a fiendlike fierceness upon it.
Straight there arose from the forest the awful sound
          of the war-whoop,
And, like a flurry of snow on the whistling wind of December,
Swift and sudden and keen came a flight of feathery arrows.

          Then came a cloud of smoke, and out of the cloud
               came the lightning,
Out of the lightning thunder; and death unseen ran before it.
Frightened the savages fled for shelter in swamp and in thicket,
Hotly pursued and beset; but their sachem, the brave Wattawamat,

Fled not; he was dead. Unswerving and swift had a bullet
Passed through his brain, and he fell with both hands
            clutching the greensward,
Seeming in death to hold back from his foe the land of his fathers.

        There on the flowers of the meadow the warriors lay, and
            above them,
Silent, with folded arms, stood Hobomok, friend of the white man.
Smiling at length he exclaimed to the stalwart Captain of Plymouth:
"Pecksuot bragged very loud of his courage, his strength, and
            his stature,---
Mocked the great Captain, and called him a little man; but I see now
Big enough have you been to lay him speechless before you!"

        Thus the first battle was fought and won by the stalwart
            Miles Standish.
When the tidings thereof were brought to the village of Plymouth,
And as a trophy of war the head of the brave Wattawamat
Scowled from the roof of the fort, which at once was a church
            and a fortress,
All who beheld it rejoiced, and praised the Lord, and took courage.
Only Priscilla averted her face from this spectre of terror,
Thanking God in her heart that she had not married Miles Standish;
Shrinking, fearing almost, lest, coming home from his battles,
He should lay claim to her hand, as the prize and reward
            of his valor....

CHARLES FRANCIS ADAMS, JR., from *THREE EPISODES of MASSACHUSETTS HISTORY* (1892)

> Eighteen years ago, the town of Weymouth had
> occasion to celebrate the 250th anniversary of its settlement,
> and I was invited to deliver an historical address in
> commemoration of the event. In preparing it, my attention
> was first drawn to the early settlement of the region about
> Boston Bay...and step by step I found myself drawn into a study
> of the history of the town [Quincy] in which I lived....
>   ...[It] might naturally be supposed [that] the slow,
> uneventful course of local narrative began. I did not find it so.
> On the contrary, the whole succession of events....with no effort
> on my part,---indeed, I might almost say in spite of me,---seemed
> to lift itself up until it became sublimated and typical. It was the
> story, not of a town, but of a people. (*Three Episodes* I: *iii-iv*)

Charles Francis Adams, Jr., was born the great-grandson of John Adams, the second President of the United States, in 1835 in Boston. Educated at private schools, at Boston Latin and Harvard University, he was admitted to the bar to begin practicing law in 1858. When his father served in Congress between 1858 and 1860 young Adams went to work with him in Washington, D.C., and directly observed the difficult political years just before the American Civil War.

Of four brothers only Charles took up military service. He joined the First Massachusetts Cavalry a first lieutenant, was posted with Union forces in occupation of Fort Royal, South Carolina, and then served in the Army of the Potomac. He took part in battle directly at Antietam and Gettysburg, in The Wilderness Campaign and other places as the years wore on. As he rose in rank, Adams found himself in command of the Fifth Massachusetts Cavalry (one of several African-American regiments) in 1865, and he retired from service as a brevet brigadier general.

After he married (Mary Hone Ogden) and traveled in Europe, Adams grew restless about resuming his career as a lawyer. Much in the tradition of his family, he believed that "education was the distinguishing requirement for positions of leadership" (Meleny 9), and he began contributing his learning to the public sphere by way of an 1867 series of articles, his ethical analysis of conflicts of interest in the then-burgeoning American railroad industries, then in competition to construct a transcontinental rail system. When a commission was established to address such problems and conflicts, Adams won appointment to it, and in time a career of national scope opened up before him. Historian Ambrose pronounced Adams during "The Gilded Age" a man "of iron rectitude and the scourge of the Union Pacific's financing" ("The Big Road" 66).

In 1871 Adams' railroad articles appeared as *Chapters of Erie and Other Essays*, he was president of the Union Pacific from 1884-90, and his works reflect expanding involvements: *Railroads: Their Origins and Problems* (1878), *The New Departure in the Common Schools of Quincy* (1879), an edition of Morton's *New English Canaan* (1883), a biography of Richard Henry Dana (1890), and countless articles, from Boston histories to his part(s) in the Anti-Imperialist League---which questioned American "annexation" of the Phillippines after the Spanish-American War. (Meleny found him "no egalitarian" while Vaughan [*Roots* xvii] relates his discontent with the "theologicoglacial" era of American history, 1637-1760.) After years of service to the Massachusetts Historical Society, Adams died in 1915. See also Kirkland's *1835-1915: The Patrician at Bay* (1965), and the bibliography in Meleny.

Richard Drinnon's landmark history *Facing West: The Metaphysics of Indian-Hating and Empire-Building* (1980; 1990) broadened the contexts of Adams' various positions. Most studies portray Adams as both involved with and "distant" from his times, and Drinnon details his stance as a "mugwump," or "fence-sitter" amid Congressional factions during strident 1890s debates over the Phillippines. Adams' Liberal-Republicans (supporters included Mark Twain and Andrew Carnegie) "failed" in "operational terms" (Drinnon 308), because "they were the 'outs,' fewer in number, and never within reach of the levers of power." But in 1898, Adams clarified certain things in his public address "Imperialism and the Tracks of Our Forefathers":

> From the earliest days at Wessagussset and in the Pequot War, down to the very last election held in North Carolina [including lynchings of African Americans],---from 1623 to 1898,---the knife and the shotgun have been far more potent and active instruments in [Anglo-Saxon] dealings with inferior races than the code of liberty or the output of the Bible Society.   (16: qtd. in Drinnon 309)

Speaking at Lexington, Mass., Adams continued that this had been "a process of extermination...but for that very reason...the salvation of the race. It has saved the Anglo-Saxon stock from being a nation of half-breeds,---miscegenates, to coin a word expressive of an idea.'"

from
CHAPTER IV
Weston's Rude Fellows

...At length, apparently some time in August [1622], the *Swan* reappeared from Boston Bay. Greene and his party[265] had, it would seem, been received in the most friendly way by the Indians, who, few in numbers and cowed in spirit, gladly welcomed those whom they hoped would prove their protectors against still-powerful neighbors; for their dealings with the Plymouth people had removed from the minds of the Massachusetts all fears of the whites, and they were sincerely anxious to have a permanent settlement near them; indeed, they had already begged Standish to establish one. Weston's agents, therefore, so far as a location was concerned, had but to choose. Exchanging presents with Aberdecest, the local sachem,[266] they finally chose for their place of settlement a site known by the **[60]** Indians as Wessagusset, near the mouth of a little stream called the Monatiquot, which empties into one of the southern estuaries of Boston Bay.[267]

While the fewness of the Indians was undoubtedly a consideration, the choice of this spot was probably due quite as much to the fact that it lay south of all the principal streams separating the Massachusetts from the Plymouth territory, thus making intercourse by land between the

---

[265] **Greene and his party**   of Richard Greene, "brother-in-law" and fellow Merchant Adventurer to Thomas Weston, "nothing is known," Adams notes [55]; but he indicates that Greene and Weston's brother Andrew were sent as advance-men "until another year" when "Master Weston" intended to come there himself

[266] **Aberdecest, the local sachem**   the Neponset Massachusett Sachem also known as "House Afire," Obtakiest, Abordikees, or Chikatawbak/Chikatawbut

[267] Adams here refers readers to the 1634 map by John Winthrop "discovered in London by Henry F. Waters," and locates the site of Weymouth "immediately north of the glacial ridge known as Hunt's Hill on the south side of the Weymouth Fore-river." He cites *Proc. Mass. Hist. Soc.* Series II. vii. 24-30. See maps

settlements comparatively easy....[268] The *Charity* had meanwhile returned from Virginia; and now Weston's enterprise might be looked upon as fairly started.

But scarcely were the newcomers seated in the place they had chosen than ominous rumors began to reach Plymouth, the poor Massachusetts complaining bitterly of them, alleging abusive treatment and theft. It was not in the power of the Plymouth magistrates [61] to do more in the premises than offer anxious remonstrances; and these, it hardly needs to be said, were of little avail. Thus matters went on until early in October. The *Charity* then returned to England, Andrew Weston and Thomas Morton, it would seem, going in her, while Richard Greene was left in charge of the plantation.[269] He was, it is said, fairly provided with supplies; but he does not seem to have been competent, and his followers were wasteful. Accordingly while the *Charity* was still almost within soundings, and before the winter's ice had begun to make, there was scarcity at Wessagusset.

Realizing at last the situation, and his own lack of capacity to deal with it, Greene wrote to Bradford proposing a joint expedition in search of food,---he furnishing the vessel, while the Plymouth people were to provide commodities for barter. A written agreement was entered into on this basis, and by the middle of October everything was in readiness for a voyage to the south side of Cape Cod. But the expedition seemed fated. At first Greene, who had gone down to Plymouth on the *Swan*, fell suddenly ill there and died. He was succeeded in command at Wessagusset by a man named John Saunders, who was apparently even more incompetent than his predecessor.

Still, realizing the pressure of growing want, Saunders' first act in authority seems to have been the writing of another letter to Plymouth urging the immediate prosecution of the voyage. So, as soon as might be

---

[268] Omitted are 14 lines describing Plymouth's "Dr." Samuel Fuller and his care for some of the sick Weymouth colonists

[269] **[Thomas] Morton**　Historian Banks found records of Morton in a minor court case c. 1622-3 in England. This and other clues suggest Morton arrived in June 1624. See Dempsey, *Morton*

after burying Greene, the *Swan* was started off, Standish going in command and Squanto acting as pilot. This was the expedition referred to at the close of the preceding chapter,---that in the course of which Squanto died. It did not start until after the month of November had begun, according to the present calendar, and the season was late for a passage round Cape Cod. The *Swan* therefore encountered easterly winds and heavy weather, and was forced to put back.

Again the party started; and again it was compelled to return. The combined exposure, fatigue and anxiety seem to have proved too much even for Standish, who now broke down under an attack of fever and gave up the command, Bradford taking his place. The outlook was bad. Though it was not yet the close of November,---though the winter was wholly before them---the want was hardly less severe at Plymouth than at Wessagusset. Indeed, it is probable that the scarcity was greatest at Plymouth; but in that patient, frugal and well-ordered community everything was eked out to the utmost, while at Wessagusset little thought was bestowed on the morrow.

But frugality and patience could only mitigate the growing need, and the Plymouth people required no urging from without to bestir themselves; so once more the expedition started, but only to give those composing it a rough experience of the "dangerous shoulds and roring breakers" which two years before had frightened the captain of the *Mayflower* into Provincetown, and which have since made what is called the backside of Cape Cod a terror to mariners. At last they found themselves off Monomoy Point, on Pollock's Rip, and were in no little danger of foundering; but the wind and tide apparently favored them, and the master of the *Swan*, thoroughly frightened, was glad enough to find himself safe in Chatham harbor.

Here a party landed, and Bradford, through the medium of Squanto, endeavored to establish friendly relations with the Indians. These were few in number, and at first very **[63]** shy; but when at last they were persuaded the strangers only wished to trade, they overcame their fear sufficiently to give them some venison and other food, and in the course of a day or two their bartering instincts were sufficiently worked upon to induce them to part with eight hogsheads of corn and beans from their scanty store.

Encouraged by this success, the party determined to attempt once more the southern passage, but Squanto's illness and sudden death, which have already been described, put an end to the project by depriving the party at once of its pilot and its interpreter; so, the wind setting in the right quarter, they rounded Cape Cod again and laid their course directly for Boston Bay. Here they got nothing. Not only did they find the savages suffering from a new outbreak of the pestilence, but the poor creatures were bitter in their complaints of the Wessagusset people. They were not only dying daily, but they were daily robbed. Nor was this all. Weston's outspoken contempt for the trading capacity of Plymouth people to the contrary notwithstanding, it was apparent that the ignorance of his own representatives had spoiled the market. They gave as much for a quart of corn as had before sufficed to buy a beaver skin.

Leaving Boston Bay, the expedition now went to the inside of Cape Cod, to see if anything could be picked up along the shores of what are now the towns of Eastham, Yarmouth and Barnstable. The stormy weather continued, and the *Swan* was at one time in no little danger of being cast away; indeed the shallop which the Plymouth people had brought along, to carry what was bought from the shore to the vessel, was swept off, and so damaged that, when found al- **[64]** most buried in the sand, it was no longer serviceable. As there was no carpenter in the party, it became necessary to leave both corn and boat in charge of the natives until at some other time they could return and fetch them away.

The partners now separated. Inasmuch as some twenty-eight or thirty hogsheads of corn and beans had been secured, the expedition could not, in view of the rough weather which had been encountered, be considered otherwise than successful. It would seem, nevertheless, that either the discomfort on board the *Swan* must have been very great, or the company little congenial; for, rather than go back in her, Governor Bradford and his party, sending word to those on board to meet them at Plymouth, set out on foot for a fifty-mile midwinter tramp home.

They presently arrived there safe, though weary and footsore, and, three days later, the *Swan* made her appearance. An equal division was made of the food the expedition had secured, and the Wessagusset party returned to their plantation; but in January another joint expedition started for Eastham, Standish, who had meanwhile recovered, being now in command. Besides being stormy, it was bitterly cold, and the suffering from exposure was aggravated by insufficiency of food; but the shallop lost in November was recovered, and a portion of the supplies then collected was secured. Another division was made, and once more the *Swan* returned to her moorings in the Weymouth fore-river.

Affairs at Wessagusset now rapidly went from bad to worse. From the beginning to the end, those living there merely demeaned themselves after the manner of their kind. Upon their first arrival, seeing the weakness of the plague-stricken savages and conscious **[65]** of their own strength, they had been arrogant and abusive. It was said that they meddled with the Indian women; what was far worse in the savages' eyes, they had certainly stolen their corn.

As the winter increased in its severity, so did the scarcity, and at last gaunt famine stared the settlers in the face. Meanwhile their bearing towards the savages had passed from one extreme to the other. Day by day their arrogance and self-confidence vanished, until, ceasing by degrees to be careless purchasers, they appeared as naturally as possible in the more congenial character of cunning thieves. Stricken, and but the shadows of their former selves though they were, the Massachusetts Indians soon realized what this change meant, and their demeanor altered accordingly. From cowering before the whites they began to despise them and domineer over them.

Alarmed at the threatening aspect of affairs, Saunders towards the middle of February renewed his efforts to purchase food. The Indians refused to sell, saying---no doubt truly enough---they had none to spare. Then he determined to take by force what he could get in no other way, and began to prepare for the hostilities sure to ensue. The plantation at Wessagusset, like that at Plymouth, seems to have consisted of a few rude log buildings surrounded by a pale, or stockade, in which were several entrances protected by gates. This stockade was now strengthened and perfected, and all the entrances save one secured.

But, before resorting to open violence, Saunders had sufficient good sense to let the Plymouth people know what he intended. They had at least to be put upon their guard. Accordingly he sent a letter to Governor Bradford informing him of the severe straits **[66]** they were in at Wessagusset, and of what they proposed to do. Restitution at some future time of whatever might now be taken was, of course, promised.

Such an unprovoked outrage as that now suggested could not fail to complicate very dangerously the relations between the Plymouth people and the natives. Seriously alarmed, Governor Bradford at once called the elders into council, and among them they drew up an answer to Saunders' communication, but addressed to his company as a whole, which they all signed. In it they labored in characteristic fashion to divert those to whom they were writing from the course proposed. They gravely pointed out that this course was not only in contravention of the laws of God and of nature, but that it was calculated to bring to nought King James' policy, both as respects the enlargement of his dominions and "the propagation of the knowledge and law of God, and the glad tidings of salvation" among the heathen.

Leaving high considerations of state and religion, they then came to particulars. The attention of those at Wessagusset was called to the fact that their case was no worse, if so bad, as that of Plymouth, where they had but little corn left, and were compelled to sustain life on ground-nuts, clams and mussels; "all which they [at Wessagusset] had in great abundance,---yea, oysters also, which we [at Plymouth] wanted." Therefore, it was argued, the plea of necessity could not be maintained. But, finally, those who put their names to the paper came to the real point in the case, and flatly informed their neighbors that, in case recourse was had to violence, those guilty of the violence would have to take care of themselves, and need look for no support from Plymouth; and, moreover, if they escaped the savages **[67]** they would not escape the gallows as soon as some special agent of the crown should come over to investigate the proceeding. In addition to this general and public reply, Bradford by the same messenger wrote privately to Saunders, warning him that he, as the recognized head of the company, would be held to a personal accountability, no matter who else might escape; and so, in a friendly way, advised him to desist in time.

These energetic remonstrances had the desired effect, and, abandoning all idea of force, Saunders now determined to stat at once for the fishing stations at Monhegan, there to procure food. Before doing so he first went to Plymouth; and the utterly destitute condition of his party was made plain by the fact that the supplies on hand did not suffice to victual a crew for the *Swan* on a short voyage of some forty leagues to the coast of Maine.

Leaving her, therefore, at Wessagusset, Saunders set out, though the winter could not yet be said to be over, in an open shallop, Governor Bradford letting him have a small supply of corn. Considering the season, the coast and the frail craft in which he went, the attempt was a perilous one, and whether he ever reached his destination does not appear, for his name is not again mentioned. Certainly he never returned to Wessagusset. Perhaps, finding himself unable to obtain supplies at the fishing stations, he had stayed there awaiting the arrival of the fleet, rightly thinking it worse than useless for him to go back empty-handed.

CHAPTER V
The Wessagusset Hanging

A few days after Saunders left for Monhegan, Standish set out on another of his winter excursions in search of food, going to Manomet, in what is now Sandwich. During the expedition of the previous November [1622], Governor Bradford had bought some corn at this place, but, owing to the loss of the shallop, had been unable to ship it. He had accordingly left it in charge of the savages; and this corn Standish now meant to bring away.

Leaving some two or three men in charge of his shallop, and taking with him as many more, he landed and went some distance inland to the habitation of Canacum, the local sachem. He had not been there long before he noticed that he was much less hospitably treated than Bradford had been, and presently a couple of Massachusetts Indians made their appearance,---one of whom, Wituwamat by name, the Plymouth men well knew. A significant interview between him and Canacum then took place in Standish's presence.

Talking violently and incoherently in his Indian dialect, Wituwamat drew a knife, which hung about his neck, from its sheath, and presented it to his host. He spoke, as it subsequently appeared, of the outrages perpetrated on the natives at Wessagusset, and of a conspiracy which had been formed to destroy the settlement there. The object of his visit now was to induce the Cape Cod Indians to join in it, and he was urging Canacum to take advantage of the occasion, which so unexpectedly offered, to cut off Standish and his party. The knife about his neck was one which he had obtained from Weston's people.

It is, of course, impossible to form any estimate of the military capacity of Miles Standish, for it was never his fortune to have the conduct of any considerable affair. His field of operations and the forces under his control were always small, and it may well be that he would have proved unequal to anything larger. Nevertheless, both on this and on other occasions presently to be described, he showed himself something more than merely a born fighter; for he rose to an equality with difficult and dangerous situations, and he did it through the easy, because instinctive, exercise of one of the most important attributes of all great commanders, -- a correct insight into the methods and characteristics of the men immediately opposed to him.

He knew what the occasion called for when the occasion presented itself. He did not need time to think the thing out; nor, seeing what the occasion called for, did he hesitate. He acted as quickly as he thought. With him it was not a word and a blow, it was a glance and a blow; but the eye was true and the blow well-directed and hard; for, in advance of delivering it, he had measured his opponent correctly.

Before he came to New England the Plymouth captain had never seen a savage; but, once he came in contact with a savage, his instinct told him, and told him correctly, how a savage should be dealth with; and he seems never to have made a mistake. In the [70] presence of savages he always bore himself boldly. He seems to have been gifted by nature with a quick ear as well as eye, for he was already more familiar than anyone else with the Indian speech; but now he could make nothing of Wituwamat's fierce harangue. It sounded to him like gibberish; but gibberish or not, he saw that harm was intended.

It was his custom always to treat the Indians he met in friendly fashion, but he suffered no liberties to be taken, and above all never evinced the slightest sign of fear. If they stole from him, he compelled immediate restitution; if they insulted him, he fiercely resented it. The neglect with which he was now treated by Canacum was in strong contrast to the consideration which the sachem showed towards Wituwamat. It was an Indian insult.

Accordingly, expressing himself in angry and defiant fashion, Standish made ready to return to his boat. Nothing further seems to have taken place at the moment, and the Indian women were induced by some trifling reward to carry the corn down to the shore. There the party had to wait until morning, and the night which followed was probably as anxious a night as Standish ever passed. The air bit shrewdly and it was very cold. Against Wituwamat in particular he was, as the sequel showed, meditating dire vengeance, and the wrath he was nursing may to a degree have counteracted the effects of the piercing wind from which he in vain sought shelter; but the events of the afternoon had alarmed him, and he wanted to get back to Plymouth with the least possible delay.

The immediate situation, also, was by no means free from danger. A mere handful of men, far from home on an exposed coast in the dead of winter, they were surrounded by savages bent on [71] their destruction. Nor were they alone. Among the others gathered at Canacum's lodge was a Paomet, or Cape Cod, Indian, whom they had seen before, but the oppressive friendliness of whose carriage now was extremely suspicious. Not only had he insisted on coming down to the shore with them, but he had voluntarily even carried some of the corn, an ignominious act for a male Indian. Neither, after so doing, had he returned to Canacum's lodge in company with the women; but, making a pretext of the cold, he remained with the Plymouth party, crouching before their fire.

Under the circumstances it is not matter for wonder, therefore, that Standish rested not at all that night, "but either walked or turned himself to and fro at the fire"; nor that, when the waking savage asked him why he did not sleep, he answered him that---"He knew not well, but had no desire at all to rest." But the watches even of that long winter night slowly wore themselves away without further cause for alarm; and, the next day, the wind coming fari, the party got safely back to Plymouth.

Meanwhile, during Standish's absence, tidings had come of the dangerous sickness of Massasoit. Winslow was at once despatched to visit him, with the Indian Hobamack as a guide, and arrived only just in time to save his life. The unfortunate man was lying in his habititation, blind and almost unconscious, while six or eight women were violently chafing his arms, legs and thighs to keep heat in him, and a crowd of men, engaged in their incantations, were, as Winslow described it, "making such a hellish noise as it distempered us that were well, and therefore unlike to ease him that was sick."

With the aid of a little sensible treatment, nature got the better of the dis- [72] order; but Massasoit, naturally attributing his recovery to the skill of his visitors, could not sufficiently express his gratitude. The sense of it was still fresh when, on the morning of the fourth day of his visit, Winslow prepared to set out on his way back to Plymouth. Seeing him about to depart, Massasoit then took aside Hobamack, who was one of his own men, and told him of a conspiracy which had been formed to destroy the Wessagusset settlement. All the tribes of southeastern Massachusetts, he said, had been induced to join in it, and he had himself been earnestly solicited to do so during the earlier days of his sickness.

Among others concerned in this plot, he named the people of Paomet and Manomet. In true Indian style he now urged decisive action, advising the Plymouth people "to kill the men of Massachusetts who were the authors of this intended mischief." All this Hobamack, as he was bid, repeated to Winslow on the way back; so that, when the latter reached home and there met the party just returned from Manomet, the presence of the two Massachusetts men at Canacum's lodge was accounted for. The full significance of the treatment Standish had received became apparent.

There could no longer be any doubt of the existence of a widespread Indian conspiracy. As yet it was directed only against the Wessagusset settlement; but it needed neither Wituwamat's defiant action nor Massasoit's warning to awaken the Plymouth people to the fact that their own fate was involved in the fate of their neighbors. Should the warwhoop ring in triumph over the smoking ruins of Wessagusset, the woods back of Plymouth would not long be quiet.

To appreciate the effect of this sudden revelation of [73] danger upon the minds and nerves of the settlers, it must be remembered that the Virginia massacre had occurred exactly one year before, and that all its harrowing details, freshly brought by the *Charity* and other vessels on their return from the scene of it, must have been uppermost in the mind of every one within the Plymouth stockade, and the constant theme of discussion. They knew whatever history now tells of the incidents of that dread 22nd of March, 1622, when at one and the same instant a merciless blow, which had been planned with impenetrable secrecy, fell upon an unsuspecting people.[270]

---

[270] Adams here cites "Bancroft, i. 142 (ed. 1876)," which relates that Native peoples of Virginia had been regarded with "contempt or compassion. No uniform care had been taken to conciliate their good-will, although their condition had been improved by some of the arts of civilized life....Powhatan, the friend of the English, died in 1618....By this time the Natives were near being driven 'to seek a stranger countrie'; to save their ancient dwelling-places, it seemed to them that the English must be exterminated. On the twenty-second of March, 1622, at mid-day, they fell upon the unsuspecting population; children and women, as well as men, the missionary, the benefactor,--all were slain with every aggravation of cruelty....[The] savages, as timid as they were ferocious, fled at the appearance of wakeful resistance....As to the Indians, [Virginia Company directors] wrote: 'The innocent blood of so many Christians doth in justice cry out for revenge. We must advise you to root out a people so cursed, at least to the removal of them far from you. Wherefore, as they have merited, let them have a perpetual war without peace or truce, and without mercy too. Put in execution all ways and means for their destruction, not omitting to reward their neighboring enemies upon the bringing in of their heads.'" Continues Bancroft: "The arrival of these instructions found the Virginians already involved in a war of extermination....In July 1623, the inhabitants of the several settlements... fell upon the adjoining savages; and a law of the general assembly commanded that in July of 1624 the attack should be repeated. Six years later, the colonial statute-book proves that ruthless schemes were still meditated; for it was enacted that no peace should be concluded with the Indians---a law which remained in force for two years." Not much further on (1892 ed.: 212),

They knew how indiscriminate the murder had been, how neither age nor sex had been spared, what atrocities had been committed on the quick and the dead. The Virginia community at the time it sustained this blow was a large one compared to what their own was now. The very dead in the massacre exceeded the whole number of the Plymouth settlers by nearly threefold; and yet, up to the hour of the Virginia attack, the savages had cunningly borne the aspect of friendliness.

So great and abiding had been the alarm caused at Plymouth by the knowledge of these things that, with the famine of the past winter and forebodings for the next never absent from their minds, the people there during that summer of want and weakness had devoted half their time and strength to building a fort of refuge. But, even when their fort was completed, they remained at most but a pitiful handful, ---not sevenscore, all told,---a speck, as it were, of civilized life between the sea on one side and that impenetrable forest, within which lurked the savage, on the other.[271]

It was true the pestilence had left but few [74] Indians in their immediate vicinity; but not far away were the Narragansetts, an unscathed and warlike tribe, whose missive of "arrows lapped in a rattlesnake's skin" had already come to them as a challenge, and in regard to whose movements and intentions rumor was constantly busy.

There is something appalling in the consciousness of utter isolation. The settlers at Plymouth were but men and women, and their children were with them, and it was impossible they should not exaggerate rather than diminish the danger. Fortunately they were a stolid, unimaginative

---

Bancroft adds that "the planters at Weymouth were saved by the wisdom of the older colony and the intrepid gallantry of Standish. It was his 'capital exploit.'"

[271] On "lurking" (Longfellow's "peeping and creeping"), see Malone, *The Skulking Way of War: Technology and Tactics Among the New England Indians* (1991: 10, 14, 21 and 23). "Mobility" was a key tactic that "fit their environment and their limited goals": Native New Englanders did at rare times of "siege" enclose themselves within a village stockade, but so preferred the refuge of "swamps" that (for ex.) Roger Williams advised Boston in the "Pequot War" of 1637 to "lay ambush between them and the swamp." As Malone points out citing Hubbard and John Eliot, by the 1670s colonists began to appreciate and adopt such tactics

race; and, even though directly from the busy life and complete security of Holland, the neighborhood of the forest seems to have soon become a thing customary and little alarming to them. Simple, straightforward and self-reliant, to them sufficient unto the day were the labors and dangers thereof. Above all else, perhaps, they were held up by that strength of endurance---that staying power, if so it may be called---which is always found associated with any deep religious feeling bred of independent thought. The grateful Massasoit, moreover, had now done for them what another of his race had done for Jamestown[272]; and, with the experience of Jamestown fresh in mind, to be forewarned at Plymouth was to be forearmed.

By this time it was the end of March [1623], and the day for the annual election of magistrates was at hand. When it came about, Governor Bradford made known the situation in open court, and it was there anxiously debated. Finally, without reaching any decision in public meeting, the matter was left in the hands of three men, Bradford the governor, Isaac Allerton the assistant, and Miles Standish; and these three were [75] authorized to call into their councils whomsoever else they saw fit, and to do whatever the common safety might seem to require. They decided on immediate and decisive action. Having so decided, they dismissed all scruples from their minds and determined to deal with the savages after a savage's own fashion. Plot was to be met with plot.

The plan of campaign was a simple one. Standish was to go at once to Wessagusset, taking with him as many men as he thought sufficient to enable him to hold his own against all the Massachusetts. When there, pretending that he was come, as he had repeatedly come before, to trade, he was first to make known his purpose to the settlers, and then, acting in concert with them, was to entrap the conspirators and kill them. The last words of his instructions showed clearly enough that they were framed by himself, and that, as revengeful as he was choleric, he retained a fresh recollection of the scene in the lodge of the sachem of Manomet. He was

---

[272] Bancroft (1892 ed: 212) mentions "a converted Indian" who warned of the 1622 attack

enjoined to forbear his blow, if possible, "till such time as he could make sure [of] Wituwamat, that bloody and bold villain before spoken of; whose head he had order to bring with him, that he might be a warning and terror to all of that disposition."

While these events were taking place at Plymouth, there was at Wessagusset a complete and wretched unconsciousness of impending disaster. Under the pressure of suffering, all pretence even at order and discipline would seem to have been abandoned after Saunders left for Monhegan. Those composing the company no longer lived together within the stockade; but, hunger overcoming the sense of fear, they had divided themselves, and were scattered about near the **[76]** Indian villages, in which, for a handful of food, they performed the most menial of services, degrading themselves into mere hewers of wood and drawers of water. Some had already bartered away their clothes and their blankets; and soon, of course, insufficient food and exposure brought on disease.

Gradually many of them became so weakened that they could hardly continue the search for something wherewith life might be sustained. What in the way of nourishment they could have found at that season is not easy to make out, for the winter had been a severe one, and the ground, full of frost, was covered with snow and ice. It is said they lived mainly on nuts and shellfish, and that one miserable wretch, while digging for the latter, got caught in the mud, and, not having strength to extricate himself, was drowned by the rising tide.

Yet, judging by the mortality among them, their sufferings, as compared with those of the *Mayflower*'s people during the winter of their arrival, would not seem to have been great. At Plymouth, out of more than 100 persons who composed the entire company in December, 1620, scarce fifty remained alive in April, 1621. At Wessagusset, during the winter of 1622-3, ten only out of sixty are reported to have died. It is true that in the one case there were many women and children, while in the other all were able-bodied men; yet, under the circumstances, the proportion of one to six cannot be looked upon as an excessive or, indeed, even as a large mortality. Considering who they were, and what they had to go through, it is, perhaps, rather matter for surprise that all of them did not die.

The bearing of the savages had meanwhile become such as was naturally to be expected. "Rude fel- [77] lows" at best, Weston's people were never calculated to command respect, and it was some time since they had ceased to inspire fear. Now they were objects of mere hatred and contempt. They counted the greater number, but the savages were the masters. As masters, too, these latter did not confine themselves to threats and insults. On the contrary, "many times as they lay thus scattered abroad, and had set on a pot with ground-nuts or shellfish, when it was ready the Indians would come and eat it up. And when night came, whereas some of them had a sorry blanket, or such like, to lap themselves in, the Indians would take it and let the other lie all night in the cold." If treatment of this kind was resented, the savages threatened the settlers, or flung dust in their faces, or even struck at them with their knives.

The natives, moreover, on their side, had good grounds of complaint. Wretchedly poor, even for New England Indians, they had nothing but a few furs, and hardly food wherewith to sustain life. Yet they had been outraged, and they were still robbed. They had complained to the Plymouth people, but their wrongs were unredressed. Under these circumstances the Indians showed in their conduct a self-restraint and respect for persons which, had the position been reversed, would assuredly have been looked for in vain among Europeans.

When pilferers were caught in the very act of stealing the hidden seed-corn, instead of inflicting punishment themselves on the spot, the Massachusetts brought the wrong-doers to the plantation, and delivered them up to be dealt with by their own people. But whippings and confinement could not hold in restraint thieves who were starving. Again the hidden stores were broken into, and again [78] with angry threats the malefactor was brought back to the block-house. Thoroughly frightened now, the settlers told the savages to take their prisoner and to deal with him as they saw fit. This they refused to do, insisting that the settlers should punish their own thieves. His companions thereupon took the culprit out, and, in full sight of those he had robbed, hanged him before their stockade.

This was that famous Wessagusset hanging, which passed into literature as a jest, and then, received back into history as a traditional fact, was long used as a gibe and reproach against New England. It happened in this wise:

Thomas Morton, who, as it has already been surmised, came out with young Weston in the *Charity* in June and returned to England in her with him in October, published, some fifteen years later, an account of his experiences in New England. Though he did not, it would appear, care to dwell upon his connection with Weston's abortive enterprise, for the obvious reason that he was then, as will presently be seen, a hanger-on of those with whom the very name of Weston was a scandal,[273] he could hardly fail at times incidentally to refer to it. Of this particular episode of the hanging he gave the following characteristic account....[274]

Thirty years after the publication of the *New English Canaan*, when its author had long been dead and the book itself was forgotten, Butler's famous satire of *Hudibras* appeared. In speaking of this work Hallam has remarked, in his *Literary History of Europe*, that the inexhaustible wit of the author "is supplied from every source of reading and observation. But these sources are often so unknown to the reader that the wit loses its effect through the obscurity of its allusions." The truth of this criticism was strikingly illustrated in the present instance. Either the author of *Hudibras* had at some time in the course of his reading come across the *New English Canaan*, or he had met Thomas Morton and heard him tell the story, which, as a highly utilitarian suggestion of vicarious atonement, appealed to Butler's sense of humor and thereafter lingered in his memory. Moreover, while in 1664 the Puritans of New England were fair game, whatever Samuel Butler found was his; and so, making, as a thing of course, those **[81]** improvements of fact which literary exigencies demanded, the incident, as finally transmuted by his wit, appeared in the following form

---

[273] that is, presumably, the Plimoth Plantation people themselves

[274] Morton's text as modernized by Adams (and which appears in full herein) now takes up the rest of *Three Episodes'* [79], all of [80] and half of [81]

in what long continued to be one of the most popular and generally read of English books:

> *Our brothers of New England use*
> *Choice malefactors to excuse,*
> *And hang the guiltless in their stead,*
> *Of whom the Churches have less need;*
> *As lately 't happened: In a town*
> *There liv'd a Cobler, and but one,*
> *That our of Doctrine could cut Use,*
> *And mend men's lives as well as shoes.*
> *This precious Brother having slain,*
> *In times of peace, an Indian,*
> *(Not out of malice, but mere zeal,*
> *Because he was an Infidel),*
> *The mighty Tottipottymoy*
> *Sent to our Elders an envoy,*
> *Complaining sorely of the breach*
> *Of league held forth by Brother Patch,*
> *Against the articles in force*
> *Between both churches, his and ours,*
> *For which he craved the Saints to render*
> *Into his hands, or hang th' offender;*
> *But they maturely having weigh'd*
> *They had no more but him o' th' trade,*
> *(A man that served them in a double*
> *Capacity, to teach and cobble),*
> *Resolv'd to spare him; yet to do*
> *The Indian Hoghan Moghan too*
> *Impartial justice, in his stead did*
> *Hang an old Weaver that was bed-rid.*

But the real humor of the thing was yet to come. The actual hanging took place in 1623. When, nearly half a century later, its memory was thus accidentally revived, the Cavalier reaction was at its height; and everything which tended to make the Puritans and Puritanism either odious or contemptible was eagerly laid hold of. They had become the **[82]** target for ribald jesting,---the standing butt of the day. The New England provinces also, and Massachusetts in particular, were known chiefly as the place of refuge of the chosen people;---there alone did they retain a secure ascendancy.

Morton's absurd fiction, as improved and embellished by Butler, was accordingly not only laughed over as a good jest forever, but, gradually passing into a tradition, it seems at last[275] to have even assumed its place as one of those historical incidents, vaguely but currently accepted as facts, which periodically reappear in spite of every effort to put an end to them. Such were, and are, the famous Blue Laws of Connecticutt;[276] and again, that limitation which prevented lords of the manor in feudal times from killing more than two serfs, after the hunt, for foot-warming purposes;[277] or, finally (a yet more familiar example in later history), that dramatic sinking of the *Vengeur*, which not even Carlyle's exposure has sufficed to exorcise.[278]

CHAPTER VI
The Smoking Flax Blood-Quenched

It has already been mentioned that the winter of 1622-3 was one of at least the average New England severity. Beginning with a succession of storms in November, the harbors had been filled with ice until early March, while the snow still lay upon the ground in April.[279] In all its

---

[275] Adams here cites his own edition of Morton's *Canaan*, pages 96 and 251n

[276] Adams here cites Jonathan Trumbull, *Blue Laws True and False* 44

[277] Adams here cites Thomas Carlyle, *French Revolution*, B. I ch. 2; New York *Nation* (No. 338), December 21, 1871, p. 400. *"Was it 'Serf' or 'Cerf'?"*

[278] Adams here cites Jules Verne, *Twenty Thousand Leagues under the Sea*, "P. II ch. 20"

[279] Adams cites Young, *Chronicles* 302, 308; and iv. *Mass. Hist. Coll.* iv. 482-3

Adams, *Three Episodes...* 153

leading features, the wintry scene at Wessagusset must then have been what it now is. The rolling hills into which the country is broken stood out against each other and the sky, offering to the view stretches of dazzling snow against which black masses of the leafless forest were sharply outlined. Groves and clumps of savin fringed the shore and crested the hills to the south and west; while northward lay the island-studded bay, an expanse of snow and ice, broken here and there by patches of water, which, according as the sky was obscured or clear, showed inky blackness or a cold-steel blue.

Immediately in front of the plantation, the swift flow and ebb of the tide must, for long weeks, have now lifted the ice until it was high upon the marshes, and then let it fall until it rested on the flats, or lay piled in huge, broken cakes in the inlets or upon the beach. The solitude and the silence were intense; for at that season both the forest and the air were devoid of animal life, unless now and again the stillness was [84] broken by the howl of a wolf, or a flock of carrion-crows were seen to wing their clumsy way in search of food.

Neither, in the case of Weston's settlement, was the presence of ice and snow merely a cause of tedium and discouragement; for, while the latter lay among the trees, making it very difficult to search for nuts and roots, the former so covered the salt marshes and beach that it must for considerable periods have been quite impossible to get at the shellfish. While the Wessagusset people were thus cut off from their two principal sources of supply, their stock of powder had also run low; nor, mere fifteenth-century London vagabonds, were they familiar with the haunts and habits of game. So there was little left for them to do through the long winter months but to hang, hungry and shivering, about the fires in their log-huts, the mud-sealed walls of which offered but a poor protection against the outer cold. And so, with the ice-bound river before them and the snow-clad wilderness behind, they awaited, with what patience men both freezing and starving could, the slow approach of spring.

The settlers mingled freely with the Indians, hanging about their villages by day and sleeping in their huts at night, thus affording them every possible advantage in case of sudden attack; but, when the feelings of hostility which had slowly been excited at length ripened into a plot, it was not only cunningly devised, but also well-concealed.

The utter destruction of the settlement was proposed; and to assure this it was necessary for the savages to seize, at one and the same moment, not only the stockade and the block-house within it, but also the *Swan*, which lay at **[85]** her moorings in the river. There would then be no place of refuge for the scattered settlers, and they could be destroyed in detail and at leisure. In furtherance of their design the Indians, it would seem, gradually edged up towards the stockade, moving their wigwams nearer and nearer to it. At the same time they were busy constructing canoes, in which latter work they were aided by some of their intended victims.[280]

By this time one at least of the settlers had become thoroughly alarmed. This was Phinehas Pratt, who, coming over in the *Swallow*, had been among the six who afterwards in May reached Plymouth in the shallop. He was now bent on making his escape from Wessagusset.

The journey he proposed for himself was both difficult and dangerous. The distance was not great,---hardly, indeed, more than twenty-five miles,---but the way was through so complete a wilderness that a few years later this region became known throughout the province as the Ragged Plain, it was such a "strange labyrinth of unbeaten bushy wayes in the wooddy wildernes."[281] It had apparently been completely depopulated by the plague of 1617; and since then the underbrush had not been burned away, the frequent watercourses stopping such fires as were set. Accordingly it was now become a tangled undergrowth of bushes and

---

[280] Adams cites Young *Chronicles of Pilgrim Fathers* 342

[281] Adams cites iv. *Mass. Hist. Coll.* iv. 482; and Wood, *New England's Prospect* 13, 61 for the quotation. So much timber had been cut for firewood that new laws against it were set up; and as Indians were soon forbidden their twice-yearly controlled burns of the undergrowth, the land soon became known as a "ragged heath" that tore settlers' clothes

brambles growing over an upland country, interspersed with swamps and cut by running streams.

Pratt may possibly have made the same journey before, though this is not probable; and now, as will be seen, he almost immediately lost his way. He had [86] neither a guide nor a compass. It was the end of March, it is true, and the rigor of the winter was broken; but great belts of snow were still lying on the north sides of the hills and in the hollows, and he was not only insufficiently clad, but weak from want of food. The sense of danger overcoming all fear, he made up a small pack and got ready to set out.

His first object was to steal away unobserved by the savages. Taking a hoe in his hand, therefore, as if he were going out in search of nuts or to dig for clams, he very early on the morning of what is now the first of April left the stockade, and made his way directly towards some wigwams standing not far off and close to the edge of a swamp. When near enough to see any movement which might be going on, he made a pretense of digging, which he kept up until he had satisfied himself that no one was stirring; then, slipping into the thicket, he hurried off towards the south.

Running and walking by turns, he made all the progress he could during the morning, but was often obliged to go out of his way to avoid the snow; though at some points he could not go around, and so was obliged to cross it,---to his great alarm, for his footprints were almost sure to reveal his course. He seems soon to have lost his way; and this probably saved his life, for when his absence became known to the savages, and they sent one of their number after him, he escaped simply from the fact that his pursuer followed the direct trail.

Until about noon the sky appears to have been sufficiently clear to enable him to make out in a general way the direction he was to take, but, as is apt to be the case in the early New England April, the clouds gathered as the day wore on, until at length the sun became so obscured that the [87] fugitive wholly lost his way, and for a time wandered aimlessly about. Later in the day it cleared again, and the glow of the setting sun both gave his bearings to the frightened wanderer, and restored to him a degree of hope and heart. Going on once more, he soon came to the North River, which he found deep and full of rocks. There was no help for it; he had to ford the icy stream, which he only succeeded in doing with much difficulty. Getting at last to its southern bank, he found it too dark to go further.

His condition was indeed pitiable. Weak and wet, cold and hungry,---worn out with his long day's tramp, ---he had but a handful of parched corn to eat, and his fear of pursuit was so great that he did not dare to light a fire. He at last came to a deep hollow in the woods, in which many fallen trees had lodged; and here he ventured to kindle a feeble blaze, before which he passed the night listening to the wolves as they howled in the forest about him. Fortunately the sky became clear, and he was able to make out the pole star, thus assuring himself of the direction he was to take.

The next morning he attempted to go on, but, whether from being too foot-sore and weary, or because of the cloudiness of the sky, he soon found himself unable to do so, and returned to his resting-place of the previous night. The third day of his journey broke clear, and once more he started on his way; but it was not until about three o'clock in the afternoon that, emerging suddenly from the forest, he found himself, to his great joy, on the outskirts of Plymouth. He had made his way by bearing to the south and east, and had come out at some point in what is now Duxbury.

His escape was a narrow one, for the next day his pursuers were lurking in the neighboring woods. Having assured themselves that their quarry had eluded them, they then turned aside and pursued their way southward, apparently intending to notify their confederates of what had happened.

Pratt had reached Plymouth on the third of April, or March 24th as it then was, the day after the annual election. The course to be pursued in crushing out the conspiracy had already been decided on, and the whole available force of the settlement placed at the disposal of Standish, who was well-acquainted with the field in which he was to operate.

His plan was to stamp the danger out at once; he did not propose to simply scare the conspirators into a temporary aspect of friendliness. Above all, it would appear, he was bent on killing Wituwamat; for

Wituwamat had affronted him in the presence of savages, and Standish meant by making an example of him to restore his own prestige in Indian eyes. Cost what it might, that prestige he proposed to maintain.

Accordingly Standish now preferred to incur additional risk rather than do anything likely to excite suspicion, and so prevent the complete carrying-out of his plan. He knew that the Massachusetts were scattered, and at most did not number more than thirty or forty fighting men; but they had been in the custom of seeing the Plymouth leader come on his trading expeditions with a few companions only, and if he now appeared with a large armed force they might be put on their guard, and the prime movers in the conspiracy at least would be careful not to trust themselves within his grasp. So he chose but eight men to go with him, and when Pratt arrived the preparations were all com- **[89]** pleted and the party ready to set out.

The news brought by the refugee was simply confirmatory of what the Plymouth people already knew, though the account he gave of the condition of affairs at Wessagusset revealed the imminence of the danger. The necessity for instant action was clearer than ever. Whatever was to be done must plainly be done at once.

The weather was wet and threatening,---in fact a dreary easterly storm, such as is not unusual in a New England spring, would seem to have prevailed. Regardless of this, on Monday (then the 25th of March, but now the 4th of April) Standish ordered his party on board their shallop and got under weigh for Wessagusset. The force consisted of ten men in all, including in the number Standish himself and the Indian Hobamack. Pratt was too weak from the effects of his journey to accompany them.

As they sailed with a fair as well as a strong wind, the party must have reached Weymouth River on the afternoon of the same day on which they left Plymouth. They soon made out the *Swan* lying quietly at her moorings, and went alongside of her, but found no one on board; nor was any one in sight on the beach. Alarmed apparently at this absence of all movement, and for the moment afraid that the blow they came to avert had already fallen, instead of at once landing at the stockade they fired a musket to attract the notice of any one on the shore near by. In answer to their signal a few stragglers, among whom was the master of the *Swan*, soon showed themselves, abandoning for the moment their anxious search for nuts. In reply to Standish's inquiry, how they dared leave the vessel so unprotected, they explained to him that they did not consider any precautions [90] necessary,---that they had no fear of the Indians, and indeed lived with them, suffering them to come and go in the settlement with perfect freedom.

Learning further that those whom Saunders had left in charge upon his departure were at the plantation, Standish landed and went thither. Finding them, he forthwith proceeded to explain the purpose of his coming. Thoroughly alarmed at what he told them, Weston's people at once became obedient, promising to do as Standish should bid, and thereupon, assuming general command, he went to work maturing the details of his counter-plot. Enjoining strict quiet and secrecy he sent out messengers to call in the stragglers, who amounted to a third part of the company, and at the same time gave notice that any one who left the stockade without permission would be put to death. Then out of his own slender supplies, taken from the little reserve kept for seed at Plymouth, the new commander rationed the entire place, causing a pint of corn a day to be served out to each man.

As the stormy weather still continued, the work of getting in the stragglers proved a somewhat long one, and an Indian meanwhile came into the plantation with some furs, ostensibly to trade, but in reality it was supposed to see what was going on. He reported Standish's arrival to the other Indians, who seem to have suspected the purpose of his coming, but failed to realize with how formidable an opponent they had now to reckon; and, moreover, it would appear that the demoralized conduct of Weston's party had inspired the savages with a feeling of contempt for Europeans generally, which had been strengthened by the apparent impunity with which Wituwamat had insulted Standish in Canacum's lodge. Accordingly, [91] when others of them presently came into the stockade, they did not hesitate to indulge in threats and insulting gestures, even flourishing their knives in the faces of the whites.

Wituwamat himself, little aware of the decree which had gone out against him, was among those who thus tempted fate. Indeed, he seems to have reenacted with variations that Manomet performance which was soon to cost him his head; for, dauntingly drawing his knife, which he carried slung about his neck, he held it up before Standish's eyes, and bade him take note of the face of a woman carved on the handle. Then he added that at home he had yet another knife on which was the face of a man; by and by the two should marry. With those knives, he boasted, he had already killed both English and Frenchmen; and presently the knife he held in his hand should see and act, but it should not speak.

Pecksuot, another brave of great size and strength, a companion of Wituwamat, was also there; and, not to be outdone in bravado, he taunted Standish, in true Indian style, on the smallness of his stature, and compared it with his own; for, though not a sachem, he boasted himself a warrior of courage and repute.

The next day (our sixth of April as it would seem), Pecksuot and Wituwamat, accompanied by two other savages, one of them a younger brother of the latter, again came into the stockade, and were permitted to enter the principal block-house. Standish was there with some four or five of his own company. His hope had been to get a larger number of the savages together before he fell upon them, but he had begun to doubt whether he could succeed in so doing. And now the two most dangerous of them were fairly within his grasp, and he seems suddenly to have resolved to **[93]** seize the occasion.

To each his work was assigned, and a signal had been agreed upon. Watching his chance to take his man unawares, with a stealth which exceeded that of the savages, Standish, suddenly giving the signal, sprang upon Pecksuot. He was the largest and most formidable of them all. Instantly the door was flung to and made fast. The struggle had begun.

It was a short fierce death-grapple. Standish had snatched the knife at Pecksuot's neck from its sheath and driven it into him. The others had fallen upon Wituwamat and his companions. Though taken wholly by surprise and at a fearful disadvantage, the savages neither cried out, nor tried to fly, nor asked for quarter. Catching at their weapons and vainly resisting, they struggled to the last. It was incredible, Winslow afterwards wrote, how many wounds the two warriors received before they died. Three out of the four were despatched on the spot; while the other one, Wituwamat's brother, and scarcely it would seem more than a boy, was overpowered and bound fast.

It remained to complete the work thus bloodily begun. A messenger was hurried off to a party at another point, bidding them at once despatch any Indian men in their power. They killed two. His boy prisoner Standish hung out of hand, killing also one more Indian found elsewhere.

There were a few women in the camp. These Standish made prisoners, placing them under the charge of some of the Wessagusset people; but they were subsequently released without any further harm being done them. Another Indian, through "the negligence," as it is expressed, of the man who should have murdered him, escaped and spread the alarm, thus preventing the full [93] accomplishment of Standish's purpose, which seems to have been the indiscriminate killing of all the males of the tribe.

Having thus disposed of those within his reach, Standish the next day took with him a party, some half dozen in number, and went out, under the guidance of Hobamack, in search of the sachem Aberdecest and the main body of his people. Word of the massacre had reached the sachem's village during the previous night, and all the men, taking their weapons, had left it. Standish had not gone far before he discovered them, apparently making their way in the direction of Wessagusset.

Both parties, getting sight of each other at about the same time, hurried to secure the advantage of a rising ground near by. Standish got their first, and the Indians, seeking at once the protection of the trees, let fly their arrows. The skirmish was hardly worthy of the name. The savages had lost their leading warriors the day before, and when Hobamack, uttering his war-cry and casting aside his garment of furs, ran upon them tomahawk in hand, they turned and fled in terror to a swamp near by, in the mire and undergrowth of which they found a hiding-place.

Only one of them seems to have been injured, his arm having been shattered by a ball from Standish's musket. It was not easy to get at the panic-stricken creatures, and neither taunts nor challenges could induce them to show themselves; nor, indeed, is it surprising that the poor wretches were reluctant to come out and be killed. Their further pursuit was therefore abandoned, and the party returned to the stockade.[282]

Though the object of the expedition was now accomplished, before Standish returned with his own company to Plymouth the course to be pursued by Weston's people had to be decided upon. They could not remain where they were; if they did not wish to **[95]** do that, they might either follow Saunders to the eastward, or, accepting an offer made by Bradford through Standish, return with the latter to Plymouth. As to the last proposition, it would seem that even the hardships of the recent winter had failed to obliterate from the memory of those "profane fellows" the

---

[282] Adams' footnote reads: "These are the incidents described by Longfellow in the Seventh Part of his poem, *The Courtship of Miles Standish*. In using his ma- **[94]** terials it cannot be too much regretted that Mr. Longfellow did not see fit to adhere more closely to the facts as they stand recorded. It certainly does not appear that for poetical effect he has improved upon them. His poem is a New England classic. Probably at least nine people out of ten, who know of these incidents at all, know of them through it. This also will continue to be the case. Nothing certainly can be more Homeric and picturesque than Pratt's struggle through the wilderness,--- than Standish's voyage in his open boat to Wessagusset, along the bleak surf-beaten shore, in the stormy eastern weather,---than the fierce hand to knife death-grapple in the rude log-house within the Wessagusset stockade. The whole is, in the originals, full of life, simplicity and vigor, needing only to be turned into verse.

"But in place of the voyage we have in Longfellow's poem a march through the woods, which never took place and contains in it nothing characteristic,---an interview before an Indian encampment 'pitched on the edge of a meadow, between the sea and the forest,' at which the knife scene is enacted, instead of in the rude block-house,---and finally, the killing takes place amid a discharge of firearms, and 'there on the flowers of the meadow the warriors' are made to lie; whereas in fact they died far more vigorously, as well as poetically, on the blood-soaked floor of the log-house in which they were surprised, 'not making any fearful noise, but catching at their weapons and striving to the last.' And as for 'flowers,' it was early in April and there was still snow on the ground.

"Reading *The Courtship of Miles Standish*, and looking at the paintings upon the walls of the Memorial Hall at Plymouth and of the Capitol in Washington, it is impossible for any one at all imbued with the real spirit of the early colonial period not to entertain a hope that the time may come when a school of historical poets and painters shall arise who will deal truthfully and vigorously with these scenes, studying the localities and the authorities carefully and in a realistic spirit, instead of evolving at once facts, dress, features and scenery from an inner and where not a weak at least a grotesque consciousness. In our early New England scenes the real facts are good enough, strong enough and picturesque enough for any one, be he historian, poet or painter. They certainly have not yet been, nor are they likely soon to be, improved upon." **[95]**

severe justice, the long prayers and the short commons of the preceding summer. They evinced small inclination to return to Plymouth.

As to remaining where they were, Standish contemptuously assured them that he would not fear to do so with a smaller force than theirs; but they were not Standishes, and felt no call to the heroic. Moreover, they were thoroughly out of conceit with the wilderness, and especially with a New England wilderness in winter. All their hopes and anticipations at coming had been disappointed, and they were tired of looking for Weston's appearance and the supplies that were to come with him.

Doubtless, too, they were terrified at the murderous deeds in which they had just taken part; and, weak and few as they knew the Indians to be, they were afraid of them. They dreaded the day of savage reckoning which might come after their energetically should be gone. In short, the single desire with most of them was to get away from the hateful place, and that as directly and quickly as possible; but in doing so they not unnaturally wished to go where there was a chance of finding something to eat. The majority therefore determined to follow Saunders,---hoping either to meet Weston at the fishing stations, or, if they failed in that, to at least work their way back to England.

Following his instructions, Standish then proceeded to supply the *Swan* as well as he could for her short voyage; and so scant was his store, that when he had **[96]** done this, he scarcely had food enough left for his own party until they could get back to Plymouth. The *Swan* and the Plymouth shallop set sail from Wessagusset in company; but when they came to the harbor's mouth they stood away on different courses, the former going off to the north and east, while the latter followed the familiar trend of the shore to the south. Standish had obeyed to the letter the stern instructions which he had himself inspired at his setting forth; for, safely stowed away in his boat, a ghastly freight, he bore back with him the gory head of Wituwamat, "that bloody and bold villain before spoken of."

Such was the ignominious end of the first attempt at European settlement on the shores of Boston Bay. When he heard of it at Plymouth the sedate Bradford gave evidence that though he was a Pilgrim and a

Separatist he was also a human being, for he sent a grim chuckle of exultation after Thomas Weston's vanishing and vagabond crew. "This was the end of these that sometime boasted of their strength," he wrote, "and what they would do and bring to pass, in comparison of the people here; and said at their first arrival, when they saw the wants here, that they would take another course, and not fall into such a condition as these simple people had come to. But a man[']s way is not in his own power; God can make the weak to stand; let him also that standeth take heed lest he fall."

Weston's attempt at a plantation certainly had fallen, for there remained of it at Wessagusset nothing but some deserted block-houses. A few stragglers, three probably in all, including one man who had thrown his lot in with the savages, abandoning civilized life and taking unto himself a [97] squaw, were left behind when the others went away. They had disregarded the summons to come in, and after the massacre could not be reached; but the Plymouth people subsequently did what they could to save them.

The savage who had followed Pratt, and, instead of stopping at Plymouth, gone on further south, had, on his return, come into the settlement and at once been secured. In manacles and under strict guard, he was confined in the new fort, that being the first day that ever any watch was there kept. When Standish safely returned, and Wituwamat's head was perched in triumph on the roof of the captive's prison, he "looked piteously" at it, and, being asked whether he recognized it, answered "Yea."

Doubtless he expected his own head would soon keep it company. But Governor Bradford, rightly concluding that enough in the way of severity had now been done, ordered the prisoner's release, sending through him a message to the sachem Aberdecest to the effect that he must at once deliver up in safety the three captive settlers, and see that no damage was done to the buildings at Wessagusset. The buildings remained undisturbed; but, before Bradford's message reached Aberdecest, the captives had already been despatched. The messenger thereupon did not dare return to Plymouth; and indeed, such was the terror felt among the Massachusetts lest the revenge they took on these men should be visited on their own heads, that for a time no one among them dared show himself.

A woman at last came in bringing a very humble message. She said that Aberdecest would fain be at peace with Plymouth, and that in obedience to their commands he would have sent the captives had they not been already dead when those commands reached him. It would seem, [98] also, that their killing was not unaccompanied by that ingenious refinement of torture which ever made death preferable to Indian captivity; for afterwards, speaking of their fate, one of the savages said,--- "When we killed your men they cried and made ill-favoured faces."[283]

Some months later the news of the Wessagusset affair reached Leyden, and by it the beloved pastor of the Plymouth church was sorely moved. He wrote an earnest letter to his people in which he took the side of the natives, and expressed himself in a way which shows at once both the high moral tone both of him who wrote the letter and of those to whom it was written. It contained all that could now, in the ripe philanthropy of two centuries and a half later, be said in condemnation of what had been done.

> *Concerning the killing of those poor Indians, of which*
> *we heard at first by report, and since by more certain*
> *relation, oh! how happy a thing had it been, if you had*
> *converted some before you had killed any; besides, where*
> *blood is once begun to be shed, it is seldom staunched of a*
> *long time after. You will say they deserved it. I grant it; but*
> *upon what provocations and invitements by those*
> *heathenish Christians? Besides, you, being no magistrates*
> *over them, were to consider, not what they deserved, but*
> *what you were of necessity constrained to inflict. Necessity*
> *of this, especially of killing so many, (and many more, it*
> *seems, they would, if they could,) I see not. Methinks one*

---

[283] Adams's citation here reads: "IV. *Mass. Hist. Coll.* iv. 486; Young, *Chron. of Pilg.* 344." These refer to Winslow's and Pratt's accounts

*or two principals should have been full enough, according
to that approved rule, The punishment to the few, and
the fear to many.*

*Upon this occasion let me be bold to exhort you
seriously to consider of the disposition of your Captain,
whom I love, and am persuaded the Lord in great mercy
and for much good hath sent you him, if you use him
aright. He is a man humble and meek amongst you, and
towards all in ordinary course. But now if this be merely
from an human spirit, there is cause to fear that by
occasion, especially of provocation, there may be wanting
that tenderness of the life of man (made after God's
image) which is meet.*

*It is also a thing more glorious in men's eyes, than
pleasing in God's, or convenient for Christians, to be a
terrour to poor, barbarous people; and indeed I am afraid
lest, by these occasions, others should be drawn to affect
a kind of ruffling course in the world. I doubt not but you
will take in good part these things which I write, and as
there is cause make use of them.*

That the Wessagusset killing amounted to a massacre, and a cold blooded one,---that it failed to include all the male Indians thereabouts simply because they could not be so entrapped that they might all be slaughtered at once,---that, so far as it went, it was a butchery,---all this admits of no doubt. The savages were the first occupants of the soil; they had sustained many and grievous wrongs at the hands of those newcomers whom they had welcomed; there was for them in this world no redress.

Had the situation been reversed, and the Indians, after similar fashion, set upon the Europeans in a moment of unsuspecting intercourse, no language would have been found strong enough to describe in the page of history their craft, their stealth and their cruelty. In this, as in everything, the European has had the last word. He tells the tale. Under these circumstances, while it is impossible to deny, it is contemptible, as is so often done, to go about to palliate. Yet, admitting everything which in harshest language modern philanthropy could assert, there is still no reasonable doubt that, in the practical working of human events, **[100]** the course approved in advance by the Plymouth magistrates, and ruthlessly put in execution by Standish, was in this case the most merciful, the wisest and, consequently, the most justifiable course.

The essential fact was, and is, that the settlers were surrounded by Indians and had to deal with them; and Indians were not Europeans. They could be dealt with successfully, either in the way of kindness or severity, only by dealing with them as what they were,---partially developed, savage, human beings. Now it has already been observed that Standish understood the Indian character, and correctly measured the savage as an antagonist. He understood the Indian, too, through no process of reasoning, for it may well be questioned whether reasoning was exactly Miles Standish's strong point. It was with him evidently a matter of intuition. In other words, he had the same natural faculty for dealing with Indians which some men have for dealing with horses, and others with dogs; and this natural faculty caused him to realize at the outset that truth which Parkman says the French,---both soldiers and priests,---though more successful than any other Europeans in dealing with the savages, learned only slowly and through bitter experience,---the truth, namely, that "in the case of hostile Indians no good can come of attempts to conciliate, unless respect is first imposed by a sufficient castigation."[284]

That the Indians in this case, however made so, were hostile, that a widespread conspiracy existed, and that their plague-stricken condition alone prevented the ill-ordered proceedings at Wessagusset from ending in a general and on the part of the savages most justifiable Indian war, can admit of no **[101]** doubt. If the Massachusetts were weak, the Narragansetts and the Pequots were strong. The movement, once successfully started, might well set the whole immeasurable wilderness in

---

[284] Adams' citation refers to Francis Parkman's "*Old Regime*, 183"

commotion. The course of true wisdom, therefore, was to extinguish the spark, and to extinguish it completely,---not to wait to fight the flame.

Least of all was the time meet for making proselytes. Stung by the wrongs they had endured, and despising those at whose hands they had suffered, the savages were in a frame of mind little receptive of gospel truths. They were thinking rather of scalps and the war-path than of conversion. Chastisement had to precede conciliation; and consequently, in the perilous case in which those composing it at Plymouth then were, John Robinson's flock stood more in need of Miles Standish, however fierce and unreasoning, than of himself, however forbearing and saintly.

It is far nobler to preach and convert than to strike; but there are times when a blow is necessary, and then it is well if one blow sufficeth. Standish struck the savages at Wessagusset in the way they best understood. Stealth, it is to be remembered, is to the Indian what strategy is to the European. It is his method of conducting war. In 1623 he saw nothing in it that was cowardly, nothing that was brutal; and he sees nothing now. On the contrary he dealt in concealments, in conspiracies, in deceits and in surprises. To take your enemy unawares, and kill him, was in his eyes the great warrior's part. To attack him openly was in his eyes folly; to have mercy on him when vanquished was weakness.

Standish therefore merely beat them, and he beat them terribly, with their own weapons. He showed himself more stealthy, more deceitful, more ferocious and more [102] daring than he among them whom, in all these regards, they most admired. With his own hand he had killed their strongest and fiercest warrior, who was also the most cunning of them all, their master in treacheries; and he had killed him with the knife snatched from the warrior's own neck.

Hence the Indians' fear of Standish now knew no bounds. Those implicated in the conspiracy against Wessagusset were at once conscience and panic stricken. Aberdecest in his terror forsook his habitation and removed daily from place to place. Canacum, remembering the scene in his wigwam, hid himself in the swamp, and there died of privation and exposure. Yet another sachem, hoping to ingratiate himself with the avenger, sent a canoe laden with peace-offerings to Plymouth. Near the mouth of the harbor it was cast away, and three of his emissaries were drowned. Thomas Morton wrote that such a terror was Standish, after this event, "that the savages durst never make to a head against them any more"[285]; while the historian of Plymouth said that "this sudden and unexpected execution, together with the just judgment of God upon their guilty consciences, hath so terrified and amazed [the savages] as in like manner they forsook their houses, running to and fro like men distracted, living in swamps and other desert places, and so brought manifold diseases on themselves, whereof very many are dead."[286]

Thus at the cost of seven lives, ruthlessly, treacherously taken, immediate Indian hostilities were averted, and the inevitable life and death struggle with the aborigines was deferred for half a century, when it had to result in the swift destruction of the inferior race. That it should also have resulted in consigning [103] to hopeless West Indian slavery the infant grandchild of that Massasoit whose friendly caution now saved Plymouth, must remain a blot on New England history in comparison with which the Wessagusset killing was an act of mercy. He, at least, might have been saved and converted, that he might have become to a Massachusetts progeny what Pocahontas is to one of Virginia. For a New-Englander to trace a descent from Massasoit would indeed be matter of family pride.[287]

Meanwhile the Wessagusset killing was Standish's last combat with the Indians, for from that time forward, as long as he lived, there was peace between them and the Plymouth colony. At Wessagusset also a few straggling settlers a little later lived for years buried deep in the solitude, and the savages did not molest them. In fact, so far as the dying tribe of the

---

[285] qtd. from the end of *Canaan*'s Book 3 Chapter 3, on the "Battle...at the Massachusetts"

[286] Adams' citation: "Young, *Chron. of Pilg.* 344-5"

[287] Adams' footnote reads: "See the volume entitled *Indian History, Biography and Genealogy: Pertaining to the good Sachem Massasoit*, prepared by Gen. E.W. Pearce and published at North Abington, Mass., in 1878, by Mrs. Zerviah Gould Mitchell. Mrs. Mitchell, who claimed to be a descendant in the seventh generation from Massasoit, was in 1888 still living at Betty's Neck on the Indian Reservation at Middleborough, Mass. She had children. The family is Indian." [104]

Massachusetts was concerned, the fierce blow struck in those early days of April, 1623, was a final one.

They could not rally from it. Out of less than twoscore warriors seven had been taken off. Massacre thus completed the work of pestilence. It may have been necessary,---almost certainly it was best; but, thinking of the terrible wasting which the broken-spirited tribe had so recently undergone at the hand of Providence, it must be admitted that, on this occasion at least, the Plymouth Fathers broke the bruised reed and quenched the smoking flax.[288] **[104]**

---

[288] **bruised reed...smoking flax**   from The Bible, *Isaiah* 42: 1-5. "Behold my servant, whom I uphold: mine elect, in whom my soul delighteth; I have put my spirit upon him: he shall bring forth judgment to the Gentiles./He shall not cry, nor lift up, nor cause his voice to be heard in the street./A bruised reed shall he not break, and the smoking flax shall he not quench: he shall bring forth judgment unto truth./He shall not fail nor be discouraged, till he have set judgment in the earth: and the isles shall wait for his law./Thus saith God the Lord...."

GEORGE F. (Findlay) WILLISON, from *SAINTS AND STRANGERS* (1945)

Being the Lives of the Pilgrim Fathers & Their Families,
with Their Friends & Foes;
& an Account of Their Posthumous Wanderings in Limbo,
Their Final Resurrection & Rise to Glory,
& the Strange Pilgrimages of Plymouth Rock

Born in Denver, Colorado in 1896, Willison attended high school and college there (U. Colorado), took his degree with honors in Greek (1918), and enjoyed his work with school debating teams. Though he enlisted for WWI with the U.S. Army Machine Gun Corps, Willison was never sent, but continued studies in Colorado until awarded a Rhodes Scholarship to Oxford in 1920. There, though interested in literature, he took up economics and politicial science, then spent a year studying history and literature in Paris. He also traveled on the Continent. This placed him amid the "lost generation" of postwar Modernist artists and expatriates, and he spent three years trying to become a writer himself; but financial success eluded him. Willison signed on as head of the Classics Department at St. John's College Annapolis. Within a year he had joined the "progressive" faculty of the Hessian Hills School at Croton on Hudson, and by 1935 was its acting director. In these years Willison wrote his first book, *Here They Dug The Gold* (1931), about early colonizers of his home state: it was reprinted more than once.

Wed in 1928, Willison retired in 1935 and published *Why Wars Are Declared*, a study of socioeconomic causes of conflict. He also became part of the Provincetown (Mass.) branch of the Depression-era's Federal Writers' Project. As he rose to its editorship, Willison came to feel that he and his countrymen knew "literally nothing" about the "real" Pilgrims of Plimoth and Puritans. For nine years he devoted himself to *Saints and Strangers*, and reviews (incl. *New York Times* and *Saturday Review of Literature*) praised its "commendable task of combining accurate scholarship, critical and unconventional in tone, with a lively and picturesque presentation" (qtd. in *Current Biography* 648). A writer/publicist for the Civil Aeronautics Administration and the Democratic National Committee (1942-45), Willison continued to publish in journals, and published *Let's Make A Play: Twelve Plays by Children* (1940); *Behold Virginia: The*

Fifth Crown (1951), and *The Pilgrim Reader* (1953). Devoting late years to fishing, "congenial friends" and "strong waters," he died in 1972. In 1945 he had remarked,

> More, perhaps, has been written about the Pilgrims than any other
> small group in our history. And yet they are still extravagantly praised for
> accomplishing what they never attempted or intended, and are even more fool-
> ishly abused for possessing attitudes and attributes quite foreign to them....Even
> Longfellow, who should have known better, dubbed Myles Standish "the Puritan
> Captain" and always referred to Priscilla Mullins as a "Puritan maid." [Standish
> had never declared himself a Puritan, and Mullins was a widow.]
>   It is about time, I think, that the Pilgrims were allowed to tell their
> own story....They were always quite able to speak for themselves, and never had
> any diffidence in doing so. They wrote marvelous letters...remarkably rich in the
> very stuff of human life. They will stand forever as a bright clear mirror of all the
> hopes and fears that lie closest to men's hearts.

None of this was immune from Willison's irony: chapters included "Purge of Joylity," "Into Ye Briars," "Diaspora," "Minister Trouble," and "Thrown by the Bay Horse." Indeed, Willison's human portrait was a maverick, his life on Cape Cod leading him to evaluate afresh the previous 250 years of "filiopietism" (see Longfellow; Young's 1841 *Good News*); with its roots in the hagiography of Morton's 1669 *Memorial* (the first New England-printed history), Mather's 1702 *Magnalia Christi Americana*, anthologies by Moses Coit Tyler, Arber, Palfrey, C.F. Adams Jr., Levermore, and Samuel Morison (of all whom only Adams detailed "The Weymouth Affair"). Willison's "human beings" broke ground and cast first doubts on records of the "Affair." His skepticism had been aroused by his mostly-mistaken reading of a "contradiction" in *Good News*, that Standish's attack had been launched *before* Plimoth received the warning of "conspiracy" via Hobbamok. (Ill, Standish had delayed a voyage for Massachusett corn.) Later, Vaughan (*Frontier* xxvii) charged that Jennings (*Invasion*) had ratified Willison's "implausible reading." Debates continue whether, in Kupperman's phrase, "the Brethren could dissemble."

The copy-text is the 1945 Reynald & Hitchcock edition of *Saints and Strangers*.

As Willison completes his Chapter XIV, "Cold Comfort for Hungrie Bellies," Plimoth's Bradford has been leading the winter 1621 search for food---and has just returned from Nauset, Nemasket, and Manomet. His chapter concludes with the following paragraph: the citation of Plimoth's minister John Robinson is Willison's.

...The results of the foraging expeditions and the friendly welcome
and generosity of the Cape Indians warmed the hearts but did little
to fill the "hungrie bellies" of the Pilgrim Fathers and their suffering families. All were thin, distraught, and irritable, a prey to many harrowing
fears. Many must have wondered at times if they would ever lay the gaunt
specter of famine. Weston's men had promised to return in the *Swan* "with
all conveniente speed" to pick up the supplies left on the Cape, but they did
not come. As the Pilgrims soon learned, things had gone from bad to worse at
Wessagusset, generating a dangerous crisis in both settlements.

CHAPTER XV
Liquidation of Wessagusset

*It is a thing more glorious in men's eyes than pleasing in God's,
or conveniente for Christians, to be a terrour to poore barbarous
people.*   ---JOHN ROBINSON

From the start the Pilgrims had looked upon Wessagusset with a
jaundiced eye. It lay uncomfortably close to Plymouth, and they feared it
as a rival in the Indian trade. They equally feared it as a source of moral
and spiritual contagion, for Weston's men---so far as they were religious at
all---professed the Anglican creed. They were "not fit for an honest man's
company," so one of the adventurers had said, and even Weston had
granted that they were "rude fellows." But he hoped, he said, "not only to
reclaime them from ye profanenes that may scandalize ye vioage, but by
degrees to draw them to God, &c." Little came of this pious [214] hope, it
appears, and now it was reported---"how truly I know not," said Bradford,
hastening as always to pass along a salacious and damaging bit of gossip---
that their governor was "keeping Indean women." Even worse, he had
"wasted" supplies on them.

Weston's men were, by all accounts, a reckless and improvident lot,
and quickly "made havoc of their provisions." Soon they were selling the
Indians their blankets, even the clothes off their backs, for a bite to eat.
Some, "so base were they," went to work for the savages and would "cutt

them woode and fetch them water for a capfull of corne." Others took to "plaine stealing, both night & day," searching out the Indians' buried stores and breaking into them as the Pilgrims had done at Corn Hill. Many were well whipped and sentenced to the pillory for this, but still the larceny continued. At length, "to give ye Indeans contente," one repeated offender was condemned to die, which gave rise to a story that long plagued the Pilgrims.

This was not the first or last time that they were castigated for the sins of others. The condemned thief, so the story ran, was a strong able-bodied young man, and as the weakened colony could ill afford to lose him, a feeble old man was substituted for him on the gallows. In their ignorance, most people in England drew no distinction between Plymouth and Wessagusset, assuming that both were Brownist colonies, and the satirist Butler in his *Hudibras* seized upon the story to blast the Separatists:

> Our brethren in New England use
> Choice malefactors to excuse,
> And hang the guiltless in their steed [stead],
> Of whom the churches have less need....

As the winter [1622-23] wore on, Weston's men reached the end of their rope. They had consumed all of their stores, even their seed corn, and could not buy, beg, or borrow any more from the Indians. The latter declared that they had scarcely enough maize and beans for their own needs, but some of the colonists refused to believe this, persuading themselves that the Massachusetts were hoarding corn out of sheer malice. At this point John Sanders, second governor of Wessagusset, called his council together and decided upon a foolhardy and fatal course **[215]** of action. He had all but one of the gates in the palisade about the town nailed up and, by Indian runner, dispatched a note to Plymouth to inform Bradford of his plan.

Wessagusset was starving, said Sanders, and therefore he was sailing immediately for Maine to see if he could procure supplies from the English fishing fleet in those waters, an idea doubtless inspired by the

Pilgrims' tale of their success there. It was doubtful, however, if his men could hold out until his return unless supplies were meantime obtained from the Indians. As the latter would not sell their corn, he was "resolved to take it by violence and waited only the return of the messenger, which he desired should be hastened, craving advice therein, promising to make restitution later"---again an echo of a Pilgrim phrase.

This threat thoroughly alarmed Bradford, who hurriedly called in Allerton, Standish, Winslow, and several others for consultation. First, they questioned the Indian messenger, pretending that they were in the market for corn, asking if the Massachusetts had any to spare. No, came his reply, for they "had already spared all they could." Convinced of the truth of this, the Pilgrim leaders rushed back to Wessagusset a strong letter of protest, signed by all of them.

"We altogether dislike your intendment," they declared, warning Weston's men not to count on them for any help in this or any such action. It was plainly "against the law of God and Nature." Why couldn't they do what those at Plymouth had often done and were now doing in want of corn? It was quite possible to "live on groundnuts, clams, mussels, and such other things as naturally the country affordeth." What if they did manage to seize a little corn? How would that help? They would soon be worse off than before, for with the Indians in arms against them they could not move about in search of supplies. And had it ever occurred to them that their raiding party might be repulsed and smashed, for they were weak from hunger, "swelled and diseased in their bodies?" All would probably be scalped by the Indians, and those who escaped would surely be punished by His Majesty's officers for such an unprincipled attack and could "expect no better than the Gaol House." Besides, said the Pilgrims, "all of us might smart for [216] it," and they should consider, too, that it would blast all hope of spreading the "glad tidings of Salvation."

Though Sanders was diverted from his foolhardy course, the fat was in the fire, for word of the plot reached the Massachusetts with unfortunate consequences for all concerned. "Yea," exclaimed Bradford indignantly, "so base were some of their company as they wente & tould ye Indians that their Governor was purposed to come and take their corne by force." Why it was "base" to warn friendly neighbors against the rankest kind of treachery on the part of a misguided few is not quite clear.

At this time, having recovered from his fever, Standish sailed for the Cape to bring back the supplies bought there by Bradford. Putting in at Nauset, he found that [Sachem] Aspinet had kept his promise to guard the stack of corn and the damaged shallop. As he was leaving, Standish discovered that "certain beads, scissors, and other trifles" on the shallop were missing. At the head of an armed party he marched back and angrily delivered an ultimatum to Aspinet. The beads and other missing articles were to be returned immediately, he declared, "or else he would revenge it on them before his departure, and so took leave for that night,...refusing whatsoever kindness they offered."

Used to the gentler and more politic ways of Bradford and Winslow, Aspinet was quite taken aback and hurried to the beach early the next morning, "accompanied with many men, in a stately manner." He saluted the Captain by licking his hand from wrist to fingertips, "withal bowing the knee, striving to imitate the English gesture," as Squanto had taught him to do, but "in so rude and savage a manner as our men could scarce forbear to break out in open laughter." According to the story brought back by Standish, or at least attributed to Standish in the Pilgrim chronicles, the chief handed back the missing "trifles" with many apologies, saying that the thief had been "much beaten," and as a peace offering fed the Pilgrims delicious cornbread baked by his squaws during the night.

Standish and his men next proceeded to Cummaquid. Overtaken by a blizzard, they spent the first night there in the open boat (frozen fast in the harbor), suffering cruelly from the [217] bitter cold. In the morning [Sachem] Iyanough and his braves spied them, brought them in, and took them to their houses, inviting them to spend the night as the storm was still raging. As at Nauset, the Indians here had carefully guarded the Pilgrims' supplies and even agreed to sell them more corn, volunteering to carry it down to the beach and help them load it in the shallop.

The Pilgrims weighed anchor and were about to depart when, curiously enough, the Captain again missed some trinkets from the shallop and in high dudgeon marched off to deliver another ultimatum. Throwing a ring of heavily armed men about the Sachem's lodge, which was crowded with people, Standish loudly demanded the return of his beads, "threatening to fall upon them without further delay if they would not fortwith restore them." Even more astonished than Aspinet, "gentle" Iyanough came out to discover the cause of the tumult and suggested to the Captain that his precious beads might perhaps have been mislaid, "desiring him to search whether they were not about the boat." A man was sent to the shallop where the beads were found "lying openly upon the boat's cuddy." But to Standish this merely proved the Indians' "knavery," for he chose to believe that Iyanough had somehow managed to have the thief surreptitiously return them. Notwithstanding all of their kindness, the Cummaquid were only "pretending their wonted love."

Quite possibly there was some friction along the Cape, for trouble usually attended the Captain's contacts with the Indians---and with many of the whites, too, for that matter. But the curious story of the beads, if true and not fabricated after the event, was a flimsy foundation for the Pilgrims' later attempt to prove a conspiracy against them in their anxious effort to justify a quite indefensible action. If Aspinet and Iyanough had been engaged in a diabolical plot against Plymouth, as the Pilgrims tried to represent, they would scarcely have begun by stealing a few beads when they had in their possession the supplies that meant life or death to the plantation. Nor would they have offered them more corn and beans from their own very limited stock and carried them down to the beach to see them quicky and safely loaded. **[218]**

Standish soon returned to the Cape, going to Manomet, where Bradford had been so well received not long before and had come away with such a favorable impression of the "grave" [Sachem] Canacum. Though he obtained the supplies he sought, the Captain was not at all impressed. On the contrary, he was very much annoyed, "not finding the entertainment he found elsewhere, and the Governor had here received." As he had doubtless heard of the martial antics at Cummaquid and Nauset, perhaps the sachem was a little cool. And he had even better reason than that to be somewhat reserved and on his guard.

Word had come, spreading like wildfire through the forests, of Sanders' proposed treachery at Wessagusset, which reminded the Cape tribes of many sad experiences with white marauders. They were aware that Sanders had been in communication with Bradford about his plan. They knew that Weston's men had lived at Plymouth for months, and it was not obvious from their joint foraging expeditions in the *Swan* that the planters at Plymouth and Wessagusset were partners? The wonder is that Standish and his party were received at all.

During the Pilgrims' visit, and to their great embarrassment, two Indians walked in---both from Wessagusset! One was a "notable insulting villain," Wituwamat by name, a renowned Massachusetts brave, who held a very low opinion of the whites, it appears, for he "derided their weakness, especially because, as he said, they died crying, making sour faces, more like children than men." And after making such insulting speeches, his "entertainment much exceeded the Captain's," which was simply insupportable, and Standish was so angry with his hosts that he "scorned at their behavior, and told them of it."

Ignoring the purplish Captain, Wituwamat drew out a long knife, presented it to Canacum, and began a long speech "in an audacious manner, framing it in such sort as the Captain, though he be the best linguist amongst us, could not gather anything from it." But Standish did not like the sound of Wituwamat's remarks, and in some mysterious manner it was "afterward discovered" just what had been said. The Massachusetts were resolved to "ruinate" Weston's colony and felt confident of success, being thirty or forty strong. But they feared Plymouth, persuaded that the planters there "would never leave the death of their countrymen unrevenged." Therefore they were come to persuade the Cape tribes to join their attack on Plymouth, for none could be safe "without the overthrow of both Plantations." As Captain Standish and his men were providentially at hand, why not begin with them?

Nothing happened.

Another visitor came in, one of the Pamet tribe, who had always been "very affable, courteous, and loving, especially towards the Captain." To all appearances he remained so, "making many signs of his continued affections." But this, it seems, was merely "to avoid suspicion," for he had "now entered into confederacy with the rest." Taken to the Pilgrim camp, he would have murdered Standish in his sleep but for the wit of the Captain, who paced up and down before the fire till dawn, the night being extremely cold. Yet the Pamet was invited to accompany the party to Plymouth the next day, and there he persuaded the Captain to go with him to the tip of the Cape to obtain more corn. They set sail together but did not arrive, being driven back by a storm.

The plot thickens, and now the scene shifts to Sowams.[289]

During Standish's absence at Manomet, the Pilgrims had received the disturbing news that Massasoit was dying. Winslow immediately departed for Sowams with Hobomok. Along the way, in Corbitant's country, they were informed tha the Big Chief was dead, to the alarm and anguish of both.

"Neen womasu Sagimus, neen womasu Sagimus!" wailed Hobomok. "My loving sachem, my loving sachem! Many have I known, but never any like thee. Whilst you live," he said, turning to Winslow, "you will never see his like among the Indians. He was no liar. He was not cruel and bloody like other Indians. In anger and passion he was soon cooled, easy to be reconciled towards such as had offended him, ruled by reason in such measure as he would not scorn the advice of mean men and governed his men better with a few strokes than others did with many, truly loving where he loved. Yea! I fear you have not a faithful friend left among the Indians."

Uneasy about the rumor that the new chief would probably [220] be "that notable politician" Corbitant, always somewhat reserved toward Plymouth, Winslow thought it wise to visit him and be the first to offer his congratulations. He therefore proceeded to Corbitant's winter headquarters at Mattapuyst, now the town of Mattapoisett, on the western shore of Buzzards Bay. Corbitant was not at home, having gone to Sowams, and Winslow sent a messenger ahead to inform him of his

[289] **Sowams**   Willison uses the Wampanoag name for the "Montop" or Mount Hope region of southeastern Massachusetts just north of Narragansett Bay, Massasoit's "permanent" residence

coming. The messenger returned at sunset to report that the Big Chief was not dead but sinking fast, and if they wished to see him alive, they would have to hurry. Winslow and Hobomok pushed on, stumbling along the forest track in the dark, and at length arrived late at night to find the sachem's lodge so full of people that they could scarcely get in and "making such a hellish noise," said Winslow, "as it distempered us that were well." The medicine men were "in the midst of their charms for him," dancing about and chanting at the top of their lungs, while the Big Chief's squaws were frantically rubbing his legs and arms.

"Oh, Winslow, I shall never see thee again!" groaned Massasoit, explaining that he had lost his vision, that everything was black before his eyes, and he was very pleased when Winslow offered to treat him. The latter had brought along a "confection of many comfortable conserves" and gave some of this to the Big Chief, feeding it to him on the point of a knife which he had great difficulty in forcing between his teeth, for the patient's jaws were almost locked. A slip here might have had serious consequences, but no blood flowed. Winslow then washed out the sachem's mouth, which was "exceedingly furred," and scraped his enormously swollen tongue. Learning that the Big Chief "had not slept in two days...and had not had a stool in five," he gave him more confection. Within a half hour, to the amazement of all, "his sight began to come back to him." Impressed with Winslow's talents, Massasoit begged him to tend all his ailing people, "saying they were good folk." Winslow agreed and washed out their mouths also, though he found it a most offensive chore, "not being accustomed with such poisonous savours."

Now the Big Chief wanted soup, some of that "good English pottage such as he had eaten at Plymouth." Winslow [221] brewed up corn, strawberry leaves, and sassafras root into something so palatable that the sachem asked for more---but with a duck or goose in it. To humor him, Winslow shot a mallard and tossed that into the pot. When it was ready, he ordered Hobomok to skim off the fat before serving, but Massasoit would not hear of this and in spite of every warning "made a gross meal of it," suffering a violent relapse, heaving and retching, again losing his sight, bleeding profusely at the nose, to the great alarm of the Wampanoag.

Winslow quieted their fears, and his own, by assuring them that he was so weak and exhausted that he would now sleep, "which was the principal thing he wanted." The sachem suffered another relapse, but within a day or two was again on his feet, "lustie" as ever, having quite forgotten his resentment at being denied Squanto's head.

"Now I see the English are my friends and love me," he told his people, "and whilst I live, I will never forget this kindness they have showed me."

Departing, Winslow accompanied Corbitant to Buzzards Bay and spent the night at his lodge there. Far from being an ogre, Corbitant proved upon acquaintance to be a very pleasant fellow, "full of merry jests and squibs, and never better pleased than when the like are returned again upon him." With a wry smile, alluding to the rumpus and shooting at Nemasket,[290] the chieftain asked if the Pilgrims would come to physic him if he were sick. Assured of this, he then inquired if Winslow were not afraid to come alone among the Indians.

"Where true love is," he was told, "there is no fear."

"But if your love be such and bring forth such fruits," Corbitant objected, "how cometh it to pass that when we visit Patuxet, you stand upon your guard with the mouths of your pieces towards us?"

"It is the most honorable and respectful entertainment we can give you," Winslow explained, trying to make sense of the military salute.

"I like not such salutations," the chief remarked and began to talk of other things. Why was it, he asked, that grace was said not only before but after meals at Plymouth? This offered a splendid opportunity for an exposition of "God's works of **[222]** Creation and Preservation, of his Laws and Ordinances, especially of the Ten Commandments," and Winslow made the most of it. Corbitant and his men listened attentively and observed that they "believed almost the same things," taking exception only to the Seventh Commandment, according to Winslow, "thinking there

---

[290] **rumpus and shooting at Nemasket**   that is, when Sachem Corbitant had "kidnapped and threatened the life of" Tisquantum/Squanto. See Editor's Introduction *xxxviii* and *liv-lv*

were many inconveniences in it, that a man should be tied to one woman, about which we reasoned a good while."[291]

The Pilgrim ambassador thoroughly enjoyed his stay and "never had better entertainment amongst any of them." Regretfully taking his leave, he set out for Plymouth next morning, and along the trail that day Hobomok told him an extraordinary story, or so Winslow reported.

Massasoit, it appears, had called Hobomok aside before his departure and "privately" informed him that the Massachusetts Indians planned to destroy Wessagusset and then fall upon Plymouth.They had persuaded the Nauset, Cummaquid, Manomet, Pamet, and even the Gayhead of Martha's Vineyard[292] to join them in the attack. Hobomok was therefore to inform his friends at Plymouth that if they wished the Big Chief's advice, they should instantly proceed against the "authors of this intended mischief" and kill them. There was not a moment to lose if they valued the lives of those at Wessagusset and their own "after-safety."

Such was the remarkable story offered by the Pilgrims as main and conclusive proof of a widespread conspiracy against them, as complete vindication of their decision to liquidage Wessagusset and put the Indian leaders to the sword. And the more one thinks about it, the more remarkable this story becomes, and the more amazing it is that the tale should ever have been taken seriously, as it always has been, even by critical historians.

First, why should Massasoit have informed Hobomok "privately" about matters so vital to Plymouth when Winslow was with him, at his elbow day and night? Under the circumstances, he might at least have offered to assist the Pilgrims as the terms of the peace pact required.[293] And why, if the Cape tribes were involved in the conspiracy, did he not offer to call them to heel, for they were his subjects [223] and looked to him in all things? The inclusion of them in the Pilgrims' story undoubtedly was

---

[291] Willison's footnote reads: "Their conclusions, unfortunately, have been lost"

[292] **the Gay [H]ead of Martha's Vineyard**   or rather, the Wampanoags of Capawac

[293] **peace pact**   that is, the Nov. 1621 "Thanksgiving" treaty (Introduction *liii*)

an afterthought, inserted to explain away several embarrassing events on the Cape---and it was a blunder. If the Cape tribes had actually been in league with the Massachusetts, then they were in revolt against Massasoit, which would have been genuinely startling news. But there is not a shred of evidence anywhere to suggest that this was true.

Was the story Hobomok's perhaps? Was he up to Squanto's trick of putting words in others' mouths to promote devious purposes of his own? It is interesting that Hobomok waited till he was two days along the trail before he told Winslow his story. But this fact must be set against another that is even more significant. One would suppose that Winslow, upon hearing such alarming news, would hasten home with all speed. Instead, he loitered along the way, stopping to spend the night at Nemasket, quite as if nothing had happened. And the next morning, while proceeding in a leisurely fashion, he met two friendly Indians coming from Plymouth who told him something which, carelessly left in the rather skilfully edited record, casts a most revealing light upon this entire business:

"Captain Standish was, that day, gone to the Massachusetts."

The decision to proceed against Wessagusset had been taken before Winslow arrived to tell Bradford what Hobomok had told him about what Massasoit had said to him "privately." Thus, unwittingly but quite effectively, the Pilgrims themselves exploded their official thesis that the attack on Wessagusset was preventive and inspired by Winslow's story. The truth is, plainly, that the tale was fabricated after the event in an effort to justify a series of treacherous actions of which the Pilgrims were always a little ashamed.

The shallop bearing Standish and his men was forced by strong head winds to turn back, arriving just as Winslow did. Then, according to the sequence of events in the Pilgrim chronicles, Bradford hurriedly called a council to discuss the terrifying news brought home by Winslow. As the governor had no authority to declare war "without the consent of the Body of the company," the question was laid before a general **[224]** meeting of the planters. The latter were quite surprised by the sudden crisis, evidently not having the slightest suspicion that anything was wrong. As they hemmed and hawed, possibly rising to ask some embarrassing questions, their leaders pressed them to stop talking and make up their minds, declaring that it was "high time to come to resolution, how sudden soever it seemed to them." In the end they decided that as "every man was not of sufficiency to know nor fitness to judge," and as there should not be another dangerous leak of information to the Indians as at Wessagusset, the decision should be left to the discretion of Bradford, Allerton, and Standish, who were to choose such others as they desired.[294]

This committee quickly drew up a secret plan of action. On pretense of trade, Standish was to go to Wessagusset with as many men as he thought necessary to deal with the Massachusetts. He was to acquaint the governor of the real purpose, but there was to be no declaration of war. Rather, he was to show himself very friendly toward the Indians until he "could take them in such traps as they lay for others." In particular, and probably at his own suggestion, he was to make sure of "that bloody and bold villain," Wituwamat, who had so insulted him at Manomet and was given to making such disparaging remarks about the prowess of the English and their childish manner of dying---"making sour faces," indeed! The wretch's head was to be cut off and brought back to Plymouth as a "warning and terrour to all of that disposition."

While preparations were under way, one Phineas Pratt arrived from Wessagusset to report that things were in a sad state there, requesting permission to stay in Plymouth for a time. Weston's men were in a pitiable condition and scattered all about the countryside in their desperate search for food. He felt sure, he said, that he had been followed from Wessagusset by one of the Massachusetts who planned to kill him along the way. But he escaped, according to the Pilgrims, because the Indian got lost in the woods!---missing Plymouth by so wide a margin that he ended up at Manomet, miles away.

On his return the savage came through Plymouth, "still pretending friendship," and Bradford promptly lodged him in the [225] Fort, chaining him to a post in the Guard Room, where he would have to be "content to

---

[294] Willison's footnote: "The names of those chosen to serve on this committee are not known. But Winslow undoubtedly was one, and Stephen Hopkins probably another"

remain," he was told, "till the return of Captain Standish from the Massachusetts." The Pilgrims did not propose to allow him any opportunity to wreck their plans by sounding the alarm.

With Hobomok and eight heavily armed men,[295] not taking more for fear of arousing suspicion, Standish again set sail and at Wessagusset found the *Swan* anchored in the harbor with not a soul on board, with "not so much as a dog therein." After the Pilgrims had fired a volley or two, the skipper and some of the crew appeared on the beach, having gone ashore to gather clams and groundnuts. How did they dare to live in such insecurity and leave their vessel thus unguarded? they were asked.

"We fear not the Indians," they replied, "but live with them and suffer them to lodge with us, not having sword or gun, or needing the same."

"If there is no cause, I am the gladder," said Standish with scarcely disguised contempt for these men "senseless of their own miserie." Marching his men into Wessagusset, he informed the governor of the purpose of his coming. Weston's men made a feeble protest but soon gave in, saying "they could expect no better." Forbidding anyone to leave the town "on pain of death" (three men preferred the Massachusetts to the Pilgrims and escaped), Standish waited patiently for the moment to strike, trucking for furs with the Indians, carrying things "as smoothly as he possibly could," but not altogether successfully. An Indian returned from Wessagusset to tell his people that from his eyes he could see the Captain was "angry in his heart."

A few days later an exceptionally tall and powerful brave named Pecksuot came in to visit Hobomok. He was aware, he said, that Standish had come to kill him and others.

"Tell him we know it, but fear him not. Neither will we shun him, but let him begin when he dare." Turning to Standish on another occasion,

---

[295] Willison's footnote reads: "Captain John Smith's army in Virginia had been almost equally small. 'When I had ten men able to go abroad, our common wealth was very strong,' Smith declared, boasting that 'with such a number I ranged that unknown country 14 weeks; I had but 18 to subdue them all, with which great army I stayed six weekes before their greatest Kings' habitations....'" Pratt counted "10 or 11" men in Standish's party

he remarked, "Though you are a great Captain, yet you are but a little man, and though I be no sachem, yet I am a man of great strength and courage."

Wituwamat also came in and was as contemptuous as ever, **[226]** drawing out and caressing a long sinister knife with the carving of a woman's face on the handle.

"I have another at home wherewith I have killed both French and English," he said, "and by and by the two must marry." All such "insulting gestures and speeches" Standish carefully noted and "bore with patience for the present." But his patience was wearing thin. Failing in his attempt to "get many of them together at once," he decided to start with Pecksuot and Wituwamat.

These two and another brave, together with Wituwamat's brother, a boy of eighteen, were lured one day into Pilgrim headquarters---by an invitation to a feast, an enemy asserted.[296] Whatever the lure, the Pilgrims were quite shockingly frank about what happened there. At a signal, the door was made fast and Standish leaped at the huge Pecksuot who had belittled him. Snatching the latter's knife from the string about his neck, he plunged it into his breast. Wituwamat and the other braves were done to death by the blades of Standish's men after a fierce hand-to-hand struggle, and even Standish remarked his admiration of the courage and strength of the trapped Indians as they hopelessly fought for their lives, saying that it was "incredible how many wounds they received before they died, not making any fearful noise, but catching at their weapons and striving to the last." Only one of the Indians escaped being cut to pieces, the Indian boy, "whom the Captain caused to have hanged."

The attack so took the Massachusetts by surprise that many of them, principally women, were caught in town. Placing these in charge of Weston's men, Standish commanded the whites to put to death every Indian warrior they could find. Weston's men killed two, Standish and his

---

[296] refers to Morton's *Canaan*, above

men added another, but a fourth escaped through "negligence"---what a pity!---"and crossed their proceedings."

Thoroughly aroused, the Captain marched his forces out of town, "still seeking to make spoil of them and theirs." He encountered and drove back a band of the Massachusetts, who let "fly their arrows amain" as they slowly retreated from tree to tree, concentrating their attack upon Standish and Hobomok. Losing his temper, the latter stripped off his coat and "being a known Pinese, chased [227] them so fast our people were not able to hold way with him." The Massachusetts finally took refuge in a swamp, hurling curses and insults at the whites as they came up, and Standish got nothing but "foul language" when he challenged their leader "to come out and fight like a man, showing how base and woman-like he was in tongueing it as he did."

Returning to Wessagusset, Standish asked Weston's men what they wished to do now, for they were afraid to stay where they were. They could come to Plymouth if they desired. Rather, they chose to sail for Maine in the *Swan*, hoping to hear of Weston there or to arrange to work their passage home in the vessels of the English fishing fleet, which most of them succeeded in doing.

With troublesome neighbors out of the way and the Indians cowed, Standish and his men set sail and were "received with joy" at Plymouth as they came triumphantly home bearing Wituwamat's head. The bloody trophy was carried to the Fort and stuck on a spike on the battlements there for all to see, one of the sights of Plymouth for many years. But they brought nothing else with them, as the Pilgrims were at pains to point out. They had refrained from looting Weston's men, "not takeing ye worth of a penny of anything that was theirs." Nor had they stripped the once giggling women of the Massachusetts when the latter were prisoners of war. Resisting temptation, Standish ordered their release and "would not take their beaver coats from them."

King Beaver, it is likely, had more of a hand in this plot than appears at first sight. The fur trade was the life blood of Plymouth, its sole profitable enterprise. It alone could provide the revenues needed to buy supplies and pay off debts. The Pilgrims did not intend to sit quietly by and see this artery of commerce cut or blocked, and Wessagusset was strategically placed for such a purpose, as that shrewd trader Weston doubtless realized in choosing the site. The town was settled only a few months before the Pilgrims noted that it was already upsetting the corn and beaver trade. On their last visit to the Massachusetts they observed that "little good could be done there," for Weston's men were "giving as much for a quart of corn as we used to do for a beaver's skin."

The Pilgrims had a way of representing the Indians as subtle and [228] dangerous whenever it served their purpose, according to a later rival in the beaver trade. "I have found the Massachusetts Indians more full of humanitie than the Christians," he declared after years of experience with both, "and have had much better quarter with them." By creating fear and mistrust of the Indians, he said, the Pilgrims hoped to keep neighboring settlers from scattering and freely going about the countryside, with the aim of bringing them "under their Lee, that none might trade for Beaver but at their pleasure."[297] Certainly the Pilgrims wept no tears when Weston's men abandoned Wessagusset and sailed for home. The scheme of their "loving freind" to dispossess them had come to naught.

When news of the "huggery" at Wessagusset reached the tribes along Cape Cod, they were terror-stricken, recalling Standish's displeasure with them and his ultimatums. They were so "amazed" that they "forsook their houses, running to and fro like men distracted, living in swamps and other desert places." Many took sick and died, including "grave" Canacum of the Manomet, "stately" Aspinet of the Nauset, and "gentle" Iyanough of the Cummaquid, who had been so helpful and friendly, winning the respect and trust of every Pilgrim leader except Standish.

---

[297] Willison's footnote reads: "This charge was made by Thomas Morton of Merry Mount, an avowed and bitter enemy. But it cannot be airily dismissed, as has been the fashion, with the remark that Morton was an 'immoral' character. The affair at Wessagusset and subsequent events elsewhere clearly reveal that a lively concern about the beaver trade was strongly operative among the Pilgrims' motives on many occasions, which was only natural. After all, their very existence depended upon it. One can only find fault with them for trying to cover needless barbarity with 'moral' pretences---and all of us, seemingly, have a weakness for that."

Well aware that recent events needed a deal of explaining, the Pilgrims entrusted their defense to the always plausible Winslow, who cleverly presented their case in *Good Newes from New England*, published in London the next year. Blandly observing that the accounts of the action at Wessagusset would no doubt be "various," as they certainly were---the Pilgrims were soon complaining about the "vile and clamorous" reports of the dispossessed Wessagusset men---Winslow apologized for the length of his story by saying that he durst not be too brief lest he "rob God of that honour, glory, and praise which belongeth to him...."

But there was one Saint, and the greatest of them, who failed to discern any sign of God's handiwork in the treacherous and bloody business and who raised a mighty voice to place responsibility squarely where it belonged.

"Concerning the killing of those poor Indians," wrote John Robinson in phrases that cut the Pilgrims to the quick, "oh! [230] how happy a thing it had been if you had converted some before you had killed any; besid[e]s, where blood is once shed, it is seldome stanched off a long time after. You will say they deserved it. I grant it, but upon what provocations and invitments by those heathenish Christians? Besid[e]s, you being no magistrates over them, were to consider not what they deserved, but what you by necessitie were constrained to inflicte. Necessitie of this, espetially of killing so many (and many more, it seems, they would if they could), I see not,...and indeed I am afraid lest, by these occasions, other should be drawne to affecte a kind of rufling course in the world...

"Upon this occasion let me be bould to exhorte you seriously to consider of ye dispossition of your Captaine, whom I love and am perswaded ye Lord in great mercie and for much good hath sent you him, if you use him aright. He is a man humble and meek amongst you and towards all in ordinarie course....But there may be wanting that tendernes of ye life of man (made after God's image) which is meete....

"It is a thing more glorious in men's eyes than pleasing in God's, or conveniente for Christians, to be a terrour to poore barbarous people." [230]

ALDEN T. (True) VAUGHAN, from *NEW ENGLAND FRONTIER: Puritans and Indians 1620-1675*
(1965: revised editions 1979, 1995)

While Vaughan's basic personal-biographical facts remain difficult to ascertain, *The Directory of American Scholars* (Detroit: Gale 1999, Vol. 1) reports that he was born in 1929, and received his B.A. in History at Amherst College, Massachusetts, in 1950. He completed his graduate studies at Columbia University in New York, earning his M.A. in Teaching and in History there in 1958, and his Ph.D. in History in 1964. Vaughan's doctoral dissertation became his first published book three years later as *New England Puritans and the American Indian*, and the title signified the main subjects of his prolific career as an historian, critic and textual editor. According to the 1999 *Directory*, Vaughan---now Professor Emeritus of History at Columbia---continues to publish new works and resides near Worcester.

Vaughan has written and edited (as well as revised and republished) as many as twelve books and numerous articles in his declared field of "British North American heritage." These have included studies of the American Revolutionary period (*America Before the Revolution* of 1967, and *Frontier Banditti and the Indians: The Paxton Boys' Legacy 1763-75* of 1984), as well as a number of accessible new editions and collections of important Early American primary texts: from *Early American Indian Documents* (1979) to *Narratives of North American Indian Captivity* (a bibliography, 1983), from his 1993 reprinting of William Wood's 1634 *New England's Prospect* to one of his latest studies in cooperation with many historians, *New England Encounters: Indians and Euroamericans 1600-1850* (published in 1999). Vaughan has also related that in the 1970s he discovered the riches of Columbia's Folger Shakespeare Library, and he has made fresh and fruitful use of those resources, including co-editing *Shakespeare's Caliban: A Cultural History*, an examination of American-colonial "slaves and slavery" that takes its inspiration from Shakespeare's problematic portrait of Caliban---a quasi-Caribbean "wild man" and resentful "servant" of magician Prospero's in *The Tempest*.

"At Columbia," Vaughan wrote (in his *Roots of American Racism*, 1995), "I had the good fortune to study history under the benign guidance of Richard B. Morris and then to be his colleague for many years. Dick's enthusiasm for early American history and his insistence on rigorous documentary research were infectious" (*xii-xiii*).

Vaughan twice revised his *New England Frontier* not least because of the controversies aroused by its basic assumptions and, according to some, "revisionist" conclusions. Hailed by *American Historical Review* as an "objective study...the standard authority on Puritan-Indian relations from the landing of the *Mayflower* through King Philip's War," Vaughan's *Frontier* stands, according to its publisher, "in contrast to most accounts of Puritan-Indian relations," for it "argues that the first two generations of Puritan settlers were neither generally hostile toward their Indian neighbors nor indifferent to their territorial rights. Rather, American Puritans---especially their religious and political leaders---sought peaceful and equitable relations as the first step in molding the Indians into neo-Englishmen."

Vaughan wished to defend colleagues whose findings proved "exculpatory" of the Puritans. Facing the "harsh revisionism of the 1970s and 1980s" (*xlv*), from such as Neal Salisbury, Richard Drinnon, and Francis Jennings (whom Vaughan found "heavily polemical," *x*), Vaughan included new Introductions to *Frontier*, and tried to reposition it as a "corrective to the shrill insistence by nearly a generation of writers that the early colonists sought to destroy the natives and appropriate their land in blatant violation of Puritan calls for Indian conversion and education, and for impartial justice" (*lxv*).

Vaughan saw around himself a "generation" of scholars he criticized as "synthetic generalists," as opposed to his own variety of "research specialists" (*lii*): the "interpretive gulf" between, Vaughan wrote, produced very different histories. "In generalists' eyes," "the Puritans provoked every clash and intended---indeed sometimes accomplished---genocide." But "specialists" like himself "viewed the causes...as less simple, less unilateral, and [found] the outcomes, though appallingly lethal, never genocidal" (*lix*).

Vaughan reiterated that the Puritans' record "before 1675 was mixed but far from the sordid story that has dominated the literature for nearly twenty years." "Were I to rewrite *New England Frontier* in its entirety, I would give more attention to the Puritans' failures, less to their fleeting virtues, and would temper its exculpatory tone. I would also further emphasize the incompatibility of the Puritans' cultural imperialism with the survival, for any appreciable time, of tribal societies."

Copy-text is from the1995 edition of *Frontier* (Norman: University of Oklahoma Press).

from **"Pilgrim Precedents, 1620-1630"**[298]

In the summer of 1622, some fifty or sixty men sent out by Thomas Weston, one of the principal "adventurers" of the Plymouth Company, arrived in New England to establish a new colony. Most of Weston's men had neither the sagacity nor the moral fiber of the Pilgrim Fathers; in the months to come the new arrivals seriously jeopardized New England's Indian-white relations and put the Pilgrims' Indian policy to its severest test.

For several weeks the new colonists lived at Plymouth while their leaders sought a place for permanent settlement. "The unjust and dishonest walking" of Weston's men and their "secret backbiting, revilings, etc." did little to endear them to the Pilgrims. And no sooner had Weston's men moved into their new quarters at Wessagusset, near the southern shore of Massachusetts Bay, than reports began to reach Plymouth that they were stealing corn and committing other abuses against the Massachusetts tribe. The Plymouth leaders reprimanded the newcomers, "advising them to better walking," but to no apparent effect.[299]

---

[298] In *Frontier* Vaughan first outlines transatlantic contacts, and gives his "overview" of Native cultures. In this his third chapter, "Pilgrim Precedents, 1620-1636," Vaughan anatomizes crucial early factors, from the Pilgrims' readings of "cruel, barbarous and most treacherous" peoples in America, to their "first encounter" at Nauset in December 1620; from the negotiation of "new harmony" (75) to the "first challenge" of summer 1621, when "at the root of the trouble was the Narragansett tribe, ever ready to encourage lesions within Massasoit's domain," and with a "willing partner" in Corbitant, Sachem of Nemasket. Vaughan then details the "awkward dilemma" in preserving both the 1621 treaty and Squanto's life; and Standish's strike against "conspirators" in Corbitant's village, which "accomplished its mission with little bloodshed" (76). Here, "messengers" with Massasoit's demand for Tisquantum's life, "disgusted at the governor's sophistry," have just "angrily withdrawn." "The emergency evaporated," Vaughan writes, and "Massasoit never again pressed the case. Still, Squanto was thereafter very careful 'to stick close to the English.'"

[299] Vaughan cites Winslow *Good News* "532-533"; and Increase Mather, *Relation of the Troubles* 82-84. See the third-to-last footnote to this excerpt

For a brief period the Wessagusset and Plymouth colonies combined efforts to procure corn from the tribes of southern New England, as both settlements were experiencing severe shortages. Perhaps the Pilgrims reasoned that Weston's men would be less likely to molest the Massachu-[82] setts Bay tribe if they could buy enough corn elsewhere, and therefore the joint expeditions promised both supply and a lessening of friction. The venture only partially achieved its end: enough corn was obtained to give both colonies minimum rations until midwinter. And even this limited success was not without its price; on a November excursion Squanto "fell sick of an Indean fever, bleeding much at the nose (which the Indeans take for a simptome of death)" and died within a few days. The loss to the English colonists was great; Squanto had done much to insure the success of New Plymouth, and his death undoubtedly gave encouragement to the latest conspirators against the colony.[300]

Hints of conspiracy began to appear in February 1623; by then the growing Indian disaffection toward Wessagusset had spread to include a distrust of Plymouth as well. Many of the Indians probably assumed that the Pilgrims condoned the actions of their English neighbors, and the sight of the two colonies working together in their search for corn must have promoted this assumption. The Pilgrims, however, remained largely unaware of the growing enmity and were hopeful that all was going moderately well---if only Wessagusset would conduct its Indian affairs with more integrity. In February a letter came to Governor Bradford from the Wessagusset leader, John Sanders, complaining of his inability to purchase corn from the natives and asking if he might not be justified in seizing enough to maintain life. Bradford vigorously objected, fearing that "all of us might smart for it," and advising his profligate neighbors to resort to shellfish and groundnuts as the Pilgrims were doing.[301] Pilgrim

---

[300] Vaughan's note: "The corn-buying expeditions are narrated in detail in Winslow 533-541, and in Bradford, *History* I, 276-284"

[301] Vaughan cites Winslow "559-560; Bradford, I, 284-287"

policy would not condone coercion so long as there remained a plausible alternative. **[83]**

What saved the English colonies from the new conspiracy was not a reformation at Wessagusset, but a repetition of the earlier successful formula: timely information from friendly Indians and vigorous action by the colonists.

This time the informant was Massasoit, and again fortune smiled on the Pilgrims at the right moment---although lady luck (or the Puritan God) took a roundabout route. In mid-March 1623, news reached Plymouth that Massasoit was ill. According to the report, his condition was grave, and he would probably not survive the week. In keeping with Indian custom, the Plymouth authorities decided to send a representative to the invalid as a sign of friendship. Edward Winslow, by now somewhat adept at the Indian tongue and familiar with the trails to Sowamet, was given the assignment; he was accompanied by Hobomock and another Englishman. At Sowamet they found the chief alive, but his medicine men were "making such a hellish noise," observed Winslow, "as it distempered us that were well."[302]

Winslow at once became Massasoit's physician. The first dose of his "confection of many comfortable conserves" restored the chief's failing eyesight; a liberal portion of English potage brought back his appetite; and a broth of corn flour, strawberry leaves, and sassafras---all strained through a pocket handkerchief---completed the cure. Massasoit was so impressed with Winslow's medical skill that he persuaded the colonist to treat all the other sick Indians in the village. Winslow's reputation for omniscience grew still greater when the chief glutted himself against his "doctor's" advice and suffered a frightening relapse. By the time medicines arrived from Plymouth, Massasoit was again clearly on the road to recovery and "brake forth into these speeches, 'Now I see the English are my friends, and love **[84]** me: and whilst I live, I will never forget this kindness they have shewed me.'"[303]

---

[302] Vaughan cites Winslow "547-550"

[303] Vaughan cites Winslow "550-552, 555"

The Wampanoag chief wasted no time in proving his sincerity, as Winslow found out a few days later. While the Plymouth envoys were plodding home, Hobomock revealed that Massasoit had told him of a plot to overthrow the English colonies. The Massachusetts, he testified, were the nucleus of the conspiracy, but they had been reinforced by the Nausets, Pamets, and several other tribes and sub-tribes in Plymouth's vicinity. Massasoit had been solicited but had refused. Now, heartened by Winslow's homemade remedies, Massasoit was ready to save the Pilgrims. He advised strong preventive action: "[']to kill the men of Massachusett' who were the authors of this intended mischief." Otherwise, Wessagusset was doomed and Plymouth's fate was dubious.[304]

The Pilgrims wasted no time in taking the Wampanoag's advice. Standish picked eight companions and prepared to sail for Massachusetts Bay, ostensibly to engage the Indians in beaver trade, but in fact to seize the ringleaders of the conspiracy. This decision had not been lightly made, for the Pilgrims knew that the Wessagusset settlers deserved little sympathy. The grievances of the Massachusetts against Wessagusset were mostly valid, and the tribe had not become hostile until severely provoked. Moreover, by their own actions the Wessagusset colony's leaders had acknowledged the justness of the accusations: the officers had publicly whipped and stocked some of the members for stealing from the natives, and one Wessagusset settler had been hanged in order to placate the Indians. Still, by the time Plymouth decided to act, the Wessagusset colony had almost disintegrated. Many of the colonists had sold all their [85] possessions for food; others had hired themselves out as servants to the Indians. The settlement was dispersing gradually as individuals

---

[304] Vaughan cites Winslow 555-556; Bradford I, 292-293; and "30-31" in E. Altham's letter (Sept. 1623) in James, *Three Visitors*. On those pages Altham reiterates Winslow's and Bradford's accounts (Pratt's came in 1658). Altham *adds* only that after Massasoit (not Hobbamock) revealed the "conspiracy," the former "told us that if we would not go fight [the Massachusetts Natives "threatening" them], he would." At this point "a messenger" (likely Pratt, unnamed) arrived to repeat the warning, and Standish with "some six or seven others" was despatched. The Weymouthers, Altham noted, "had no civil government amongst themselves, much less were they able to govern and rule Indians nearby them."

moved out of the palisaded village and foraged for themselves.[305] Clearly Weston's men were ill suited for their task and had ignored the example of diligence and foresight established by their Plymouth neighbors.

On the other hand, there was also no doubt as to the existence of a scheme to wipe out Plymouth as well as the offending Wessagusset. Massasoit's disclosure of the conspiracy was corroborated at this time by the brother of the Massachusetts' sachem,[306] and overt unfriendliness on the part of some of the Indians lent further credence. Here were reasons enough for Plymouth's decision to take preventive action. But before Standish departed for Wessagusset, further evidence appeared. Learning of the cabal from a loquacious squaw, Phineas Pratt, a Wessagusset settler, had slipped away to warn Plymouth of the impending attack.[307] According to Pratt, the blow would fall as soon as the snow disappeared and the Indians had constructed enough canoes to assault the Wessagusset ship that lay in the harbor. Then the Wessagusset men "would all be knokt in the head." Pratt's tale undoubtedly stirred fresh memories of the recent horrendous massacre in Virginia that had taken the lives of more than three hundred colonists.[308]

The battle of Wessagusset, when it finally materialized, was a short but sanguine affair. Standish and his little army went to Wessagusset, but the Indians there immediately suspected his designs and would not congregate in the presence of the Pilgrim soldiers. Standish therefore decided to cut down the most obnoxious of the enemy and hoped that the

---

[305] Vaughan cites: Winslow, 559-564; Bradford, I, 288-291; Pratt 482; Morton's *Canaan* (Adams edition, 96, 251n; and Adams *Three Episodes* 79-82

[306] On **Wassapinewat** see Note 119 to Winslow's *Good News*

[307] **loquacious squaw**　　see Editor's Introduction Part 4; and Pratt (95) herein

[308] Vaughan cites Pratt 474-487; Winslow 530, 561-562, 572-573; Bradford, I, 276, 293-294; and "Great Britain, Public Record Office, *Calendar of State Papers, Colonial Series, America and the West Indies*, I (London 1860), 31." This last refers to a scolding letter from directors of the Virginia Company to its colonists just after the 1622 "uprising" against Virginia plantations (see Note 175 *Good News*, and Adams' citation of Bancroft). Its *contemporary* analysis of the causes of the 1622 "massacre" mainly decried the colonists' "own supine negligence"

rest would heed the lesson. His chance came in late March when Chief Witawamet, the leading conspirator, **[86]** and three other Massachusett braves came to Wessagusset. At a signal from Standish each Englishman attacked an Indian. All but one of the natives were slain on the spot; the lone survivor was Witawamet's eighteen-year-old brother, "whom the Captain caused to be hanged." Before the day was over, three more Massachusetts warriors paid with their lives the price of conspiracy. The Pilgrims carried Witawamet's head to Plymouth and triumphantly impaled it on their fort. While none of the Plymouth contingent was seriously injured, three of Weston's men who had previously moved out of the village were slain by the Massachusetts a few days later.[309]

The Wessagusset affair ended the cabal against the English colonies. Plymouth found it unnecessary to attack any of the other conspiring tribes; fear had thrown them into confusion. As Winslow wrote:

> This sudden and unexpected execution, together with
> the just judgment of GOD[310] upon their guilty consciences,
> hath so terrified and amazed them as, in like manner, they
> forsook their houses, running to and fro like men distracted,
> living in swamps and other desert places: and so brought
> manifold diseases amongst themselves, where of very many
> are dead.

Among the dead were several of the sachems who had abetted the conspiracy. Members of the offending tribes who did not flee were too frightened to spring planting, and so famine weakened them further.

Much to the Pilgrims' relief, the cause of the conspiracy evaporated at the same time that its perpetrators did. Weston's men, discouraged by their sad experience, decided to abandon their plantation. Captain

---

[309] Vaughan cites Winslow 565-74; "Emmanuel Altham to Sir Edward Altham (Sept. 1623) in James, *Three Visitors to Early Plimoth*, 31-32; I. Mather, *Relation of the Troubles*, 91-93. Cf T. Morton, *New English Canaan*, 252-255." The full title of Mather's treatise (Boston: John Foster 1677) suggests the nature of its argument: *Relation of the Troubles which Have Happened by Reason of the Indians There from the Year 1614 to the Year 1675*"

[310] This capitalized form of the word comes not from an original copy of Winslow's *Good News* but from the 1897 edition by Edward Arber, wherein for some reason it is often printed this way

Standish gave them adequate provisions for a journey to Maine, where they could [87] obtain passage to England on the fishing vessels. Once again Plymouth's bold action, with a generous assist from fortune, had restored interracial harmony.[311]

---

[311] **Once again**   Likely refers to the first "bold action" taken by Standish against the Nemasket village of Sachem Corbitant: see Introduction *lviii*

KAREN ORDAHL KUPPERMAN, "THOMAS MORTON, HISTORIAN" (1977)

Kupperman was born April 23, 1939 at Devil's Lake, North Dakota, and received her B.A. in History from the University of Missouri in 1961. She pursued her Master's at Harvard (1962), and wed Joel Kupperman in 1964. Her declared fields of study included the "Early Modern Atlantic World" and "American Indian-European relationships in early America" (Velasquez ed., *Directory of American Scholars*). Kupperman earned her Ph.D. at Cambridge University, England (Lucy Cavendish College) in 1978; and, just before her degree, she published "Thomas Morton, Historian," plus another article whose even-handedness, immersion in primary texts, and sophisticated multicultural analysis were to become trademarks: "English Perceptions of Treachery, 1583-1640: The Case of the American 'Savages'" (see Editor's Introduction).

Kupperman became a Mellon Fellow at Harvard (1980-81) while Assistant Professor from 1978-95. She has since been affiliated with University of Connecticutt and a Professor of History at New York University, while receiving multiple fellowships including The National Endowment for the Humanities and The National Humanities Center. Residing on New York's Washington Square, she also works with Yale's Institute for the Advanced Study of Religion.

Kupperman's first book, *Settling With The Indians: The Meeting of English and Indian Cultures in America 1580-1640* (1980) provided vast documentation on which she continues to build: one goal was "to demonstrate the broad agreement among eyewitness English writers about the essential humanity and high level of organization among the Indians" (*Facing Off* x). New work found her in Italy on a fellowship when her 1988 *Captain John Smith: A Selected Edition of His Writings* appeared. While publishing many short articles, Kupperman expanded the breadth of her studies, not wanting to be "bounded by anachronistic national entities," with new analysis of Europe's "first" voyages in her 1992 *North America: The Beginnings of European Colonization*. 1993 also proved fruitful. She edited *Major Problems in American Colonial History*, seeking "to open the field...to regions and peoples left out in the traditional English-centered approach," and so to work toward "a more representative and coherent field" of Early American studies. Also in 1993, in *Providence Island* (on the 1630 Puritan colony that failed off Nicaragua), Kupperman described the comparative methods evolving in her works:

> Working on the history of Providence Island made me see that we have artificially cut up the early English colonial effort into hermetically-sealed little units...and have ignored massive evidence of an integrated colonial vision that was widely shared on both sides of the Atlantic....[W]e have allowed the unusually parochial vision of John Winthrop to dominate anachronistically ....This comparative treatment was not the book I intended to write: the sources forced it on me....(x)

What some lamented as "fragmentation," Kupperman called "unprecedented opportunity." As she delved into European "world views" to address the fact that "far more historical inquiry has been devoted to the consequences for America of the 'discovery' of 1492 than to the consequences for Europe" (ix), she also showed how "self-presentation...shaped relationships" with Native peoples (*Facing Off* ix). Seeking out the past on its own terms ("The key...to sweep away our knowledge of the eventual outcome," *Facing Off* x), her editing of 1995's *America in European Consciousness 1493-1750* revealed in part the cultural-symbolic struggle that arose from "the uncertainty and fear in which all sides lived" (*Facing* x). Kupperman continues to weave together European documents and visual arts with archaeology, Native orature and postmodern concepts of language and culture, into complex multicultural history---from *Scandinavian Colonists Confront the World: New Sweden in America,* to *Indians and English: Facing Off in Early America* (2000). As Vaughan described "the current historiography" (*Roots* xxii),

> ...[T]he new scholars are less concerned with challenging the wisdom of their elders (though there is inevitably a bit of that) than in asking questions ignored or only tangentially answered....What changes in belief and practice did Puritanism undergo in New England? What influence did Puritanism have on the attitudes of New England colonists towards their environment and toward non-Puritan inhabitants of their [*sic*] territory?

Dynamically committed to "new comprehension" and our "enhanced ability to interpret" the transatlantic world(s), Kupperman reiterates in her latest work that "This is a propitious moment [of] new awareness."

NOTE: The copy-text for "Historian" was that published in *The New England Quarterly*, Vol. 50, December 1977; pp. 660-664.

"Thomas Morton, Historian"

Although the record of English treatment of the American Indians during the earliest years of colonization is dismal, historians have always been glad to point to one bright spot---the record of Plymouth colony. John Demos, the social historian of seventeenth-century Plymouth, writes of the "impressive" record of forty years of "peace, even of amity" between Pilgrims and Indians.[312] Howard Peckham speaks of the Pilgrims as "good neighbors," because they "wanted nothing so much as to be left alone."[313] David Bushnell's "The Treatment of the Indians in Plymouth Colony" strikes a similar note.[314]

Cracks have appeared in this happy picture. Francis Jennings has recently pointed out that historians have preferred to ignore the reconstruction of the events leading up to the Wessagusset incident presented by George Willison in his *Saints and Strangers* first published in

---

[312] Kupperman cites John Demos, *A Little Commonwealth: Family Life in Plymouth Colony* (New York, 1971), 14-15

[313] Kupperman cites Howard H. Peckham, *The Colonial Wars, 1689-1762* (Chicago, 1964), 19

[314] Kupperman cites David Bushnell, "The Treatment of the Indians in Plymouth Colony," *New England Quarterly*, XXVI, 193-218 (1953). From his p. 193-5: "We know...the lurid tales of Indian savagery then circulating through Europe...but [the Pilgrims] seem to have trusted in Captain Miles Standish to improvise a system of defense....For their other relations with the natives, they trusted in The Ten Commandments....[Standish] hurried off to stage a preventive massacre at Massachusetts Bay. No further punishment was inflicted....The natives were given to understand that treachery would not be tolerated....But it was also made clear that the Pilgrims bore the Indians no ill will, and that the aborigines had nothing to fear so long as they behaved themselves....[The] Indians had nothing to offer save their labor, their land, and a few furs....Even on a practical level, Indian claims to the greater part of Plimoth Colony were extremely weak, since most of their territory was used only intermittently as a game preserve."

1945.[315] Wessagusset colony had been founded in 1622 by a man who had formerly been one of the merchants supporting Plymouth colony. At first the Pilgrims helped these new colonists, though they were not Puritans, but they soon became convinced that the Wessagusset colonists' laziness and improvident ways, as well as their rivalry in the lucrative fur trade, forecast trouble for Plymouth. Joint expeditions to buy food from the Indians continued, but the Plymouth men attempted to make it clear that they were separate colonies. Ultimately, the Pilgrim leaders, saying that they had received information of an Indian conspiracy to eliminate the Wessagusset colonists and then attack Plymouth, traveled to Wessagusset and invited some of the Indian leaders to meet with them, during which meeting they locked the doors and killed the Indians. The trickery was justified as a preemptive strike, an explanation that historians have accepted ever since. **[660]**

Willison demonstrates that the plot story is singularly unconvincing, especially as the supposedly conspiring Indians had just sold the desperate colonists large quantities of corn. Moreover, the Pilgrim leaders also acted in ways which are inexplicable if they had in fact just been informed of a widespread conspiracy against them. Willison concludes that the story was constructed after the fact by Edward Winslow in an attempt to justify the colonists' conduct to supporters in England.[316] Clearly, Winslow was very successful, as his explanation of the events has stood for over three hundred years. The result of the action at Wessagusset was that it was no longer safe for that small colony to continue in the midst of the now-hostile Indians and therefore the colony was disbanded. Plymouth could not pay off its debts to its English backers without control of the New England fur trade. The main threat to that control was now gone. The Wessagusset colonists refused the further protection of Plymouth, most of them sailing

---

[315] Kupperman cites Francis Jennings, *The Invasion of America: Indians, Colonialism, and the Cant of Conquest* (Chapel Hill, 1975), 186-187

[316] Kupperman cites Winslow, *Good News from New-England* (London 1624), 31-47 (Page numbers show she worked with an original copy)

for Maine in hopes of finding passage back to England with fishing ships.[317]

Neither Jennings nor Willison point out that much of the story had been told once before. Another Plymouth rival, Thomas Morton, wrote indignantly of the episode and offered an analysis of its motivation which was very similar to that of these two modern historians.

Morton alleges that the Wessagusset colonists were unwelcome at Plymouth from the beginning. Since they were "no chosen Separatists," and since they planned to recompense investors with beaver skins, they "would hinder the present practice, and future profit." He specifically charges that the attack on the unsuspecting Indians was intended as a blow at Master Weston, the backer in England of the Wessagusset colony and formerly a Plymouth backer. The immediate effect of this "plott from Plimoth" was that revenge was taken on other unsuspecting Englishmen. "But if the Plimmouth Planters had really intended good to Master Weston, or those men, why had they not kept the Salvages alive in Custody, untill they had secured the other English? Who by meanes of this evill mannaginge of the businesse lost their lives and the whole plantation was dissolved thereupon, as was likely for feare of a revenge to follow, as a relation to this cruell antecedent." From this time forward, the Indian name for Englishmen [661] was "Wotawquenange, which in their language signifieth stabbers or Cutthroates." When Master Weston did arrive in New England, the Pilgrims tried to convince him that the incident had proceeded from "the Fountaine of love & zeale to him; and Christianity...." They used their "glosse upon the false text" to argue "that the Salvages are a dangerous people, subtill, secreat, and mischievous, and that it is dangerous to live separated, but rather together, and so be under the Lee, that none might trade for Beaver."

Morton clearly had an important interest in this development, because he, like the Wessagusset planters, chose to live separately in the neighborhood of the Pilgrims and he participated successfully in the fur

---

[317] Kupperman cites Willison, *Saints and Strangers* (rev. ed. (London 1966), 122-131

trade. They scorned him and considered him dangerous for his relationship with his Indian friends and they accused him of selling guns and liquor to the Indians. Plymouth's scorn for Morton has stuck, just as Winslow's version of the Wessagusset massacre has been accepted.

He is widely pictured as an irresponsible libertine, attempting to create a fanciful version of some classical pagan paradise, and wrapping himself in a disguise of orthodox Anglicanism.[318] The settlement he presided over was composed of "brawling drunkards and unscrupulous traders."[319] His name is rarely mentioned without an adjective such as "notorious."[320] He is always "Morton of Merrymount" or "Mine Host of Merrymouth," his plantation never being referred to by the name he gave it---Ma-re-mount, mountain by the sea. The Pilgrim influence is again seen in the fact that their construction, Merrymount, stuck.[321] **[662]**

All of this works subtly to discount Morton's worth as a historical source. Though many writers agree that this "gay gentleman" wrote the most lively and entertaining account of early New England, his lack of value as a source on its history is assumed.[322] It is still entirely possible to write the history of Plymouth colony without taking account of Morton's version of events. Perhaps it is time to change all this. If Morton was accurate in his analysis of causation and intention in the Indian deaths at Wessagusset, then there is reason to believe his reports on the broader area

---

[318] Kupperman cites Morton's *Canaan* (edition in Force's *Tracts* Vol. II, 71-79)

[319] Kupperman cites Bushnell, 201; Slotkin, *Regeneration Through Violence*, 59-60; Larzer Ziff, *Puritanism in America: New Culture in a New World* (New York, 1973), 41; Zolla, *Morphology of the American Indian*, 24-25

[320] Kupperman cites J. Gary Williams, "History in Hawthorne's 'The Maypole of Merrymount,'" *Essex Institute Historical Collections*, CVIII, 184-185 (1972); Vaughan, *New England Frontier* (1965 ed.), 89

[321] Kupperman cites Vaughan 187; James Truslow Adams, *The Founding of New England* (1921; rpt. Boston, 1949), 148. See also the 30-odd examples of such opinions of Morton and *Canaan* in Dempsey, "A Sampler of Remarks" in *Thomas Morton* (2000)

[322] Kupperman cites Samuel Eliot Morison, *Builders of the Bay Colony*, 2nd. ed., revised (Boston, 1958), 14; which repeats the above-mentioned "Remarks"

of relationships on Cape Cod may also be worth looking at. Control of the fur trade may reasonably be seen to be at the bottom of the controversies between the Pilgrims and individual planters there. Individual traders may have given guns to their Indian hunters in order to increase their productivity. Leaving aside the question of the ecological effects of such hunting, it is clear that both the individual planter-traders and the men of Plymouth colony were reaching far out into the mainland to establish that trade. Morton's giving of guns to the Indians, if he did so, was offensive because of the greater share of the fur trade that it meant for him as well because of fears of Indian attacks.

Historians who feel that Morton's expropriation by the Plymouth colonists was justified because he endangered English settlements with his gun sales are making the wholly unwarranted assumption that Indians equipped with seventeenth-century matchlock guns were much more dangerous than Indians whose weapons were bows and arrows.[323] Each weapon had a similar range and a bowman could make many more shots per minute than could a man with a gun. Further, the necessity of keeping a match burning to ignite the gunpowder contrasted unfavorably with the silence and inconspicuousness of a man armed with a bow and arrows.[324] Many writers from New England wrote to praise the power of the Indians' weapons and several, including the leaders of Plymouth colony, indicated that the arrows were headed with points of brass, bird claws, and horn.[325] Bows and arrows were **[663]** clearly not a negligible weapon. It is difficult to believe that the possession of guns would make a significant difference

---

[323] Kupperman cites Morison, 16; Vaughan, *Frontier*, 89-90

[324] Kupperman's note reads: "This argument is developed fully and documented in Kupperman, 'English Perceptions of Treachery, 1583-1640: The Case of the American 'Savages,'" *Historical Journal*, XX, 263-287 (1977)." (See Editor's Introduction)

[325] Kupperman cites *Mourt's Relation* (London 1622), 20; John Brereton, *A Brief and True Relation of the Discoverie of the North Part of Virginia*, 2nd ed. (London 1602), 4; Higginson, *New England's Plantation* in Force I, 12; Martin Pring, *A Voyage Set Out from the City of Bristoll*, in Samuel Purchas, *Hakluuytus Posthumus or Purchas His Pilgrimes* (1625; rpt. Glasgow, 1906), XVIII, 325; James Rosier, *A True Relation of the Most Prosperous Voyage...by Captaine George Waymouth* (London, 1605), sig. C-Cv; Wood, *Prospect* (London, 1634), 90

in the degree to which a lightning attack on an outlying settlement was to be feared.

The argument thus returns to the motives of the Pilgrims. Unprovoked attacks on Indians, such as that at Wessagusset, were likely to produce Indian attacks where none had formerly been experienced. If their primary concern was security, then their behavior is difficult to explain. It is time to drop the bundle of attitudes, toward both the Pilgrims and Morton, appropriate to "those, that did not know the Brethren could dissemble."[326]

---

[326] Kupperman cites the edition of Morton's *Canaan* in Force *Tracts* II, 78

Wanakia,
"Suffering Fools:
A Stand-up Historian
Shoots (Back) from the Hip" (2001)

Wanakia (Eastern Algonquian "wa-na-kee-YAH," Peace Maker) describes himself as "a writer, a person adopted by the Quinnipiac, people still living in the southern Connecticutt country about New Haven, The Quinnipiac River and Thimble Islands."

When this editor sought out Native American points of view, and was directed to this "extra-academic acquainted with Wessagusset," he learned "new" things from several sharp blows of the man's tomahawk---or was it a double-axe?---and withdrew most of his stock in notions of ethnicity. Discussions ensued. The editor respects Wanakia's privacy---"the piece, if you want it, tells enough," he insisted. Indeed, told of this intended new edition of Winslow's *Good News*, he first-replied:

"Fast Eddie?" With a complex comedian's glance: ambivalent seeing it all resurrected, optimistic something might emerge. The glance fit Wanakia's nickname, "stand-up historian." "Got no place to sit down," he explained, citing Thomas Morton (1637) that people not in favor with "new" England seemed to find food and shelter more (and more) difficult to arrange. He added, "Well, Permanent-Part-Time-Professor, what about Mine Host, that prickly partydogpoet and propheteer?"

"He's getting righter," was the impecunious reply. "Show me some work?"

"Same old question, you people," he smirked. "In the trunk behind you."

So-called unpublished amateurs investigating the early Northeast have made important contributions---researched, sensible, fieldwork-correlated. Naturalist Mike McWade agrees that "professionals" still turn to them when on-campus resources go dry. This is part of what makes Wanakia "crazy"---that those with "institutional support" hunker around unintelligible models while the vital foundations, *material evidences*---dozens of known Native and colonial sites undug, close-to-the-land "unlettered" sources speaking plain, unheard language---remain "invisible." This editor will not "probe" Wanakia's formal education. "Suffering Fools" is "about Weymouth," and qualified

What *would* it "mean" to "explain" these pages---their love-song, their troubling consistencies and unrighteous compassion---in terms of Wanakia's readings and influences, his ways of wresting "food and shelter" from America's "prosperity," his ethnicity, experience? From what "position" in a downsized world do "Soft Cynics" dismiss a Hard one, whose "Indian speech" is yet within their own "Classical" vein of "lyrical diatribe" and "serio-comic satirical analysis"---especially when that speech is an attempt to heal suffering? Why, after all, is *literature*, like *academic*, an American synonym for *irrelevant*?

This "omni-outsider" seems abreast of Europe's past. Despite 50 years of fresh archaeology obfuscated on both sides of the Atlantic today, Wanakia sees that the "colonizers"---whose own earliest, longest-continuous civilizations *were* a multicultural "garden"---abandoned that past, yet still pursue "The Garden"; but in almost *any* direction *except* toward its actual "trail," the evidence. Only *all* the "facts" can ground what he calls Americans' authentic hunger for spiritual life in a vibrant relation with a living Earth. Is there some other sustainable course? As noted below, "Utopia" is one wing of the Western ghetto for all stripes of Difference, whose mention seems to provoke such embarrassment and wrath.

Wanakia asks us to wonder why today's Plimoth Plantation---whose excellence owes "worlds" to "amateurs"---still censors the presence of the blood-soaked "flag" and Wituwamat's piked head above its fort. Who is being protected from a sophisticated grasp of ambiguity? What *is* being defended through even the seasoned "postmodern distrust of all authority," if it adopts the same old career-promoting scorn for "uncomfortable" knowledge?

Wanakia "takes Weymouth by the horns" and provokes us to interrogate *for real* the Western past. To fear not; to believe that because of the goodness of *all* human beings, we will rise from that endeavor as did the ancients *on both* sides of the Atlantic, "fresh as the morning star." To act---as if we *really* know that Death and History will ask us, too, the meaning of having lived. Full of respect, he asks if "the greatest generation" shed the blood of world war to sustain courageous cultural growth; or for a Disneyed-down delusion that, in favor of coy grandmas, "consumers" and corporate crustaceans, engenders more doomed acts of injustice. Amid the conformity of calls "back to fundamentals" that *created* the crushing confusions of "suffering fools," Wanakia shoots (back).

The copy-text was Wanakia's original unpublished manuscript.

"SUFFERING FOOLS:
A Stand-Up Historian
Shoots (Back) from the Hip"

*...This is what archaeologists have learned from
their excavations in the land of Israel: the Israelites
were never in Egypt, did not wander in the desert, did not
conquer the land in a military campaign and did not pass
it on to the 12 Tribes of Israel...*

> *It turns out that part of Israeli society is ready
to recognize the injustice that was done to the Arab inhabitants of the country and is willing to accept the principle
of equal rights for women---but it is not up to adopting the
archaeological facts that shatter the Biblical myth. The
blow to the mythical foundations of the Israeli identity is
apparently too threatening, and it is more convenient to
turn a blind eye.*

Israeli archaeologist Ze'ev Herzog,
qtd. in "Archaeology vs. The Bible,"
Chronicle of Higher Education 1/21/2000

*This is a fight among children over who has the best
imaginary friend.*

Palestinian leader Yassir Arafat

An artist is just like everybody else, only more so.

Charlie Parker

Ah-Ho.

Phew! Thanks, it's great to be here. Just in from the New England
powwow circuit---That's where I follow the crowd, where we go to feel
good, the gatherings of People of the Dawn, in that sweet country along

the oceanside where every sunrise bathes your spirit in The Creator's First Thought, fresh as the morning-star. Where the salt air washes a bad heart clean and red-tailed falcon fly the summer blue. We come together with families and friends to dance with The Earth, to say our prayers with our noisy hands and feet, to talk and listen, be, touch home in the circle. Feels good to be there because that is where the ancient human world is: our origin, and the bosom where we'll sleep in peace forever. Springboard and goal: common destiny as civilized individuals. "Job," playground, cathedral. Each creature there stands strong in their own wild concentric center, need never lift a validating finger. The ancient world and the future live in our veins, ours, the living, in each eternal pulse of drum, the resonant circles of our love. (Hope this blows off the hackademics and hardened psychos right away.)

I smudge, wash away the world(s) of no account, and people touch me, and soon I think no more about the crazy colonists driving over us these prosperous days, barreling so-important down their highways in armored "sport utility" halftracks, two and three abreast (raging up my bumper or crawling in front), in a consuming race to the bottom of an oil-barrel. Phinehas Pratt on steroids. Familiar note, history-buffs? Except that Ms. Colonist, liberated housefrau-consumer, is now "free" also to roughshod the country the same way, alone (so alone) with a cell-phone full of money and melodrama crammed to her ear, captain at last of a mobile house (seats six with the comforts of home) going noplace, maybe the mall (same thing), very fast. Of course blunt brutality is part of occupation. What really kills is "omnipresent and fierce stupidity," as Mr. Those-Who-Forget-The-Past Santayana said it.

Sometimes---I cannot help it as one of "the conquered"---I hate. They took our world, deny that they took it, and squander it, stuffing their faces with "development" painful even to their eyes. They couldn't believe just the codfish swamping their boats, the profits of one beaver-pelt: it made them Greed-Junkies, and every Dow Jones withdrawal fetches out the sword of Captain Wild-Eyes businessman. I *have* a World, The Dawn Land----so would I be half-out of my mind if I did not care about his victims?

But, you say justly, are these your conquerors, offending-nobody families come a weekend afternoon to the refuge of powwow? Are they not beautiful too, innocent? Can you find one, Peace Maker, who speaks face-to-face for injustice?

Then why outside The Circle do my "liberal progressive" ears burn? All that means is that my struggle to be free and happy should make the next person's easier---You'd think there's a *reason* "we all have to scratch our way up"...

Articulate the innocent "lifestyle" that has devoured, since 1970, one full third of the entire Earth's biota. Forty percent of its 3 percent total fresh water. Sing me the innocence of my tiny lifetime's "missile gap," Vietnam's liberators, Watergaters, "Morning in [senile] America," Iran-Contra, government shutdowns, impeachment under the Presidential Penis Clause, and now, fresh hordes of gun-and-Bible-toting, land-wasting imbeciles high on *The Boastin Glob*'s proclaimed "instant diversity"---under the dopiest cracker in a dog's age, a corporate dirtbag posing as mediocrity? Tell us *The Glob*'s inability to correlate lead-stories of "booming prosperity" with its sidebar-statistical whimpers on the daily-worse poverty of working people (that means "people who do the work").

Mistake not: since your Empire of Profit At Any Cost bounced off the Vietnamese, I have never felt such care for "Americans" of every stripe--It's a selfish thing, of course, because I know how little any of them enjoy post-Nam America, being treated like Indians "in their own country"...

What *do* the scientists call creatures that swarm in, devour everything and then move on? Tooling up to siphon the last of this continent into the private plantations of soul-dead gastropods, from the "public lands" of Alaska to your own "reformed" pittance of old-age funds soon bound for unaccountable Wall Street. This "innocence" forgets that "Wall" Street was built to keep "Indians" off Manhattan; forgets even yesterday's Senatorial Cheshire grin as the new "Defense" Secretary mocked the very idea of accounting for 1/3 of its 2000 budget: *a trillion dollars* of one year's public money, "lost." These are the folks who want to get government off our backs. "Missile Defense": a high-tech Pilgrims' Palisade erected in advance of guilty selfishness. Teachers and children starve in schools like factories, mental wards, war-zones, prisons: tell us this locust innocence---

And yet when we see these colonists' painful confusion we do not look down. We do not rejoice when human beings hurt because of a mistake. Is there a people more unhappy since they "forgot" their own actual, extremely beautiful, historical origins *as* Europeans? Instead they remain what the palisades keep them, colonists-still, starving for a *home*, real-rootless people misled like sheep of an intoxicated shepherd, day-in, year-out, this way/back the other and round again, their memory and so their feelings and their lives confused by a slop-feed of free-floating "symbols." Got a Jesus for everybody, or at least the daily numb-numb of subsistence that looks to The Joneses like power and wealth. Power *over*; yet over nothing, yet "symbolically" everything. (Find out how many "believers" have ever traveled outside The United Snakes.)

But the real world, and there *is* a real world in the midst of *all* our human Imaginaries, keeps poking through the razorwire. People want to know (anew) where the hell is the center of the relative world. I never thought People of the Dawn should answer for their problems, and I do not much understand The Great Spirit. I only know that Those Powers are greater and that nothing out of Harmony lasts. What makes my heart bad is to see them grow more harmfully crazy, the needless fearful greed. I think they feel the demographics of the races shifting out from under them at last, like sand under castles in air, toward the undoing of their vast apparatus of privilege. Every child born since the plunging Baby-Boom will yield the bankers their old-time growths of profit, or else. How much more violent denial before the world does make them realize: there is nothing to be afraid of, and everything to gain, in sharing?

Go watch TV, honey. Peter Jennings will take care of it.

The central fire crackles and the smoke of sweetgrass climbs the sky. The Circle opens. Our Elders enter two by two behind the Medicine People (those most adept at handling power)---and that's *all* our Elders entering, from the first of the Past to this afternoon's. The Shamans and Elders bless The Circle: they thank, that is, The Creator, the Four Directions, the World Above and Earth too, from the Four-Leggeds to the Two-. For everything.

It takes a few moments. They thank The Ancestors, and the Veterans, and I look around and see the wounds and memories of people who gave more of their people to World War II than any others. And I see the Stars and Stripes and the Turtle Flag flying in unequal freedom under the sun---and I know that our documented status as the poorest peoples on this continent (except where we imitate colonists and swindle gambling-money from the desperate) is not only a "political remnant" of "social policy." It is a *symbolic* status: like a lampshade made from human skin, it is *a comforting symbol* to "masters" trapped in their own Empire...

And then the Intertribal; and then the Fancy Dancers come out; and as I give in to my flexing knees and give myself to what's before my eyes and spirit, "I" dissolve...thank God...

Like the once-master race of South Africa, whose guilt feared democracy as a bloodbath, America does not understand that the great historical *reckoning* in progress simply proclaims that, after all, each is equal. No doubt it's a come-down, like any withdrawal, but this "crisis" comes straight from their colonies' sole unifying trait, you might say: the claim that *they* are civilization in their sacred separateness, that their God *is* God, that *better* is at bottom who they are.

Look at them pouring in, drawn by drums and flashing dancers of that *real* old-time religion. Overpowered, just as we are, by the beauty of a young girl as she kicks up her novice heels and her shawl flies. She---*just as in ancient Europe*---is the human balance-point and image of living Spirit, shy, proud, fierce, loving, miraculous---and here they come, sheepish refugees and indentured servants drawing up to our shores in their *Rangers* and *Explorers*, like old Mary Rowlandson and her frontier-sister for whom The Bible did not suffice: the cutting-edge of colonial commodification camouflaged as harmless suburban white family. Their visible culture a pastiche of other peoples' or a sanded-down persona fashioned from resonance with nobody. Careful clean ass-mortgaged middle class, a few aloof hackademics, blue-collar clans out for fun on the cheap, confused-rebel bikers with haggard hard-drinking babes, professionals with a wide-eyed toddler and beepers at the belt where other frontier-tools once rode...

They wash up here wild-eyed hungry, now they scarce know what to do with it all and still they starve. How would you feel, your ancient home occupied by people who *don't want to know* how they came here or the nature of *Manit* that The Great Spirit planted, as in a garden---so long as it hands over the harvest? Am I going too fast? Feel around you this high-tech rampage, people racked with the drugs of futility, connected by their Web to other lonely souls who ignore *their* neighbors too: I go out of my mind trying to describe what surrounds me and that is not "natural": carefully negligent, most-proud of their humility, blind visionaries, vicious philanthropics, nature-and-woman-worshipping rapists---and *By the sword we seek peace* quoth the seal of their "commonwealth" Massachusetts. Before that they cartooned other words in our mouths: *Come over and help us...*

If they so grieve for The Garden why do they not want to know they are *in* it? By what "logic" did they murder us rather than marry? They had "separated": they would not understand where they were...

> The wonders of inanimate [*sic*] nature leave [Americans] cold, and, one may almost say, they do not see the marvelous forests surrounding them until they begin to fall beneath the ax. What they see is something different. The American people see themselves marching through wildernesses, drying up marshes, diverting rivers, peopling the wilds, and subduing nature. It is not just occasionally that their imagination catches a glimpse of this magnificent vision....[It] is always flitting before their mind....   (Alexis de Tocqueville, *Democracy in America* 1835)

1835! If that's not an ad for a 2001 S.U.V., I'll eat my peace-pipe.

From the soil of Connecticutt comes a king's-ransom hoard of exquisite ceremonial goods (carbon-dated 3200-900 years ago): a stone-carved sea turtle that sits in your palm, a foot-long ceremonial pipe (itself unheard-of in New England) with serpents twined round its stem, an "Indian" head looking back at you between the serpents' gaze, and on his carved headband the *exact* image of Ohio's spirally Serpent Mound. A trove of Native-copper discs (from a garment? an instrument?) incised with concentric circles, gorgets, more pipes---and "That shouldn't be there," quoth the State archaeologist who still squats his funded inert ass upon the dig.

My friends, *It's only beauty!* And what about the "new" fact that America's first poet in English created his works directly from his actual intimacies with Native peoples? Nothing---But soft! What's this upon which *The Washington Post* bestows its Thanksgiving Day gaze? Why, it's the *actual post-holes* of an English fort, and some shards of ceramics, from Sagadahoc's 1607 "Popham Colony"! Quoth the Professor, "It's a no-brainer that this site is nationally significant. It's of just absolutely supreme importance." Post-holes and bits of pots from another "needless watch-house" ---and the journalists, sure there will be nothing "upsetting" to Grandma Sponsor, swarm safely in.

Almost a hundred years now since old Santayana, driven back to Europe by his sanity, said So Long to this genteel tradition:

> A Californian whom I had recently the pleasure of meeting observed that, if the philosophers had lived among your mountains, their systems would have been different from what they are. Certainly, I should say, very different...for these systems are egotistical; directly or indirectly they are anthropocentric, and inspired by the conceited notion that man, or human reason, or the human distinction between good and evil, is the centre and pivot of the universe. That is what the mountains and the woods should make you at last ashamed to assert. From what, indeed, does the society of nature liberate you, that you find it so sweet? It is hardly (is it?) that you wish to forget your past, or your friends, or that you have any secret contempt for your present ambitions....They suspend your forced sense of your own importance not merely as individuals, but even as men. They allow you, in one happy moment, at once to play and to worship....   (1913: 109)

Why will you not allow yourselves the very thing you hunger for? The Dawn Land is an Earth-centered Communal Matrifocy.

Earth-centered means that we understand, respect, and celebrate that Earth is the doorway of The Great Mystery. Earth is not an option in a symbolic national imaginary. It is where all people came from and where we are going. Inhabiting Earth with body, heart, mind and spirit, we reach the goal of being, "Glory Here" as your own radicals used to say---live surrounded by a sublime, infinite act of love made freely by a forever-mysterious Power, whose children we and Earth together are, family. Earth is mother, sister, and home of body and spirit. She has many husbands so we have many grandfathers. She is our substance, support and teacher, center and fate. Except and after that, most else is moot.

The colonists call this Utopia, meaning "Nowhere," or "You seem to need our assistance."

Communal means that we share (each person is expected to give something), rather than profit (someone gets something more than what they gave). The Great Mystery gave and The Earth gives everything freely. We did not earn the blessings of the past nor do we own the future. For one creature or group of creatures to try to "get away with" less at the expense of all others and call it either a culture or an economy is Cosmic Crass. A person who demonstrates power by fashioning *property*, and property into domains of power over others, is a failed human being, a criminal embarrassment to the family. We *shame* our "criminals"---*You powerless fuck-up! We made you an equal to our greatness that comes from our harmony with The Greater, and this is what you do with it?* Here, to live is to owe, and the strong and the wise sing celebration. A savage is a delusional man who has abandoned all human bearings in favor of selfishness. From him the universe takes away its music. He imagines he owes nothing, kills anything that "re-minds" him, and wastes his life (and yours) crashing ass-backwards into everything. We live The Earth. The garden grows *because* it grows that way. If they didn't like it, why didn't they go back where they came from?

Matrifocy---Well, somebody had to coin it (*ma-tri-folk-y*). It means that where Life is the Center, so is Woman. The colonists themselves had such a word (which they learned to despise), *matriarchy*; but to us too that smacks of overbearing. Our women and men are equals. It's just that, well, maybe we're a bit more *interested* in woman, her point of view, the way she feels her way along. Focused on her, Matrifocy means that she is where we feel and find our deepest heritage, she is the flesh of our families past and future, touchstone of right and wrong, center of our harmony with all other harmonies, mother of our thousand forms of love. Been enjoying, as you should, the life-giving fruits of this world, been working on your fancy-dance feathers all year, have you? Fine, unless you've been neglecting the kids; and if you have, your name is Mudd, and you do not enter The Circle, you do not dance. Man: a lump of a word. *Hu*-man: where The Spirit breathes. Woman is unsounded intelligence, source, pride and strength, who carries tradition and makes new tradition, tradition new. The proof of our power is hers. She moves us from the heart of memory to our best selves.

Is this not the "natural freedom" that colonists surrendered in exhange for "civility," for a heap of exclusive bric-a-brac piled upon the still-inevitable grave? Funny: once they knew Her too by a thousand names: Isis, Queen of Heaven and Earth, whose lap was the mountain-throne where sat the first Pharaoh. He literally chiseled Her Eternities away over a period of narcolepsy called patriarchal time; and here we be...

I guess it's inevitable these pages tell my spirit's chancred anger. It was forced on. When I ask the ocean, I do not hear that I need this, enjoy it, am its cause. I am sick of it. Hungry brothers and sisters from across the sea, so are you.

How we love your restless search for "a better life"---Why did you give up, then, improving your own home? How we love this "hate of tyranny"---but can you not see that there was only "cultural crisis" where colonists forced their symbols down other throats? Every people is certainly entitled by The Creator to limit themselves. But colonists are deluded to suppose that we---the peoples *outside* their self-limiting symbols---will not resist their reforms and reductions to the death. We are not (only) them: we "identify" with Life; and so, even dancing among ourselves *a thousand miles* from white sight, we "troubled" their dream of themselves. Their missionaries taped the mouths of children who dared to speak their families' tongues. Do you know that the "American" and "Mexican" governments together crushed early 1800s Fredonia, a Jeffersonian democracy founded by all the "loser" tribes in wasteland "Territories"? Why were you not told? Why does the meticulous Mr. Vaughan tell us in footnote-one to Wood's *Prospect* that the Mohawks are located "near Albany," when it was Albany who "located" near *them*? It is still too much to bear that The Dance go on *any*where outside Profit...

But as the great (and by tradition, ridiculed) poet Susan Griffin has said: Delusions are not innocent. The mind that believes in a delusion must ultimately face reality. And when faced, she says, with the actual nature of the world, he must act. He must either come to terms with that world, or force the world to resemble his delusion---

And now we understand that colonists did not generate their mountains of "literature" to justify killing "Indians": they killed "Indians" to "justify" their literature. They did not rape an American wilderness: they *made* America *into* the wilderness they still need to "believe in"...

Seen Texas lately? Or The East Coast, for that matter...

Home is freedom. You want to be where you are accepted whatever you are and you defend that life with your life. Without *home*, "power" and "I" mean nothing. Centered in home, everything means: it is infinite concentric connection, where a joke of a small temporary *I* becomes not a feary father to menace the young from greed-gilded walls---but a thinking pulsing Joy in the center of Space, Time and Always. Standing in that, do I need any monument but love to remember my name? What price Abercrombie & Fitch? What's *primitive* about a life devoted to ever-greater achievements in play, food, sex, sleep, children, ceremony, gratitude, arts and crafts? I've done some heavy reading and want to cite an authoritative bumper-sticker:

You Wouldn't Understand: It's an Indian Thing

But I think some would. Some sense that "their" civilization in body, mind and spirit never did "cross the Jordan." If they did not "see" the ancient Canaanites, how then could their psyche and soul have "crossed" the Atlantic? Ask Indochina (*Come over and help us*) who it was that came across the Pacific...

Powwow is a family event and a dance of culture. But when these people come and cruise the tents, well, it's our own fault that powwow becomes too much another mall, a circuit for shopping under the big sky. "Have to make a living." The land of liberty prospers on loss of options. ("Freedom," observed amateur-historian Orwell: "the right to exploit others for profit.") Consumers consumed with consumption are the norm, now, yet it's something when one of them keeps finding their knees a-flexing with the rhythms, and musters up Hello. Rarer, the old refugee motto: how they "admire this culture and would like to learn."

As a pain in the ass myself I have inquired whether they've studied their own culture. By their faces, you'd think they *have*, and that's why they are here, hungry for a life as big as life, tentatively tasting "alternatives" to the "development, progress and prosperity" closing in---

Great Spirit, bless and feed the *post* children: Post-Christians, who've realized what shepherds have in mind for sheep; Post-Capitalists, living creatures ever-uneasier with money's plans for their children; and post-Patriarchs, the ones beginning to detox from addiction to group-bonding with testosterone. Where *have* their parents spiritually "been" that in 25 generations they have invaded The Middle East twice with "holy war" in the name of The Prince of Peace and Exxon; invaded Africa and, for money, there inflicted 60 million deaths, 10 million more than in all of World War II; invaded Central, North and South America to the deaths of uncounted millions more; gave their own "peasants" the right to fight for a "dream" on others' lands, gave The Earth World Wars I and II, tried to invade Asia from the Hollywood side, poisoned more Earth with Cold War, and build now a "global economy" starring the downsized us? And they "worry" for children to whom they feed-by-default the pearl of that history: *Whatever you can get away with*; or, *I want what I want when I want it...*

I know I talk too much, like all the crazy. We ache. To get out, get somehow beyond that past into the---*New World*? We mean them well and would give much to help ourselves in helping them and it does not "make us feel good or better." For if these brothers and sisters did look *into their own past*---beyond the moronic mainstream and corporate generations of spineless textbooks swilled them---they'd be home now...

Send your book-results of 15 years' research and sacrifice aimed at healing to, among others, National Public Radio and its *All Things Considered,* care of star reporter Ms. Margot Adler. In a few months, she sends you a postcard inviting you to call her about it, at home. When you do, she says her "friend" has read the first page and "wasn't grabbed" by it. She's also very busy waiting for the wisdom-packed confessions of mass murderer Timothy McVeigh. As you see what is edging this work out of her attention, and as she insists she has no time for what she invited with her card, try the diplomatically-desperate. "Hold the phone, I'll go shoot up the local McDonald's. Will you 'talk to me' then?" "Ohh," Adler laughs, "I'd *have* to then." End of conversation.

You miss her eventual report on how much we learned from McVeigh. A few months later NPR runs a filler asking "Where was The West" the last time the Hale-Bopp Comet swung by Earth (about 4000 years ago, smack at the height of Minoan Crete). The answer? "Nowhere: utterly primitive." So was McVeigh, and his hobbies are "news."

How can it be otherwise, then, that these powwow-peekers are so well "educated" that most have not an inkling that, in the original worlds of most of their own ancestors, they and we "Indians" believed, as the Sachem said, "almost all the same things." *The Europeans too* all built their earliest *thousands of years* of civilization as Matrifocal, Earth-loving People who knew (from Her) how to cooperate. I don't understand people who erase and forget that their own mothers---according to *archaeology,* my friends, a science scarcely 100 years old---their own mothers built them a heritage largely egalitarian, sexy *and* spiritual, a high-tech network of international trading cultures born and thriving for ages before the rule of men; before Judeochristianity; before capitalism. Don't understand people who still refuse to try another road, come to new life, refuse to claim so much of a real inheritance of human achievement...

They do not know the names, the worlds or their own highest achievements of the free human spirit within the names, Minoan Crete, the Aegean, the Land of Canaan before it was "promised" to one "special" people (whose priests became priests by "killing one his brother, another his friend, another his neighbor": *Exodus* 32: 25-29). They do not know the dazzling technologies and paradisal, this-world "afterlife" of the Etruscans and the Celts, before the great ass-backward steps "forward" of Classical Greece and the Romans. They do not know that the very "need" for "democracy" was created the moment they deposed the great women of their ancient world, Pasiphae the "nymphomaniac," her "romantic fool" daughter Ariadne (and both the victims of their own "hero" Theseus!). Once you've rejected Woman you've got to do *some*thing to bind the tribe against "his-story"---that long succession of egomaniacs, butchers and would-be Alexanders...

Free people not allowed, by design and negligence, to peep over the palisades. Not allowed, by businessmen, brain-dead "reporters" and school boards who take no risks on "different" *any*thing. Not allowed to know the achievements and wild dancing spirits of their own ancestors, whose worlds full of color, variety, wealth, art, sex and humor throve longer than any other period in their shopworn, tragi-proud parade of "inspired" sociopaths. But suppose you *did* know that for the vast majority of The Earth's human time, its various families prayed through sharing the creation of, yes, cosmic orgasms? You'd lose the sweet numb-numb of "necessity" off your colonial predicament: it begins to hurt and demand explanation, life as infantilized tyrants, prisoners of prosperity, and most contemptible, inmates of an identity built from what the darkies (nor woman neither) ain't entitled to...

Back to basics, then? Here's some basics (*Wisdom* 12: 3-11):

> The ancient inhabitants of your holy land you [Yahweh] hated
> for their loathsome practices, their deeds of sorcery and unholy rites, hated
> as ruthless murderers of children, as eaters of entrails at feasts of human
> flesh, initiated while the bloody orgy goes on....You determined to destroy
> them at our fathers' hands, so that this land...might receive a colony of God's
> children worthy of it. Even so, since these were men, you treated them
> leniently...to destroy them bit by bit...although you knew very well they
> were inherently evil...and fixed in their cast of mind; for they were a race
> accursed from the beginning...

You don't want to go back there, Americans...

This planet is all we *can* know of Paradise. The beautiful, loving, genius-children on your arms understand. Come forth and breathe the sunshine. The living do not hunker ever-deeper in the palisaded privacy of TV dens, cathode-irradiated, engrossed in DVD reruns of *Lost In Space*: featuring the intergalactically-asexual, crypto-pilgrim family of no less than---Dr. John Robinson! Or what is it now, *Survivor*? Needless competition on a paradisal island with plenty for everybody...and like the losers at old Weymouth, you perish stuck in the mud, starve because you will not leave your needless guardpost...

If we could get rid of them, we would be suffering fools not to. We can't. So we have suffered fools because Europe's "neurotic suicide-note" (as Frederick Turner called history) gave us no choice but to endure. Why don't people "lost in a Roman wilderness of pain," as *another* drunken exiled poet sang, try to understand that The Creator gave us vast cycles of love and realms of beauty and each other to help us being born, and living, and dying amid The Great Mystery? You will never find *that* in stained-glass, in malls and catalogs...

It's only beauty. Suffering fools refuse to learn, in favor of stuffing the starving place inside them with our world. They suffer fools to rob their living of truth; fools whose private negligence makes crazy cracker-kings, and choirs of fools who shout where Spirit whispers. That is, I repeat, their right. It is not their right to make other peoples hard of hearing.

We would not say even these things to you; but we are where the harm falls. Government and business acknowledge us as *Externalities*---we are the costs and consequences "out in the world someplace" of what they do in their Internalities-world of producing profit.

We are not a term. We *never* wanted to "depend" on anybody. Who is it won't let that go? We are living people and a universe created as neither raw material for others' "dream" nor a dump for their poisons. The map at the mortgage office is not the territory. We ask you, not to hate the voice of this world, this pain and, yes, compassion that would speak with you, brothers and sisters who search the skies for "other civilizations"---

We do not ask you to be like us, but to find out and reclaim the goodness that you really are, the goodness that you have been for the *greatest part* of your own history. *It's only beauty!* You would no longer take the tales of cowards for the truth about yourself, but blossom and bloom again, in tears, and then eternal glory in the holy ambiguity of sunshine...

We remember your families' houses in the earliest days of your Crete, where no blood-boltered deeds of kings ruled the painted walls, but flowers, sunny meadows full of animals and birds, woman (who else?) dancing your prayers with her curls and her flounces and her bare breasts whirling out music of the spheres. This gentle wild brilliance is all yours. I would say, here are good things forgotten at the birth of your spirit, colonists, take them to heart and build not a colony, but a home.

Do not forget where you turned in the road, but go back, and turn again. What your heart seeks is real, and waiting for you and for all of us. Too many suffer for too much nothing. Let Death have only what is not Life, not in Harmony, with Earth, with The Living, with The Dead and the worlds to come. Remember.

No one who invades is a victim. No one who defends *Home* is a savage.

We are still here.

Ah-Ho.

****
***

Works Cited & Selected Bibliography

Abbreviations Used In This Book

FBH	*The History of Plimoth Plantation,* by William Bradford (Worthington C. Ford *et als'* 2-volume edition)
WPF	*The* [John] *Winthrop Papers,* edited by Forbes
WJH	*Winthrop's Journal,* edited by Hosmer
ENEV	*The English New England Voyages* by David Beers Quinn
H15	Vol. 15 (*Northeast*) of Trigger, ed., *Handbook*
MHSC/P	*Mass. Historical Society Collections/Proceedings*

"A., J. T.," "Massachusetts." *Encyclopedia Britannica.* Vol. 14, 1028-1033. Chicago: William Benton Publishers 1966

Acosta, Jose de, *The Natural and Moral History of the Indies.* Madrid 1589. London 1604, trans. Edward Grimston. Rpt. London: The Hakluyt Society, Clements R. Markham, ed. 1930

Adams, Charles Francis, Jr., and Henry Adams, *Chapters of Erie and Other Essays.* Boston: Osgood 1871

Adams, Charles Francis, Jr., "The May-Pole of Merrymount." *Atlantic Monthly Magazine* 39 (May 1877), 557-567; (June 1877), 686-697

---, ed., *Prince Society Edition of New English Canaan.* New York: Burt Franklin 1883

--- and Henry W. Haynes, *The Site of the Wessagussett Settlement in 1622 at Weymouth, Massachusetts.* Cambridge MA: J. Wilson & Son. University Press. 1891 (Copy via the G. Stinson Lord Collection, Quincy Historical Society)

---, *Three Episodes Of Massachusetts History: The Settlement of Boston Bay.* 2 Vols., New York 1892. Rpt. New York: Russell & Russell 1965

---, *Imperialism and The Tracks of Our Forefathers* (lecture). Boston: Estes 1899

Agnew, Jean-Christophe, *Worlds Apart: The Market and the Theater in Anglo-American Thought 1550-1750.* Cambridge: Cambridge University Press 1986

Albanese, Catherine L., *Nature Religion in America: From the Algonkian Indians to the New Age.* Chicago: Chicago University Press 1990

Alexander, Sir William, *An Encouragement to Colonies* and other works collected in Prince Society, eds., *Sir William Alexander and American Colonization.* Boston: Prince Society 1873. Rpt. Burt Franklin 1967

Allen, Paula Gunn, *The Sacred Hoop: Recovering the Feminine in American Indian Traditions.* Boston, Beacon Press 1986

---, "Where I Come From God Is A Grandmother." *Prisma: A Multicultural Forum.* Boston: University of Massachusetts Publications, Vol. 2 #1, Spring 1991

Altham, Emmanuel, Letter of "to Sir Edward Altham, September 1623." In James ed., *Three Visitors to Early Plymouth* 23-36

Ambrose, Stephen E., "The Big Road." *American Heritage Magazine* October 2000, 56-66

Anderson, Benedict, *Imagined Communities: Reflections on the Origin and Spread of Nationalism.* London: Vero 1983

Andrews, K.R., N.P. Canny and P.E.H. Hair, eds., *The Westward Enterprise: English Activities in Ireland, the Atlantic and America 1480-1650.* Detroit: Wayne State University Press 1979

Arber, Edward, ed., *Travels and Works of Captain John Smith, President of Virginia and Admiral of New England 1580-1631.* 2 vols., Edinburgh: John Grant 1910

---, ed., *The Story of the Pilgrim Fathers as Told By Themselves, Their Friends and Their Enemies 1606-1623.* Boston: Houghton Mifflin 1897

Armstrong, Nancy and Leonard Tennenhouse, *The Imaginary Puritan: Literature, Intellectual Labor and the Origins of Personal Life.* Berkeley: University of California Press 1992

Ashcraft, Richard, "Leviathan Triumphant: Thomas Hobbes and the Politics of Wild Men." In Dudley, ed., *The Wild Man Within*

Ashley, Leonard R.N., *Elizabethan Popular Culture.* Bowling Green State University Press, Ohio 1988

Axtell, James, *The European and the Indian: Essays in the Ethnohistory of Colonial North America.* New York, Oxford University Press 1981

---, *The Invasion Within: The Contest of Cultures in Colonial North America*. New York, Oxford University Press 1985

Bailey, Alfred Goldsworthy, *The Conflict of European and Eastern Algonkian Cultures 1504-1700* . Toronto 1969

Baker, Brenda J., "Pilgrim's Progress and Praying Indians: The Biocultural Consequences of Contact in Southern New England." In *In the Wake of Contact: Biological Responses to Conquest*. Larsen, Clark Spencer and George R. Milner, eds. New York: Wiley-Liss 1994

Bancroft, George, *The History of the United States of America from the Discovery of the Continent*. 2 Volumes. New York: Appleton 1892

Banks, Charles Edward, *History of York, Maine*. 2 volumes. Boston 1931. Rpt. Baltimore: Reginal 1967

Barbour, Philip L., ed., *The Complete Works of Captain John Smith*. Chapel Hill: University of North Carolina Press (3 vols.) 1986

Barker, Francis, Peter Hulme, Margaret Iverson and Diana Loxley, eds., *Europe and Its Others: Proceedings of the Essex Conference on the Sociology of Literature*. Colchester: University of Essex 1985

Barrett, Louise K., *The Ignoble Savage: American Literary Racism 1790-1890*. Westport CT: Greenwood Press 1975

Barsh, Russell Lawrence, "The Nature and Spirit Of North American Political Systems." In *American Indian Quarterly*, Vol. X #3, Spring 1986

Baym, Nina, *Feminism and American Literary History: Essays*. New Brunswick: Rutgers Univesity Press 1992

Beck, Horace P., *Gluskap the Liar and Other Indian Tales*. Freeport ME: Cumberland Press 1966

Beisner, Robert L., *Twelve Against Empire: The Anti-Imperialists 1898-1900*. New York: McGraw Hill 1968

Benes, Peter, ed., *New England/New France 1600-1850*. Vol. 14 of The Dublin Seminar for New England Folklife. Boston University 1992

---, ed., *Medicine and Healing*. Vol. 15 of The Dublin Seminar for New England Folklife. Boston University 1992

---, ed., *Algonkians of New England: Past and Present*. The Dublin Seminar for New England Folklife. Boston University 1993

---, ed., *New England's Creatures: 1400-1900*. Vol. 18 of The Dublin Seminar for New England Folklike. Boston University 1995

Bennett, John W., *The Ecological Transition*. New York: Pergamon 1976

Bennett, M.K., "The Food Economy of the New England Indians 1605-1675." In *Journal of Political Economy* 63 (1955), 369-397

Bercovitch, Sacvan, *The American Puritan Imagination: Essays in Revaluation*. Cambridge: Harvard University Press 1974

---, *The Puritan Origins of the American Self*. New Haven: Yale University Press 1975

Biggar, H.P., ed., *The Early Trading Companies of New France*. University of Toronto Library 1901

Bolgar, R.R., ed., *Classical Influences on European Culture AD 1500-1700*. Proceedings of an International Conference Held at King's College, Cambridge, England April 1974. Cambridge University Press 1976

Borque, Bruce and R.H. Whitehead, "Tarrantines and the Introduction of European Trade Goods in the Gulf of Maine." In *Ethnohistory* 32: 327-341

Bradford, William, *History of Plimoth Plantation*. (Mass. Secretary of State Edition) Boston: Wright & Potter 1898

---, "A Letter of William Bradford and Isaac Allerton, 1623." *American History Review* Vol. VIII Oct. 1902-July 1903. New York: Macmillan 1903

---, *History of Plimoth Plantation 1620-1647*. Charles Francis Adams, Arthur Lord, Morton Dexter, Gamaliel Bradford Jr., and Worthington C. Ford, eds. 2 vols., Boston: Houghton Mifflin 1912

---, "A Dialogue" in Young, *Chronicles* 416-17

---, "Letter Book" in MHSC I, series III (1794), 27-76

---, "A Descriptive and Historical Account of New England in Verse, from the Manuscripts of Williams Bradford," (a.k.a. "Verse History"). In MHSC I, series III (1794), 82-3

Bradley, James W., "Native Exchange and European Trade: Cross Cultural Dynamics in the Sixteenth Century." In *Man in the Northeast* 33 (Spring 1987): 31-46

Bragdon, Kathleen J., "'Emphaticall Speech and Great Action': An Analysis of 17th-Century Native Speech Events Described in Early Sources." In *Man in the Northeast* 33 (1987), 101-11

---, "Vernacular Literacy and Massachusetts World View 1650-1750." In Benes, ed., *Algonkians* (1993), 26-35

---. *Native People of Southern New England 1500-1650*. Norman: Oklahoma University Press 1996

--- and Ives Goddard, *Native Writings in Massachusett*. 2 vols. Philadelphia: American Philosophical Society 1988

Brasser, T.J., "Early Indian-European Contacts," in H15

Brooks, Cleanth, R.W.B. Lewis, R.P. Warren and David Milch, eds., *American Literature: The Makers and the Making*. New York: St. Martin's Press 1973

Bruchac, Joseph, and Michael s. Caduto, eds., *Keepers of the Earth: Native American Stories and Environmental Activities for Children.* Golden CO: Fulcrum 1988

---, eds., *Keepers of the Animals: Native American Stories and Wildlife Activities for Children.* Golden CO: Fulcrum 1991

---, eds., *Native American Gardening: Stories, Projects and Recipes for Families.* Golden CO: Fulcrum 1996

Burrage, Henry S., ed., *Early English and French Voyages.* New York: Scribner's, Original Narratives of Early American History 1906

Burrell, Chris, "Wopanaak Spoken Here." *The Boston Globe.* November 5, 2000: E5-E6

Bushnell, David, "The Treatment of the Indians in Plymouth Colony." *New England Quarterly* xxvi (1953), 193-218

Calloway, Colin G., "The Abenakis and the Anglo-French Borderlands." In Benes, ed, *New England/New France*

Canny, Nicholas P., "The Ideology of English Colonization." In *William and Mary Quarterly*, 3rd series vol. XXX (OCt. 1973) #4, 575-98

---, "The Permissive Frontier: The Problem of Social Control in English Settlements in Ireland and Virginia." In Andrews, *The Westward Enterprise* 17-44

Carpenter, Dolores Bird, ed., *Early Encounters: Native Americans and Europeans in New England. From the Papers of Warren Sears Nickerson.* East Lansing: Michigan State University Press 1994

Carlin, Norah, "Ireland and Natural Man in 1649" in Barker, ed., *Europe and Its Others*

Carlson, Richard G., ed., *Rooted Like the Ash Trees: New England Indians and the Land.* Naugatuck, CT: Eagle Wing Press 1987

Carroll, Joseph, *Evolution and Literary Theory.* Columbia: University of Missouri Press 1995

Carson, Dale, *Native New England Cooking.* Madison CT: Sachem Press 1986

Cassirer, Ernst, P.O. Kristeller and J.H. Randall, Jr., eds., *The Renaissance Philosophy of Man.* Chicago University Press 1948

Cave, Alfred E., *The Pequot War.* Amherst: University of Massachusetts Press 1996

Ceci, Lynn, "Native Wampum as a Peripheral Resource in the 17th Century World System." In Hauptmann *Pequots* 48-63 (1990)

---"Squanto and the Pilgrims: On Planting Corn 'in the manner of the Indians.'" In Clifton, ed., The Invented Indian 71-90 (1994)

Champlain, Samuel D., *Voyages of Samuel de Champlain 1604-1618*. W.L.Grant, ed. New York: Scribner's 1907

---, *The Works of Samuel de Champlain*. 1626. Hentry P. Biggar, ed. 6 vols. Toronto: The Champlain Society 1922-1936

Charvat, William, *The Origins of American Critical Thought 1810-1835*. Philadelphia: University of Pennsylvania Press 1936

Chiappelli, Fredi, Michael J.B. Allen and Robert L. Benson, eds., *First Images of America: The Impact of the New World on the Old*. 2 Vols. Berkeley: University of California Press 1976

Chilton, Elizabeth S., "In Search of Paleo-Women: Gender Implications of Remains from Paleoindian Sites in the Northeast", in *Bulletin of the Massachusetts Archaeological Society*, Vol. 55 (1), Spring 1994, 8-17

Connor, Sheila, *New England Natives*. Cambridge: Harvard University Press 1994

Cook, Sherburne F., "The Significance of Disease in the Extinction of the New England Indians." *Human Biology* 45 (3) (1973): 485-508

Cowan, William, ed., *Papers of the Seventh Algonquian Conference*. Ottawa: Carleton University 1976

Cox, Edward G., ed. *A Reference Guide to The Literature of Travel* (3 vols: Old World, New World, England). Seattle: University of Washington Press 1935-49

Cronon, William, *Changes in the Land: Indians, Colonists and the Ecology of New England*. New York: Farrar Straus & Giroux 1983

Crosby, Connie, "The Algonkian Spiritual Landscape." In Benes, *Algonkians of New England*, 35-41 (1993)

(authors/editors unspecified), *Current Biography: Who's News and Why*. New York: H. W. Wilson 1947

Cushman, Robert, "On the State of the Colony, and the Need of Public Spirit Among the Colonists." 1622-1623. Rpt. in Young 255-268

Davenport, Francis Gardner, *European Treaties Bearing on the History of the United States and Its Dependencies*. Washington D.C.: Carnegie Institute Publication 254. 3 vols. 1917

David, Richard, ed., *Hakluyt's Voyages*. Boston: Houghton Mifflin 1981

Davies, Horton, *The Worship of the American Puritans 1629-1730*. New York: Peter Lang 1990

Davies, Stevie, ed., *Renaissance Views of Man*. Manchester University Press 1979

Davis, William A., "Digging It In Massachusetts." *The Boston Globe* June 6, 1992

Day, Gordon M., "Western Abenaki" in H15 148-159

Deagan, Kathleen A., "Spanish Indian Interaction in Sixteenth Century Florida and Hispaniola." In Fitzhugh, ed., *Cultures in Contact*

Deane, Charles F., ed., *Records of the Council for New England*. American Antiquarian Society Proceedings, 1875. (John Hay Library Metcalf Collection, Brown University, Providence RI)

Deetz, James and Patricia Scott Deetz, "Rocking the Plymouth Myth." *Achaeology Magazine*. November-December 2000, 16-18

Delgado-Gomez, Angel, "The Earliest European Views of the New World Natives." In Williams, ed., *Early Images of the Americas* (1993)

de Molina, Don Diego, "Letter of Don Diego de Molina." 1613. In Tyler, ed., *Narratives of Early Virginia*. New York: Scribner's 1907

Dempsey, John [Jack], *Thomas Morton and the Maypole of Merrymount: Disorder in the American Wilderness 1622-1647*. 2-hr. video documentary (1992) distributed by the producer (see front of book)

---, Jack, *Nani: A Native New England Story*. 1-hr. videodocumentary (1998) distributed by V-Tape, 401 Richmond St. West, Suite 452, Toronto, Canada M5V 3A8 (456-351-1317); and by Shenandoah Film Productions, Arcata CA

---, ed., *New English Canaan by Thomas Morton of "Merrymount. Text and Notes*. Scituate MA: Digital Scanning Inc. 2000

---, *Thomas Morton: The Life and Renaissance of an Early American Poet*. Scituate MA: Digital Scanning Inc. 2000

Densmore, Frances. *How Indians Use Wild Plants for Food, Medicine, and Crafts*. New York: Dover 1974

de Rasieres, Isaac, Letter of "to Samuel Blommaert, c. 1628." In James, ed., *Three Visitors* 65-80

Dexter, Lincoln A., *Maps of Early Massachusetts: Prehistory Through the 17th Century*. Springfield MA: New England Blue Print Paper Company 1979

Dickason, Olive Patricia, *The Myth of the Savage and the Beginnings of French Colonialism in the Americas*. Edmonton: University of Alberta Press 1984

Dincauze, Dena F., "A Capsule Prehistory of Southern New England." In Hauptmann and Wherry, *The Pequots*

Drake, Samuel G., ed., *The Book of the Indians: or, Biography and History of the Indians of North America, from Its First Discovery to the Year 1841*. Boston: Antiquarian Bookstore 1841

Drinnon, Richard, *White Savage: The Case of John Dunn Hunter*. New York: Schocken 1972

---, *Facing West: The Metaphysics of Indian-Hating and Empire-Building*. New York: Schocken 1980

230

Dudley, Edward and Maximilian E. Novak, eds., *The Wild Man Within: An Image in Western Thought from the Renaissance to Romanticism.* University of Pittsburgh Press 1972

Duncan, Roger F., *Coastal Maine: A Maritime History.* New York: Norton 1992

Dunn, Jerome P., "Squanto Before He Met the Pilgrims." In *Bulletin of the Massachusetts Archaeological Society,* Vol 54, #1, Spring 1993

Dyer, Gwynne, *War.* New York: Crown Press 1985

Eccles, W.J., *France in America.* East Lansing: Michigan State University Press 1990. [Ch. 1: "False Starts 1500-1632"]

Eddy-Snow, Stephen, *Performing the Pilgrims: A Study of Ethnohistorical Role-Playing at Plimoth Plantation.* Jackson: University Press of Mississippi 1993

Edmundson, George, *Anglo-Dutch Rivalry During the First Half of the 17th Century.* Oxford UP 1911

Elson, Ruth Miller, *Guardians of Tradition: American Schoolbooks in the 19th Century.* Lincoln: University of Nebraska Press 1964

Empiricus, Sextus, *The Outlines of Pyrronhism* (c. 150-225 AD) Rpt. in Hallie, Philip P., ed., and Etheridge, Sanford G., trans., *Scepticism, Man and God: Selections from the Major Writings of Sextus Empiricus.* Middletown CT: Wesleyan University Press 1964

Erickson, Vincent O., "Maliseet-Passamaquoddy" in H15 123-36

Etienne, Mona, and Eleanor Leacock, eds., *Women and Colonization: Anthropological Perspectives.* New York: Praeger 1980

Fausz, J.F., "Patterns of Anglo-Indian Aggression and Accomodation." In Fitzhugh, ed., *Cultures in Contact*

Felt, Joseph B., *Annals of Salem, From Its First Settlement.* Salem: W. and S.B. Ives 1827

Fiedler, Leslie, *Love and Death in the American Novel.* 1960: rpt. New York, Anchor 1992

Fischer, David Hackett, *Albion's Seed: Four British Folkways in America.* New York: Oxford University Press 1989

Fiske, John, *The Dutch and Quaker Colonies in America.* 2 vols. Boston: Houghton Mifflin 1903

Fitzhugh, William, "Early Contacts North of Newfoundland Before 1600: A Review." In Fitzhugh ed., *Cultures in Contact*

---, ed. *Cultures in Contact: The Impact of European Contacts on Native American Cultural Institutions.* Washington D.C.: Smithsonian Institution Press 1985

Force, Peter, ed., *Tracts and Other Papers Relating Principally to the Origin, Settlement, and Progress of the Colonies in North America, From the discovery of the country to the Year 1776*. Washington: 3 vols., Peter Force printer, 1836

Freeman, Stan, and Mike Nasuti, *The Natural History of Eastern Massachusetts*. Florence MA: Hampshire House 1998

Frost, Jack, ed., *Immortal Voyage...And Pilgrim Parallels: Problems, Protests, Patriotism 1620-1970*. North Scituate, MA: Hawthorne Press 1970

Fumerton, Patricia, *Cultural Aesthetics: Renaissance Literature and the Practice of Social Ornament*. University of Chicago Press 1991

Gardner, Russell H. (*aka* Great Moose: Wampanoag Tribal Historian/Gay Head Aquinnah), "Genesis of New England's Sacred Landscape and Our Spiritual Legacy." Unpublished text of lecture to Massachusetts Archaeological Society, Robbins Museum, Middleboro MA: April 5, 1997; read from aloud by Gardner in Dempsey, *Nani*

---, "Anthropomorphic and Fertility Stoneworks of Southeastern New England: A Native Interpretation." Illustrated. To be published 1999 by *The Massachusetts Archaeological Society Bulletin*. Generously shared in mss.

Gathorne-Hardy, G.M., *The Norse Discoverers of America: The Wineland Sagas*. 1921. Rpt. London: Oxford University Press 1970

gkisedtanamoogk, and Frances Hancock, *Ceremony Is Life Itself*. Portland, ME: Astarte Shell Press 1993

Gookin, Daniel, *Historical Collections of the Indians in New England*. 1674. 1806 Rpt. in MHSC 3 series vol. 1, 141-229

Gookin, Warner F., and Philip L. Barbour, *Bartholomew Gosnold: Discoverer and Planter*. London: Archon 1963

Gorges, Sir Ferdinando, *A Brief Relation of the Discovery and Plantation of New England*. London 1622. MHSC 2nd series ix (1823), 1-25

---, *A Brief Narration of the Original Undertakings, for the Advancement of Plantations in America*. [1658]. Maine Historical Society Collections, I ser II, 1847, 1-65

Grafton, Anthony, *New Worlds, Ancient Texts: The Power of Tradition and the Shock of Discovery*. Cambridge: Harvard University Press 1992

Grant, W.L., and James Munroe, eds., *Acts of the Privy Council, Colonial Series 1613-1783*. Hereford, England: 2 vols. 1908

Gray, Edward F., *Leif Eriksson: Discoverer of America AD 1003*. New York: Oxford University Press 1930. Rpt. New York: Kraus 1972

Greenblatt, Stephen J., *Renaissance Self-Fashioning: From More to Shakespeare*. Chicago: University of Chicago Press 1984

232

Griffin, Susan, *Pornography and Silence: Culture's Revenge Against Nature*. New York: Harper & Row 1981

Grumet, Robert Steven, "Sunksquaws, Shamans and Tradeswomen: Middle Atlantic Coastal Algonkian Women During the 17th and 18th Centuries." In Etienne *Women and Colonization*

Guillette, Mary E., ed., *American Indians in Connecticutt: Past to Present. A Report Prepared for the Connecticutt Indian Affairs Council*. State of Connecticutt, Department of Environmental Protection 1979

Hakluyt, Richard, ed., *Divers Voyages Touching the Discoverie of America and the Islands Adjacent Unto the Same*. London: T. Woodcocke 1582. Rpt. John W. Jones, ed., London: Hakluyt Society 1850

---, ed., *The Principall Navigations, Voyages, Traffiques, and Discoveries of the English Nation*. Rpt. (12 vols). Glasgow: 1903-05

Hale, Edward Everett Jr., ed., *Notebook Kept by Thomas Lechford, Esquire: Lawyer in Boston, Massachusetts Bay 1638-1641*. Camden, ME: Picton Press 1988

Haller, William, *The Rise of Puritanism*. New York: Columbia University Press 1938

Hallett, Leaman, F., "Medicine and Pharmacy of the New England Indians." *Mass. Archaeological Society Bulletin*, Vol. 17 #3 (1956)

Halpern, Richard, *The Poetics of Primitive Accumulation: English Renaissance Culture and the Genealogy of Capital*. Ithaca, NY: Cornell University Press 1991

Hammond, Jeffrey A., *Sinful Self, Saintly Self: The Puritan Experience of Poetry*. Athens: University of Georgia Press 1993

Hammell, George, "Mythical Realities and European Contact in the Northeast During the Sixteenth and Seventeenth Centuries." In *Man in the Northeast* 33 [1987]: 63-87

Hariot, Thomas, *Brief and True Report of the New Found Land of Virginia*. London 1588. Rpt. New York: Dover 1972

Harris, John, *Saga of the Pilgrims: From Europe to the New World*. Chester, CT: Globe Pequot [1983]1990

Harris, Laurie Lanzen, ed., *Nineteenth Century American Literary Criticism*. 41 Volumes. Detroit: Gale Research 1981-1990

Harris, Marvin, *The Rise of Anthropological Theory*. New York: Crowell 1968

Harris, Tim, ed., *Popular Culture in England 1500-1850*. New York: St. Martin's 1995

Haskins, George, *Law and Authority in Early Massachusetts*. Hamden CT: Archon 1960

Hauptmann, Laurence M. and James O. Wherry, *The Pequots in Southern New England: The Fall and Rise of an American Indian Nation*. Norman: University of Oklahoma Press 1990

Hazard, Ebenezer, ed., *Historical Collections*. 2 vols. Philadelphia: 1792

Heard, J. Norman, *Handbook of the American Frontier: Four Centuries of Indian-White Relationships*, Vol. II *The Northeastern Woodlands*. Metuchen, NJ: Scarecrow Press 1990

Heath, Dwight, ed., *Mourt's Relation: A Journal of the Pilgrims at Plymouth*. New York: Corinth 1963

Higginson, Francis, *New England's Plantation*. London 1630. Rpt. in Force, *Tracts* 1

Hill, Christopher, *The World Turned Upside Down: Radical Ideas During the English Revolution*. [1972] New York: Viking 1973

---, *Change and Continuity in Seventeenth Century England*. Cambridge: Harvard University Press 1975

Holly, H. Hobart, "Wollaston of Mount Wollaston." Quincy [MA] Historical Society Publication. Rpt. from *The American Neptune*, Vol. XXXVII, #1, Jan. 1977

Honour, Hugh, *The New Golden Land: European Images of America from the Discoveries to the Present Time*. London: Allea Lane 1976

Horner, George R., "Squantum, Moswetusett, Mattachusett, Massachusetts, Neponset, Chikkatawbut." In *Quincy History*. Quincy, MA: Historical Society #21, Winter 1989, 1-4

Hosmer, James Kendall, ed., see *Winthrop's Journal "History of New England"*

Hubbard, William, *The History of the Indian Wars in New England*. 1677. (1865) Samuel G. Drake, ed., Roxbury: W. Eliot Woodward. Rpt. 1969, New York: Kraus Reprint Co.

Huddleston, Lee, *Origins of the American Indians 1492-1729*. Austin: University of Texas Press 1967

Hulme, Peter, "Polytropic Man: Tropes of Sexuality and Mobility in Early Colonial Discourse." In Barker, ed., *Europe and Its Others*

Hutchinson, Thomas, *A Collection of Original Papers Relative to the History of the Colony and Province of Massachusetts Bay*. Boston: Fleet 1769 Original copy in John Hay Library, Brown University, Providence RI . Rpt. Cambridge: Harvard University Press 1936

Hutton, Ronald, *The Rise and Fall of Merry England: The Ritual Year 1400-1700*. New York: Oxford UP 1994

Ingram, Martin, "From Reformation to Toleration: Popular Religious Cultures in England, 1540-1690." In Harris, ed., *Popular Culture in England*

James, Sydney V., ed., *Three Visitors to Early Plymouth: Letters About the Pilgrim Settlement in New England During Its First Seven Years*. Plymouth MA: Plimoth Plantation Inc. 1963

234

Jameson, J. Franklin, ed., *Narratives of New Netherland 1609-1664*. New York: Barnes and Noble 1909

Jantz, Harold S., *The First Century of New England Verse*. (1944) Rpt. New York: Russell and Russell 1962

Jennings, Francis, *The Invasion of America: Indians, Colonialism and the Cant of Conquest*. Chapel Hill: University of North Carolina Press 1975

---, *The Founders of America*. New York: W.W. Norton 1993

Johannessen and Hastorf, eds., *Corn and Culture in the Prehistoric New World*. Boulder: Westview Press 1994

Johnson, Edward, *Johnson's Wonder-Working Providence 1628-1651*. [1653] J. Franklin Jameson, ed., New York: Scribner's, 1910

Johnson, Frederick, ed., *Man in Northeastern America*. Andover, MA: *Papers of the Robert S. Peabody Foundation for Archaeology* 3, 1946

Johnston, Alexandra F., "English Puritanism and Festive Custom." *Renaissance and Reformation* (New Series) 1991, Vol. XV, #4, 289-99

Jones, Colin, "Plague and Its Metaphors in Early Modern France." *Representations* 53 (Winter 1996): 97-127

Jones, James Rees, *The Anglo-Dutch Wars of the 17th Century*. New York: Longman 1996

Josselyn, John, *New-Englands Rarities Discovered*. 1672. In Transactions and Collections of the American Antiquarian Society [Archaeologia Americana], IV (1860), 130-238

---, *An Account of Two Voyages to New-England*. 1674. Rpt. in Lindholdt, ed., *John Josselyn, Colonial Traveler*

Kaplan, Justin, *Walt Whitman: A Life*. New York: Bantam 1980

Kearney, Hugh, "The Problem of Perspective in the History of Colonial America." In Andrews, ed., *Westward Enterprise* (290-302)

Kelso, Ruth, *The Doctrine of the English Gentleman in the Sixteenth Century*. University of Illinois Press 1929

Kennedy, J.H., *Jesuit and Savage in New France*. New Haven: Yale University Press 1950 (Ch. 2: "Canada 1608-1629")

Kirkland, Edward C., *Charles Francis Adams, Jr. 1893-1915: The Patrician at Bay*. Cambridge: Harvard University Press 1965

Kolodny, Annette, *The Lay of the Land: Metaphor as Experience and History in American Life and Letters*. Chapel Hill: University of North Carolina Press 1975

Krech, Shepard III, ed., *Indians, Animals and the Fur Trade: A Critique of Keepers of the Game.* Athens: University of Georgia Press 1981

Kricher, John C., *A Field Guide to Eastern Forests.* Boston: Houghton Mifflin 1988

Kristeva, Julia, "Oscillation Between Power and Denial," in *New French Feminisms: An Anthology,* E. Marks *et als,* eds. New York: Schocken 1981

Kupperman, Karen Ordahl, "English Perceptions of Treachery 1583-1640: The Case of the American 'Savages.'" *Historical Journal* xx, 263-287 (1977)

---, *Captain John Smith.* Chapel Hill: University of North Carolina Press 1988

---, *North America and the Beginnings of European Colonization.* Washington, D.C.: American Historical Association 1992

---, ed., *Major Problems in American Colonial History: Documents and Essays.* Lexington MA: Heath 1993

---, *Providence Island 1630-1641: The Other Puritan Colony.* New York: Cambridge University Press 1993

---, ed., *America In European Consciousness 1493-1750.* Chapel Hill: University of North Carolina Press 1995

---, *Indians and English: Facing Off in Early America.* Ithaca NY: Cornell University Press 2000

---, *Settling With the Indians: The Meeting of English and Indian Cultures in America 1580-1640.* Totowa NJ: Rowman and Littlefield 1980

---, "'Brasse without but Golde within': The Writings of Captain John Smith." In *Virginia Cavalcade* (Winter 1989), 38:3, 134-43

---, "Thomas Morton, Historian." *The New England Quarterly,* Vol. 50, Dec. 1977, 660-64

Lamphere, Kim and Dean Snow, "European Contact and Indian Depopulation in the Northeast: The Timing of the First Epidemics." In *Ethnohistory* 35, #1, 1988: 15-33

Lauter, Paul, gen. ed., *The Heath Anthology of American Literature.* 2 Vols. Lexington MA: Heath 1994

Leahy, Christopher, John H. Mitchell and Thomas Convel, eds., *The Nature of Massachusetts.* Reading MA: Addison Wesley 1996

Lee, Sidney, *The French Renaissance in England: An Account of the Literary Relations of England and France in the 16th Century.* New York: Scribner's 1910

Leland, Charles G., *Algonquian Legends.* Boston 1884. Rpt. New York: Dover 1992

---, *Kuloskap the Master and Other Algonkin Poems.* New York: Funk & Wagnalls 1902

Lescarbot, Marc, *Nova Francia, or A Description of Acadia*. 1606. Henry P. Biggar, ed., London: George Routledge & Sons 1928

---, *The History of New France*. 1618. W.L. Grant, trans. Toronto: Champlain Society 1907-14

---, "The Conversion of the Savages." Paris 1610. Rpt. in Thwaites, ed., *The Jesuit Relations* 1

---, *The Theatre of Neptune in New France*. [1606] Harriette T. Richardson, ed. Boston: Houghton Mifflin 1927

Levermore, Charles Herbert, ed., *Forerunners and Competitors of the Pilgrims and Puritans*. 2 Vols. Brooklyn NY: New England Society 1912

Levett, Captain Christopher, *A Voyage into New England*. London 1628. Rpt. in Levermore, ed., *Forerunners* Vol. 2

Lewis, Clifford M. and Albert J. Loomie, eds., *The Spanish Jesuit Mission in Virginia 1570-1572*. Chapel Hill: University of North Caroline Press 1953

Lindholdt, Paul J., ed., *John Josselyn, Colonial Traveler: A Critical Edition of Two Voyages to New-England*. Hanover: University Press of New England 1988

Loftfield, Thomas C., "The Adaptive Role of Warfare Among the Southern Algonquians." In Cowan, ed., *Papers of the Seventh Algonquian Conference*

Longfellow, Henry Wadsworth (no editor named), *The Complete Poetical Works of Henry Wadsworth Longfellow*. Boston: Houghton Mifflin 1893

Major, Minor Wallace, "Thomas Morton and His *New English Canaan*." Unpublished Ph.D. Dissertation, University of Colorado 1957

---, "William Bradford Versus Thomas Morton." *Early American Literature* Vol. V, #2, Fall 1970, 1-13

Malone, Patrick M., "Changing Military Technology Among the Indians of Southern New England 1600-1677." *American Quarterly* 25 (1973), 50-53

---, *The Skulking Way of War: Technology and Tactics Among the New England Indians*. New York: Madison Books 1991

Marten, Catherine, *Occasional Papers in Old Colony Studies* #2. December 1970. Plimoth Plantation Inc. publication

Martin, Calvin, "Fire and Forest Structure in the Aboriginal Eastern Forest." In *The Indian Historian* 6 (1973), 23-26

---, "The European Impact on the Culture of a Northeastern Algonquian Tribe: An Ecological Interpretation." *William and Mary Quarterly* 31, #1 (1974): 3-26

---, *Keepers of the Game: Indian Animal Relations and the Fur Trade*. Berkeley: University of California Press 1978

Mates, Benson, ed. and trans., *The Skeptic Way: Sextus Empiricus' Outlines of Pyrrhonism*. New York: Oxford University Press 1996

Mathes, Valerie, "A New Look at the Role of Women in Indian Society." *American Indian Quarterly* 2 (Summer 1975), 131-9

Matthiessen, F. O., *American Renaissance: Art and Expression in the Age of Emerson and Whitman*. New York: Oxford University Press 1941, rpt. 1968

Maverick, Samuel, *A Brief Description of New England and the Severall Towns Therein, together with the present government thereof.* Rpt. in MHSP, second series Vol. 1 (1884-5), 231-249

---, Letter to the Earl of Clarendon. 1661. In "The Clarendon Papers." *New York Historical Society Collections II*, 1869, 40-41

Mavor, James W. Jr., and Byron E. Dix, *Manitou: The Sacred Landscape of New England's Native Civilization*. Rochester VT: Inner Traditions 1991

McBride, Kevin A., "'Ancient and Crazie': Pequot Lifeways During the Historical Period." In Benes, ed., *Algonkians of New England* 63-75

McCann, Franklin T., ed., *English Discovery of America to 1585*. New York: Octagon 1969

McGrath, Patrick, "Bristol and America, 1480-1631," in Andrews, ed., *The Westward Enterprise*

McPherson, John and Geri McPherson, *Primitive Wilderness Living and Survival Skills*. Randolph, KS: Prairie Wolf Press 1993

Meleney, John C., "Charles Francis Adams, Jr." In *The Dictionary of Literary Biography* Volume 47, 7-16

Merchant, Carolyn, *Ecological Revolutions: Nature, Gender and Science in New England*. Chapel Hill: University of North Carolina Press 1989

Miller, Perry, ed., *The Puritans: A Sourcebook of Their Writings* (1938). Rpt. (2 vols.) New York: Harper & Row 1963

Montaigne, Michel de, *The Essayes of Michael Lord of Montaigne*. (1580-1588) London 1603, John Florio, trans. 3 vols. London: J.M. Dent & Sons 1910

Moody, Robert E., ed., *The Letters of Thomas Gorges, Deputy Governor of the Province of Maine 1640-1643*. Portland: Maine Historical Society 1978

More, Sir Thomas, *Utopia*. 1516. Northbrook IL: AHM Publishing 1949, H.V.S. Ogden, trans.

Morgan, Edmund S., *The Puritan Dilemma: The Story of John Winthrop*. Boston: Little Brown 1958

Morison, Samuel Eliot, *Builders of the Bay Colony* . New York: Macmillan 1952

238

---, ed., *Of Plimoth Plantation, by William Bradford*. [1952] New York: Random House 1981

Morton, Thomas, *New English Canaan*. See Adams and Dempsey editions

Morrell, William, *Nova Anglia; or New-England*. London 1625. Rpt. in MHSC Vol I, 1792, 125-139

Morton, Nathaniel, *New-England's Memorial*. [1669] 5th ed. John Davis, ed., Boston: Crocker & Brewster 1826

Mourt's Relation: A Journal of the Pilgrims at Plimoth (anonymous, London 1622). D.B. Heath, ed., Chester CT: Globe Pequot Press 1963

Nabokov, Peter, ed., *Native American Testimony: A Chronicle of Indian-White Relations from Prophecy to the Present 1492-1992*. New York: Penguin 1992

Nanepashemet (*aka* Anthony Pollard), personal interview in Rolbein, Seth, "The Thanks-giving Myth: The head of Plimoth Plantation's Wampanoag site gives his people's view of this popular American feast." *Boston Sunday Herald*, "Sunday People Magazine," Nov. 17, 1991; p. 6 (incl. "jumps" to pp. 8 and 19)

---, personal interview on Native New England culture and history in Dempsey video-documentary, *Thomas Morton* 1992

---, "Smells Fishy to Me: An Argument Supporting the Use of Fish Fertilizer by the Native People of Southern New England." In Benes, ed., *Algonkians of New England* (1993)42-50

---, "Hobbomock: A Special Instrument Sent of Massasoit for Their Good Beyond Their Expectation." Unpublished paper delivered at Northeastern Anthropological Association, Danbury CT March 1993

New England Begins: The Seventeenth Century. Vol. 1. Boston: Museum of Fine Arts, Department of American Decorative Arts and Sculpture Publications 1982 (no listed authors)

Nickerson, Frederick Sears, *Early Encounters: Native Americans and Europeans in New England*. Dolores Bird Carpenter, ed. East Lansing: Michigan State University Press 1994

NOVA. *The Lost Red Paint People*. Film production of the WGBH-Boston Educational Foundation 1987 (Program #1420)

Nova Britannia: [attrib. Robert Johnson *Offering Most Excellent Fruites by Planting in Virginia. Exciting all such as be well affected to further the same*. Printed for Samuel Matcham, London 1609. Rpt. in Force, *Tracts* 1

Numbers, Ronald L., ed., *Medicine in the New World: New Spain, New France and New England*. Knoxville: University of Tennessee Press 1987

O'Gorman, Edmundo, *The Invention of America: An Inquiry into the Historical Nature of the New World and the Meaning of Its History*. Bloomington: Indiana University Press 1961

Oleson, Tryggvi J., *Early Voyages and Northern Approaches 1000-1632*. Canadian Centenary Series: Toronto: McClelland & Stewart 1963

Pagden, Anthony, *Spanish Imperialism and the Political Imagination*. New Haven: Yale University Press 1990

Palfrey, John Gorham, *The History of New England During the Stuart Dynasty*. (3 vols.) Boston: Little Brown 1890

Payne, Edward John, ed., *Voyages of the Elizabethan Seamen to America: Select Narratives from the 'Principall Navigations' of Hakluyt*. Oxford: Clarendon Press 1900

Peacock, John, "Principles and Effects of Puritan Appropriation of Indian Land and Labor." *Ethnohistory* 31, #1 (1984): 39-44

Pearce, Roy Harvey, *Savagism and Civilization: A Study of the Indian and the American Mind*. (1953) 2nd ed. Baltimore: Johns Hopkins University Press 1965

Pennington, Loren E., "The Amerindian in English Promotional Literature 1575-1625" in Andrews, ed., *The Westward Enterprise*

Perkins, William, *The Arte of Prophesying*. [1613] Rpt. in *Works of That Famous and Worthie Minister of Christ in the University of Cambridge, M. William Perkins*. 2 vols. Cambridge, England: John Legat 1608-9. Original copy in the Brown University Hay Library, Star Collection

Petegorsky, David W., *Left-Wing Democracy in the English Civil War: A Study of the Social Philosophy of Gerrard Winstanley*. New York: Haskell House 1972

Peters, Russell, *The Wampanoags of Mashpee: An Indian Perspective on American History*. Somerville: Media Action Press 1987

---, *Clambake: A Wampanoag Tradition*. Minneapolis: Lerner Publications 1992

Peterson, Harold L., *Arms and Armor in Colonial America 1526-1783*. New York: Bramhall House 1956

---, *Arms and Armor of the Pilgrims 1620-1692*. Plymouth MA: Plimoth Plantation Inc. and Pilgrim Society 1957

Plane, Anne Marie, "Childbirth Practices Among Native American Women of the Northeast and Canada, 1600-1800." In Benes, ed., *Medicine and Healing*

Pollard, H.B.C., *A History of Firearms*. Boston: Houghton Mifflin 1933

Popkin, Richard H., *The History of Scepticism from Erasmus to Spinoza*. Berkeley: University of California Press 1979

Pory, John, Letter of "to the Earl of Southampton, Jan. 13, 1622/1623, and Later." In James, ed., *Three Visitors* 5-13

240

Pratt, Phinehas, "Declaration of the Affairs of the English People that First Inhabited New England." c.1658-1662. In MHSC IV, 474-487

Preston, Richard Arthur, *Gorges of Plymouth Fort*. Toronto: University of Toronto Press 1953

Pribek, Thomas, "The Conquest of Canaan: Suppression of Merrymount." *Nineteenth Century Literature*, Dec. 1985, 40:3, 345-54

Price, Richard, *Ethnographic History, Caribbean Pasts*. Working Papers #9. Department of Spanish and Portuguese, University of Maryland, College Park 1990

Pritchard, Evan, *Algonguin Eagle Song*. Woodstock NY: Center for Algonquin Culture, Resonance Communications 2000

Quinn, David Beers, *The Newfoundland of Stephen Parmenius*. Toronto: University of Toronto Press 1972

---, *England and the Discovery of America 1481-1620. from the Bristol Voyages of the 15th Century to the Pligrim Settlement at Plimoth*. New York: Knopf 1974

---, "Renaissance Influences in English Colonization." In *Transactions of the Royal Historical Society*, 5th series, XXV 73-93

---, *North America from Earliest Discovery to the First Settlements: The Norse Voyages to 1612*. New York: Harper & Row 1977

Quinn, David Beers and Alison M. Quinn, eds., *The English New England Voyages 1602-1608*. London: Hakluyt Society 1983

Rabb, Felix, *The English Face of Machiavelli*. London: Routledge & Keegan Paul 1964

Rabb, Theodore K., *Enterprise and Empire: Merchant and Gentry Investment in the Expansion of England, 1575-1630*. Cambridge: Harvard University Press 1967

Raesly, Ellis Lawrence, *Portrait of New Netherland*. New York: Columbia University Press 1945

Ranlet, Philip, *Enemies of the Bay Colony*. New York: Peter Lang 1995

Ray, Arthur J., *Indians in the Fur Trade*. Toronto: University of Toronto Press 1974

Reynolds, Barrie, "Beothuk" in H15, 101-108

Reynolds, David S., *Beneath the American Renaissance: The Subversive Imagination in the Age of Emerson and Melville*. New York: Knopf 1988

Robinson, Paul A., "Lost Opportunities: Miantonomi and the English in 17th Century Narragansett Country." In Grumet *Lives* 13-28

Rosensteil, Annette, *Red and White: Indian Views of the White Man 1492-1982*. New York: Universe Books 1983

Rowe, John Howland, "Ethnography and Ethnology in the 16th Century." Kroeber Anthropological Society Papers 30, 1-19

Rowse, A. L., *The Elizabethans and America*. New York: Harper & Rown 1959

Russell, Howard S., *Indian New England Before the Mayflower*. University Press of New England 1980

Salisbury, Neal, *Manitou and Providence: Indians, Europeans and the Making of New England 1500-1643*. New York: Oxford UP 1982

---, *The Indians of New England: A Critical Bibliography*. Bloomington: Indiana University Press 1982

Salwen, Bert, "Indians of Southern New England and Long Island: Early Period." In H15, 160-176

Santayana, George, "The Genteel Tradition in American Philosophy." 1913. Rpt. in Hollinger, David A. and Charles Capper, eds., *The American Intellectual Tradition*. (Vol. 2 of 2) New York: Oxford University Press 1993

Saum, Lewis O., *The Fur Trader and the Indian*. Seattle: University of Washington Press 1965

Scarry, C. Margaret, ed., *Foraging and Farming in the Eastern Woodlands*. Gainesville: University Press of Florida 1993

Schama, Simon, *The Embarrassment of Riches: An Interpretation of Dutch Culture in the Golden Age*. New York: Knopf 1987

Scholes, Robert, *Textual Power: Literary Theory and the Teaching of English*. New Haven: Yale University Press 1985

Scottow, J., "A Narrative of the Planting of the Massachusets-Colony &c" [1628] Rpt. in MHSC XXXIV, 279-330

Shurtleff, Nathaniel E., *The Records of the Governor and Company of the Massachusetts Bay in New England*. (5 Vols.) Boston: William White 1853

Shrewsbury, J.F.D., *A History of Bubonic Plague in the British Isles*. London: Cambridge UP 1970

Shuffelton, Frank, ed., *A Mixed Race: Ethnicity in Early America*. New York: Oxford University Press 1993

Simmons, William S., *Cautantowwitt's House: An Indian Burial Ground in the Island of Conanicut in Narragansett Bay*. Providence: Brown University Press 1970

---, "Southern New England Shamanism: An Ethnographic Reconstruction." In William Cowan, ed., *Papers of the Seventh Algonquian Conference*, Ottowa: Carleton University Press 1976

---, "Narragansett" in H15, 190-197 (1978)

242

---, *Spirit of the New England Tribes: Indian History and Folklore 1620-1984.* University Press of New England 1986

Slack, Paul, *The Impact of Plague in Tudor and Stuart England.* Boston: Routledge and Keegan Paul 1985

Slafter, Edmund F., ed., *Sir William Alexander and American Colonization.* Boston: Prince Society 1873. Rpt. New York: Burt Franklin 1967

Slavin, Arthur J., "The American Principle from More to Locke." In Chiappelli, ed., *First Images*

Slotkin, Richard, *Regeneration Through Violence: The Mythology of the American Frontier 1600-1860.* Wesleyan University Press 1973

Slow Turtle (a.k.a. John Peters; Medicine Man of the Wampanoag Nation [Mashpee], Director of Massachusetts Center for Native American Awareness), personal interview in Dempsey video-documentary *Thomas Morton* 1992

Smith, Abbot Emerson, *Colonists in Bondage: White Servitude and Convict Labor in America 1607-1776.* Chapel Hill: University of North Carolina Press 1947

Smith, John, *Description of New England.* London 1616. Rpt. in Arber, ed. *Travels and Works*

---, *New Englands Trials.* London 1622. Rpt. in Force *Tracts* Vol. 2

---, *Description of New England.* London 1616. Rpt. in Barbour, Philip L, ed., *The Complete Works*

---, *Captain John Smith: Works.* Edward Arber, ed. Westminster, England 1895

Smith, William and John Lockwood, eds., *Chambers Murray Latin-English Dictionary.* London: Chambers 1995

Snow, Dean R., *The American Indians: Their Archaeology and Prehistory.* London: Thames and Hudson 1976

---, "Late Prehistory of the East Coast," in H15, 58-69

---, "Eastern Abenaki" in H15 142-147

---, "The Solon Petroglyphs and Eastern Abnaki Shamanism." In Cowan, ed., *Papers of the Seventh Algonquian Conference* 281-288

Speck, Frank G., "The Family Hunting Band as the Basis of Algonkian Social Organization." *American Anthropologist* 17 (1915)

---, "Medicine Practices of the Northeastern Algonquians." In *19th International Congress of Americanists: Proceedings* (Dec. 27-31, 1915) Washington D.C., 1917: 303-321

---, "Penobscot Shamanism." *Memoirs of the American Anthropological Association,* Vol. VI #4, Oct.-Dec. 1919

---, *Penobscot Man: The Life History of a Forest Tribe in Maine*. Philadelphia: University of Pennsylvania Press 1940 (rpt. 1970)

Speck, Grank G., and R.W. Dexter, "Utilization of Marine Life by the Wampanoag Indians of Massachusetts." Washington D.C.: Washington Academy of Sciences, *Journal*, XXXVIII (1948), 257-265

Speiss, Arthur J. and Bruce D. Speiss, "New England Pandemic of 1616-1622: Cause and Archaeological Implication." In *Man in the Northeast* 34 (Fall 1987), 71-83

Spengemann, William C., *A Mirror for Americanists: Reflections on the Idea of American Literature*. Hanover NH: University Press of New England 1989

---, *A New World of Words: Redefining Early American Literature*. New Haven: Yale University Press 1994

Starkey, David, *The Reign of Henry VIII: Personalities and Politics*. New York: Franklin Watts 1986

Starna, William A., "The Pequots in the Early 17th Century." In Hauptmann and Wherry *The Pequots* 33-47

Stone, Lawrence, *The Crisis of the Aristocracy 1558-1641*. New York: Oxford University Press 1967

---, *The Past and the Present*. Boston: Routledge & Keegan Paul 1981

Strong, Pauline Turner, "Captivity in White and Red: Convergent Practice and Colonial Represenation on the British-American Frontier, 1606-1736." *Crossing Cultures: Essays in the Displacement of Western Civilization*, Daniel Segal, ed. Tucson: University of Arizona Press1992

Tantaquidgeon, Gladys, *Folk Medicine of the Delaware and Related Algonkian Indians*. (1972) 2nd ed. Harrisburg: Commonwealth of Pennsylvania: Pennsylvania Historical and Museum Commission 1977

Tetel, Marcel, *Montaigne*. New York: Twayne Publishers 1974

Thirsk, Joan, ed., *The Agrarian History of England and Wales 1500-1640*. 5 vols. London: Cambridge University Press 1967

Thomas, Keith, *Religion and the Decline of Magic*. New York: Scribner's 1971

Thomas, Peter A., "The Fur Trade, Indian Land, and the Need to Define Adequate 'Environmental' Parameters." *Ethnohistory* 28, #4 (1981): 359-79

Thwaites, Reuben Gold, *The Jesuit Relations and Allied Documents: Travels and Explorations of the Jesuit Missionaries in New France, 1610-1791*. 73 Vols. Cleveland, Ohio: Burrows Brothers 1896

Tompkins, Jane, *West of Everything: The Inner Life of Westerns*. New York: Oxford University Press 1992

Tooker, Elisabeth, *Native American Spirituality of the Eastern Woodlands*. New York: Paulist Press 1979

244

Trigger, Bruce G., *The Children of Aataentsic: A History of the Huron People to 1660.* 2 Vols. Montreal: McGill-Queen's University Press 1976

---, editor of *Volume 15: The Northeast. The Handbook of North American Indians.* William C. Sturtevant, General Editor. Washington, D.C. 1978

Trinkaus, Charles, "Renaissance and Discovery" in Chiappelli, ed., *First Images of America*

Trumbull, J. Hammond, ed., *Plain Dealing or News from New England,* by Thomas Lechford. Boston: Wiggin & Lunt 1897

---, *Natick Dictionary.* Smithsonian Institution Bureau of American Ethnology Bulletin #25, 1903

Tuck, James A., "Regional Cultural Development 3000 to 300 BC" in H15, 28-43

--- and Robert Grenier, *Red Bay, Labrador: World Whaling Capital A.D. 1550-1600.* St. John's University Press, Newfoundland, Canada 1989

---, "The Maritime Archaic Tradition." Publication of the Newfoundland Museum 1996. Internet *source:* http://www.stemnet.nf.ca/-cshea/note12.html

Tuchman, Barbara, *The First Salute.* New York: Knopf 1980

Tyler, Moses Coit, *A History of American Literature.* (2 Vols.) New York: G.P. Putnam's Sons 1880

Underdown, David, *Revel, Riot and Rebellion: Popular Politics and Culture in England 1603-1660.* New York: Oxford University Press 1985

---, "The Taming of the Scold: The Enforcement of Patriarchal Authority in Early Modern England." In Fletcher and Stevenson, eds., *Order and Disorder* 1985

Vanderbilt, Kermit, "The Literary Histories of Moses Coit Tyler." In Voloshon, Beverly R., ed., *American Literature, Culture and Ideology: Essays in Memory of Henry Nash Smith.* Series XXIV, Vol. 8. New York: Peter Lang 1990

Van Wassenaer, Nicolaes, *Historisch Verhael.* 1924. Rpt. in Jameson, ed., *Narratives of New Netherland*

Vastokas, Joan M and Romas K. Vastokas, *Sacred Art of the Algonkians: A Study of the Peterborough Petroglyphs.* Peterborough, Ontario: Mansard Press 1973

Vaughan, Alden T., *The Puritan Tradition in America 1620-1730.* New York: Harper & Row 1972

---, *New England Frontier: Puritans and Indians 1620-1675.* Boston 1965. Rpt. Norman: University of Oklahoma Press 1995

---, ed., *New England's Prospect* by William Wood. 1634. Amherst: University of Massachusetts Press 1977

---, ed., *The Roots of American Racism: Essays on the Colonial Experience*. New York: Oxford University Press 1995

Vecsey, Christopher and R. W. Venables, eds., *American Indian Environments* Syracuse: Fadiman 1980

Velasquez, Rita C. ed., *Directory of American Scholars*. Detroit: Gale Group 1999

Verrazzano, Giovanni da, *The Voyages of Giovanni da Verrazzano 1524-28*. 2 Vols. Lawrence C. Wroth, ed., New Haven: Yale UP 1970

---, "Soderini Letter, The": *Letter to Piero Soderini, Gonfaloniere, the year 1504*. Princeton: Princeton UP 1916, George Tyler Northrup, trans.

Vogel, Virgil J., *American Indian Medicine*. Norman: University of Oklahoma Press 1970

Wagner, David R., "The Ekonk Hill Petroglyphs." January 1996 unpublished article (available from the author at Box 373, Thompson CT 06277)

--- and David Ostlowski, "The Stone Mounds of the Eastern Woodland People." January 1997 unpublished survey/article (available as above *Wagner*)

Wallace, Anthony F.C., "Woman, Land and Society: Three Aspects of Aboriginal Delaware Life." *Pennsylvania Archaeologist* 17 (1947), 1-35

---, *The Death and Rebirth of the Seneca*. 1969. Rpt. New York: Random House 1972

Wassenaer, Nicolaes van, *Historisch Verhael* (1624) in Jameson ed., *Narratives of New Netherlands*

Watson, Patricia A., "'The Hidden Ones': Women and Healing in Colonial New England." In Benes, ed., *Medicine and Healing*

Weiss, Roberto, *The Renaissance Discovery of Classical Antiquity*. Oxford: Basil Blackwell 1969

Westbrook, Perry D., *William Bradford*. Boston: Twayne Publishers 1978

White, Richard and William Cronon, "Ecological Change and Indian-White Relations" in H15, 417-429

White, Hayden, "The Noble Savage Theme as Fetish." In Chiappelli, ed., *First Images of America*

Wilbur, C. Keith, *The New England Indians*. Chester CT: Globe Pequot Press 1978

---, *Indian Handcrafts*. Chester, CT: Globe Pequot Press 1990

Williams, Jerry M. and Robert E. Lewis, eds., *Early Images of the Americas: Transfer and Invention*. Tucson: University of Arizona Press 1993

Williams, Roger, *A Key Into the Language of America*. London 1643. John J. Teunissen and Evelyn J. Hinz, eds. Detroit: Wayne State University Press 1973

---, *Letters of Roger Williams*. John Bartlett, ed., Narragansett Society Publication. North Providence RI

---, *Complete Writings*. 7 vols. John Russell Bartlett, ed. New York: Russell and Russell 1963

---, "Letter of Roger Williams Relative to the Purchase of Lands at Seekonk and Providence." (December 13, 1661) In Bartlett, ed., *Complete Writings*

Willison, George F., *Saints and Strangers: The Story of the Mayflower and the Plymouth Colony*. New York: Reynal and Hitchcock 1945

Willoughby, Charles C., *Antiquities of the New England Indians*. Peabody Museum of American Archaeology and Ethnology. Cambridge: Harvard University Press 1935

Winslow, Edward, *Good News from New-England*. London 1624. Rpt. in Arber, ed. *The Story of the Pilgrim Fathers*

---, *Hypocrisie Unmasked: A True Relation of the Proceedings of the Governor and Company of the Massachusetts vs. Samuel Gorton....*London 1646. Rpt. Providence Club for Colonial Reprints #6 (1916)

Winthrop, John, *Journal* in *The Winthrop Papers*. Worthington C. Ford *et als*, eds. 3 Vols. Boston: Massachusetts Historical Society, Plimpton Press 1931

---, *The Winthrop Papers*. Allyn B. Forbes, ed. Massachusetts Historical Society. Boston: Merrymount Press 1943

---, *Winthrop's Journal*. *"History of New England" 1630-1649*. James K. Hosmer, ed. 2 Vols. New York: Scribner's 1908

---. "Christian Experience" [1607] in Vol 1: 154-68 of Ford, ed.

---, "A Model of Christian Charity" [1630] in Forbes, ed., Vol. II

Witherspoon, Alexander M., and Frank J. Warnke, eds., *Seventeenth Century Prose and Poetry*. (1929) Rpt. New York: Harcourt Brace Jovanovich 1982 (2nd enlarged edition)

Wood, William, *New England's Prospect*. London 1634. Alden T. Vaughan, ed., Amherst: University of Massachusetts Press 1977

Woolf, Eric, *Europe and the People Without History*. Berkeley: Univeristy of California Press 1982

Woolverton, John Frederick, *Colonial Anglicanism in North America*. Detroit: Wayne State University Press 1984

Wright, Louis B., *The Elizabethans' America: A Collection of Early Reports by Englishmen on the New World*. London: Edward Arnold Publishers 1965

Wrightson, Keith, *English Society 1580-1680*. Rutgers University Press 1982

---,"Alehouses, Order and Reformation in Rural England 1590-1660." In E. Yeo, ed., *Popular Culture and Class Conflict*. Hassocks, England: Harvester Press 1981

Young, Alexander, *Chronicles of the Pilgrim Fathers of the Colony of Plymouth 1602-1625*. New York: DeCapo 1971

Youngken, Heber H., "The Drugs of the North American Indians." *American Journal of Pharmacy* 97 #3 (1925)

Zolla, Elemire, *The Writer and the Shaman: A Morphology of the American Indian*. R. Rosenthal, trans., New York: Harcourt Brace Jovanovich 1969

Zuckerman, Michael, "Pilgrims in the Wilderness: Community, Modernity and the Maypole of Merry Mount." *New England Quarterly* 50 (1977), 255-77

---, "The Fabrication of Identity in Early America." *William and Mary Quarterly*, 3rd series, Vol. 34: April 1977, 183-214

ILLUSTRATIONS

1) Historical marker at First Encounter Beach, Samoset Road, Eastham Cod),
Massachusetts. "Follow the asphalt path to the top of the hill to see this
monument" (Eastham Tourism Guide)

2) "Landing of the Pilgrims at Plimouth 11th December 1620." In Nathaniel
Morton's New England's Memorial

3) Monument topped with conceived likeness of Captain Myles Standish (just
north of Plymouth, Massachusetts)

4) Photo of the remains of a Native woman and baby (Lord's "squa and papoose
burial" – see his notebook entries following). Discovered during construction at
Weymouth's Bicknell School, the collection was purchased by Mr. Matthew
Popowitz from original "owner" Walter Duncan (both of Weymouth and
photographed by the former; a copy of which photo appears in a unique private
collection edition of Frost. (Further information unavailable; this courtesy of
Bill Bowman of Weymouth.)

5, 6, 7, 8) Excerpted pages from the "Diary" of 1930s archaeologist G. Stinson Lord,
indicating the location of Weymouth Colony and detailing his investigations into the
"Affair" and its aftermath. (from Frost, Immortal Voyage)

NOTE: The archaeology of Weymouth Colony has included 3 main digs: 1) 43
Bicknell Road, where remains of 7 colonists were "entombed"; 2) 136 or 236 Sea
Street, where the "headless" and other Native remains were found; and 3) The
Bicknell School, where the Native woman's and baby's remains were discovered.
Ms. Jodi Purdy Quinlan of Weymouth was a great help and encouragement to this
editor in these (and other) regards.

LANDING OF THE PILGRIMS AT PLIMOUTH 11ᵗʰ DEC. 1620.

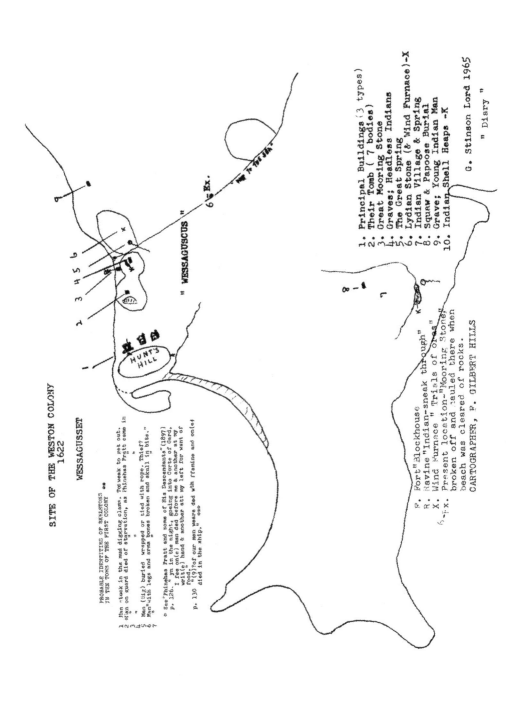

SITE OF THE WESTON COLONY
1622

WESSAGUSSET

PROBABLE IDENTITIES OF SKELETONS
IS THE TOMB OF THE FIRST COLONY **

1. Man "stuck in the mud digging clams, foo weak to get out.
2. Man on guard died of starvation, as Phineas Pratt came in *
3.
4.
5. Man (Sig) buried wrapped or tied with rope, Thief?
6. "Man" with legs and arms bones broken and skul in bits."
7.

* See "Phineas Pratt and some of His Descendants" (1897)
p. 126. "...gun in the night, going into Corte of Gard,
I fee on(e) man ded before me & another at ye
write(e) hand & another sitt my left for want of
food."
p. 130 "(9)of our men weare ded with ffamine and on(e)
died in the ship." ***

1. Principal Buildings (3 types)
2. Their Tomb (7 bodies)
3. Great Mooring Stone
4. Graves; Headless Indians
5. The Great Spring
6. Lydian Stone (& Wind Furnace)-X
7. Indian Village & Spring
8. Squaw & Papoose Burial
9. Grave; Young Indian Man
10. Indian Shell Heaps -K

G. Stinson Lord 1965

"Diary"

F. "Fort"Blockhouse
R. Ravine "Indian-sneak through"
X. Wind Furnace " Trials of Ores"
6-Ex. Present location-Mooring Stone;
broken off and dauled there when
beach was cleared of rocks.
CARTOGRAPHER, F. GILBERT HILLS

"WESSAGUSCUS"

HUNT'S HILL

HAUNTED HOUSE OF SEVEN SKELETONS
AND GHOST OF THE GIANT INDIAN PECKSUOT

MRS. WALTER LANG, JR. STRONGLY E.S.P.
AND USED TO SEE HIS GHOST IN HER HOUSE
AT #43 BICKNELL ROAD, SO DID HER CHILDREN -
STORY TOLD TO MR. LORD, WHEN THE LANGS JUST
MOVED INTO THE HOUSE AND KNEW NOTHING OF
WEYMOUTH HISTORY, WOULD WAKE UP AT NIGHT TO
FIND HIM GLOWERING ACROSS THE ROOT AND COULD
SEE HIM AFTER AWAKENED AND EITH FAMILY

* North Weymouth,
Massachusetts

** Jeremiah Spencer's story of the skeletons"dug up."
It would seem that from this tomb at #43 Bicknell
Road,to the graves of the headless Indians at 136
Sea Street, must have been the First Burying Ground.
The skeleton dug up, with an "awful long neck" in the
cellar of the next house on the south of Cecil Evans,
Cecil thought was of the young brother of Whituwamat.
The freshest "teen-ager" that ever lived! Or rather--
died." a fourth, a youth of eighteen, was overpowered and secured; Mm. Standish subsequently hung."
The papoose skeleton found in the 1930" by workers
putting in the flagpole for the Bicknell School, had
its skull bashed in. Later enlargement of diggings
brought to light the Squaw with her head in the same
condition. One wonders if this could be the child of
the man who married an Indian Squaw at Weston's Colony. No doubt he suffered a worse fate-in the game
of "Tit-for-tat, typical of those rough (?) times. A³

A - THE HOUSE OF SKULLS

(House haunted by ghost
of giant Indian Pecksuot.)

THE HOUSE OF SKULLS

Built over the tomb of the first colony at Wessagusset 1622
by Waldo Turner and Jeremiah Spencer, Civil War Veterans-
probably sometime shortly after the turn of this century.

They placed five of the seven skulls found into the jog of an
eastwardly well of the cellar. One of the owners of this #43
Bicknell Road property had the skulls chopped out of the
concrete wall and handfulls of cement pressed into openings. *

Stin Lord's Diary-1931

* Told to me by "Jerry" Spencer, Edward L. Rand, and others.
Spencer had metal buckles from shoes, belts(hats?) in his
cellar on overhead beam

F. Gilbert Hills, Pl...

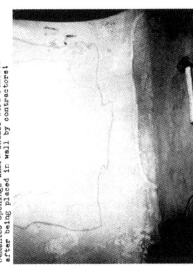

Five Skeletons All in One Family Closet!

Cemented openings where skulls were removed after being placed in wall by contractors!

Edge of one of the slabs of rock that covered the tomb. It was not shoved far enough north to clear cellar wall

Stin Lord's Diary
1931-1963

Hunt's Hill and Hunt's Hill Plain, usually considered as one and the same, but separated by a 'Ravine" Charles Francis Adams was under this impression, as most people were. This Ravine was the source of much annoyance to the Weston Colony as it was a "sneak-through" used by the Indians. Note hull of ship in N. Porter Keen's Shipyard at Hunt's Hill. Site of the Principal Buildings. The lower one near the shore was the Blockhouse.

WEYMOUTH, MASS. 1880. (Bird's eye view)

Much like Plymouth!

Of glacial origin—in two sections divided by a "gully."

Man drowned in mud. "Plastow's(?) Clam Flats

STATEMENTS IN REGARD TO THE
1622-23 WESSAGUSSET COLONY

" The Wessagusset Plantation was much like Plymouth, Buildings and stockade, Ftc. page 31; vol. I. Hist. Wey. (1923)

" Hunt's Hill, which is now known as the Site of the Weston Colony, was a ridge of glacial origin projecting into Fore River Bay at the Mouth of the Monatiquot River and rose to a considerable height. IT WAS DIVIDED INTO TWO SECTIONS BY A SORT OF GULLY OR SMALL ANCIENT (GLACIAL) CHANNEL WHIC WAS GIVEN THE NAME OF THE " RAVINE," AND PLAYED AN IMPORTANT PART IN SOME EVENTS OF WEYMOUTH HISTORY. page 29, 1880.

* In one case a man, who was weak from the want of food, was caught in the mud, and not being strong enough, to pull himself out was drowned when the tide came in." page 32.

" Truth about the Hanging at Wessagusset." page 32.

Rev. William Hyde, Wey. Hist. Soc. 1923.

THE HOUSE OF THE HEADLESS INDIANS

Built by Edward Blanchard in the early part of the Nineteenth Century.
The headless skeletons of the Sachem Wituwamat and the giant Pecsuot were exhumed when the cellar hole was dug.
M. P. Koopman House, 236 Sea St.1970.

G. Stinson Lord Foto

Friday 13, 1970

Mr. Donald H. Blanchard, 230 Sea Street, North Weymouth. 02191
found a coin while excavating for his new home in cellar hole.

Face of coin states GULIELMUS TERTIUS (1697)
Back " " " BRIT XXI4 1697

GULIELMUS TERTIUS (WILLIAM III) ruled Britian, in overall time from 1689 to 1702 , so this coin does not "positively and absolutely" predate all known artifacts of the white men in Weymouth and is not dated" 1697." James I, ruled Britian 1607-1697 (1697) so this is not 1607.

I interviewed Mr. Blanchard, 8-15-1964
G. Stinson Lord Historian
Weymouth Historical Society,
at that time'
G. Stinson Lord

North Weymouth Cemetery

The bones of Wituwamat and Pecksuot were reinterred here, in the embankment of his own family lot, by the late Edward Blanchard in what was a remarkably kindly act! Embankment terraced later. Skeletons removed? Told me by John H. Leighton, owner; J. Spencer and others, 1930s. Also Herbert Porter Keene, 1970.

Stin.Lord's Diary
1931-1963

FINIS?

" That Site no longer exists: and it will ever be a matter of profound regret to me that the spot was not known, and the exact location fixed, a few years earlier, at the time of the Celebration of 1874.... It might have been secured, and dedicated forever as a public water park fronting on the Fore River. A Permanent Memorial should there HAVE BEEN erected. p. 124," WEYMOUTH THIRTY YEARS LATER, Charles F. Adams.(1904) 1905. This paper sums up and settles this question, as far as I am concerned. G. Stinson Lord. November 28, 1970.

Lightning Source UK Ltd.
Milton Keynes UK
UKHW010628260120
357616UK00001B/140